EXPORT CONTROLS

A Contemporary History

Bert Chapman

University Press of America,® Inc.
Lanham · Boulder · New York · Toronto · Plymouth, UK

Copyright © 2013 by
University Press of America,® Inc.
4501 Forbes Boulevard
Suite 200
Lanham, Maryland 20706
UPA Acquisitions Department (301) 459-3366

10 Thornbury Road
Plymouth PL6 7PP
United Kingdom

Library of Congress Control Number: 2013949573
ISBN: 978-0-7618-6233-8 (clothbound : alk. paper)
eISBN: 978-0-7618-6234-5
ISBN: 978-0-7618-6591-9 (pbk : alk. paper)

To Becky.
I won't trade you for anyone or anything!

Contents

Acknowledgments

Writing a book on a subject of such enormous interdisciplinary complexity and depth is challenging and I want to acknowledge those helping me. I especially want to thank Lindsay MacDonald and Piper Owens of University Press of America for patiently guiding me through the intricacies of their publishing procedures. In this era of drastically expanded public access to government information, I'd like to thank the large variety of U.S. and international government organizations who provide readily available Internet access to their export control policy-making documents. Additional thanks goes to the Hathitrust catalog which provides access to significant amounts of historical U.S. Government information on this topic for the post-World War II time period covered by this work.

I want to thank Purdue Economics Professor David Hummels for his guidance on this topic and Purdue Research Security Administrator Michael Reckowsky for providing his perspective on how the complexity of U.S. Government export controls affects the research activities of a major research university with global instructional and research connections and aspirations. I also want to thank Dorothy Albritton for her typesetting and editorial assistance and expertise. Additional thanks are due to Purdue University Libraries for providing an environment conducive to scholarly research and for providing access to an incredible variety of information resources to meet faculty and student research and instructional needs and Robert Swanson for indexing.

I am also grateful to my wife Becky for her love and understanding the time commitment involved in writing a book. Most importantly, I thank God for the opportunities He gives me to pursue projects such as this through my work.

Introduction

International trade is a vitally important engine of American and international economic prosperity. National and international economic growth is highly dependent on exports which can be affected by fluctuating exchange rates, domestic and international consumer demand, domestic and international economic policies, and international security conditions. During calendar year 2011, the U.S. exported $2,105,046,000,000 in goods and services to all countries representing 13.74% of its $15,319,400,000 of national Gross Domestic Product for that year.[1]

These goods and services cover economic sectors such as agriculture, industry, manufacturing, services, and technology and help influence the economic health of U.S. companies, shareholder investments, the overall U.S. economy, and the overall health of the international economy, the economic performance of companies in other countries, and the profitability of their shareholders. The overwhelming majority of goods and services exported by the U.S. to other countries are for economically legitimate non-military purposes. However, the U.S. and other countries also export goods and services that have strictly military or dual-use civilian and military applications. In some cases, such exports are part of normal trade and legitimate intellectual information exchange between foreign countries and private sector institutions. In numerous cases, though, this trade involves the illegal and/or imprudent sales and transfers of goods and services, along with financial transfers to, countries or transnational terrorist or criminal organizations, with interests antagonistic to U.S. national security and economic interests.[2]

The United States, other nations, and international government organizations, seek to restrict, disrupt, and stop the export of militarily sensitive technologies and financial transfers to hostile countries and transnational groups through export controls. This work seeks to provide

a contemporary history of export controls, primarily from a U.S. perspective, and show how the U.S. and international government organizations have sought to restrict the exports of national security related products and services, with varying degrees of success and failure, from the
post-World War II period to the present.

It begins by covering the legal and legislative history of U.S. Government export control laws in this time period, with a retrospective look
back to the 1918 Trading With the Enemy Act, and show how the multifaceted, labyrinthine, and multiagency bureaucratic morass of government agencies involved in export control activities was established and
sustained. One chapter will address the often contradictory roles played
by the Commerce and Defense Departments in sculpting U.S. export
control policy.[3]

Subsequent chapters will address the roles played in American export control policy by agencies as diverse as U.S. Customs and Border
Protection within the Department of Homeland Security,[4] the Energy
and Justice Departments,[5] and Treasury Department.[6] The multifaceted
and problematic role of congressional oversight or lack of oversight of
U.S. export control policy will also be examined.[7] The highly political
nature of this topic and the efforts of non-governmental organizations
such as export oriented businesses and their interest group advocates to
influence U.S. international trade and export control policy will be analyzed in another chapter.[8] The role of international government organizations such as the Australia Group, Missile Technology Control Regime, and Wassenaar Regime, along with their effectiveness or lack of
effectiveness in regulating the export of militarily sensitive technology,
including weapons of mass destruction and their component parts, to and
from countries such as China, Iran, North Korea, Pakistan, Russia, and
Syria will also be examined.[9]

Recent Obama Administration attempts to streamline the U.S. export
control system and examine the overall effectiveness of export controls
in national and international foreign economic and national security policy
will also be reviewed. This work will also assess whether export controls
are desirable and feasible in a constantly evolving global economic, security, and technological environments. Its conclusion is that carefully
targeted export controls are desirable and realistic despite economic globalization and widespread scientific and technological information dissemination due to ongoing international security threats involving Weapons of Mass Destruction (WMD) proliferation, cybersecurity, and actively

ongoing sensitive technology espionage involving China, Russia, and other countries.

This is a subject ripe for interdisciplinary research. It involves U.S. and international history, domestic and international economics including economic sanctions, international law, and various political science fields, the roles played by interest groups, administrative bureaucratic cooperation and competition, international relations, legislative oversight, and security studies. It does not strive to be the definitive scholarly historical assessment on this topic. However, it aspires to illustrate the vital link between national and international economic growth and security and how countries such as the United States tend to oscillate back and forth between vigorously promoting exports to fuel economic growth and promoting national security interests through restrictive export controls depending on domestic political factors within their countries and continually evolving domestic and international economic, political, and security environments.

Notes

1. See U.S. Census Bureau, Foreign Trade Division, "U.S. Trade in Goods and Serivces-Balance of Payments (BOP) Basis," (2012) www.census.gov/foreign-trade/statistics/historical/gands.pdf; Accessed April 11, 2012; and U.S. Department of Commerce, Bureau of Economic Analysis, *News Release: Gross Domestic Product: Fourth Quarter and Annual 2011 (Third Estimate) Corporate Profits: Fourth Quarter and Annual 2011*, (March 29, 2012); www.bea.gov/newsreleases/national/gdp/2012/pdf/gdp4q11_3rd.pdf; Accessed April 13, 2012.

2. See Richard T. Cupitt, *Reluctant Champions: Truman, Eisenhower, Bush, and Clinton: U.S. Presidential Policy and Strategic Export Controls*, (New York: Routledge, 2000); Evan S. Medeiros, *Chasing the Dragon: Assessing China's System of Export Controls for WMD-Related Goods and Technologies*, (Santa Monica: Rand Corporation, 2005); U.S. National Research Council, *Beyond "Fortress America": National Security Controls on Science and Technology in a Globalized World*, (Washington, DC: National Academies Press, 2009; U.S. Congress, House Committee on Foreign Affairs, *Export Controls, Arms Sales, and Reform: Balancing U.S. Interests*, (Washington, DC: GPO, 2011); and U.S. Congress, House Committee on Oversight and Government Reform, *Implementation of Iran Sanctions*, (Washington, DC: GPO, 2011) for examples of the burgeoning literature on this topic.

3. See Mitchell B. Wallerstein, "Losing Controls," *Foreign Affairs*, 88 (6)(November/December 2009): 11-18; and John C. Rood, "Improvements to the Defense Export Trade Control System," *DISAM Journal*, 30 (4)(December 2008): 83-89.

4. See U.S. Department of Homeland Security, Office of Inspector General, *Review of Controls over the Export of Chemical and Biological Commodities,* (Washington, DC: DHS OIG, 2005); and Ibid., *Audit of Export Controls for Activities Related to China,* (Washington, DC: DHS OIG, 2006).

5. See U.S. Department of Energy, Office of Inspector General, *The Global Threat Reduction Initiative's Molybdenum-99 Program,* (Washington, DC: DOE IG, 2012); http://energy.gov/sites/prod/files/OAS-L-12-07.pdf; Accessed January 3, 2013; and U.S. Department of Justice, *Summary of Major U.S. Export Enforcement and Embargo-Related Criminal Prosecutions: 2007 to the Present,* (Washington, DC: Department of Justice, 2011); www.justice.gov/nsd/docs/summary-eaca.pdf; Accessed April 13, 2012.

6. See U.S. Congress, Senate Committee on Banking, Housing, and Urban Affairs, Subcommittee on International Finance and Monetary Policy, *International Affairs Functions of the Treasury and Export Administration Act,* (Washington, DC: GPO, 1981); and U.S. Department of the Treasury, Office of Foreign Assets Control, "About," (2012); http://www.treasury.gov/about/organizational-structure/offices/Pages/Office-of-Foreign-Assets-Control.aspx; Accessed April 13, 2012.

7. Kenneth W. Abbott. "Defining the Extraterritorial Reach of American Export Controls: Congress as Catalyst," *Cornell International Law Journal*, 17 (Winter 1984): 79-158.

8. See Dirk De Bièvre and Andreas Dür, "Constituency Interests and Delegation in European and American Trade Policy," *Comparative Political Studies*, 38 (10)(December 2005): 1271-1296; and Teng Kun Wang, "Lobbying Paradox of Strategic Export Policy in a Differentiated Duopoly," *International Economics and Economic Policy*, 8 (3)(September 2011): 323-336.

9. See U.S. Congress, Senate Committee on Governmental Affairs, Subcommittee on International Security, Proliferation, and Federal Services, *The Role of Bilateral and Multilateral Arms Control Agreements in Controlling Threats from the Proliferation of Weapons of Mass Destruction,* (Washington, DC: GPO, 2003); and U.S. Congress, House Committee on Foreign Affairs, *Nuclear Cooperation and Non-Proliferation after Khan and Iran,* (Washington, DC: GPO, 2010).

Chapter 1

U.S. Legal and Legislative History

Nations have attempted to use export controls and other economic sanctions to achieve strategic objectives throughout history. During the Peloponnesian War, Athenian leader Pericles sought to impose a trade embargo on the Spartan-allied state Megara banning it from access to Athenian markets and ports in 433/432 BC for killing an Athenian emissary and cultivating land consecrated to the Athenian harvest goddess Demeter.[1]

Subsequent centuries have seen many nations seek to implement economic sanctions such as export controls on their military and political adversaries in order to achieve desired national objectives. Export controls have been part of the multifaceted and interdisciplinary history of individual countries and their international trade policy and the multiple domestic and international political factors influencing individual countries trade and foreign policies.[2]

This chapter focuses on export controls and economic sanctions the U.S. has sought to implement to achieve national strategic objectives during the 20th and 21st centuries with particular emphasis on the era since World War II. It will present a list and explanation of major laws and presidential executive orders the U.S. has enacted to try to get countries and transnational organizations such as terrorist groups to comply with or respond more favorably to U.S. diplomatic, economic, military, and political objectives and interests without requiring the use of U.S. military power.

The first major example of the U.S. seeking to impose export controls is the Trading With the Enemy Act (TEA) signed by President

Woodrow Wilson on October 6, 1917.[3] Enacted during World War I, provisions of this statue, some remaining in force today, sought to preclude the provision of materials which would benefit the warfighting capabilities of other countries. These included contraband war items with examples being:

A. Arms, guns, ammunition, explosives, and ingredients used in their production;
B. Air, land, and water transport components and accessories required to use them;
C. Clothing and food destined to be controlled by enemy governments and personnel;
D. Tools, implements, instruments, equipment, maps, documents, and machinery required to carry out hostile operations; and
E. Monetary assets, metals, and machinery required to manufacture these assets.[4]

This legislation defined enemies of the U.S. as individuals, partnerships, or other groups of individuals of any nation the U.S. is at war with along with the government of any nations the U.S. is at war with including that government's officials and agents.[5] Trading was defined by this statute as:

A. Paying, satisfying, compromising, or giving security for paying or satisfying any debts or obligation;
B. Drawing, accepting, paying, presenting for acceptance or payment, or endorsing negotiable instruments;
C. Entering into, carrying on, completing, or performing any contract, agreement, or obligation;
D. Buying, selling, loaning, or extending credit, trading in, dealing with, exchanging, transmitting, transferring, assigning or disposing of or receiving any form of property;
E. Having any form of business or commercial communication with enemy countries.[6]

This legislation updated Wilson's statement from earlier that year that export controls would be pursued with provisions for providing generous supplies of materials to allied and neutral nations while also mentioning that the presence of export controls was not intended to restrict normal trade patterns and that an export licensing system "which will be as simply organized and administered as possible, so as to constitute no impediment to the normal flow of commerce."[7]

Enforcing the TEA would be carried out by the War Trade Board (WTB) established by Executive Order (EO) 2729-A on October 12, 1917. WTB responsibilities included licensing exports and imports, rationing supplies to neutrals, conserving commodities and shipping facilities for U.S. and allied use, seeking to keep strategic goods out of enemy hands, and prohibiting the use of enemy credit and financial holdings in the U.S.[8]

WTB carried out its responsibilities until it was terminated by EO 3059 on March 3, 1919 which transferred this entity's functions to the State Department.[9] The State Department, as will be described in a later chapter, has become one of the major U.S. Government entities administering export control policy and the Treasury Department's Office of Foreign Assets Control (OFAC), established in December 1950, following China's entry into the Korean War, is now the federal agency responsible for administering U.S. economic sanctions against other countries and transnational organizations which is a role it assumed from predecessor Treasury Department offices of Foreign Funds Control and Office of International Finance. OFAC replaced the Office of Foreign Funds Control established following Germany's 1940 invasion of Norway and can be seen as the successor agency to the WTB.[10]

The U.S. would partially be involved with other international export controls and economic sanctions up and through World War II. These would include a somewhat successful venture to get Greece to back down from a 1925 military operation in Bulgaria and the failure of the League of Nations to persuade Italy to withdraw from Ethiopia in the middle-1930s.[11] Concern over increasing conflict in Europe and Asia and the U.S.' desire to maintain neutrality in these conflicts, lead it to pass Neutrality Acts in the 1930s prohibiting weapons sales and military supplies to warring nations. The 1940 National Defense Act sought to impose munitions controls consistent with U.S. policy in World War II at presidential discretion with violators being subject to a maximum fine of $10,000 and/or imprisonment for up to two years.[12]

The modern statutory infrastructure of U.S. export control policy would begin in earnest following World War II as the wartime alliance with the Soviet Union collapsed and the Cold War began. Concerns within the U.S. and other western democracies about Soviet expansionism in Eastern Europe and the emergence of a nuclear-armed Soviet Union lead the west to adopt numerous policies to restrict access to militarily sensitive western technologies by the Soviet bloc. The 1949 Export Control Act was the first major Cold War statutory instrument giving the U.S. the authority to restrict exports to the emerging Soviet bloc. Specific provisions of this statute, combining domestic protectionism and national security concerns, included:

A. Protecting the U.S. economy from excessive draining of scarce materials and reducing the inflationary impact of abnormal formal demand;
B. Furthering U.S. foreign policy and helping the U.S. fulfill its international responsibilities; and
C. Exercising necessary vigilance over exports as they affect national security.[13]

The unilateral approach of this legislation was augmented by the multilateral approach embodied by the Coordinating Committee (COCOM) which was the leading example of western efforts to control and restrict the transfer of militarily sensitive technologies to the Soviet Union and its allies.[14] Beginning in part with the European Recovery Program or Marshall Plan, COCOM saw these countries, consisting of every NATO nation except Iceland and non-NATO member Japan, establish a strategic trade control system in 1950 and 1951 focusing on embargoing a list of commodities and technologies to Soviet bloc countries. COCOM member countries were prohibited from licensing export of these items to Communist countries without unanimous COCOM approval. This structure had sporadic effectiveness as Western European countries eventually saw the Soviet bloc as an increasingly desirable trade partner while the U.S. tended to favor more restrictive export controls. Subsequent decades would see increasing tensions between the U.S. and its European allies over COCOM and this organization would eventually end in 1994.[15]

U.S. attempts to restrict the export of militarily sensitive technologies would accelerate as the Cold War exploded into combat with the 1950 onset of the Korean War. This conflict saw North Korean forces, aided by the Soviets and Chinese, invade and conquer a significant portion of South Korea before being pushed back by a U.S. lead United

Nations response into a bloody stalemate lasting three years and leaving the territorial status quo in place at the 38th parallel. On June 28, 1950, the U.S. imposed a comprehensive embargo on exports to North Korea based on authority derived from the 1949 Arms Export Control Act (AECA) with the Commerce Department imposing the most restrictive controls. These sanctions were further strengthened by Treasury Department Foreign Assets Control Regulations forbidding financial transactions involving North Korea and China along with transactions relating to travel and North Korean assets subject to U.S. jurisdiction.[16]

The U.S. also sought to impose economic sanctions on China's military and technological capabilities with the China Committee (CHINCOM) regime beginning in 1952 as a result of U.S. displeasure over the 1949 Communist triumph in China, and Chinese military intervention during the Korean War. In 1954 COCOM members agreed to continue export controls against China despite relaxing controls on the Soviet Union and Eastern Europe. However, the increasing attractiveness of China as an export market for Western Europe and continued strong Sino-Soviet relations during the 1950s weakened CHINCOM's effectiveness. For instance, the value of items allowed for export to China increased from $3 million to $79 million between 1954-1956 with the British and French often violating COCOM rules to permit exports to China.[17] This wholesale erosion of CHINCOM sanctions is further illustrated by free world exports to China starting in 1947 at $672.2 billion, falling to $272.5 billion in 1952, before rising to $523.2 billion in 1957 and free world imports from China going from $417.9 million in 1947 to $623.5 billion in 1958. That year saw China came under COCOM controls which would become increasingly lax in subsequent decades. Ultimately, the gradual improvement in Sino-U.S. relations beginning in the 1970s and partially stemming from the Sino-Soviet split of the previous decade, would cause the U.S. to liberalize many of its export restrictions on China before the collapse of the Soviet Union and COCOMs demise.[18]

A second effort to strengthen early Cold War export control architecture was enacting the 1954 Mutual Security Act. This sought to regularize U.S. military assistance objectives including promoting U.S. national security interests, preventing proliferation of weapons of mass destruction, and regulating and reducing the amount of arms and military forces with sufficient safeguards to protect complying nations against violations or evasions of these restrictions by other countries. Section 414 of this law directed the President to regulate the export and imports of arms, ammunition, and technical data while also requiring individuals engaged in exporting, importing, and manufacturing defense items to register with the U.S. Government. Individuals violating Section 414 provisions were subject to fines of up to $25,000 and/or imprisonment of up to two years.

The State Department's Office of Munitions Controls (OMC) was designated for this purpose and its activities will be covered in a subsequent chapter.[19] U.S. export controls have also been directed against individual countries seen as acting contrary to U.S. interests as well as blocs of nations. An example of this is provided by Egypt's July 26, 1956 decision to nationalize the Suez Canal in response to a July 19, 1956 decision by Secretary of State John Foster Dulles (1888-1959) to withdraw U.S. funding for the Aswan Canal. This eventually produced British, French, and Israeli military intervention in Egypt. The U.S., already coping with a presidential election campaign, Soviet repression in Hungary, and seeking to bolster its ties with newly independent countries such as Egypt to prevent them from becoming allied with the Soviet bloc, responded by imposing economic and political sanctions against Britain, Egypt, France, and Israel. These sanctions included an embargo on oil supplies to these nations causing a diminution of their oil reserves and an international run on the British pound, including the precipitous fall of British gold reserves, which caused the these three powers to withdraw from Egypt and eventually produced the collapse of British Prime Minister Antony Eden's (1895-1977) government.[20]

These sanctions achieved mixed results as has been the case with most export controls. They were most effective against Britain since British leaders had enhanced their vulnerability by placing so much reliance on the pound. Sanctions against Egypt, France, and Israel were less successful. In Egypt's case this was because U.S. pressure against President Gamal Abdel Nasser (1918-1970) was limited since it did not block private Egyptian bank accounts, attempt to decrease the prices of Egypt's largest export cotton, the U.S.' desire to maintain open communications with Egypt, and financial support provided to Egypt by China, India, and the Soviet Union. France proved resistant because its government was able to borrow money from the International Monetary Fund in October 1956 to weather the financial storm. Israel was forced to withdraw from the territory it captured from Egypt in November 1956. While it could economically withstand U.S. sanctions, it needed U.S. support in a hostile neighborhood due to the increased weaknesses of Britain and France.[21]

The 1959 Mutual Security Act sought to strengthen international military assistance programs while also limiting support for dictatorial regimes and ensuring that these weapons exports were necessary for U.S. national interests and the recipient countries national security interests. Language in this statute explicitly stated that Western Hemisphere countries receiving U.S. military assistance could only use it for common hemispheric defense purposes and promoting national economic development. The President had to annually review this assistance to determine if it was necessary for these countries. In addition, the President was also given the authority to waive congressional restrictions on military assistance to these countries if he determined that such military assistance was necessary for their internal security.[22]

The victorious Cuban Communist revolution lead by Fidel Castro (1926-) enhanced U.S. security concerns over the presence of a hostile nation just 90 miles from U.S. shores. It prompted various controversial attempts by the U.S. to overthrow the Castro regime and limit its financial sustainability by restricting U.S. trade to that country, settle claims for U.S. property, and discourage Cuba from militarily attempting to export its revolution. These sanctions, with various modifications, remain in effect half a century later and are the subject of considerable controversy over their effectiveness.[23]

The 1961 Foreign Assistance Act (FAA) barred any assistance to Cuba and authorized the President to establish and maintain an economic embargo. Section 620(a) of this statute prohibited any U.S. foreign assistance to the "present" Cuban Government and authorized the President to maintain a complete embargo on all trade between the U.S. and Cuba to enforce this provision.[24] This embargo was set in motion by Proclamation 3447 on February 6, 1962 when President John Kennedy (1917-1963) authorized and directed the Treasury Department to prohibit the importation of Cuban goods and goods imported through Cuba. This proclamation also directed the Commerce Department to continue existing prohibitions on exports to Cuba under the 1949 Export Control Act while allowing Commerce to made adjustments to the export prohibition.[25]

On July 8, 1963 the Treasury Department issued Cuban Assets Control Regulations (CACR) under presidential authority given by TEA Section 5(b) and the FAA. CACR prohibited persons subject to U.S. jurisdiction from engaging in transactions involving property in which Cuba or a Cuban national had interests, including those related to travel, trade, and personal remittances, without a government license. These regulations are currently administered by the Treasury Department's Office of Foreign Assets Control (OFAC) and now includes 12 categories of activities covering circumstances when OFAC authorizes some travel-related transactions including travel for family visits, journalism, and professional research in Cuba. Controversy over the efficacy of this trade embargo continues until today. For instance, between 65-75% of Cuban trade was conducted with the U.S. prior to 1960, but starting in 1961 Cuba sent 75% of its exports to the communist bloc, received 86% of imports from these nations, and received considerable technical and monetary aid from the Soviet Union.[26]

Berlin became a key crisis center during the Cold War as the former German capital was divided into separate American, British, French, and Soviet divisions as an enclave surrounded by the Soviet controlled puppet state of East Germany. The greater economic opportunities and political freedoms in Berlin's western sectors attracted an increasing number of refugees from East Berlin and compelled panicked East German authorities to erect a wall between their sector and the Berlin's western sectors stopping the flow of refugees on August 13-14, 1961. This prompted a protracted and dangerously tense standoff over Berlin between the Soviets and the western powers headed by the United States with diplomatic, economic, intelligence, military, and political implications.[27]

As this crisis was building during the summer of 1961, the allied powers foreign ministers agreed to consider an economic embargo of the Soviet bloc as a countermeasure. The U.S. imposed economic sanctions on East Germany and its Soviet bloc allies, including not signing a bilateral air agreement with the Soviets, and recommending that the State Department take the widest possible range of actions against Warsaw Pact countries for supporting East German construction of the wall and ensuring unobstructed western power access to East Berlin.[28] U.S. and NATO policymakers also recognized that Soviet bloc vulnerabilities to economic sanctions were particularly prevalent in areas such as production inefficiencies, research and development, and agricultural productivity.[29]

Various policy options were proposed in response including a proposal for a sea blockade of East Germany by West German Chancellor

Konrad Adenauer (1876-1967) which was rejected as being unrealistic.[30] An October 23, 1962 CIA assessment on West Berlin's ability to withstand a Soviet economic blockade, taken in response to U.S. actions in Cuba, said that this city was economically prepared for a total blockade and had sufficient food, fuel, medicine, and industrial supplies. This assessment went on to maintain that a quick and sustained western response to such a blockade was essential if West Berliners morale was to be sustained but that their morale would collapse if there was no sign the blockade would be broken.[31]

These proposed East German sanctions were modest and would have produced limited results if implemented. Agreement clarifying the Berlin's legal status was reached, but the East Germans and Soviets refused to remove the wall and it remained in place until 1989. Western powers were unwilling to risk war with the Soviet bloc due to tensions between NATO and the three allied powers responsible for West Berlin although NATO's conventional forces were strengthened. The wall's construction remained a fait accompli and Berlin's new status quo existed for nearly three decades until the collapse of the Soviet bloc.[32]

The 1961 FAA sought to reorganize the structure of U.S. foreign assistance programs by separating military from non-military assistance and creating the U.S. Agency for International Development to implement non-military economic assistance programs. This statute also contained language stating that no assistance could be provided to governments engaging in gross human rights abuse unless such assistance directly benefited needy individuals in these countries; that U.S. annual arms sales to these countries could not exceed $3 million unless the country conformed to United Nations Charter principles; that the recipient country only used these weapons in self-defense; and that the country's ability to enhance its self-defense was important to U.S. security.[33]

The 1962 FAA sought to prohibit selling or furnishing surplus agricultural commodities to Communist countries. Additional provisions of this statute enhanced property rights protections by granting presidential authority to suspend assistance to any governments nationalizing, expropriating, or seizing ownership or control of property owned at least 50% by U.S. citizens, corporations, partnerships, or associations and imposing or enforcing discriminatory taxes or other restrictive maintenance or operational conditions which effectively nationalize, expropriate, or seize ownership or control of U.S. owned properties.[34]

The domestic and foreign policies of newly independent African countries extended the geographic scope of U.S. export control efforts and also illustrated the multiple political difficulties of the U.S. attempting to work its will on them. The 1967-1970 civil war between Nigeria and Biafra represents an example of this. On May 30, 1967, Nigeria's oil rich region of Biafra proclaimed its independence. Nigeria's central government sought to militarily defeat this secessionist movement and used a series of economic sanctions including imposing an economic blockade by suspending air and sea access to Biafra. A particularly important and effective form of economic leverage used by the Nigerians was changing its currency making it impossible for the Biafrans to use Nigerian currency to pay for the war. The blockade succeeded in starving two million Biafrans to death (1/6th of the population), but did not undermine their morale and they continued fighting until a December 24, 1969 breakthrough by Nigerian forces cut the secessionist region in half eliminating military resistance.[35]

U.S. policy toward this conflict was often confused. The U.S. was very concerned with its adverse humanitarian effects and did not want to see a major African country disintegrate. At the same time, it was extremely reluctant to intervene militarily because it did not consider this a vital strategic interest. The U.S. also kept technical assistance and volunteer personnel in Biafra which enhanced the secessionists political legitimacy and provided humanitarian assistance. However, both the Johnson and Nixon Administrations were reluctant to explicitly support Biafran aspirations despite significant domestic U.S. pressure to intervene in their favor. The U.S. ultimately did not impose sanctions on either party in this conflict due to the complexities of Cold War politics and conflicting domestic political pressures. Nigeria's economic sanctions and military actions against the Biafrans assumed preeminence in this tragic conflict without U.S. intervention.[36]

The 1968 AECA was produced out of a background of concern about what was seen as the liberal availability of U.S. weapons through credit purchases by developing countries and a desire to limit U.S. weapons sales to countries seeking to use these weapons to enhance national prestige, increasing regional military competition, be used on domestic military spending instead of domestic social needs, and be transferred to third parties antagonistic to the U.S. This legislation gave the Secretary of State authority for determining U.S. foreign military policy and integrating the sales of other U.S. items with broader U.S. foreign policy objectives. It also directed recipient countries to pay for weapons from Defense Department stocks at current market values within 120 days of delivery and that the President had to transmit semiannual reports to Congress on sales to developing countries including forecasts of anticipated future sales and credit extensions.[37]

During the 1960s, international trade became increasingly important to the U.S. economy and its allies began to exert significant political pressures on the U.S. to liberalize existing export control statutes. This trend was further strengthened by lessening hostilities with the Soviet Union. Congress responded to this trends and pressures by passing the 1969 Export Administration Act (EAA). Provisions of this act gave enhanced authority to the Commerce Department to inform the business sector of export control policy changes and procedures to encourage maximum possible trade. It also administered penalties of $10,000 and/or one year imprisonment for violators of this act and penalties of three times the value of the exports involved or $20,000 (whichever is greater), and/or five years imprisonment for second and subsequent violations.[38]

Additional provisions of this legislation included declaring U.S. export policy involved:

1. Encouraging trade with all countries it has diplomatic or trading relations with except those countries where the President determines such trade to be against the national interest;
2. Restricting the export of goods and technologies which would significantly enhance the military potential or any nation or nations which would be injurious to U.S. national security;
3. U.S. policy will use export controls to protect its economy from excessive drain of scarce materials and reduce the inflationary impact of excess foreign demand; advance U.S. foreign policy and international responsibilities; and exercise vigilance over how exports effect U.S. national security;
4. U.S. policy will formulate and apply export controls in coordination with other countries the U.S. has defense treaty commitments with;
5. The U.S. will use its economic resources and trade potential to enhance sound national economic growth and stability while furthering foreign and national security policy objectives; and

6. U.S. policy will oppose restrictive trade practices or boy-
    cotts advocated or imposed by foreign countries against coun-
    tries allied to the U.S. and encourage export oriented U.S.
    businesses to refuse to take part in such actions against U.S.
    allied countries.[39]

South Africa's minority white government became a target for U.S.
and international export control efforts during the 1970's. Some of this
was enmity was due to this country's support for the minority white
government in Rhodesia which separated from the United Kingdom in
1965. The vast majority of this enmity toward Pretoria was due to the
country's racially restrictive apartheid policies and its efforts to subvert
what it saw as hostile governments in neighboring countries including
Angola and Mozambique.[40]

A key target of U.S. and international critics of South Africa was its
nuclear weapons program based in the Kahlahari Desert which had
achieved significant progress, including some U.S. support, until Washington stopped enriched uranium sales in 1975 when this program was
detected by a Soviet satellite in August 1977. The Soviets relayed their
findings to the U.S. and other countries and these countries responded
with such hostility that South Africa had to reduce its nuclear ambitions
although Pretoria did conduct a nuclear weapons test in the Atlantic Ocean
around this time.[41]

Sanctions imposed by the international community and the U.S. on
South Africa included United Nations Security Council Resolution 418
including a mandatory arms embargo against South Africa on November
4, 1977[42] and a February 22, 1978 Commerce Department embargo on
exports and reexports of U.S.-origin commodities and unpublished technical data that could be used by South African or Namibian military or
police forces to enforce apartheid.[43] The U.S. imposed additional financial sanctions on South Africa in 1978 when it enacted legislation prohibiting the Export-Import Bank from guaranteeing, insuring, extending
credit, or participating in extending credit in supporting any export which
would enable South Africa to enforce apartheid unless the President determines in writing that significant progress has been made in eliminating apartheid. This law also required the State Department to verify that
South African purchasers of U.S. exports were working to achieve non-
segregated work forces, equal pay for all employees regardless of race,

and equal opportunity for employees of all races to participate in supervisory or leadership positions within their workplaces.[44]

The next significant piece of U.S. export control legislation was the 1976 International Security Assistance and Arms Export Control Act. This legislation sought to regulate commercial arms sales and the dangers these could promote military conflict while also seeking to increase U.S. leverage over their recipients. It was prompted by concern over growing U.S. arms sales to Mideast countries including Iran and Saudi Arabia who sought to purchase air-to-air missiles and jet fighter planes.[45]

This legislation also mandated the State Department provide extensive reporting on estimated U.S. arms sales to individual countries and how these transactions advanced U.S. foreign and national security policy interests while also relating to regional arms control efforts and impact on regional stability. It made it illegal to export weapons without a license and to make false or misleading applications in license applications with penalties of up to $1 million and ten years imprisonment. Section 38 of the statute also gave the President the authority to select items regarded as defense articles and services and promote regulations for importing and exporting them. These items are called the United States Munitions List (USML) and are part of the International Traffic in Arms Regulations (ITAR) which the State Department uses to enforce this law.[46]

Another significant revision of U.S. export control laws was the 1977 International Emergency Economic Powers Act (IEEPA). This legislation amended TEA giving the President the authority to investigate, regulate, and prohibit the following in the event of a national emergency:

1. Any foreign exchange transactions; credit or payment transfers through banking institutions involving the interests of foreign countries or nationals; and importing or exporting currencies or securities;
2. Investigating, regulating, compelling, nullifying, and prohibiting financial transfers involving foreign countries or nationals;
3. The President stating why these actions must be taken due to national security threats to U.S. economic prosperity, foreign policy, or national security;
4. The President reporting to Congress every six months on why such actions are necessary.[47]

IEEPA has become the key legal authority by which the President imposes export controls or other economic sanctions against hostile foreign countries or transnational organizations due to periodic failures to reauthorize the Export Administration Act (EAA). These reports are regularly issued by presidential administrations to Congress and are readily accessible.[48]

The Carter Administration's concern over the potential proliferation of nuclear weapons and enabling technologies to hostile countries prompted Congress to include nuclear non-proliferation in its efforts to promote international stability and advance U.S. export control objectives. Receiving impetus from India's 1974 nuclear weapons test, this concern was demonstrated in 1977 Nuclear Proliferation Amendments to the 1961 FAA. Provisions of this statute included prohibiting military assistance, education, and training to any country delivering nuclear enrichment equipment, materials, or technology to another country or receives these items from another country without agreeing to place them under multilateral management and agreeing to place these nuclear materials and facilities under International Atomic Energy (IAEA) safeguards. These amendments also required the recipient country to not acquire nuclear weapons or assist other countries in acquiring such weapons. Violation of these provisions could subject these nations to termination of U.S. economic and security assistance unless the President certified to Congress that terminating such assistance would jeopardize U.S. national security and nonproliferation objectives.[49]

Political influence peddling and economic corruption such as bribery can influence international business transactions and this is particularly true of weapons sales. U.S. concern over the requirements of providing bribes or other financial incentives to enable U.S. businesses to acquire contracts in some foreign countries prompted Congress to enact the Foreign Corrupt Practices Act (FCPA) in 1977. Provisions of this legislation made it illegal for employees of U.S. companies subject to Section 30A of the 1934 Securities Exchange Act to corruptly use the mails or other interstate commerce instruments to offer payment, promise of payment, or authorize payment of money, offers, gifts, promises, or any items of value to any foreign officials to:

A. Influence any of their acts or decisions including deciding not to perform their duties;

B. Induce these officials to use their influence with a foreign government or business interest to influence decisions by these entities in obtaining or retaining business for or with, or directing business to any person, foreign political party or political candidate to obtain business opportunities for U.S. companies.[50]

Criminal penalties for violating this act included fines of up to $1 million for company violations and up to $10,000 fines and/or maximum five years imprisonment for individual violators. Efforts to strengthen foreign anti-bribery laws through the Organization of Economic Cooperation and Development (OECD) Anti-Bribery Convention resulted in FCPA being amended in 1998 by adding international government organization officials to the list of individuals who could not be subject to lobbying influence by U.S. individuals and organizations. This amended legislation increased company fines to $2 million and individual fines to up to $100,000 while retaining existing incarceration penalties.[51]

Continuing U.S. concern over the nuclear "arms race" and the proliferation of nuclear weapons and related technology lead to passage of the 1978 Nuclear Non-Proliferation Act (NNPA). This legislation sought to develop a stronger framework for international energy cooperation to meet global energy needs and encourage the peaceful development of nuclear activities while also ensuring that exporting nuclear technology did not contribute to weapons proliferation. NNPA also sought to encourage other countries to ratify the United Nations Nonproliferation Treaty and to ensure that the U.S. had effective export controls of nuclear equipment, materials, and technology.[52]

Additional NNPA commitments made by the U.S. included having the long-term capacity to meet international nuclear fuel supply commitments as long as they are consistent with U.S. non-proliferation policies and domestic energy needs; strengthening the IAEA's safeguard system to ensure the timely detection of possible diversions of nuclear sources or materials which could be used for nuclear explosions; providing timely information dissemination about such diversion; timely implementing internationally agreed procedures if such diversion occurs; and encouraging the IAEA to provide nations supplying nuclear materials and equipment with essential data to ensure these nations adhere to relevant bilateral nuclear supply agreements. This law also gave authority to federal agencies such as the Arms Control and Disarmament Agency, Commerce, Defense, and Energy Departments, and Nuclear Regulatory Commission to participate in consultations on the possible international licensing and export of nuclear materials.[53]

The 1979 Export Administration Act (EAA) reflected an attempt to balance the conflict between advocates of expanding U.S. exports of defense sensitive goods and technologies and those favoring continuing restrictions on exporting these products due to concern they would benefit the Soviet Union and other U.S. enemies. EAA sought to minimize uncertainty in U.S. export control policies by encouraging trade with all countries the U.S. has diplomatic relations with unless the President determined such trade was injurious to U.S. interests. Statute requirements included having the Commerce Department maintain a Commodities Control List (CCL) describing licensing administrations for exporting strategic goods and technologies and confronting the problem of state-sponsored terrorism by requiring a specific license to export critical goods and technologies with countries having documented records of supporting international terrorism.[54]

Other EAA provisions included declaring that U.S. export control policy involved:

1. Opposing restrictive trade practices or boycotts of foreign countries against U.S. allied countries or any U.S. nationals;
2. Encouraging or requiring U.S. nationals in the export industry to refuse to participate in or support these trade practices or boycotts;
3. Having export controls by reviewed by appropriate U.S. Government agencies and private industry;
4. Using export controls, including license fees, to get foreign countries to remove supply access restrictions when such restrictions may have serious domestic inflationary impact, cause serious domestic shortage, or seek to influence U.S. foreign policy;
5. Using export controls to encourage other countries to take immediate steps to prevent use of their territories or resources to support or provide sanctuary to those supporting or participating in international terrorism;
6. Cooperating with other countries the U.S. has defense treaty obligations with to restrict goods and technology exports which

would be detrimental to the security of the U.S. and these countries; and

7. Minimizing restrictions on exporting agricultural commodities and products.[55]

The ink on EAA's more liberalized U.S. export control statute would barely be dry before international events would result in a tightening of U.S. export control screws. On December 27, 1979, the Soviet Union invaded Afghanistan to prop up a failing puppet government. The U.S. responded by imposing various economic and political sanctions against the Soviet Union including expanding CCL export controls to the Soviet Union for certain lasers, silicon materials and deposition equipment, and semiconductor sawing and furnishing equipment. The Carter Administration also imposed an embargo on U.S. agricultural exports to the Soviet Union which proved extremely unpopular with the U.S. agricultural industry and was eroded by other countries increasing their grain sales to the Soviet Union, and decided to boycott U.S. participation in the 1980 Moscow Summer Olympics.[56]

1981 saw the Carter Administration replaced by the Reagan Administration and renewed concern on the national security implications of western bloc technology transfers to the Soviet Union. A major challenge to U.S. export control policy and the complex relationships between the U.S. and its European allies was posed by the December 13, 1981 declaration of martial law in Poland by that nation's leader General Wojciech Jaruzelski (1923-) in an effort to thwart a Soviet invasion of Poland due to the rise of the Solidarity trade union movement.[57]

The U.S. imposed a variety of sanctions on Poland and the Soviet Union including suspending $100 million in agricultural assistance, withdrawing Polish fishing rights in U.S. waters, and refusing to extend Poland's Export-Import Bank Credit line. The Reagan Administration later added energy transmission and refining items to its list of foreign policy controlled commodities which affected contracts signed by Caterpillar and General Electric totaling $575 million for a Siberian pipeline. Western European allies such as the British, French, and West Germans were concerned with Polish events, but were more concerned with imposing economic sanctions due to their closer trade ties with and geographic proximity to the Soviet bloc. The U.S. was also concerned that construction of this pipeline would enhance Western European dependence on the Soviet bloc for crucial natural gas and petroleum supplies.

These differences of opinion imposed acute strains on U.S.-Western European relationship for nearly a year until an alternative approach was devised and vividly demonstrated that divergent economic interests can make broader allied cooperation on export control issues extremely difficult.[58]

Although the Reagan Administration would end the Carter Administration's agricultural exports embargo against Moscow, it also tried increasing U.S. efforts to prevent the export of sensitive technologies to the Soviet bloc. Washington also sought to promote economic relations with the Soviet Union which coincided with its strategic and foreign policy goals. These were elaborated on in *National Security Decision Directive (*NSDD*)* 75 issued on January 17, 1983 which served as a template for U.S. relational objectives toward the Soviet Union. Key points of this document emphasizing economic aspects included:

A. Ensuring East-West economic relations do not enhance Soviet military buildup by preventing equipment and technology transfers making substantial direct or indirect contributions to Soviet military power.

B. Avoiding subsidizing the Soviet economy or unnecessarily reducing Soviet resource allocation decisions in order to encourage systemic structural change.

C. Minimizing the potential for Soviet exercise of reverse leverage on Western countries stemming from energy supply, financial, and trade relationships.

D. Permitting mutually beneficial trade with the USSR in nonstrategic areas such as agriculture without Western subsidization or creating Western dependence.[59]

NSDD 75 sought to leverage U.S. economic strengths toward the Soviet Union by exhausting it to the point of collapse and achieved eventual success in this. Overall Reagan Administration export control policy toward the Soviet Union was more pragmatic. For instance, the U.S. did not impose economic sanctions on the Soviet Union following the 1983 shoot-down of Korean Airlines Flight 007 and economic sanctions against Poland were gradually eliminated as the 1980s proceeded.[60]

Export control issues confronting the Reagan Administration were not limited to the Soviet bloc. Congress sought to reauthorize the EAA in 1985 based on concerns within the private sector and Congress that the

Reagan Administration had been excessively successful in reversing the course of détente in its export control policies. This concern was based on evidence that U.S. companies were losing market share to rivals because U.S. export controls were stricter and comprehensive than other CoCom countries. In addition, evidence existed that a substantial number of export controlled items were becoming available through non-CoCom and non-Communist contries and evidence that other CoCom countries were not enforcing controls on "low-end" items without convincing the U.S. that these items were no longer strategic all combined to prompt pressure for change to the 1979 EAA.[61]

Congress responded to these export industry generated concerns by passing a new version of EAA in 1985. This statue included additional liberalization in U.S. export control laws such as requiring the President to annually certify the need and justification for continuing export foreign policy controls, requiring the President to consult with Congress and American business organizations before imposing foreign policy controls, and directing the President to determine that reasonable efforts had been made to use diplomatic or other alternative means to achieve the purpose of these export controls. 1985 EAA amendments also directed the President to gain cooperation from other countries governments in establishing comparable export controls, prohibiting the imposition of foreign policy controls on previously agreed contracts or agreements unless the President determines the export would jeopardize peace or endanger national security, controlling exports on goods or substances hazardous to public health and the environment which are banned or severely restricted in the U.S., and calling for limits on licensing requirements for exporting "low end" items to CoCom countries and attempting to place specific limits on executive branch ability to deny licenses in situations where the items are available internationally.[62]

Concerns over nuclear proliferation also marked U.S. export control policy during the 1980s. This applied to countries hostile to the U.S. and even to ostensibly friendly countries. An example of this was the Pressler Amendment passed in 1985. Introduced by Senator Larry Pressler (R-SD)(1942-), this amended the 1961 FAA by declaring that Pakistan could not receive U.S. military equipment or technology unless the President certified in writing to the Speaker of the House and the Senate Foreign Relations Committee chair that Pakistan did not possess nuclear weapons and that any military assistance Pakistan receives will significantly reduce that country's ability to possess nuclear weapons. This legislation would not be fully implemented until 1990, but reflected U.S. concern over the dangerous consequences of exporting weapons of mass destruction and their supportive technologies to volatile global regions like South Asia.[63]

The next target of U.S. export control efforts was South Africa. Although, the white minority government was not a regional security threat or a threat to U.S. national security interests, its racially oppressive Apartheid policies had been the target of U.S. and international displeasure for many years. This displeasure with South African domestic policies culminated in the Comprehensive Anti-Apartheid Act of 1986. This legislation sought to encourage U.S. employers operating in South Africa to actively oppose apartheid by recruiting and training black and colored employees for management responsibilities. It also sought to injure South Africa's economy by prohibiting the import of Krugerrand gold coins; the import of South African weapons and military vehicles; and products produced by South African government owned corporations or 15 parastatals unless they were agricultural products or strategic minerals essential for U.S. economic supply and national security and unavailable from other reliable and secure suppliers.[64]

This statute also imposed numerous export control and export related economic sanctions against South Africa including prohibiting computer exports to government and military agencies enforcing apartheid; direct or indirect loans or credits to the South African government; licensing nuclear products or technology determined to have nuclear proliferation potential; prohibiting U.S. financial institutions from holding non-diplomatic deposit accounts from South African government agencies; prohibiting U.S. nationals from making new investments in South Africa unless in black South African owned firms; prohibiting the export of USML items; crude oil and petroleum product exports; and non-intelligence related cooperation with the South African military. Penalties for violating these provisions range from $50,000 to $10 million and maximum imprisonment of ten years.[65]

This legislation can arguably be said to have played a significant role in injuring South Africa's economy and leading to the end of apartheid in 1994 due to their widespread domestic and international support though their utility has been debated.[66]

Using financial assistance as export control leverage was demonstrated by additional 1986 legislation. This statute saw the Export-Import Bank (Exim-Bank), the U.S. Government's export credit agency, prohibited from providing economic assistance to Communist countries unless the President determines that such assistance is in the national interest or that the country is no longer adheres to Communist principles. This law also sought to restrict U.S. companies from doing business with Angola's Communist government, supported by Cuban and Soviet troops, which possessed significant oil reserves and because the U.S. supported that country's opposition political and military movement. It ultimately sought to encourage the President to use his 1979 EAA authorities to restrict U.S. business transactions in Angola conflicting with national security interests.[67]

China's economic liberalization during the 1980's made it an increasingly attractive market for U.S. and international exporters and the U.S. and other countries a major outlet for Chinese exports which have helped fuel China's economic growth and political power. Unfortunately during 1989, China's totalitarian government reacted to student unrest, including demands for greater democratization, with a savage crackdown in Beijing's Tiananmen Square killing at least several hundred people. This action compelled the U.S. and other major countries to walk a delicate diplomatic tightrope as they sought to punish China for its bloody repression while also seeking to retain their increasingly lucrative economic engagement and some level of political leverage with the Middle Kingdom.[68]

The U.S. responded with a series of sanctions in 1990 that sought to balance these sometimes conflicting objectives. These sanctions included suspending exports of all items on the USML including arms and defense related equipment; suspending high level governmental contacts between these two countries; instructing U.S. representatives to international financial institutions to delay consideration of loan requests which would benefit China; suspend Overseas Private Investment Corporation action on applications for issuing new insurance and financing investments in China by U.S. investors; opposing further liberalization of COCOM trade guidelines with China; suspending implementation of a nuclear energy agreement with China foreclosing issuance of new licenses; suspending export licenses for U.S. manufactured satellites for Chinese-owned launch vehicles; and requiring the President to certify to Congress that China has provided clear assurance to the U.S. that it is not assisting and will not assist any non-nuclear state in acquiring nuclear explosive devices and the materials and components for such devices.[69]

Additional sanction provisions allowed for the potential lifting of these controls if the President reported to Congress that China had progressed on political reform by lifting martial law; halting executions and reprisals against individuals for peacefully expressing their political views; releasing political prisoners; increasing respect for internationally recognized human rights standards such as freedom of the press, assembly, and association; and permitted the freer flow of information including ending the jamming of the Voice of America and allowing greater access for foreign journalists.[70]

The duration and effectiveness of these sanctions was ephemeral. Just over three weeks after the Tiananmen Square crackdown, National Security Advisor Brent Scowcroft (1925-) and Assistant Secretary of State Larry Eagleburger (1930-2011) made a secret trip to China in an unsuccessful attempt to get China to adopt more favorable policies. Other subsequent U.S.-Sino diplomatic démarches would occur in the next few months.[71] Trade sanctions would also have an ephemeral effect on burgeoning Sino-U.S. trade. After dipping from $5.755 billion in 1989 to $4.806 billion between 1989-1990, U.S. exports to China steadily rose throughout the subsequent decade to reach $19.182 billion in 2001 and U.S. imports from China steadily rose from $11.990 billion in 1989 to $102.278 billion in 2001.[72]

Some European Union (EU) countries which also imposed an arms embargo against China were considering ending this sanction as of 2005 in their desire to develop a "strategic partnership" with China despite U.S. concerns that resuming such exports could threaten U.S., European, and Asian interests in peace and stability.[73] The U.S. would end its restrictions on satellite launch exports to China during the Clinton Administration eventually igniting a scandal that China had enhanced its nuclear weapons and space launch capabilities through espionage from the Energy Department and the commercial U.S. space launch industry with the complicity of these agencies and companies.[74]

These controls have done little to deter Chinese proliferation of weapons of mass destruction and supportive technologies. Beijing has sold chemical, missile technology, and nuclear technologies to countries as diverse as Libya, Iran, North Korea, Pakistan, and Syria and actively sought to promote cyberwar capabilities to enhance its own military capabilities and threaten military vulnerabilities of the U.S. and its allies.[75]

New post-Cold War security threats involving the potential use of weapons of mass destruction by regional powers in the Mideast also became the target of U.S. export controls and military action. The 1990 Iraqi invasion of Kuwait was an example of this. The U.S. initially responded to this event by ending commercial licenses to transfer defense articles and services to Iraq and Kuwait under AECA Section 38.[76] Soon after President George H.W. Bush issued EO 12724 blocking Iraqi government property and prohibiting transactions with Iraq. Examples of this included prohibiting the export to Iraq of goods or technologies requiring issuance of U.S. Government licenses and prohibiting U.S. citizens from performing or financing contracts supporting commercial, industrial, governmental, or public utility projects in Iraq.[77]

Further efforts to strengthen economic coercion against Iraq in light of what was the inevitable military conflict of Operation Desert Storm, reflected concerns over potential Iraqi access to weapons of mass destruction. On December 11, 1990, the Commerce Department's Bureau of Export Administration issued guidelines on export transactions involving equipment, materials, and technical data for producing biological agents. These guidelines urged U.S. commercial and governmental entities to watch out for individuals from countries such as Iran, Iraq, Syria, and Libya who sought to enroll as students or be involved working in courses or projects involving biological agents technical data and to be especially wary when individuals from these countries sought consultations and advice concerning such data and offered extremely generous payments for such information.[78]

Additional efforts to strengthen U.S. economic sanctions against Iraq occurred while military operations were underway. The Treasury Department's Office of Foreign Assets Control (OFAC) issued regulations calling for a census of blocked Iraqi government assets and a census of claims against Iraq's government. Detailed enumeration of items to be included in these censuses included descriptions of property, security or bullion, letters of credit, real and tangible property locations and descriptions, and reports of U.S. nationals documenting financial assets seized by the Iraqi Government.[79]

Concern over the proliferation of weapons of mass destruction to rogue regimes would dominate U.S. export control policy in the two decades following Operation Desert Storm. The first example of this was the Iran-Iraq Non-Proliferation Act of 1992. This statute imposed mandatory sanctions on any foreign individual or government transferring or retransferring goods or technology that enhance efforts by Iran or Iraq to acquire biological, chemical, or nuclear weapons or destabilizing types and numbers of certain advanced conventional weapons. If foreign governments transferred these materials to Iran or Iraq they would be subject to a one year suspension of U.S. assistance (except for urgent humanitarian assistance); suspension of collaborative dual-use and military technical exchange agreements; be ineligible to receive exports of items on the USML; and the U.S. would oppose multilateral bank assistance to these countries. Such sanctions could be waived if the President determined the waiver was "essential to U.S. national security interests."[80]

Although ostensibly a U.S. ally, Pakistan remained and remains a continuing country of U.S. nonproliferation concern. This was particularly reflected in the Glenn Amendment to the 1994 AECA incorporated by Ohio Senator John Glenn (1921-). This provision required the President to impose a series of economic sanctions when a then non-nuclear country such as Pakistan detonated nuclear explosive devices or transferred nuclear weapons technology to individuals, groups, or countries for developing nuclear weapons. These sanctions included terminating foreign aid programs except for food and other humanitarian assistance; denying export credits and guarantees issued by U.S. Government agencies; terminating military sales and foreign military financing; opposing non-humantarian international financial institution economic assistance; prohibiting U.S. banks from making loans to the detonating country except for food and agricultural commodities; and prohibiting exports of specific goods and technologies having civilian, military, and strategic uses and subject to Commerce Department export licensing. This legislation would not be implemented until 1998 when both India and Pakistan explored nuclear weapons and even then the Clinton Administration waived some of this amendment's financial assistance provisions.[81]

The Soviet Union's collapse between 1989-1991 also signaled the end of the need for COCOM as the premier western export control regime. COCOM lingered until March 31, 1994 when participating countries agreed to let it lapse until a new multilateral export control infrastructure was established. COCOM member countries, including the U.S., agreed to retain existing export control lists and focus on controlling exports of critical strategic concern until a new international export control regime was established. This occurred in July 1996 when the Wassenaar Arrangement was established as the primary western export control regime. This multilateral arrangement will be profiled in a subsequent chapter.[82]

Maintaining the trade embargo against Cuba's Communist Castro regime has been a hallmark characteristic of U.S. export control policy since the Kennedy Administration. The February 24, 1996 shootdown of the humanitarian organization Brothers to the Rescue plane by Cuba prompted additional enhancements to the U.S. embargo through the Helms-Burton Act sponsored by North Carolina Senator Jesse Helms (1921-2008) and Indiana Representative Dan Burton (1938-). Provisions of this statue included reaffirming that the President should encourage foreign countries to restrict trade and credit relations with Cuba and that sanctions should be applied against countries assisting Cuba; giving the U.S. the authority to seize any funds or materials used to trade with Cuba; prohibiting indirect financing of Cuban property confiscated from U.S. nationals; maintaining continuing U.S. opposition to Cuban membership in international financial institutions; and requiring the President to submit an annual report to congressional commerce committees on trade with and assistance provided to Cuba by other countries during the preceding 12 months including joint ventures and military assistance. This legislation proved highly unpopular internationally as demonstrated by challenges to it from the European Union and World Trade Organization.[83]

Ongoing problems with international terrorism, whether carried out by state sponsors or transnational terrorism groups, prompted Congress to enact the Antiterrorism and Effective Death Penalty Act in 1996. This legislation sought to optimize U.S. power to prevent individuals within the U.S. and subject to U.S. jurisdiction from providing material support or resources to foreign organizations engaging in terrorist activities. Provisions of this statute included giving the Treasury Department the authority to require U.S. financial institutions holding or controlling assets of foreign organizations involved in supporting terrorism to block all financial transactions involving these assets; penalizing individuals or organizations assisting or attempting to materially assist foreign terrorist organizations with up to 10 years imprisonment and civil penalties of $50,000 per violation; giving the President the authority to use covert and overt means to disrupt, dismantle, and destroy international terrorist infrastructures; and prohibiting economic and military assistance to countries providing assistance to states supporting terrorism and not fully cooperating with U.S. antiterrorism efforts as determined by the State Department.[84]

1996 also saw Congress enact additional nonproliferation and anti-terrorism related sanctions against Iran and Libya. The Iran and Libya Sanctions Act (ILSA) sought to limit Iran's ability to acquire weapons of mass destruction and financially sustain support for such weapons and terrorist activities and to keep Libya from supporting international terrorism and acquiring weapons of mass destruction. Specific provisions within this legislation included prohibitions of annual investments in exceeding $40 million that enhance development of Iranian and Libyan petroleum resources; directing the Export-Import Bank to not provide financial assistance to individuals sanctioned for violating this act; and requiring the President to file semiannual congressional reports on efforts to persuade countries to pressure Iran to stop supporting international terrorism and developing weapons of mass destruction while also documenting Iran's use of governmental, military, and quasi-governmental institutions to develop and promote international terrorism and sustain that country's weapons of mass destruction programs.[85]

Concern over the lack of religious freedom in many countries prompted the U.S. Government to implement export controls and other forms of economic and political pressure against these governments to get them to change their policies. This was demonstrated by the International Religious Freedom Act of 1998. Relevant sections of this statute included directing appropriate U.S. Government agencies not to issue export licenses for goods and technologies to foreign governments, agencies, companies, or officials committing religious freedom violations; directing U.S. trade assistance agencies such as the Export-Import Bank to not approve financial guarantees or credit to foreign governments, agencies, companies, or officials committing religious freedom violations; prohibiting military assistance to such countries; prohibiting U.S. financial institutions from making loans or providing credits of over $10 million annually to religious freedom violators; and prohibiting U.S. Government agencies from procuring from or contracting with any foreign government, entities, or officials determined by the President to be violating this law's religious freedom provisions.[86]

U.S. export control efforts also reflected an increasing emphasis on transnational terrorism as personified by the Al Qaeda terrorist group headed by Osama bin Laden (1957-2011). This group had been involved in attacks against U.S. military facilities in Saudi Arabia in 1996, U.S. embassies in Kenya and Tanzania in 1998, and had been sheltered for several years by Afghanistan's Taliban regime with the U.S. unsuccessfully attempting to extradite Bin Laden from Afghanistan. In EO 13129 on July 4, 1999, President Clinton declared Afghanistan's sheltering of Bin Laden and Al Qaeda constituted a national emergency and an unusual and extraordinary threat to U.S. foreign policy and national security. This document went on to seize Taliban property and interests in the U.S. and cut off financial, material, and technological support for Taliban assets in the U.S.; and prohibited U.S. exports to Taliban-controlled territory in Afghanistan and importation into the U.S. of Taliban products, services, and technologies. This order was reinstated by EO 13224 signed by President George W. Bush on September 23, 2001 in the aftermath of the 9/11 terrorist attacks against the U.S.[87]

Afghanistan was not the only rogue nation impacting U.S. export control policy during the late 1990s. North Korea's reclusive Stalinist regime maintained a large conventional military which threatened South Korea and surrounding nations, promoted terrorism and drug trafficking, and sought to develop a nuclear weapons program despite being unable to feed its own people. The North Korea Threat Reduction Act of 1999 sought to prevent North Korea from enhancing its nuclear weapons program. Provisions of this statute included prohibiting the transfer of nuclear components, material, and infrastructure to North Korea unless:

1. North Korea fully complies with its safeguards agreement with the International Atomic Energy Agency (IAEA);
2. Permits the IAEA to have full access to ALL of its nuclear facilities;
3. Consistently takes steps to implement the Joint Declaration on Denuclearization and adheres to the 1994 Agreed Framework between it and the U.S. in which Pyongyang agreed to shut down its nuclear weapons program in exchange for U.S. delivery of fuel and construction materials for two light water nuclear reactors;
4. North Korea does not have uranium enrichment or nuclear reprocessing facilities and is not making progress in acquiring and developing such facilities;
5. North Korea does not have nuclear weapons and is not trying to acquire, deploy, develop, purchase, or test these weapons; and
6. Transferring key nuclear components to North Korea under the Agreed Framework is in the U.S. national interest.[88]

Iran's nuclear weapons development aspirations and terrorism promotion remained U.S. foreign and national security policy concerns as the new millennium dawned. These concerns continue to the present and were reflected at this time in the 2000 Iran Nonproliferation Act. Relevant export controls provisions of this legislation included the President reporting to Congress credible information about foreign individuals transferring to Iran nuclear-related goods, services, and technologies listed on international export control regimes such as the Nuclear Suppliers Group Guidelines, Missile Technology Control Regime, Australia Group, and the Wassenaar Arrangement list of Dual Use Goods and Technologies and Munitions List; prohibiting U.S. Government weapons sales to foreign nationals of items on the USML, terminating sales of defense articles and services to such individuals under AECA; denying and suspending existing licenses enabling them transfer dual use items to other countries under the EAA; and requiring a Presidential determination that Russia continues adhering to its policy of not allowing the proliferation to Iran of weapons of mass destruction and missile systems capable of delivering such weapons. The consistency and effectiveness of these sanctions remains questionable.[89]

Following the 9/11 terrorist attacks, Congress enacted the USA Patriot Act as the main statutory foundation for responding to these attacks and preventing further attacks in the U.S. This legislation included various provisions for enhanced terrorist communication surveillance and tracking and seizing terrorist financial assets as well as various criminal penalties. Export control provisions within this legislation included amending the Trade Sanctions Reform and Export Enhancement Act of 2000 (Public Law 106-387) to include prohibitions facilitating the design, development, or production of weapons of mass destruction; including Taliban and Afghanistan in areas covered by this 2000 law; harmonizing the USA Patriot Act with the 1996 Antiterrorism and Effective Death Penalty Act by including smuggling and export control violations involving items on the USML and Export Administration Regulations (EAR) into U.S. anti-money laundering statutes; strengthening Treasury Department data collection on financial transactions such as exporting monetary instruments involving potential terrorist activity; and prohibiting restricted individuals from possessing, shipping, or receiving biological agents in interstate or foreign trade.[90]

The African country of Zimbabwe was another source of frustration for U.S. foreign policy during the early 2000s. This was due to the squandering of this country's resources and absence of political reform and democratization by Zimbabwean dictator Robert Mugabe's regime. In an effort to move this country in a more positive direction, the U.S. enacted the Zimbabwe Democracy and Economic Recovery Act in 2001. This legislation required the U.S. to vote against multilateral international financial assistance to Zimbabwe until the President certified that the rule of law, property rights, and various constitutional rights were restored in that country and that the U.S. should consider imposing international travel restrictions and economic sanctions against Zimbabweans responsible for these repressive conditions. These travel restrictions and economic sanctions were imposed by President George W. Bush through EO 13288 on March 6, 2003. Order provisions included blocking transactions made by these Zimbabweans with Americans as were any transactions initiated by Americans to economically benefit these individuals whose names and positions were listed in this executive order.[91]

Other transnational terrorist groups and their financial assets have been the target of U.S. export controls and economic sanctions. The Islamist terrorist group Hamas is one such example. Initially designed as a foreign terrorist organization by the State Department in 1997,[92] additional export controls including financial assets freezes have been taken by the U.S. against this Palestinean organization and its supporting entities such as the Holy Land Foundation including 2002 action freezing their U.S. property and prohibiting U.S. citizens from doing business with them unless licensed by the Treasury Department's Office of Foreign Assets Control (OFAC).[93]

Iran and Iraq were not the only Mideast countries economically targeted by the U.S. Syria has been a long-standing concern for the U.S. due to its hostility to the Middle East peace process; support for terrorism including fighters attacking U.S. forces in Iraq, the repressive Assad regimes, territorial aggrandizement in Lebanon; its close ties with Iran and North Korea; and its unsuccessful attempts to obtain nuclear weapons from the latter country until this infrastructure was destroyed by Israel in 2007. In response, Congress enacted the Syrian Accountability and Lebanese Sovereignty Restoration Act of 2003. This legislation called on Syria to immediately stop supporting terrorism and close the Syrian offices of Hamas, Hizballah and other terrorist organizations; stop supporting individuals going to fight in Iraq; withdraw its military and paramilitary forces from Lebanon; halt the development of weapons of mass destruction; and enter into serious peace negotiations with Israel.

Penalties to be imposed on Syria for not adhering to these requirements included prohibiting the export to Syria of any items including
those on the USML or the Commerce Control List (CCL) of dual-use
items in EAR; and the President being given the authority to impose at
least two of the following sanctions:

1. Prohibiting the export of U.S. products besides food and
    medicine;
2. Prohibiting U.S. businesses from investing or operating in
    Syria;
3. Restricting the travel radius of Syrian diplomats at the United
    Nations in New York and in Washington, DC;
4. Prohibiting Syrian owned or controlled aircraft from landing
    in, taking off, or overflying the U.S.;
5. Reducing U.S. diplomatic contacts with Syria to those re-
    quired to protect U.S. interests or implement this legislation;
    and
6. Blocking property transactions in which the Syrian govern-
    ment has an interest subject to U.S. jurisdiction.[94]

North Korea's unrelenting desire to defy international opinion and
build nuclear weapons would continue bedeviling the George W. Bush
Administration during its second term. Hope that North Korea was willing to surrender its nuclear aspirations rose when Pyongyang agreed to
participate in the Six-Party talks with South Korea, Japan, China, Russia, and the United States between 2003-2007. A goal of these talks was
providing North Korea with economic assistance in exchange for its dismantling its nuclear program. The U.S. ended TEA sanctions against
North Korea in 2008 as a positive incentive for Pyongyang to become a
more internationally responsible stakeholder.[95]

Unfortunately, North Korea proved unwilling to keep its word in
these negotiations. It continued participating in international drug trafficking; tested long-range ballistic missiles; attacked South Korean targets such as the naval ship *Cheonan*; and conducted nuclear weapons
tests on October 9, 2006 and May 25, 2009.[96] This misbehavior forced
both the Bush and Obama Administrations to take additional export control sanctions against North Korea. EO 13466, issued on June 26, 2008,
declared that Pyongyang's nuclear program constituted a national security and foreign policy threat to the U.S under IEEPA.[97] Detailed regu-

lations for implanting this order were approved on November 4, 2010 and included blocking the property and interests of the North Korean Government and North Korean nationals determined to trafficking in arms and related materials, restricting North Korean acquisition of luxury goods, or engaging in illegal activities such as money laundering, counterfeiting goods and currency, cash smuggling, and narcotics trafficking. These regulations also block U.S. citizens and institutions from transferring, paying, exporting, withdrawing, or dealing in property or property interests of individuals named in EO 13551.[98]

Ongoing U.S. concerns about Iran's nuclear programs and promotion of international terrorism continued to make Tehran the target of U.S. diplomatic enmity and the subject of economic sanctions. This enmity was further exacerbated by Iranian President Mahmoud Ahmadinejad's visceral expressions of hostility toward the U.S. and Israel such as calling for Israel to be "wiped off the map", denying the Holocaust, building diplomatic ties with anti-American leaders such as Venezuela's Hugo Chavez, and aiding anti-U.S. insurgents in Iraq.[99]

During the Bush's Administration's second term, the U.S. sought to increase already existing pressure on Iran by passing the Iran Freedom Support Act in 2006. This statute amended various features of ILSA by allowing the President to investigate imposing sanctions against individuals conducting investment activity in Iran and imposing sanctions against individuals, nations, or organizations who knowingly export, provide knowledge, or transfer to Iran goods, services, or technologies that would enable Tehran to acquire or develop weapons of mass destruction and related technologies along with destabilizing numbers and types of advanced conventional weapons. This law also declared that the U.S. would not cooperate with any country or government assisting Iran in developing its nuclear program or transferring advanced conventional weapons to it unless the President certifies that Iran has suspended all enrichment-related and reprocessing-related activity, commits to refrain from such activity in the future, and abides by strict international safeguards for peaceful nuclear energy development.[100]

The subsequent five years saw the Bush Administration replaced by the Obama Administration along with continued displeasure within the U.S. toward Iran's nuclear program and its overall foreign and national security policies. In an effort to avoid controversial and costly military action against Tehran, the U.S. attempted to increase economic pressure on Iran with the passage of additional sanctions in late 2011. One section of this legislation required the United States Comptroller General to conduct a study of any gaps between Iranian conventional and anti-access capabilities and the U.S.' capabilities to overcome these gaps. The heart of this legislation directed at Iran, however sought to impose a variety of crippling financial sanctions including:

1. Designating Iran's financial sector, including the Central Bank of Iran, as a primary money laundering concern due to the Iranian Government's pursuit of nuclear weapons, support for international terrorism; and efforts to deceive responsible financial institutions and evade international sanctions;
2. Giving the President the power under IEEPA to freeze Iranian financial institution assets and blocking their property and property interests if these are within the U.S. or come within possession or control of U.S. nationals;
3. Prohibit the opening in the U.S. of correspondent accounts or payable-through accounts of foreign financial institutions which have conducted or facilitated significant financial transactions with Iranian financial institutions;
4. Requiring the Energy Information Administration to submit to Congress reports on the availability and price of petroleum products produced in countries other than Iran every 60 days and whether this makes it possible for countries purchasing Iranian petroleum and petroleum products to significantly reduce their purchases from Iran;
5. Requiring the President to carry out multilateral diplomatic initiatives to persuade countries purchasing Iranian oil to limit Iranian use of oil revenue to purchasing non-luxury consumer goods from the oil-purchasing country; prohibiting Iranian purchases of military or dual use technology that could enhance Iranian conventional or weapons of mass destruction programs; and encourage petroleum producing countries to increase their production to increase non-Iranian oil supplies and minimize the international impact on oil prices from these sanctions.[101]

Regulations for implementing these sanctions were specified in EO 13599 on February 5, 2012.[102]

Syria's descent into bloody civil war in 2011-2012 between Bashir Assad's regime and his opponents continues to horrify the world. It has also brought additional U.S. sanctions against Syria as the U.S. and international community struggle to find something approximating a favorable outcome to this internecine conflict. On August 17, 2011, President Obama issued EO 13582 blocking Syrian Government property and prohibiting certain transactions. This order also prohibited new U.S. investment in Syria; exporting, reexporting, selling, or supplying from the U.S. any services to Syria; importing Syrian petroleum or petroleum products into the U.S.; any transactions by U.S. nationals related to Syrian petroleum or petroleum products; and any approval, financing, facilitation, or guarantee by foreign individuals of Syrian products or services within the U.S.[103]

EO 13606 issued on April 22, 2012 saw the Obama Administration seek to sanction individuals and organizations providing products and technologies enabling the Iranian and Syrian governments to stop the free flow of information through computer networks and provided goods, services, and technologies these countries could use to facilitate computer or network disruption or serious human rights abuses.[104] EO 13608 issued on May 1, 2012, went on to impose sanctions on individuals and organizations seeking to evade existing U.S. economic and financial sanctions on Iran and Syria including suspending their immigration into the U.S.[105]

The 20th and 21st centuries have seen the U.S. Government create a surfeit of export control legislation and regulations to advance U.S. national security, foreign policy and economic objectives. These laws and regulations have mandated the compilation and dissemination of numerous reports and data on U.S. export control activities to assist researchers and inform the public. They have also created an enormously complicated statutory and organizational structure consuming significant sections of the United States Code including portions of Titles 7, 10, 15, 19, 22, and 50. Regulations for implementing and enforcing these laws, including the CCL, EAR, USML, and various financial sanctions cover Titles 15, 22, and 31 of the Code of Federal Regulations covering 1,294 pages of often excruciating detail as of 2011.[106]

These laws and regulations have granted export control responsibilities to numerous federal officials and agencies including the President, Commerce Department, Defense Department, Justice Department, State Department, Treasury Department, and U.S. Customs and Border Protection. These agencies have achieved mixed success and effectiveness in enforcing U.S. export control policies.[107] Involvement of these multi-faceted agencies also creates oversight opportunities and challenges for multiple congressional committees and subcommittees which export oriented industries seek to influence in their efforts to promote expanded U.S. export opportunities. Conversely, individuals and organizations favoring more restrictive controls on foreign policy and national security grounds also lobby Congress to promote their objectives. Subsequent chapters will address how various U.S. Government agencies have carried out their responsibilities in recent decades and how the U.S. has interacted with various international government export control organizations in the continuing challenge to promote international economic development and trade while restricting the proliferation of destructive military and dual-use technologies to rogue nations and transnational terrorist groups.

Notes

1. See Christopher Tuplin, "Thucydides 1.42.2 and the Megarian Decree," *The Classical Quarterly*, 29 (2)(1979): 301-307; and Charles Fornara, "Plutarch and the Megarian Decree," in Donald Kagan, *Studies in the Greek Historians*, (New York: Cambridge University Press, 2009): 213-228.

2. See Richard Rosecrance, *The Rise of the Trading State: Commerce and Conquest in the Modern World,* (New York: Basic Books, Inc., 1985); Ronald Findlay and Kevin H. O'Rourke, *Power and Plenty: Trade, War, and the World Economy in the Second Millenium,* (Princeton: Princeton University Press, 2007); and William J. Bernstein, *A Splendid Exchange: How Trade Shaped the World,* (New York: Atlantic Monthly Press, 2008).

3. Public Law 65-91, "An Act to Define, Regulate, and Punish Trading With the Enemy, and for Other Purposes," 40 *U.S. Statutes at Large* 411-426.

4. U.S. Department of State, *Papers Relating to Foreign Relations of the United States: The Lansing Papers 1914-1920,* (Washington, DC: GPO, 1940): 2: 10-11.

5. C.H. Hand, Jr., "The Trading With the Enemy Act," *Columbia Law Review,* 19 (2)(April 1919): 115-116.

6. Ibid., 123-124.

7. U.S. Committee on Public Information, *Official Bulletin,* 1 (40)(June 26, 1917): 1.

8. See U.S. National Archives and Records Administration, "Records of the War Trade Board," (Washington, DC: National Archives and Records Administration, 1995); http://www.archives.gov/research/guide-fed-records/groups/182.html#182.1>; Accessed May 3, 2012; and U.S. War Trade Board, *Report of the War Trade Board, June 1917-June 1919*, (Washington, DC: GPO, 1920); http://babel.hathitrust.org/cgi/pt?id=mdp.39015006987500; Accessed May 3, 2012.

9. Ibid., "Records of the War Trade Board.

10. See U.S. Department of the Treasury, "Office of Foreign Assets Control (OFAC)" (2012): 1; http://www.treasury.gov/about/organizational-structure/offices/Pages/Office-of-Foreign-Assets-Control.aspx; Accessed May 3, 2012; and U.S. Treasury Department Foreign Funds Control, *Administration of the Wartime Financial and Property Controls of the United States Government*, (Washington, DC: Treasury Department, 1942); http://catalog.hathitrust.org/Record/001122826; Accessed May 3, 2012.

11. U.S. Department of the Treasury, "Office of Foreign Assets Control (OFAC)" (2012): 1; http://www.treasury.gov/about/organizational-structure/offices/Pages/Office-of-Foreign-Assets-Control.aspx; Accessed May 3, 2012; and U.S. Treasury Department Foreign Funds Control, Administration of the Wartime Financial and Property Controls of the United States Government, (Washington, DC: Treasury Department, 1942); http://catalog.hathitrust.org/Record/001122826; Accessed May 3, 2012): 10.

12. See John H. Henshaw, *The Origins of COCOM: Lessons for Contemporary Proliferation Control Regimes*, (Washington, DC: Henry C. Stimson Center, 1993); *Neutrality Act of 1937*, House Report 75-363, Serial 10083; (Washington, DC: GPO, 1937); Public Law 76-703, "National Defense Act of 1940," 54 *U.S. Statutes at Large* 714; and Stuart L. Weiss, "American Foreign Policy and Presidential Power: The Neutrality Act of 1935," *The Journal of Politics*, 30 (3)(August 1968): 672-695.

13. See Public Law 81-11, "Export Control Act of 1949," 63 *U.S. Statutes at Large*, 7-8; and Paul H. Silverstone, "The Export Control Act of 1949: Extraterritorial Enforcement," *University of Pennsylvania Law Review*, 107 (3)(January 1959): 331-362.

14. Morris Bornstein, *East-West Technology Transfer: The Transfer of Western Technology to the USSR*, (Paris: OECD, 1985).

15. See U.S. Department of State, *Foreign Relations of the United States 1950: Volume IV: Central and Eastern Europe; The Soviet Union*, Roger P. Churchill, Chales S. Sampson, and William Z. Slany, eds., (Washington, DC: GPO, 1980): 65-260; for COCOM's documentary foundations. See also Public Law 82-213, "Mutual Defense Assistance Control Act of 1951, 65 *U.S. Statutes at Large*, 644-647; Michael Mastanduno, *Economic Containment: COCOM and the Politics of East-West Trade*, (Ithaca: Cornell University Press, 1992); Frank M. Cain, "Exporting the Cold War: British Responses to the U.S.A's

Establishment of COCOM: 1947-1951," *Journal of Contemporary History*, 29 (3)(July 1994): 501-522; Ibid., "The U.S.-Led Trade Embargo on China: The Origins of CHIMCOM, 1947-1952, *Journal of Strategic Studies*, 18 (4)(1995): 33-54; Richard T. Cupitt, *Reluctant Champions: U.S. Presidential Policy and Strategic Export Controls, Truman, Eisenhower, and Clinton*, (London: Routledge, 2000): 96-105; Tor Egil Førland, *Cold Economic Warfare: CoCom and the Forging of Strategic Export Controls, 1948-1954*, (Dordrecht: Republic of Letters Publishing, 2009); and James K. Libbey, "CoCom, Comecon, and the Economic Cold War," *Russian History*, 37 (2)(2010): 133-152.

16. See Dianne E. Rennack, *North Korea: Economic Sanctions*, (Washington, DC: Library of Congress, Congressional Research Service, 2003): 5, 12; and *Economic Sanctions Against a Nuclear North Korea: An Analysis of United States and United Nations Actions Since 1950*, Suk Hi Kim and Semoon Chang, eds., (Jefferson, NC: McFarland, 2007): 34-55.

17. See Mastanduno, 98-99; and *Foreign Relations of the United States, 1955-1957: Foreign Aid and Economic Defense Policy Volume X*, Robert J. McMahon, William F. Sanford, and Sherrill B. Wells, (Washington, DC: GPO, 1989): 420-421.

18. See U.S. Department of State, *The 1958 Revision of East-West Trade Controls Mutual Defense Assistance Control Act of 1951: Twelfth Report to Congress*, (Washington, DC: GPO, 1959): 38; Frank Cain, "The U.S.-Led Trade Embargo on China: The Origins of CHINCOM, 1947-1952," *Journal of Strategic Studies*, 18 (4)(1995): 33-54; and Gary Clyde Hufbauer, et. al. eds., *Economic Sanctions Reconsidered*, 3rd ed., (Washington, DC: Peterson Institute for International Economics, 2007): 11, 21.

19. See Public Law 83-665, "Mutual Security Act of 1954," 68 *U.S. Statutes* 832-833, 848-849; U.S. Congress, House Committee on Foreign Affairs, *Mutual Security Act Extension*, (Washington, DC: GPO, 1953); 77-118; and U.S. Department of State, *Foreign Relations of the United States, 1955-1957 Volume X: Foreign Aid and Economic Defense Policy*, John P. Glennon, Editor in Chief, (Washington, DC: GPO, 1989): 17-25, 118-119, for coverage of this act's development and implementation.

20. See U.S. Department of State, *Foreign Relations of the United States, 1955-1957 Suez Crisis, July 26-December 31, 1956, Volume XVI*, Nina J. Noring, ed., (Washington, DC: GPO, 1990); Peter L. Hahn, *United States, Great Britain, and Egypt: Strategy and Diplomacy in the Early Cold War, 1945-1956*, (Chapel Hill: University of North Carolina Press, 1991; and Diane B. Kunz, *The Economic Diplomacy of the Suez Crisis*, (Chapel Hill: University of North Carolina Press, 1991).

21. Kunz, 192-194.

22. See Public Law 86-108, "Mutual Security Act of 1959," 73 *U.S. Statutes at Large*, 246-247; U.S. Congress, *Senate Committee on Foreign Relations, Mutual Security Act of 1959. Hearings on S. 1451 to Amend Further the*

Mutual Security Act of 1954, as Amended, and for Other Purposes . . . (Washington, DC: GPO, 1959); http://catalog.hathitrust.org/Record/009862897; Accessed May 10, 2012; President of the United States, *Report on the Organization and Administration of the Military Assistance Program Submitted to the President on June 3, 1959*, House Document 86-186, Serial 12228, (Washington, DC: GPO, 1959); and John Duncan Powell, "Military Assistance and Militarism in Latin America," *The Western Political Quarterly*, 18 (2)(June 1965): 382-392.

23. See Irving Louis Horowitz, *The Long Night of Dark Intent: A Half Century of Cuban Communism*, (New Brunswick, NJ: Transaction Publishers, 2008); U.S. Government Accountability Office, "U.S. Embargo on Cuba: Recent Regulatory Changes and Potential Presidential or Congressional Actions," (Washington, DC: GAO, 2009); http://purl.access.gpo.gov/GPO/LPS119709; Accessed May 10, 2012; and *Foreign Relations of the United States, 1961-1963, Volume X, Cuba, January 1961-September 1962*, Louis J. Smith, ed., (Washington, DC: GPO, 1997).

24. Public Law 87-195 "Act for International Development of 1961," 75 *U.S. Statutes at Large*, 424, 444-445.

25. President of the United States, "Proclamation 3447: Embargo on All Trade With Cuba," 27 *Federal Register* (February 7, 1962): 1085.

26. See U.S. Department of the Treasury, "Cuban Assets Control Regulations: Control of Financial and Commercial Transactions Involving Cuba or Nationals Thereof," 28 *Federal Register* (July 9, 1963): 974; U.S. Government Accountability Office, (2009): 4; Michael P. Malloy, Eric M. Lieberman, Dennis M. O'Connell, and Steven M. Schneebaum, "Are the U.S. Treasury's Assets Control Regulations a Fair and Effective Tool of U.S. Foreign Policy?: The Case of Cuba, *Proceedings of the Annual Meeting (American Society of International Law)*, 79 April 25-27, 1985): 169-189; U.S. Government Accounting Office, *Economic Sanctions: Effectiveness as Tools of Foreign Policy*, (Washington, DC: GAO, 1992): 2.

27. See U.S. Department of State, *Documents on Germany, 1944*-1985, (Washington, DC: U.S. Department of State, 1986): 773-775; U.S. Department of State, *Foreign Relations of the United States, 1961-1963: Volume XIV: Berlin, 1961-1963*, Charles S. Sampson, ed., (Washington, DC: GPO, 1993); David Murphy, Sergei A. Kondrashev, and George Bailey, *Battleground Berlin: CIA vs KGB in the Cold War*, (New Haven: Yale University Press, 1997).

28. See *Foreign Relations of the United States, 1961-1963*, 14:317; U.S. Joint Chiefs of Staff, "Statements of Generals Watson and Clarke on Berlin Wall Situation 13-31, August 1961," (Washington, DC: Joint Chiefs of Staff, 1962): 3; <http://www.jfklibrary.org/Asset-Viewer/Archives/JFKPOF-117-008.aspx>; Accessed May 14, 2012; and David Klein, "Memorandum for Mr. Bundy: Berlin Discussions at Geneva," (Washington, DC: National Secu-

rity Council, 1962): 2-3; http://www.jfklibrary.org/Asset-Viewer/Archives/JFKPOF-117-008.aspx; Accessed May 14, 2012.

29. U.S. Central Intelligence Agency, "Notes on Soviet Vulnerabilities," (Washington, DC: CIA, July 7, 1961): 9-13; www.foia.cia.gov/BerlinWall/1961-Summer/1961-97-07d.pdf; Accessed May 15, 2012.

30. U.S. Department of State, "Incoming Telegram To: Secretary of State," (Washington, DC: U.S. Department of State, February 18, 1962): 1; http://www.jfklibrary.org/Asset-Viewer/Archives/JFKPOF-117-008.aspx; Accessed May 14, 2012.

31. "Survivability of West Berlin," in *On the Front Lines of the Cold War Intelligence War in Berlin 1946 to 1961*, Donald Steury, ed., (Washington, DC: Center for the Study of Intelligence, 1999): 633-634.

32. See Hufbauer, 86, 123; and Gregory W. Pedlow, "NATO and the Berlin Crisis of 1961: Facing the Soviets While Maintaining Unity," (Washington, DC: Central Intelligence Agency, 2011): 7-13; www.foia.cia.gov/BerlinWall/Essays/NATOandBerlinCrisis.pdf; Accessed May 15, 2012.

33. See Public Law 87-195, "Act for International Development for 1961," 75 *U.S. Statutes at Large*, 424, 434-438; and President of the United States, "Executive Order 10973: Administration of Foreign Assistance and Related Programs," 26 *Federal Register* 215 (November 7, 1961): 10469-10470.

34. See Public Law 87-565, "Foreign Assistance Act of 1962," 76 *U.S. Statutes at Large*, 255, 260-261; and "Foreign Assistance Act of 1962: Provisions Regarding Certain Restrictions on U.S. Aid," *International Legal Materials*, 1 (1)(August 1962): 118-120.

35. See John J. Stemlau, *The International Politics of the Nigerian Civil War 1967-1970*, (Princeton: Princeton University Press, 1977); and Robert A. Pape, "Why Economic Sanctions Do Not Work," *International Security*, 22 (2)(Autumn 1997): 102, 111-112.

36. See Stemmlau, 62-66, 290-294; and *Foreign Relations of the United States, 1964-1968: Volume XXIV, Africa*, Nina Davis Howland, ed., (Washington, DC: GPO, 1999): 610-690; and *Foreign Relations of the United States, 1969-1976, Volume E-5, Part I, Documents on Sub-Saharan Africa, 1969-1972*, Joseph Hilts and David C. Humphrey, eds. (Washington, DC: GPO, 2005): http://history.state.gov/historicaldocuments/frus1969-76ve05p1; Accessed May 16, 2012.

37. See Public Law 90-629, "Foreign Military Sales Act," 82 *U.S. Statutes at Large*, 1320-1328; and U.S. Congress, House Committee on Foreign Affairs, *The Foreign Military Sales Act*, (Washington, DC: GPO, 1968).

38. See Public Law 91-184, "Export Administration Act of 1969," 83 *U.S. Statutes at Large*, 842-844; and Ian F. Fergusson, *The Export Administration Act: Evolution, Provisions, and Debate*, (Washington, DC: Library of Congress, Congressional Research Service, 2009): 2.

39. See Public Law 91-184, 83 *U.S. Statutes at Large*, 841-842; and U.S. Congress, House Committee on Banking and Currency, Subcommittee on International Trade, "*To Extend and Amend the Export Control Act of 1949*," (Washington, DC: GPO, 1969); http://catalog.hathitrust.org/Record/008466898; Accessed May 16, 2012.

40. United States Congress, House Committee on International Relations, Subcommittees on Africa and International Organizations, *United States Policy Toward South Africa*, (Washington, DC: GPO, 1978).

41. See U.S. Congress, House Committee on International Relations, Subcommittee on Africa, *U.S.-South Africa Relations: Nuclear Cooperation*, (Washington, DC: GPO, 1978); United Nations, Department for Disarmament Affairs, Report of the Secretary General, *South Africa's Nuclear-Tipped Ballistic Missile Capability*, (New York: United Nations, 1991): 9; Roy E. Horton III, *Out of (South) Africa: Pretoria's Nuclear Weapons Experience*, (Colorado Springs: USAF Institute for National Security Studies, 1999): 8; Timothy J. Stapleton, *A Military History of South Africa from the Dutch-Khoi Wars to the End of Apartheid*, (Santa Barbara: Praeger, 2010): 158; and *Foreign Relations of the United States, 1969-1976 Volume XXVIII: Southern Africa*, Myra F. Burton, ed., (Washington, DC: GPO, 2011): 173-177.

42. United Nations Security Council, *Resolution 418 of 1977 of November 4, 1977*, (New York: United Nations Security Council, 1977): 5-6; http://daccess-dds-ny.un.org/doc/RESOLUTION/GEN/NR0/297/01/IMG/NR029701.pdf?OpenElement>; Accessed May 16, 2012.

43. U.S. Department of Commerce, "Restriction of Exports to the Republic of South Africa and Namibia," 43 *Federal Register* 36 (February 22, 1978): 7311.

44. Public Law 95-630, "Financial Institutions Regulatory and Interest Rate Control Act," 92 *U.S. Statutes at Large* 3641, 3727.

45. See Public Law 94-329, "International Security Assistance and Arms Export Control Act of 1976," 90 *U.S. Statutes at Large* 729-769; U.S. Congress, House Committee on International Relations, *International Security Assistance and Arms Export Control Act of 1976*, (Washington, DC: GPO, 1976); http://catalog.hathitrust.org/Record/003220332; Accessed May 17, 2012; and Ibid., *Arms Export Control Act*, (Washington, DC: GPO, 1976); http://catalog.hathitrust.org/Record/003220393; Accessed May 17, 2012.

46. See Ibid., 90 *U.S. Statutes at Large*, 734, 739, 744; Peter Swan, "A Road Map to Understanding Global Export Controls: National Security in a Changing Global Environment," *American Business Law Journal*, 30 (4)(February 1993): 616; U.S. National Archives and Records Administration, *Code of Federal Regulations Title 22: Foreign Relations: Parts 1-299*, (Washington, DC: National Archives and Records Administration, 2011): 464-571. USML is listed in 22 CFR 121.

47. See Public Law 95-223, "With Respect to the President in Time of War or National Emergency," 91 *U.S. Statutes at Large* 1625-1628; U.S. Congress, House Committee On International Relations, Subcommittee on International Trade and Commerce, *Trading With the Enemy: Legislative and Executive Documents Concerning Regulation of International Transactions in Time of Declared National Emergency*, (Washington, DC: GPO, 1976); http://catalog.hathitrust.org/Record/003220307 > ; Accessed May 17, 2012; and U.S. Congress, Senate Committee on Banking, Housing, and Urban Affairs, Subcommittee on International Finance, *Amending the Trading With the Enemy Act*, (Washington, DC: GPO, 1977); http://catalog.hathitrust.org/Record/002941349; Accessed May 17, 2012.

48. See Joel B. Harris and Jeffrey P. Bialos, "The Strange New World of United States Export Controls under the International Emergency Economic Powers Act," *Vanderbilt Journal of Transnational Law*, 18 (Winter 1985): 71-108; and Jason Luong, "Forcing Constraint: The Case for Amending the International Emergency Economic Powers Act," *Texas Law Review*, 78 (5)(April 2000): 1181-1213. For an example of recent presidential use of IEEPA see President of the United States, *An Executive Order Clarifying Certain Executive Orders Blocking Property and Prohibiting Certain Executive Transactions*, House Document 109-10, (Washington, DC: GPO, 2005); < http://purl.access.gpo.gov/GPO/LPS59800 > ; Accessed May 17, 2012.

49. See Warren H. Donnelly and Barbara Rather, *Nuclear Weapons Proliferation and the International Atomic Energy Agency: An Analytical Report*, (Washington, DC: Library of Congress, Congressional Research Service, 1976); http://catalog.hathitrust.org/Record/003222211; Accessed May 18, 2012. Public Law 95-92, "International Security Assistance Act of 1977," 91 *U.S. Statutes at Large* 614, 620-621; and U.S. Government Accountability Office, *An Evaluation of the Administration's Proposed Nuclear Non-Proliferation Strategy: Report to the Congress*, (Washington, DC: GAO, 1977); http://catalog.hathitrust.org/Record/011408757; Accessed May 18, 2012.

50. See Public Law 95-213, "Foreign Corrupt Practices Act," 91 *U.S. Statutes at Large,* 1495-1497; and U.S. Congress, House Committee on Interstate and Foreign Commerce, Subcommittee on Oversight and Investigations, *Foreign Corrupt Practices Act*, (Washington, DC: GPO, 1979).

51. Ibid., 1497; Public Law 105-366, "International Anti-Bribery and Fair Competition Act of 1998," 112 *U.S. Statutes at Large 3301-3304;* U.S. Congress, House Committee on Commerce, Subcommittee on Finance and Hazardous Materials, *The International Anti-Bribery and Fair Competition Act of 1998*, (Washington, DC: GPO, 1999).

52. See Public Law 95-242, "Nuclear Non-Proliferation Act of 1978," 92 *U.S. Statutes at Large,* 120-121; and U.S. Congress, Senate Committee on Energy and Natural Resources, Subcommittee on Energy Research and Devel-

opment, *Nuclear Non-Proliferation Policy Act of 1977*, (Washington, DC: GPO, 1977.)

53. Ibid., 92 *U.S. Statutes at Large*, 124-126, 141.

54. See Public Law 96-72, "Export Administration Act of 1979," 93 *U.S. Statutes at Large*, 503-536; and U.S. Congress, Senate Committee on Banking, Housing, and Urban Affairs, *U.S. Export Control Policy and Extension of the Export Administration Act*, (Washington, DC: GPO, 1979); http:// catalog.hathitrust.org/Record/002947441; Accessed May 21, 2012.

55. Ibid., 504-505.

56. See U.S. International Trade Administration, "Revisions to Reflect Identification and Continuation of Foreign Policy Export Controls," 45 *Federal Register 5*, (January 8, 1980): 1595-1598; U.S. International Trade Administration, "Revisions to Reflect Identification and Continuation of Foreign Policy Export Controls," 45 Federal Register 5, (January 8, 1980): 1595-1598; U.S. International Trade Administration, "Request for Comments on Effects of Foreign Policy Controls," 45 *Federal Register 173*, (September 4, 1980): 58562; U.S. Congress, Senate Committee on Agriculture, Nutrition, and Forestry, *Embargo on Grain Sales to the Soviet Union*, (Washington, DC: GPO, 1980); and Alan P. Dobson, "From Instrumental to Expressive: The Changing Goals of the U.S. Cold War Strategic Embargo," *Journal of Cold War Studies*, 12 (1)(Winter 2010): 98-119.

57. See *From Solidarity to Martial Law The Polish Crisis of 1980-1981: A Documentary History*, Andrzej Paczkowski and Malcolm Byrne, eds., (Budapest: Central European University Press, 2007); and *Preparing for Martial Law: Through the Eyes of Col. Ryszard Kuklinski*, (Washington, DC: Central Intelligence Agency, 2009); http://purl.fdlp.gov/GPO/gpo15351; Accessed May 21, 2012.

58. See U.S. International Trade Administration, "General Orders; Suspension of Licensing for All Orders to the U.S.S.R.," 47 *Federal Register 2* (January 5, 1982): 141-146; Ibid., "Amendment of Oil and Gas Controls to the U.S.S.R.," 47 *Federal Register 122*, (June 24, 1982): 47250-47252; U.S. Department of State, *Siberian Gas Pipeline and U.S. Export Controls*, (Washington, DC: Department of State, 1982); U.S. Congress, Joint Economic Committee, *Soviet Pipeline Sanctions: The European Perspective*, (Washington, DC: GPO, 1983); http://catalog.hathitrust.org/Record/011336860; Accessed May 21, 2012; Bruce W. Jentleson, *Pipeline Politics: The Complex Political Economy of East-West Energy Trade*, (Ithaca: Cornell University Press, 1986); Mastanduno, 244-263; and Alan P. Dobson, "From Instrumental to Expressive: The Changing Goals of the U.S. Cold War Strategic Embargo," *Journal of Cold War Studies*, 21 (2)(Winter 2010): 117-118.

59. See National Security Council, "NSDD-75 on U.S. Relations With the USSR," (Washington, DC: The White House, 1983): 3; www.fas.org/irp/

offdocs/nsdd/nsdd-75.pdf; Accessed May 24, 2012; Norman A. Bailey, *The Strategic Plan That Won the Cold War" National Security Decision Directive 75*, (Maclean, VA: The Potomac Foundation, 1999); and Alan P. Dobson, "The Reagan Administration, Economic Warfare, and Starting to Close Down the Cold War," *Diplomatic History*, 29 (3)(June 2005): 531-556.

60. Ibid., 547-551.

61. *Finding Common Ground: U.S. Export Controls in a Changed Global Environment*, (Washington, DC: National Academy Press, 1991): 317.

62. See Ibid., 64, 318; and Public Law 99-64, "Export Administration Amendments Act of 1985," 99 *U.S. Statutes at Large* 120.

63. See Public Law 99-83, "International Security and Development Cooperation Act of 1985," 99 *U.S. Statutes at Large* 190, 267-268; and Public Law 101-513, "Foreign Operations, Exporting Financing, and Related Programs Appropriations Act, 1991," 104 *U.S. Statutes at Large*, 1979, 2042; and U.S. Congress, Senate Committee on Foreign Relations, *Interpreting the Pressler Amendment: Commercial Military Sales to Pakistan*, (Washington, DC: GPO, 1992).

64. Public Law 99-440, "Comprehensive Anti-Apartheid Act of 1986," 100 *U.S. Statutes at Large*, 1086, 1093, 1099.

65. Ibid., 100 *U.S. Statutes at Large*, 1099-1102, 1104-1106.

66. See Hufbauer, 54, 68, 79; Philip I. Levy, "Sanctions on South Africa: What Did They Do?" *American Economic Review*, 89 (2)(May 1999): 415-420; and *How Sanctions Work: Lessons from South Africa*, Neda C. Crawford, and Audie Klotz, eds., (London: Macmillan Press Ltd., 1999).

67. See Public Law 99-472, "Export-Amendment Bank Amendments," 100 *U.S. Statutes at Large* 1200-1203, 1210; and U.S. Congress. Senate Committee on Banking, Housing, and Urban Affairs, *Department of Commerce's First Annual Report on Foreign Policy Export Controls*, (Washington, DC: GPO, 1986); http://catalog.hathitrust.org/Record/007604044>; Accessed May 25, 2012.

68. See U.S. Congress, Senate Committee on Finance, *Extending Most-Favored-Nation Status for China*, (Washington, DC: GPO, 1991); and James A.R. Miles, *The Legacy of Tiananmen: China in Disarray*, (Ann Arbor: University of Michigan Press, 1996).

69. Public Law 101-246, "Foreign Relations Authorization Act, Fiscal Years 1990 and 1991," 104 *U.S. Statutes at Large*, 15, 81, and 84.

70. Ibid., 85.

71. James A. Baker III with Thomas M. DeFrank, *The Politics of Diplomacy: Revolution, War & Peace, 1989-1992*, (New York: G.P. Putnam's Sons, 1995): 108-114.

72. See *Historical Statistics of the United States Millenial Edition*, Susan B. Carter et. al. eds., (New York: Cambridge University Press, 2006): Table Ee533-550; 5:538; and Table Ee 551-568; 5:544.

73. Kristin Archick, Richard F. Grimmett, and Shirley A. Kan, *European Union's Arms Embargo on China: Implications and Options for U.S. Policy*, (Washington, DC: Library of Congress, Congressional Research Service, 2006): 1.

74. See U.S. Congress, House Select Committee on U.S. National Security and Military Concerns with the People's Republic of China, *Report*. House Report 105-851, (Washington, DC: GPO, 1998): 1:ii-xxxvii.

75. See Shirley A. Kan, *China and Proliferation of Weapons of Mass Destruction and Missiles: Policy Issues*, (Washington, DC: Library of Congress, Congressional Research Service, 2002): 1-14; and United States-China Economic and Security Review Commission, *China's Proliferation Practices and the Development of its Cyber and Space Warfare Capabilities*, (Washington, DC: GPO, 2008).

76. U.S. Department of State, Bureau of Politico-Military Affairs, "Revocation of Munitions Export Licenses to Iraq; Suspension of Munitions Exports to Kuwait," 55 *Federal Register* 150 (August 3, 1990): 31808.

77. Title 3-The President, "Blocking Iraqi Government Property and Prohibiting Transactions With Iraq: Executive Order 12474 of August 9, 1990," 55 *Federal Register* 156 (August 13, 1990): 33089.

78. U.S. Department of Commerce, Bureau of Export Administration, "Guidelines for Export Transactions Involving Equipment, Materials, and Technical Data for Producing Biological Weapons," 55 *Federal Register* 242 (December 17, 1990): 51740.

79. U.S. Department of the Treasury, Office of Foreign Assets Control, "Iraqi Sanctions Regulations; Census of Blocked Iraqi Government Assets and Claims Against Iraq and Iraqi Government Entities," 56 *Federal Register* 128 (February 11, 1991): 5636.

80. See Public Law 102-484, "National Defense Authorization Act for Fiscal Year 1993," 106 *U.S. Statutes at Large*, 2315, 2571-2575; and Mary Beth Naitkin, Paul K. Kerr, and Steven A. Hildreth, *Proliferation Control Regimes: Background and Status*, (Washington, DC: Library of Congress, Congressional Research Service, 2006): 25.

81. See Public Law 103-236, "Foreign Relations Authorization Act, Fiscal Years 1994 and 1995," 108 *U.S. Statutes at Large* 382, 512, 516-519; and U.S. International Trade Commission, *Overview and Analysis of the Economic Impact of U.S. Sanctions With Respect to India and Pakistan, Investigation 332-406*, (Washington, DC: USITC, 1999): iii and v.

82. See U.S. Department of Commerce, Bureau of Export Administration, "Establishment of New General License for Shipments to Country Groups QWY and the People's Republic of China," 59 *Federal Register* 64 (April 4, 1994): 15621; and Richard F. Grimmett, *Military Technology and Conventional Export Controls: The Wassenaar Arrangement*, (Washington, DC: Library of Congress, Congressional Research Service, 2006): 1-2.

83. See Public Law 104-114, "Cuban Liberty and Democratic Solidarity (LIBERTAD) Act of 1996," 110 *U.S. Statutes at Large* 785, 792-794, 798-799; and U.S. Congress, House Committee on International Relations, Subcommittee on International Economic Policy and Trade, *Interfering With U.S. National Security Interests: The World Trade Organization and European Union Challenge to the Helms-Burton Law*, (Washington, DC: GPO, 1997); and Ibid., *Helms-Burton; Two Years Later*, (Washington, DC: GPO, 1998).

84. Public Law 104-132, "Antiterrorism and Effective Death Penalty Act of 1996," 110 *U.S. Statutes at Large* 1214-1215, 1247-1248, 1250, 1255-1258.

85. Public Law 104-172, "Iran and Libya Sanctions Act of 1996," 110 *U.S. Statutes at Large* 1541-1551.

86. Public Law 105-292, "International Religious Freedom Act of 1998," 112 *U.S. Statutes at Large* 2787, 2806-2808.

87. See "Executive Order 13129 of July 4, 1999: Blocking Property and Prohibiting Transactions With the Taliban," 64 *Federal Register* 129 (July 7, 1999): 36759-36761; U.S. Department of State, *Patterns of Global Terrorism 1999* (Washington, DC: GPO, 2000): 7-8; "Executive Order 13224 of September 23, 2001," Blocking Property and Prohibiting Transactions With Persons Who Commit, Threaten to Commit, or Support Terrorism," 66 *Federal Register* 186, (September 25, 2001): 49079-49083; and Michael John Garcia and Charles Doyle, *Extradition To and From the United States: Overview of the Law and Recent Treaties*, (Washington, DC: Library of Congress, Congressional Research Service, 2010).

88. Public Law 106-113, *North Korea Threat Reduction Act of 1999*, 113 *U.S. Statutes at Large* 1501A-472.

89. See Public Law 106-178, "Iran-Nonproliferation Act of 2000," 114 *U.S. Statutes at Large* 38-39, 41; and U.S. Government Accountability Office, *Iran Sanctions: Impact in Furthering U.S. Objectives is Unclear and Should Be Reviewed*, (Washington, DC: GAO, 2007); http://www.gao.gov/new.items/d0858.pdf; Accessed June 18, 2012.

90. See Public Law 107-56, *USA Patriot Act*, 115 *U.S. Statutes at Large* 292, 308-309, 330-331; Charles Doyle, *USA Patriot Act: A Legal Analysis*, (Washington, DC: Library of Congress, Congressional Research Service, 2002); Ray Banoun, Derrick Cephas, and Larry Fruchtman, "USA Patriot Act and Other Recent Money Laundering Developments Have Broad Impact on Financial Institutions, *Journal of Taxation and Regulation of Financial Institutions*, 15 (March/April 2002): 17.

91. See Public Law 107-99, *Zimbabwe Democracy and Economic Recovery Act of 2001*, 115 *U.S. Statutes at Large* 962-965; and "Executive Order 13288 of March 6, 2003: Blocking Property of Persons Undermining Democratic Processes or Institutions in Zimbabwe," 68 *Federal Register* 46 (March 10, 2003): 11457-11461.

92. U.S. Department of State, Office of the Coordinator for Counterterrorism, "Designation of Foreign Terrorist Organizations," 62 *Federal Register* 195, (October 8, 1997): 52650-52651.

93. See Ibid., "Designations of Terrorists and Terrorist Organizations Pursuant to Executive Order 13324 of September 23, 2001," 67 *Federal Register* 53 (March 19, 2002): 12633; and Trifin J. Roule, "Post 9-11 Financial Freeze Dries Up Hamas Funding," *Jane's Intelligence Review*, 14 (5)(May 2002): 17-19.

94. See Public Law 108-175, "Syria Accountability and Lebanese Sovereignty Restoration Act of 2003," 117 *U.S. Statutes at Large*, 2486-2489; U.S. Central Intelligence Agency, *Unclassified Report to Congress on the Acquisition of Technology Relating to Weapons of Mass Destruction and Advanced Conventional Munitions 1 January to 31 December 2006*, (Washington, DC: CIA, 2006): 6-7; U.S. Office of the Director of National Intelligence, *Background Briefing with Senior U.S. Officials on Syria's Covert Nuclear Reactor and North Korea's Involvement*, (Washington, DC: ODNI, 2008); http://www.dni.gov/interviews/20080424_interview.pdf; Accessed June 19, 2012; and U.S. Congress, House Committee on International Relations, Subcommittee on the Middle East and Central Asia, *Syria Accountability and Lebanese Sovereignty Restoration Act Two Years Later*, (Washington, DC: GPO, 2006).

95. See Emma Chanlett-Avery, *North Korea: U.S. Relations, Nuclear Diplomacy, and Internal Situation*, (Washington, DC: Library of Congress, Congressional Service, 2012): 9-11; and Presidential Documents, "Proclamation 8271 of June 26, 2008: Termination of the Exercise of Authorities Under the Trading With the Enemy Act With Respect to North Korea," 73 *Federal Register* 125 (June 27, 2008): 36785.

96. See Chanlett-Avery, 16-17; and Jonathan Medalia, *North Korea's 2009 Nuclear Test: Containment, Monitoring, Implications*, (Washington, DC: Library of Congress, Congressional Research Service, 2010): 1-5.

97. Presidential Documents, "Executive Order 13466 of June 26, 2008: Continuing Certain Restrictions With Respect to North Korea and North Korean Nationals," 73 *Federal Register* 125 (June 27, 2008): 36787.

98. See Department of the Treasury, Office of Foreign Assets Control, "31 CFR 510: North Korea Sanctions Regulations," 75 *Federal Register* 213 (November 4, 2010): 67912-67918; and Presidential Documents, "Executive Order 13551: Blocking Property of Certain Persons With Respect to North Korea," 75 *Federal Register* 169, (September 1, 2010): 53837-53841.

99. See U.S. Congress, Senate Committee on Foreign Relations, *Iran's Political/Nuclear Ambitions and U.S. Policy Options: A Compilation of Statements by Witnesses*, (Washington, DC: GPO, 2006); Sasan Fayazmanesh, *United States and Iran: Sanctions, Wars, and the Policy of Dual Containment*, (New York: Routledge, 2008); and Jalil Roshandel and Nathan Chapman Lean, *Iran,*

Israel, and the United States: Regime Security vs. Political Legitimacy, (Santa Barbara: Praeger, 2011).

100. Public Law 109-293, "Iran Freedom Support Act," 120 *U.S. Statutes at Large* 1344-1350.

101. See Public Law 112-81, "National Defense Authorization Act for Fiscal Year 2012," 125 *U.S. Statutes at Large* 1636, 1647-1649; and U.S. Congress, Senate Committee on Homeland Security and Governmental Affairs, *Iran Sanctions: Why Does the U.S. Government Do Business With Companies Doing Business in Iran?*, (Washington, DC: GPO, 2011).

102. Presidential Documents, "Executive Order 13599: Blocking Property of the Government of Iran and Iranian Financial Institutions," 77 *Federal Register* 26 (February 8, 2012): 6659-6662.

103. Ibid., "Executive Order 13582 of August 17, 2011: Blocking Property of the Government of Syria and Prohibiting Certain Transactions With Respect to Syria," 76 *Federal Register* 162 (August 22, 2011): 52209-52210.

104. Ibid., "Executive Order 13606 of April 22, 2012: Blocking the Property and Suspending Entry into the United States of Certain Persons With Respect to Grave Human Rights Abuses by the Governments of Iran and Syria via Information Technology," 77 *Federal Register* 79 (April 24, 2012): 24571-24574.

105. Ibid., "Executive Order 13608 of May 1, 2012: Prohibiting Certain Transactions With and Suspending Entry Into the United States of Foreign Sanctions Evaders With Respect to Iran and Syria," 77 *Federal Register* 86 (May 3, 2012): 24609-24611.

106. Personal search of the *U.S. Code and Code of Federal Regulations*.

107. *Economic Sanctions Reconsidered*, 158-178.

The foundation of modern U.S. export controls grew out of wartime conflicts, U.S. neutrality, and interests in restricting war profiteering. Following WWII, the leading interests were driven by non-proliferation efforts, directed at cold war objectives to maintain strategic advantages in military and intelligence.

Since the collapse of the USSR, these aims have continued to evolve to serve foreign policy objectives, using or attempting to use U.S. economic strength to force policy objectives.

Results have been mixed, as proliferation of many technologies, and sometimes failures of western allies to apply or maintain firm and like controls have created some holes in the impact of such control tactics.

Chapter 2

Commerce and Defense Departments

Numerous federal departments and agencies have been given executive responsibility for implementing the multifaceted export control statutes enacted by Congress listed in the previous chapter. Two of these agencies are the Department of Commerce and Department of Defense and their attempts to execute U.S. Government export control policy will be detailed in this chapter.

Department of Commerce

The Commerce Department is primarily concerned with promoting domestic and international trade, economic growth, fostering a globally competitive free enterprise system, and supporting fair trade practices while also regulating the licensing of U.S. exports to ensure they don't injure national security.[1] Since the Truman Administration, numerous and continually changing offices within the Commerce Department have been responsible for these often contradictory missions as they have sought to adapt to continually evolving domestic and international economic, political, and security conditions. Examples of some of these organizations include the Advisory Committee on Export Policy, Bureau of East-West Trade, Bureau of Export Administration, Bureau of Industry and Security, Export Control Investigations Staff, International Trade Administration, and Office of Export Supply.[2]

These Commerce Department entities have not conducted export control policymaking in a vacuum as they have needed to carry out this policy in interaction with agencies and officials such as the Departments of Agriculture, Defense, Homeland Security, Justice, and State, and the National Security Council (NSC) and President.[3]

The 1949 Arms Export Control Act (AECA) represents the beginning of U.S. unilateral attempts to impose a national statutory export control infrastructure on U.S. companies seeking to trade with the emerging Soviet bloc. The Coordinating Committee (COCOM) beginning the following year represented a multilateral attempt by most North Atlantic Treaty Organization (NATO) and Japan to embargo or restrict exports to Soviet bloc countries.[4]

Soon after AECA's enactment, Commerce began drafting regulations seeking to enforce this statute. It began setting up a licensing system requiring prospective exporters to fill out various customs forms and dividing countries and commodities into various groups based on whether their destination was to countries with governments compatible with or antagonistic to U.S. interests. Commerce Department permission was also required before delivering items to these countries.[5] October 12, 1949 regulations listed detailed paperwork requirements for license applicants including information about individuals and organizations in other countries who would receive these exports and their end use upon arrival. These regulations would also see the U.S. attempt to regulate the end use of these exports once they reached their destinations including possible transfers to third countries, which has proven to be a source of immense controversy in the international trading community, in bilateral and multilateral relations between the U.S. and allied countries, and proven impossible to manage effectively.[6]

1950 saw the beginning of the detailed enumeration of the Commerce Department's regulatory control system which would become known as the Commerce Control List (CCL) and the Export Administration Regulations (EAR). These broke U.S. export controls down into specific categories such as listings of countries not subject to export restrictions, listings of countries subject to export restrictions, and breakdowns by different commodities and services such as weapons and financial instruments.[7]

The CCL has been incorporated into Title 15 Part 774 of the Code of Federal Regulations (CFR) which is the cumulative body of U.S. Government regulations agencies use to enforce federal laws. CCL includes military use oriented items whose export is subject to Commerce Department jurisdiction and broken up into the following categories:

1. Nuclear Materials, Facilities, & Equipment
2. Materials Processing
3. Electronics
4. Computers
5. Telecommunications and Information Security
6. Sensors and Lasers
7. Navigation and Avionics
8. Marine
9. Aerospace and Propulsion

The 2012 CFR edition of the CCL is 214 pages long.[8]

EAR consists of dual use items having both civilian and military applications and covers Titles 15 Parts 730-774 of the CFR. Totaling 683 pages in 2012, EAR includes procedural information on applying for export licenses, delivering products and services to other countries, descriptions of the Export Control Classification Number (ECCN) system contained in CCL such as ECCN 3A225 Frequency Changers (also known as converters or inverters) or generators, the names of entities subject to end use and end user based control policy restrictions under 15 CFR 744 such as China's Citron Electronics Company and their date of sanctioning in the *Federal Register*, the review process for export license applications by the Commerce Department and other federal agencies, descriptions of short supply controls which are CCL items requiring export control licenses such as crude oil and other petroleum products to protect the U.S. economy from excess draining of scarce materials and reducing the serious inflationary impact of foreign demand, procedures for restricting foreign national access to sensitive information on national security grounds, penalties for violating the EAR, and numerous other areas. These regulations are the subject of continual contentiousness, evaluation, and revision involving U.S. and foreign companies, U.S. and foreign governments, the U.S. military, and academic institutions.[9]

The next section of this chapter will examine Commerce Department export control actions in presidential administrations from Eisenhower to Obama. It will seek to demonstrate the multiple governmental and non-governmental factors influencing the U.S. export control policy landscape on an ongoing basis.

Eisenhower Administration

Not long after COCOM, CCL, and EAR were implemented, pressure to eliminate or ease its restrictions soon came from U.S. companies, foreign companies and governments, and other U.S. Government agencies. Unanimity on how to best enforce U.S. Government and allied government export control began to fall apart immediately in the early years of the Eisenhower Administration. Many factors contributed to this collapse in export control policy unanimity including different threat perceptions of the Soviet bloc by the U.S. and its allies, the desire of U.S. businesses to trade with Soviet bloc countries, and the desire and need for companies in Western European countries to increase trade with Soviet bloc countries in order to bolster their still fragile domestic economic and political conditions in the aftermath of World War II and the early years of the Cold War.[10]

This conflict between using export controls as a means of restricting the Soviet bloc's military potential and the desire of U.S. and allied businesses and governments to increase domestic and international economic well-being and competitiveness, along with the hope that increased trade would improve Soviet bloc economic and political conditions, began in earnest during the Eisenhower Administration. A February 11, 1953 National Security Council (NSC) meeting saw this conflict start when President Eisenhower stressed that the U.S. should have an affordable defense policy. When the Defense Department stressed that proposed defense cuts could cripple national security, Eisenhower warned that national bankruptcy could be as fatal as a foreign enemy.[11]

The Commerce Department has tended to favor a more liberalized approach to exports to other countries in order to benefit U.S. businesses. An example of this more permissive attitude was reflected by Secretary of Commerce Sinclair Weeks (1893-1972) in a May 21, 1954 letter to Secretary of State John Foster Dulles (1888-1959) who referred to British desires to increase trade with the Soviet Union:

> The present negotiations in COCOM, which will inevitably lead to increased trade with Soviet Russia and her satellites on the part of our partners in Europe and presumably on our part as well, seem to me to have been given insufficient attention from the standpoint of their value as a factor for over-all negotiations with the Russians. I understand some brief mention was made during the course of the Berlin Conference of Russia's desire to increase her imports from the United King-

dom, but as far as I know no use was made of their desire at that Conference. We well understand the motives behind the British pressure to dismantle a portion of the controls as they see dangling before them some profitable orders for machinery and equipment. It seems to me obvious that the Russians are very anxious to make these purchases because they are short of the equipment and materials they seek to buy, and we ought to take full advantage of any multilateral willingness on the part of the West to accede to these desires and to use that willingness as a means of getting some other advantage at the Geneva Conference or in some other way.[12]

Soon after this dispatch, a COCOM conference in Paris reflected increase export control policy division within allied ranks as a Commerce Department policymaker asserted that the U.S. was facing opponents instead of teammates and that concessions made on some items to produce agreement on others only produced additional disagreements.[13] More detailed context on the conflicts involved in U.S. export control policy during the Eisenhower Administration was reflected in a June 11, 1954 National Security Council (NSC) memorandum. According to this document, problems with U.S. policy in this area included whether the U.S. should have stricter or more extensive controls than other COCOM countries; another NSC document calling for "gradual and moderate relaxation" in U.S. controls over exports to the Soviet bloc while also advocating stricter criteria in determining what strategic commodities could be exported; inconsistency in how the U.S. defined "military capabilities" and "war potential" in assessing export control criteria; concern that such inconsistencies may produce severe congressional and public criticism that the U.S. is permitting strategic goods to be shipped to a potential enemy; and the double standard applied to strategic exports to the Soviet bloc with the 1951 Battle Act embargo list being significantly shorter than the embargo list denying exports from the U.S. to the Soviet bloc.[14]

Alternatives to these problems proposed by this NSC document included:

1. Maintaining U.S. controls only over strategic commodities agreed for international control in COCOM.
2. Maintaining U.S. controls plus additional strategic commodities which could be effectively controlled by the U.S. alone

and commodities, regardless of their strategic nature, presented special political problems for the U.S. e.g. scrap,
petroleum.

3. Maintain U.S. controls, as in the previous point, and controlling their shipment to prevent the U.S. from being the
source, even though these commodities are available to the
European Soviet bloc from other free world sources.[15]

While one Commerce Department hand was promoting expanded
U.S. trade with the Soviet bloc and other trading partners, the other
Commerce Department hand was seeking to enforce U.S. export control
laws restricting unauthorized trade by American companies. In August
1954, Commerce determined that Pacific States Laboratory of San Fran-
cisco violated the 1949 Export Control Act by filing ten false Customs
declarations for licenses to export the drugs sulfathiazole and
dihydrosteptomycin to a Manila drug corporation to be used for resale to
and consumption by Philippine laboratories, pharmacists, and hospitals.
These products were actually transshipped to a Bangkok drug company.
Commerce sanctioned Pacific States Laboratory and the individuals involved in this transaction lost their export licenses and were prohibited
from being able to export products and services from the United States to
any country except Canada until July 20, 1955.[16]

An additional export license revocation and export privilege denial
was issued by the Commerce Department against Italian Nova Works of
Milan, Italy in February 1955. This firm was convicted of violating the
1949 Export Control Act by making false statements about a license to
export a boring and turning mill from the United States to Italy. In reality, this mill was never received by Italian Nova Works but was transshipped to Hungary. Consequently, this company and additional Swiss
and Italian companies involved in this illicit transshipment lost their U.S.
export licenses and privileges for periods ranging from six months to
two years.[17]

The Eisenhower Administration sought to ease some export controls
as its tenure progressed. A January 31, 1956 report on economic penalties caused by trade controls said that eliminating export controls against
the Soviet bloc and China for all commodities, except weapons and nuclear
energy materials, could increase Free World exports to this area by nearly
$350 million. Even though this amount would be too small to signifi-
cantly benefit the U.S. and Western Europe, it would be very beneficial

to Japanese firms. This report went on to maintain that Western imposition of trade controls has caused the Soviet bloc to rapidly expand its capability to export commodities in categories similar to those controlled by the Free World and that eliminating most trade controls would probably produce increases in Soviet bloc purchases of certain metals, ships, electronics, and complex industrial equipment.[18]

Eisenhower himself expressed frustration on April 5, 1956 that many laws restricting trade on Soviet bloc countries had been enacted in a state of hysteria during the McCarthy era. The President went on to speculate that it might be advisable to revisit these trade restrictions now that the "hysteria" had ended. Dulles said we could use our food and agricultural surpluses against the Soviets by offering to distribute them in the Soviet bloc while Secretary of Defense Charles Wilson (1890-1961) doubted the Soviets would barter strategic materials in return for surplus U.S. agricultural products.[19]

Continuing concern over the inconsistent application of U.S. export controls by federal agencies and concern over the negative impacts of these controls on U.S. relations with allies, characterized the Eisenhower Administration's later years. These concerns were reflected in a July 7, 1958 memo by the Assistant Secretary of Commerce Henry Kearns (1911-1985) to Clarence Randall (1891-1967) the Presidential Assistant and Chairman of the Council on Foreign Economic Policy.

Trenchant questions posed by Kearns in this memo on this topic which remain valid today include:

1. Are our relations with friendly countries being so seriously adversely affected by our controls over their corporate citizens that changes in these controls are warranted on foreign policy grounds? What would be the over-all impact of a changed U.S. position?
2. Can the U.S. maintain its embargo policy on direct U.S. transactions with Communist China and at the same time permit a significant amelioration of the impact of controls respecting foreign corporations subject to control by private U.S. interests?
3. How serious a problem of discrimination would arise if U.S.-controlled firms off-shore were permitted to engage in trade but this privilege were denied to firms operating in the U.S?

4. Would our economic defense position be strengthened or weakened by adopting a more conciliatory approach respecting off-shore operations of firms controlled totally or partially by U.S. private interests?
5. Is there a domestic political problem to be considered?[20]

The Commerce Department, according to this memorandum, reached the following conclusions about these multifaceted dilemmas:

1. U.S. foreign transactions controls as applied to foreign firms controlled by U.S. interests are becoming an irritant in our government-to-government commercial relations with a number of countries.
2. These controls, except as applied to strategic goods, are difficult to justify on economic defense grounds.
3. U.S. private firms in their relations with friendly foreign governments are subject to embarrassment as a result of these regulations.
4. Private U.S. investment abroad, directly and through licensing agreements, may be adversely affected.
5. Our relations with friendly countries respecting the China embargo have undergone a fundamental change since the adoption of the Treasury regulations, and therefore these regulations should be evaluated in the context of other U.S. commercial policy objectives, particularly that of expanded trade and investment in friendly countries.

These conclusions lead Commerce to believe that it is in the U.S.' national interest to reexamine its position on trade with the Sino-Soviet bloc by foreign-based U.S. subsidiaries and affiliated firms. Factors which should be involved in this reexamination would include threats to future private investment abroad, the overall impact on U.S. foreign relations, economic defense consequences, and political implications.[21]

Kennedy Administration

New presidential administrations seek to make their policymaking marks by changing or revising the policies of previous administrations. This occurred in the early part of 1961 as the Kennedy Administration sought to implement its policymaking imprimatur on U.S. export control policy. The mechanism for this was Executive Order (EO) 10945 which created the Export Control Review Board (ECRB) on May 24, 1961. This entity consisted of the Secretary of Commerce, who served as the Board's chair, the Secretary of State, and Secretary of Defense. ECRB's mission was addressing export license matters involving national security questions or other policy issues as selected by the Secretary of Commerce. It could also address matters referred to it by other Board members and any government department or agency having interests in export control matters and the Secretary of Commerce was directed to periodically report to the President on ECRB actions.[22]

During the early months of the Kennedy Administration Secretary of Commerce Luther Hodges (1898-1974) was under heavy pressure from Rep. John Moss (D-CA)(1915-1997) to provide information on the company names, product, and country of destination for all of the 12,000 export licenses issued each month. Commerce gathered opinion on this from businesses and the State and Treasury Departments and decided not to release this information. Its rationale for not releasing this information was based on competitive intelligence and the fact that many companies feared local public opinion if revealed they were selling to Soviet bloc countries. Commerce also decided not to release this information because nearly 70% of licenses issued for exports to Soviet bloc countries were not followed by actual product shipments.[23]

During the summer of 1961, Commerce withdrew export licensing privileges from the Swiss firm Ferrochemie SA for violating the Export Control Act by ordering 2,500 tons of titanium scrap from a Cologne, West Germany firm which had imported it from the U.S. making it subject to the U.S. export license process. Ferrochemie SA proceeded to violate U.S. law by transmitting this titanium to South Africa and filed false documentation on this transfer causing it to receive this sanction.[24]

U.S. technological superiority in many areas of international trade helped COCOM achieve at least relative stability and unanimity during much of the 1960s. The U.S. worked to preserve CCL by bringing most list addition proposals to COCOM for its approval and assumed responsibility for insuring compliance by non-COCOM suppliers such as Sweden and Switzerland through informal intergovernmental agreements and threats of sanctions against private firms. Particular emphasis was placed on restricting the export of items with military potential or significance to the Soviet bloc.[25]

Kennedy Administration policymakers, however, recognized there was a fine line in promoting East-West trade and coping with public opposition to such trade. This was reflected in a Sept. 18, 1961 Hodges memo to Secretary of State Dean Rusk (1909-1994) and Secretary of Defense Robert McNamara (1916-2009). Hodges stressed that the administration maintained a "business as usual" export policy toward Soviet bloc countries despite the ongoing Berlin Crisis. He also mentioned that the U.S. has withheld announcement of its decision not to ship subsidized agricultural commodities to the Soviet bloc because of congressional opinion against trade with these countries. Hodges went on to mention that export license application approvals have been reduced without being announced, that the U.S. should avoid reacting to strings the Soviets may pull at given points in time, and that there must be unified political and trade policy action among NATO allies including a decision by these allies that there is compelling support by them for discontinuing trade with the Soviet bloc.[26]

Bilateral Anglo-U.S. trade control talks were held in Washington from February 19-23, 1962. These centered around interpreting COCOM embargo criteria. While wanting to retain existing COCOM atomic energy and military criteria, the British believed other sections of the CCL were obsolete and needed to be reduced in items and scope. Concerns the British had included believing that the common pattern of a product's use in the Soviet bloc, instead of its alleged use, should determine if it's to be regarded as having a principally military application; that an item's importance should be considered as well as its descriptive nature before determining if its end use is warfighting or producing military equipment and cited jacketed liquefied gas storage containers as an example; and that equipment control should be relaxed when such equipment has been in normal commercial use long enough that its "know-how" is considered common property. The British believed this was especially applicable to commercial electronics which they felt could no longer be credibly embargoed after two to four years. The U.S. expressed broad agreement with these British reform proposals.[27]

This relative Anglo-American comity on export controls could not hide continuing differences between Commerce and State over European Communist bloc export licensing. During 1961, U.S. sales to the European Soviet bloc were $133 million with the Soviet Union accounting for $42 million with trade being an instrument of overall U.S. policy toward the Bloc and export licensing needing to be consistent with that trade policy. A key U.S. policymaker said denying export license applications would be counterproductive to our attempts to establish sober communications with the Soviet bloc and that the underlying objective for national export control policy should be that trade is one of the few forms of leverage we have to influence the Soviets to adopt an attitude that will make it a more peaceful and responsible international community member. This official went on to note the pressures within allied countries against increasing the stringency of U.S. exports controls:

> Our friends and allies are entirely opposed to an increase in the severity of existing trade controls at this time. As a practical matter, domestic political forces in Western Europe and Japan leave the governments there with little ability to strengthen the control mechanism. The United States should therefore have no illusions that restrictions by us would be effective in preventing such trade between the Soviet bloc and the rest of the free world.[28]

Unilateral trade blocks ineffective, hurt U.S. economic interest more

In contrast, the Commerce Department suggested that multilateral export controls should be maintained over non-Communist countries exports of materials, equipment, supplies, and technical data (including plants, processes, designs, components, parts, production equipment, and production in specific areas to prevent these items from substantially enhancing Communist countries military or economic potential to take actions inimical to the free world's economic and national security. Specific categories proposed by Commerce for such multilateral controls included electronics, chemical and petrochemical, transportation, new materials, advanced research and development, aircraft, advanced types of electrical equipment, metal working machinery, pipelines and pipeline equipment, and steel industry.[29]

This policymaking document went on to add that principles of a more effective U.S. economic defense policy should include the following criteria:

1. Since U.S. and free world security continues being threatened by the Sino-Soviet bloc, economic defense pressures need to be applied against the bloc to retard its war-making potential and reduce its unity while retaining U.S. and allied flexibility.

2. Decisions to restrict or promote trade with the Bloc should be coordinated with other foreign policy decisions so that foreign trade policy serves overall foreign policy goals.

3. Acknowledge and support forces for fragmentation within the bloc when opportunities allow such as the case of Poland and selective support bloc countries desirous of enhancing their self-determination and national interests.

4. Economic defense systems can achieve optimal effectiveness by representing the cooperative efforts of the principal trading nations and be coordinated within a larger system of political and military alliances.

5. A trade control system should be selective and concentrate on denying commodities and technologies which directly increase the Bloc's net military strength.

6. Continue to seek, maintain, and, if necessary extend bilateral arrangements with Free World countries to obtain support for multilaterally agreed export controls.

7. Continually seek adoption of effective measures to enforce the agreed scope and severity of multilateral controls[30].

Concern over the complexities and dilemmas in U.S. export control policy was also reflected in a May 16, 1963 memorandum from Kennedy to the ECB. Kennedy asked whether the U.S. should deal with the Soviets on exporting advanced machinery and equipment in a way that protects U.S. interests; expressed concern that there are many cases where no clear security issues are involved yet the Soviets use U.S. machinery and equipment to copy U.S. technology and questioned whether the U.S. is being properly compensated in such sales; whether the U.S should consider the entirety of its Soviet trade in light of trade between Western Europe and the Soviet bloc; and whether a less restrictive policy would be within U.S. security interests[31].

ECB responded to Kennedy's questions on August 15, 1963. Its recommendations included:

1. Initiating a study to determine if the U.S. could organize arrangements permitting it to seek higher compensation for technology sold to Communist nations without incurring greater costs than advantages from such sales.

2. The U.S. should not make significant change over goods or technical data in its Soviet export control policy although there should be greater control rationalization between the Commerce and Treasury in technology.

3. If there is significant relaxing of tensions with the Soviet Union, the U.S. should be willing to take all necessary steps to remove obstacles to trade except for items determined by COCOM to be of direct strategic importance, if such action produces equally constructive Soviet moves.

4. The U.S. should consider establishing a U.S. Commercial Corporation to keep better track of U.S. trade balances with Soviet bloc countries and prepare legislation for Congress which would give the President the needed administrative authority to use trade as an effective political instrument for dealing with the Soviets and their allies.

5. The U.S. should consult with its allies on the potential effect such trade policy changes would have on multilateral export controls and make it clear that such potential changes do not affect China or Cuba[32].

Soviet-centric policy / multilateral Approach

Johnson Administration

Following Kennedy's assassination, the Johnson Administration came to power and the Vietnam War became its all consuming foreign and national security policy priority. The same concerns about the effectiveness of U.S. export controls toward the Soviet bloc remained as the new administration dealt with the foreign economic policy. In 1964, a presidential Task Force on Foreign Economic Policy issued a report addressing these concerns. This group expressed doubt about the efficacy of such controls in the following paragraph:

> Experience has shown that we, and even the West as a whole, have little capacity to affect the viability of Communist countries by denying the trade. The economies of Russia and China are relatively little dependent upon outside trade and the Bloc, as a whole could, if necessary, satisfy its minimum requirements at least to the extent required to prevent defection. Unless the West acts together, the force of trade restriction is marginal. Efforts to achieve this unity of action have not been particularly effective except in times of actual hostilities, and they have been a continuing source of friction within the Alliance.[33]

economic/business issues among Euro allies

Key-- cannot get cooperation/agreement

Trade restriction Alliance ineffective in peace time against ideological opponents-- only in time of warfare are real enforcement and unity of restrictions attainable

Additional conclusions reached by this Task Force included that U.S. policy should actively encourage trade in both directions with the Soviet bloc without contributing to Communist military potential; that East-West trade has a large political component and there should be an East-West trade Act giving the President power to grant most-favored-nation treatment and negotiate trade agreements with Communist countries when he determines such agreements are in the public interest; that allied cooperation with U.S. trade policy has not been successful except for the Korean War; that the U.S. trade policy towards the Soviet resources should encourage them to shift resources away from the military which would have positive effects for U.S. security; and that there should more flexibility in the Export Control Act for the President to determine if exports significantly enhance the economic or military potential of countries to threaten the U.S.[34]

The Johnson Administration's desire to publicly communicate desirable benefits of increased trade with the Soviet bloc was reflected in the following June 21, 1965 letter from Secretary of Commerce John Connor (1914-2000) to National Security Advisor McGeorge Bundy (1919-1996):

> If trade with Communist countries is to be used for these objectives, the U.S. public, the Congress and the executive branch must have a thorough understanding of the problem, the opportunities that trade affords, and U.S. national objectives in this field. The U.S. Government should take every opportunity to make explicit what it intends to do and what it seeks to accomplish. It should act to remove any stigma from trade with Communist countries where such trade is determined to be in the national interest. The foreign policy advantages of such trade to the United States are not widely enough appreciated. With greater public awareness of both facts and objectives, the United States will be in a stronger position to use this trade as it must be used-for national purposes and to support national policy.[35]

Although the Johnson Commerce Department may have been determined to promote greater trade with Soviet bloc countries, it still had to contend with skeptical allies such as the British who believed existing U.S. export controls were to rigid. A December 9, 1966 dispatch from U.S. Ambassador David Bruce (1898-1977) vividly reflected British concerns. Bruce mentioned that while the British were in broad agreement with strategic trade controls, they take a more liberal and commercial view toward items they consider as strategic. He went on to maintain that due to Britain's historic orientation toward and dependence on foreign trade, which accounts for a high percentage of their economic performance, it is much less inclined to sacrifice export earnings for strategic geopolitical advantage.

Bruce's missive also mentioned that the British believe that if an item is not restricted by COCOM that licensing it for export is subject to their discretion regardless of where its components originated; that the U.S.' insistence on stringent trade controls is an overreaction that has not worked well historically; that trade embargoes have limited western trade market opportunities; and that the extraterritorial jurisdiction U.S. export control laws strive for is extremely unpopular in Britain and elsewhere and viewed as U.S. infringement on national sovereignty.[36]

This desire to liberalize export controls during the Johnson Administration culminated with the liberalization of nearly 500 items between October 1966-July 1968 covering products such as central computer processing units and export licensing practices for U.S. owned subsidiaries, although this liberalization ended with the Soviet intervention into Czechoslovakia in August 1968 to crush reforms enacted by that country's reformist Communist government.[37]

Nixon Administration

Numerous domestic and international problems impacted Nixon Administration export control policymaking including the Vietnam War, the desire to improve relations with the Soviet Union and increase trade with the Soviet bloc, the beginnings of a thaw in Sino-U.S. relations, domestic economic problems such as increased inflation which prompted consideration of restricting agricultural exports, and the 1973 Arab oil embargo.[38]

Nixon's Secretary of Commerce Maurice Stans (1908-1998) sought to continue the policy of promoting expanded trade with the Soviet bloc. In an April 9, 1969 memo to Nixon he mentioned that direct U.S. trade with Eastern Europe accounted for less than $420 million divided roughly equally between imports and exports and that the removal of some existing export controls would only modestly enhance this trade. Stans went on to mention that most U.S. businesses feel existing U.S. controls are excessive and favor relaxing them while also recognizing some segments of congressional and public opinion oppose relaxing export controls while the Vietnam War continues. He also asserted that congressional restrictions prohibiting Export-Import Bank financing of Eastern European export transactions and extending Most Favored Nation (MFN) treatment to Eastern European imports are more critical obstacles to improved trade with Eastern Europe than export controls. Additionally, he concluded that Eastern European countries needed to improve their products and marketing to meet U.S. requirements, open up their own markets to U.S. traders, provide better industrial technology and property rights protection, and continue opening up their economies.[39]

An NSC paper issued at this time asked whether the U.S. should continue maintaining an export control list more restrictive than the COCOM list, whether Soviet bloc countries should be treated differently in how U.S. export controls are applied, and whether U.S. firms should be licensed to design and install a $26 million oil extraction and gathering system for the USSR and a $60 million engine foundry to expand a Moscow truck factory. This treatise also addressed possible causal relationships between U.S. export control policy and Communist economic and military capabilities concluding:

> We can be reasonably confident that export controls, particularly as they apply to the transfer of technology critical to the development of advanced weapons systems, have imposed a heavy cost on the Communist countries in special areas such as computer facilities. We can also be reasonably confident that the strictest and broadest export controls could not be expected to impose more than a moderate effect on the Communist economies as a whole, since those economies do not depend heavily on trade with the non-Communist world. Trade controls have had an adverse impact on the quality of economic growth in Communist countries, however, and the cost of the differential controls unilaterally imposed by the United States has added marginally to this impact.[40]

However, another document by National Security Advisor Henry Kissinger to Nixon argued that existing East-West trade policy hurts Communist countries marginally; is a source of irritation between the U.S. and its allies and the U.S. business community; and that increased trade could help improve East-West political relations. Kissinger went on to mention the existence of three contrasting approaches to liberalizing present U.S. export control policy:

1. The Defense Department view of seeking political concessions from the Soviet bloc prior to seeking congressional
   authority for liberalizing U.S. laws;
2. The State Department view of requesting congressional authority prior to negotiations but *then* liberalizing in expecta-
   tion it will produce a better political climate; and
3. The Commerce Department view of seeking authority *then*
   liberalizing for purely *economic* concessions.[41]

Kissinger himself said he agreed with the view the U.S. should liberalize the export control list of goods and data to COCOM standards
except for areas such as advanced computers where the U.S. can effectively maintain unilateral controls.[42]

Numerous individual export decisions are taken during presidential
agencies with the participation of multiple agencies. The desire to increase U.S. trade and political ties with non-Soviet Eastern European
countries motivated Nixon Administration policymaking in this area. An
example of this occurred in 1970 when the Commerce Department requested permission to issue export licenses to sell petroleum refining
technology and energy services to Poland and Romania. Both the Commerce and State Departments favored these sales while the Defense and
Interior Departments opposed them because of their concerns that Poland and the Soviet Union could convert this technology to jet fuel production in case of war. The decision to approve the export license was
granted due to the administration's belief that there were insufficient
foreign policy and national security concerns for denying the license.[43]

Commerce also sought to enhance U.S. exports to Eastern Europe
and the Soviet Union based on Stans' concerns over the U.S. small percentage of this area's trade market share. In a November 19, 1970 memo
to Nixon, Stans expressed his concern that Western European and Japanese penetration into that market could be insurmountable without con-
certed U.S. action. He mentioned that in 1969, less than $250 million of
Eastern European imports of $8.5 billion came from the U.S. with $5.8
billion of this coming from Western Europe. Stans referred to the greater
freedom of action in export controls granted by the 1969 Export Administration Act (EAA) amendments and urged the administration to do everything possible to minimize export license denials. He cited as an example of an unacceptable export license denial as Camco of Houston not

being allowed to supply $3 million in petroleum equipment to a Siberian field which required Camco to manufacture and ship the equipment from the United Kingdom.[44]

The potential economic costs of U.S. export controls on potential trade with the Soviet bloc were revealed in a July 7, 1971 memo to Nixon from the President's Assistant for International Economic Affairs Pete Peterson (who would be Secretary of Commerce from 1972-1973). This memo said that if existing U.S. trade restrictions continued that total U.S. exports to this region would be $440 million and imports would be $360 million. It went on to project that if the U.S. removed all unilateral trade restrictions by the end of 1971 that U.S. exports would reach $1 billion by 1975 and imports would reach $600 million.[45]

Export controls continued to be imposed despite this rhetorical emphasis on increasing U.S. exports to Soviet bloc countries. On May 7, 1971, Commerce continued a prohibition on exporting petroleum and petroleum products to North Korea and North Vietnam on foreign vessels larger than 500 gross registered tons departing from the U.S. that are controlled or chartered by these countries or their nationals[46]. Concern over nuclear weapons proliferation and the desire to adhere to the 1963 Nuclear Test Ban Treaty prompted an April 20, 1972 Commerce Department edict prohibiting the export of certain aerial films and plates to countries which were not treaty signatories.[47]

The 1973 Arab Oil embargo demonstrated the increasing importance of energy resources as international economic weapons. Congress responded by giving the President the authority to issue regulations to regulate petroleum allocation and issue export and price controls on this commodity in the 1973 Emergency Petroleum Allocation Act. These export and price controls were motivated by concern with protecting the U.S. economy from being drained of scarce resources and reducing inflationary pressures from foreign demand. Consequently, this legislation was used to restrict U.S. petroleum exports on a quarterly basis with exceptions allowed for foreign policy and national security reasons.[48]

Concern over ongoing domestic inflationary pressures prompting increases in food prices, caused the Nixon Administration to consider taking measures to restrict agricultural exports. This process involved the Agriculture, Commerce, and Treasury Departments. In order to invoke export controls, the Secretary of Agriculture had to determine that the commodity was in short supply. However, Secretary of the Treasury George Shultz argued against issuing export controls on foods. He maintained it could reverse favorable movement in the U.S. trade balance; undermine the dollar in foreign exchange markets; put the U.S. in an extremely bad position for international trade negotiations; affect our reliability as a supplier for current and potential foreign customers; and cause complications in our efforts to improve relationships with Communist countries.

While Nixon imposed a temporary price control program on June 13, 1973, there was considerable debate within the Administration as to whether it had the legal authority to impose agricultural export controls under the EAA. Nixon said he would keep national export commitments while also asking Congress for the authority to impose export controls which could be applied to grains. On June 27, the administration issued a temporary embargo on soybean and cottonseed exports which was lifted on July 2 when export controls were instituted on scrap metal. On July 5 the administration restricted the export of an additional 41 agricultural commodities, but announced on July 18 that these agricultural export controls would be rescinded once the new harvest was ready for sale. Nixon himself suggested that there further export controls would be unnecessary if there were no major crop failures or large increases in foreign demand.[49]

Technology transfer is a perennially sensitive issue in export control policymaking. The Commerce Department seeks to promote high technology of exports of U.S. companies while the Defense Department is concerned that cutting edge technology with military potential might benefit U.S. adversaries. Consequently, the U.S. has to engage in a delicate balancing act to promote U.S. exports without jeopardizing national security with many export transactions. An example of this balancing is provided by National Security Decision Memorandum (NSDM) 247 issued by the NSC on March 14, 1974. This document allowed the export of computers to Communist countries having a processing power of 8 million bits per second to be raised to 32 million bits per second and for the decontrol of exports of electromechanical peripheral equipment and spare parts for this equipment. However, this continued restrictions on the export or transfer to these countries of computer technology, production facilities, and comprehensive programming services including mechanisms to design, develop, and produce computers, peripheral storage devices and storage media, displays, high speed memories, and electronic components. Finally, NSDM 247 directed Commerce and Defense to simplify administrative procedures for processing computer export license applications.[50]

Ford Administration

Commerce Department export control activities during the Ford Administration were carried out by the Bureau of East-West Trade. Key divisions within this bureau included the Operations Division and Compliance Division. Operations Division responsibilities included processing licensing applications; developing internal operating procedures; preparing analytical and statistical reports on export control activities; publishing export control regulations and procedures; and collecting requests made to U.S. exporters to cooperate in restrictive trade practices or boycotts such as the Arab League boycott of Israel. Compliance Division responsibilities included ensuring compliance with export administration regulations; developing intelligence information about areas of possible export violations; preparing cases on violations for referral to the Hearing Commissioner in Commerce's Office of General Counsel; promoting compliance with export administration clearance regulations; working with other U.S. Government agencies and private organizations on export administration compliance; and collecting intelligence on overseas individuals and companies to evaluate their suitability and reliability as recipients of products under EAR.[51]

This Bureau was involved in approving $133 million in export licenses to the Soviet Union, Eastern Europe, and China between October 1975-March 1976 and denying $20,517,544 worth of export licenses to these countries under COCOM export security controls. This same period saw the review of 2,702 export licenses to Communist countries with 1,365 being exempt from the Defense Department review at that agency's determination. This period also saw the October 20, 1975 announcement of a five year agreement with the Soviet Union for Moscow to purchase at least six million metric tons of corn and wheat annually. Enforcement actions taken by the Bureau included having 159 export violation cases under investigation or criminal proceedings during this time period and imposing export control penalties against firms as varied as Air Trans Africa of Gabon for illegal transactions with Rhodesia, Hewlett-Packard of Vienna for illicit transactions with Czechoslovakia, and Getty Oil Company for receiving a request from a Kuwaiti company that effectively promoted the anti-Israel boycott.[52]

Despite these enforcement successes, U.S. export control activities encountered numerous problems during the closing years of the Nixon and Ford Administrations. A 1972 General Accounting Office (GAO) report mentioned that Commerce and State had not developed effective country market trade promotion programs and general commercial strategies; that Commerce direction contained only limited and short-term strategies and lacked a clear focus as to what the U.S. is trying to accomplish and how to achieve such objectives; and that Commerce export promotion efforts did not include active and aggressive searching for the commercial intelligence export oriented companies seek.[53]

The following year another GAO report revealed concerns with monitoring of U.S. munitions exports. This document revealed that munitions exports are approved more on the basis of the country the items are going to than who receives the items; that there are inadequate port inspections to determine whether prohibited items are being exported; that it's not possible to determine whether exported munitions may be reexported to other countries; and that the Commerce and Treasury Departments need to determine which agency would be the most effective at monitoring munitions export shipments.[54]

A 1976 GAO report was extremely critical of the multiple agencies involved in determining U.S. export control policy and their often conflicting and overlapping objectives and administrative policymaking:

> There is no basic interagency agreement on criteria for export controls and whether foreign policy, commercial, or defense considerations should dominate trade policy with Communist states. Executive branch agencies have fundamental differences regarding licensing standards and procedures to be followed in administering controls. Agency reactions appear to result from the priority of their concerns and the nature of their constituencies.

> Executive branch agency disagreements over export control review and operating procedures are caused essentially by a lack of substantive agreement on détente. Defense's Office of Strategic Trade wants a voice in every control decision. Defense is reluctant to relinquish or delegate any authority to Commerce's Office of Export Administration because it believes that office does not have the technical capability to insure that licensing restrictions are properly applied. Commerce has conflicting priorities and coordination problems. Its Bureau of East-West Trade cooperates closely with State in promoting trade with Com-

munist countries, but OEA, part of the Bureau, shares many of the concerns of Defense and has coordination problems with Commerce's Office of International Marketing.[55]

Additional report findings include U.S. export controls with Communist countries being frustrated by reexports of American strategic goods by non-Communist countries; incorporation of U.S.-origin components in foreign strategic products for direct exports to Communist countries; and exports of foreign strategic products to Communist countries derived from U.S.-origin technical data. Consequently foreign customs service have insufficient expertise to recognize evaluations of approved technical specifications and are unfamiliar with U.S. export controls concerning reexports. In addition, interdepartmental delays in U.S. approval of COCOM country exception requests have produced foreign ultimatums to approve the request or accept the foreign country's withdrawal from COCOM; U.S. Embassy officials have minimal confidence in the willingness of other COCOM countries to uphold multilateral security controls as they pursue international trade competitive advantage; and the report found inconsistencies with U.S. requests for exceptions to export high-technology items to Communist states while opposing exports for similar but less sophisticated items other COCOM members propose for export to these countries.[56]

This report concluded that Commerce should become the primary agency for enforcing export commodity controls; that it should create an overseas export verification and enforcement capability; that the Defense Department should limit its export control deliberations to priority cases and that its current narrow technical criteria should focus on probable instead of possible military uses; and that this agency's Office of Strategic Trade should narrowly redefine its review responsibilities or acquire enough staff to carry out its reviews promptly.[57]

Carter Administration

The export control paradox continued during the Carter Administration. This was demonstrated by a continued desire by the Commerce Department to promote and expand U.S. trade with the Soviet bloc and by the administration's desire to limit nuclear weapons proliferation and promote international human rights. Carter Administration export control policymaking was also complicated by Congress' desire to assert its constitutional prerogative to regulate international trade by making various amendments to the EAA in 1977 and 1979.[58]

1977 EAA amendments affected the Commerce Department by explicitly introducing the concept of foreign policy controls into the export process. Language in this statute declared U.S. policy involved encouraging trade with all countries except for those "with which such trade has been determined by the President to be against the national interest." It went on to assert the need to use U.S. export control policy "to the extent necessary to further significantly the foreign policy of the United States and to fulfill its international obligations." The President was given the authority to implement foreign policy controls by prohibiting or curtailing exports through administrative rules.[59]

Purposes of foreign policy controls included denying economic benefits to countries considered threatening to the U.S. foreign policy interests; expressing moral outrage at a target country's behavior; fulfilling international obligations; avoiding enhancements to the military capacity of countries affecting U.S. security or allied countries security; and seeking to limit human rights violations. Foreign policy controls are much vaguer than national security policy controls, but this did not stop the Carter Administration from making widespread use of them.[60]

Examples of Carter Administration use of these controls included a February 16, 1978 announcement requiring a validated license for exporting U.S. origin commodities and technical data for South African military and police use; suspending $400 million in sales of trucks, aircraft, and spare parts to Libya to discourage it from supporting international terrorism; refusing to license selling a Sperry-Univac computer to the Soviet news agency Tass to express displeasure with trials of Soviet dissidents and U.S. newspaper reporters; withholding export to the Soviet Union by Dresser Industries of technical data and equipment for a rock drill bit manufacturing facility; and imposing special controls on exports of oil field equipment and technology to the Soviet Union.[61]

1979 EAA provisions were discussed in greater detail in the previous chapter. Where the Commerce Department is concerned, this statute sought to reduce export licensing delays by encouraging use of a qualified general license in place of a validated license along as such use is consistent with national security. EAA also sought to remove controls from goods and technologies if these have become obsolete in terms of possible threats to U.S. national security. This statute also gave the Commerce Department the exercise of export control national security authority in consultation with the Defense Department and other stakeholders.[62]

U.S. trade with the Soviet bloc and China continued experiencing gradual growth during the Carter Administration. During the first seven months of 1978 aggregate U.S. exports to communist countries were $2.825 billion which was a 61.8% increase above the same period in 1977. U.S. imports from these countries were $868.9 million and increased 26.2% from the previous time during 1977.[63]

U.S. trade with communist countries began accelerating further with the January 1, 1979 establishment of diplomatic relations with China.[64] This would begin the process of drastically expanding the U.S. trading relationship with China which continues unabated three decades later. Between 1979 and 1980, U.S. exports to China increased from $ 1.716 billion in 1979 to nearly $3.749 billion in 1980. During 1980, U.S. exports to Eastern Europe increased 13.2% while exports to the Soviet Union declined 58.1% due, in part, to the Carter Administration's domestically unpopular agricultural trade embargo in response to the December 27, 1979 Soviet invasion of Afghanistan.[65]

A more positive Carter Administration export control initiative was the August 1980 issuance of a framework to regulate the export of hazardous substances whose use is banned or significantly restricted in the United States. Additional factors prompting these regulations were concerns that exporting these goods and technologies might injure national security; that restricting their export was necessary to prevent excess drain of scarce materials from the U.S; and that restricting export of these items would enhance U.S. foreign policy objectives.[66]

Reagan Administration

The Reagan Administration assumed power in 1981 confronting difficult domestic economic conditions which it desired to rectify through expanding exports, but also concerned with the continued growth in Soviet military power which it sought to restrain through increasing U.S. military spending and limiting Soviet access to western high technology. These would prove to be often contradictory objectives.

The administration lifted the Carter Administrations' controversial and unpopular Soviet grain embargo imposed in the aftermath of the 1979 invasion of Afghanistan.[67] In some respects, trade with Soviet bloc countries continued experiencing growth. During the first six months of

1982, U.S. exports to Communist countries increased to nearly $4.335 billion which was 3.5% higher than this same period in 1981 and the U.S. experienced trade surpluses with Soviet bloc countries and China.[68]

Despite this increasing trade, the Reagan Administration was acutely concerned with Soviet acquisition of Western technology and concerned with inconsistency in COCOM export controls. Particular concern was expressed with proposals to export oil and natural gas pipeline equipment to the Soviets at two summer 1981 NSC meetings. Arguments for allowing the export of this equipment included helping the Soviets overcome potential energy and hard currency shortages to reduce their temptation to pursue aggression in the Persian Gulf, increasing the world oil supply and reducing pressure on world oil prices, and providing substantial export and employment benefits for the U.S. and allies. Arguments against allowing such exports included stressing that is was unlikely the Soviets would ever become dependent on the world oil market for oil imports, that Soviet intervention in the Persian Gulf would be more likely to deprive the west of oil, that western equipment and technology reduces their energy development costs and enables them to free resources for military appliations, and such assistance would increase Soviet energy exports to the West and enhance European dependence on the Soviet Union.[69]

A July 9, 1981 NSC meeting demonstrated vivid differences between the Commerce, Defense, and State Departments on these possible equipment exports. Commerce Secretary Malcolm Baldridge (1922-1987) argued that it was not practical to stop the export of compressors, pipelayers, and other equipment needed for the pipeline; that news reports were announcing a Japanese sale of 500 pipelayers to the Soviets; that Caterpillar Corporation had been told by the Soviets they would lose the sale if they did not have a license by July 30, and that the Soviets had other purchasing alternatives besides the U.S. and Japan. Defense Secretary Caspar Weinberger (1917-2006) argued against selling the pipeline saying it would produce major hard currency earnings for the Soviets, increase European dependence on the Soviets, and that seeing the pipeline built would produce the impression of the U.S. as a weak and undecided country. Secretary of State Alexander Haig (1924-2010) warned of the inconsistency of the U.S. decontrolling its own energy markets while increasing controls on its allies energy supplies and favoring giving them an alternative energy package involving Alaskan oil.[70] U.S. exports to stop pipeline exports to the Soviet Union would prove unsuccessful in 1982.[71]

U.S. concern over Soviet bloc attempts to acquire western technology was documented in an April 1982 Central Intelligence Agency (CIA) report. This analysis mentioned that Soviet efforts to acquire western technology dated back to at least the 1930s. They involved significant financial and manpower resources to acquire technology which would enhance its military power while also improving military manufacturing technology efficiency. This technology acquisition came through legal means including scientific and technological agreements and legally purchasing uncontrolled advanced technologies with military industrial application and illegal means such as spending hard currency to illegally purchase controlled equipment and directing intelligence services to acquire classified and export controlled U.S. and western technologies Soviet technology acquisition efforts.[72]

Licit and illicit Soviet bloc technology acquisition efforts involved intelligence agencies such as the KGB and GRU, the Ministry of Foreign Trade, Soviet State Committee for Science and Technology. Mechanisms used include open literature; legal trade channels; scientific and technological exchanges at conferences; through trade channels evading COCOM export controls; and intelligence service acquisitions using recruited agents and industrial espionage. The Soviet Kama Truck facility which was built over seven years with imports of $1.5 billion in U.S. and Western European automotive production equipment and technology was used by Soviet forces in Afghanistan and Soviet military units in Eastern Europe.[73]

Western technology sectors of key interest to the Soviet bloc, which can be acquired through foreign purchasing agents and dummy corporations include: Computers, materials, semiconductors, communications, navigation and control, vehicular/transportation, lasers and optics, nuclear physics, and microbiology. Examples of specific applications within these sectors include: pattern recognition, robots, metallurgy, superconductors, computer assisted design, satellite communications, signal processing, fiber optics, tunable lasers, superconductors, and genetic engineering. Areas where the Soviets and Eastern Europeans achieved significant military technology enhancements from western sources include: computers, microelectronics, signal processing, manufacturing, communications, lasers, guidance and navigation, structural materials, acoustical sensors, electro-optical sensors, and radars. These acquisitions enabled the Soviet bloc to:

A. Save hundreds of millions of dollars in R&D costs and development lead time;
B. Modernize critical military industry sectors and reduce engineering risks by following or copying western designs to limit military production cost increases;
C. Achieve greater weapons performance than relying solely on indigenous technology;
D. Incorporating countermeasures to Western weapons early in their own weapon development programs.[74]

Commerce continued promoting U.S. exports and attempting to work with U.S. allies on export control policy coordination while also issuing penalties to U.S. and foreign firms violating export control laws. On June 11, 1982, it denied export privileges to a Madrid-based engineering firm for purchasing U.S. origin goods for use in Cuba and attempting to re-export these items in violation of Export Administration Regulations (EAR).[75] Approximately two weeks later, it issued a proposed rule seeking to restrict exports and re-exports to the Soviet Union of U.S. and non-U.S. origin oil and gas goods and technical data in what would ultimately prove to be an unsuccessful effort to stop the export of these goods and technologies.[76]

Commerce's export control activities often involved collaboration with other federal agencies like the Energy Department (DOE). This resulted in a proposed September 17, 1982 regulation on export criteria for sensitive nuclear material as part of the 1978 Nuclear Non-Proliferation Act (NNPA). This particular rulemaking dealing with exporting sensitive nuclear technology for peaceful purposes and involved enhanced reporting requirements on the activities of individuals engaged in peacefully using nuclear technology to design, construct, fabricate, operate, or maintain uranium enrichment or nuclear fuel reprocessing facilities in countries adhering to NNPA.[77]

Eighteen months later saw proposed regulations issued for exporting and importing nuclear fuel equipment in material. This rulemaking's primary objective was harmonizing U.S. policy of facilitating nuclear cooperation with countries sharing U.S. nonproliferation goals. Consequently, it proposed permitting nuclear exports to all countries except Cambodia, Cuba, North Korea, and Vietnam with export restrictions imposed on countries such as Libya, Iran, and Iraq.[78] These regulations were ultimately adopted on December 3, 1984.[79]

A significant change in Commerce Department export control administrative organization was establishing the Bureau of Export Administration (BXA) on October 1, 1987. BXA was given responsibility for processing license applications and enforcing export control laws with particular emphasis on fighting proliferation along with pursuing other national security, short supply, and foreign policy goals.[80]

The Reagan Administration's later years saw the weaknesses in U.S. export control architecture and contentiousness between the U.S. and its allies vividly revealed with the Toshiba-Kongsberg affair. This incident involved Toshiba's subsidiary Toshiba Machine Company sell propeller milling machinery to the Soviet Union through Norway's Kongsberg corporation violating COCOM rules. This sale drastically increased the quietness of Soviet submarines, reduced Soviet research and development expenditures, and enhanced U.S. submarine difficulty in detecting and tracking Soviet submarines in their tense Cold War undersea rivalry.[81]

Revelation of this export control violation resulted in the 1988 enactment of the Multilateral Export Control Enhancement Act (MECA) which required the President to apply sanctions of two to five years against individuals violating COCOM munition list rules if the violations substantially enhanced Soviet bloc submarine or antisubmarine warfare capabilities along with other critical missile and missile defense technology and strategic technologies as determined by the President and NSC.[82]

This time period also saw additional revelations of weaknesses and bureaucratic dysfunctionality in Commerce Department export control programs. A GAO report noted that Commerce approved about 65% of the export license applications DOD wanted to deny while denying about 1% of the licenses DOD wanted to approve. This report also revealed that the major policy differences between these two agencies during the 1985-1986 review period of this report included the appropriateness of issuing export licenses when their foreign purchasers intended to resell these items to customers U.S. licensing authorities were unaware of.[83] A March 17, 1987 statement by a GAO official to the Senate Banking Committee's Subcommittee on International Finance and Monetary Policy revealed the number of items requiring national security licensing is to large and nearly half of them could be eliminated without compromising national security, that foreign policy export controls are largely symbolic and negatively impact potential U.S. export sales, and that U.S. export licensing requirements are increasingly less effective due to the availability of comparable products from new industrializing countries such as Brazil and South Korea who are not part of COCOM.[84]

More significant criticism of U.S. export controls was revealed by the 1987 National Academy of Sciences (NAS) report *Balancing the National Interest: U.S. National Security Export Controls and Global Economic Competition.* This report recognized that there was a significant problem with a massive, well-financed, and effective Soviet espionage acquisition of western technology; that international trade is increasingly important to the U.S. economy; noted declining U.S. advanced technology dominance; and observed that it is difficult to precisely estimate the costs and benefits of export controls. *Balancing the National Interest* went on mention that nearly 40% or $62 million of all U.S. nonmilitary goods shipped in 1985 required an export license; that 52% of U.S. companies lost sales in the year before May 1986 due to export license requirements; that 38% of U.S. businesses had customers who preferred shifting to non-U.S. suppliers to avoid entanglement with U.S. export controls; and that U.S. export control administrative efficiency is hampered by shared responsibility between Commerce, DOD, and State and exacerbated by Commerce and State not making as much progress as DOD in upgrading their human and technical resources and automating their licensing process.[85]

Reforms recommended by NAS included:

A. Strengthening COCOM by having the U.S. take the lead in making it a more effective multilateral export control regime for dual use technologies.

B. Seek controls within COCOM on exports to third countries and negotiate comprehensive understandings with these third countries.

C. Remove export controls from items where such control is no longer feasible.

D. Maintain unilateral controls on a temporary basis for limited unique national security circumstances.

E. Eliminate Export Re-export authorization requirements in countries participating in common international dual-use export technology standards.

F. Maintain current COCOM control procedures on transferring sensitive information and technical data.

G. Maintain clear separation between foreign policy and national security export controls.
H. Balance protecting national security with promoting national economic vitality through affirmative policy direction.
I. Give the Commerce and State Departments sufficient resources and authority to fulfill their export control responsibilities.
J. Develop reliable data regarding U.S. national security export controls operation and impact.[86]

The Reagan Administration's final significant export control action recognized the increasing importance of computer technology in international economics, scientific research, and international security. On December 5, 1988, BXA issued a proposed rule seeking to define supercomputers. This definition reads:

> The term 'supercomputer' refers to advanced architecture, very high speed computer systems that can solve highly complex problems in strategically relevant time frames. Because of their high-speed problem solving capabilities, supercomputers have unique applications in a variety of critical military areas. The United States and certain of its western allies have a commanding edge in supercomputer technology over the Soviet Union and its allies. This technological edge translates into a specific strategic military advantage. If this technological edge were eroded by diversion of a supercomputer system to the Soviet bloc, our national security could be seriously jeopardized. Accordingly, the Bureau of Export Administration licenses the export of a supercomputer only when it is satisfied that special security safeguards—covering security during shipment, physical security of the system, and computational access security—are in place and will be adhered to.[87]

George H.W. Bush Administration

Epochal geopolitical changes during the George H.W. Bush Administration produced the collapse of the Soviet bloc, China's growing importance as a trading partner and strategic competitor, seismic transformations in information technology dissemination, and the growing emergence of weapons of mass destruction in the developing world. These changes would ultimately produce significant changes in U.S. and international multilateral export control structures such as COCOM and lead to different emphases in export control policymaking.[88]

This period between 1989-1992 saw bilateral U.S. trade with soon to be former Soviet bloc countries change (excluding Albania and Yugoslavia) with U.S. exports to bloc countries outside the Soviet Union/Russian Federation being approximately $20.93 billion with imports from these countries being approximately $6.615 billion. In contrast, U.S. exports to China were $24.309 billion, despite an ephemeral 1990 downturn due to the 1989 Tiananmen Square massacre, and U.S. imports from China during this period totaled approximately $94.683 billion.[89]

Bush Administration export control policies sought to align with what administration policymakers saw as the emergence of a new world order emphasizing the emergence of new trade markets in the former Soviet bloc and China, the need to enhance U.S. international economic competitiveness through export driven growth, and the desire to prevent proliferation of weapons of mass destruction to volatile global regions such as the Middle East. In August 1991, BXA issued a rule removing certain prepeg production equipment (e.g. reinforcing or modeling materials such as paper or class cloth containing synthetic resin) from national security export controls in the Commodity Control List (CCL).[90]

In Executive Order (EO) 12735 issued on November 16, 1990, President Bush declared chemical and biological weapons proliferation constituted an unusual and extraordinary threat to U.S. national security and directed the Commerce Department to prohibit the export of goods, technology, or services which would assist foreign countries in acquiring the capability to deliver, develop, produce, stockpile, or use these weapons and work with the State Department to develop an initial list of these items. In partial contrast to this, National Security Directive (NSD) 53 on December 10, 1990 granted a presumption of approving export licenses applications unless an agency opposing such licensing on national security grounds presents enough evidence to overcome this burden. Supplemental rulemaking in October 1991 saw some dual-use items removed from the State Department's United States Munitions List (USML) and transferred to the CCL.[91]

A detailed listing of biological and chemical items whose export was controlled under CCL was published by BXA in July 1992 and included chemical processing equipment such as reactor vessels and certain storage tanks;items capable of detecting USML listed chemical warfare agents or precursors; and specific viruses or genetically modified organisms containing DNA sequences associated with pathogenicity including Ebola virus, Monkey pox virus, yellow fever virus, clostridium botulinum, botulinum toxins, and ricin.[92]

These enhancements to U.S. export controls on potential weapons of mass destruction did not stop additional criticism of the U.S. export control architecture. A 1991 NAS report *Finding Common Ground: U.S. Export Controls in a Changed Global Environment* determined that the collapse of the Soviet bloc required new changes in the U.S.' export control strategy. It reiterated many of its 1987 report findings including noting exports increasing importance to U.S. economic vitality; recognizing the Soviet Union's increasing transparency; that increasing Western economic assistance to Eastern Europe gives the west a greater stake in the success of Eastern European economic and political reforms; that while China could emerge as a national security threat the U.S. should encourage Beijing to enhance its participation in major international nonproliferation regimes; and that the increasing spread of weapons proliferation mandates creation of new international nonproliferation regimes.[93]

Explicit export control recommendations made by this NAS panel include continuing to restrict Soviet access to weapons technology that could significantly contribute to enhancing their weapons capabilities; coordinating export control regimes to the unique circumstances of proliferation threats and make them multilateral to achieve optimum effectiveness; the intelligence community needing to develop reliable assessments of Soviet technology acquisition efforts; foreign policy controls should be classified as "proliferation controls" to distinguish them as key elements of U.S. national security policy; the U.S. should analyze the usefulness, advantages, and disadvantages of alternative export controls for divergent proliferation or security concerns; eliminate re-export reauthorization requirements for goods being re-exported out of fully cooperating third countries; seek a common licensing and export enforcement processing standards for trade with non-proscribed countries; presidential National Security Directives should be the explicit U.S. statutory vehicle for export control formulation and implementation; establish an interagency Export Control Policy Coordinating Committee EC/PCC to formulate and review policy recommendations and resolve interagency disputes; consolidate export control administration within BXA; and enhance industry participation in this process.[94]

Further criticism of Commerce Department export controls during the first Bush Administration was also provided by GAO reports. A June 1989 report identified over 25 federal offices and divisions with programs tracking foreign dual-use technologies. Examples of this duplication of effort within the Commerce Department included BXA tracking foreign technology to comply with EAA provisions assessing the foreign availability of commercial products subject to U.S. export controls while the International Trade Administration tracks technologies for use in trade and domestic policy formulation, trade promotion, and gauging U.S. competitiveness. GAO also was unable to find a single source identifying activities tracking foreign technologies while revealing that this dispersal of federal agencies involved in tracking foreign dual-use technologies also included the Defense, Energy, and State Departments, NASA, and National Science Foundation.[95]

A June 1990 GAO report examined U.S. participation in the international Missile Technology Control Regime (MTCR) which seeks to regulate and restrict the dissemination of ballistic missile technology. This assessment found that Commerce and State have different guidance and procedures for determining which export license applications may be subject to MTCR restrictions. Commerce focuses its reviews on certain countries developing nuclear capable missiles while State examines license applications in the context of possible technology transfer and diversion to a country that may develop nuclear-capable missiles.[96]

This same assessment also revealed that during MTCR's first two and half years, Commerce identified 128 license applications subject to MTCR controls involving 13 countries while the Defense Department (DOD) reviewing applications referred to it by State identified 1,450 missile technology license applications for over 70 countries. The U.S. denied 29 of these licenses with Commerce only denying three of them and GAO also revealed that MTCR had failed to obtain adherence to its guidelines by countries which are major sources of missile technology. In addition, Commerce had only incorporated about 100 of 500 names associated with missile technology concerns from State into its computer database because of limited computer storage capacity. Finally, Commerce had no one devoting more than half of their time to addressing MTCR export concerns while State had three employees with full-time missile technology control responsibilities.[97]

Clinton Administration

The Clinton Administration saw a continuation and further liberalization of Bush administration export control policies. A particular emphasis of Clinton export control policymaking was taking advantage of U.S. advantages in high technology industries such as computers and satellites to expand sales to traditional export markets while also taking advantage of economic growth and increased purchasing power among newly emerging powers such as Brazil, India, and China. These initiatives would achieve some success, but also produce acute controversy as demonstrated by illicit Chinese acquisition of U.S. nuclear technology from the Energy Department and satellite technology from the U.S. private sector. Concerns over the U.S.' ability to restrict proliferation of weapons of mass destruction and the continued sclerotic and dysfunctional nature of U.S. export control policymaking also persisted during these years. This era also illustrated the increasing complexities of the conflict between scientific and commercial openness and national security in formulating export control policy.[98]

During the Clinton Administration, U.S. exports to Russia declined slightly from $2.970 billion in 1993 to $2.092 billion in 2000 and the U.S. trade position going from a surplus of $1,226.9 billion to a deficit of $5.566 billion during this period. U.S.-China bilateral trade figures during this period vividly demonstrate China's increasing importance to U.S. trading patterns. In 1993, the U.S. exported $8.762.9 billion to China and in 2000 U.S. exports nearly doubled to $16.185.2 billion while the U.S. trade deficit with Beijing increased from $22.777 billion to $83.833 billion and remains a continuing source of economic tension between these countries.[99]

The Clinton Administration sought to promote what it claimed would be more efficient governmental operations through the National Performance Review (NPR) programs under the public stewardship of Vice-President Al Gore. Where Commerce Department export controls were concerned, NPR recommended:

A. The President direct the overhaul of the export licensing dispute and resolution system.

B. The President direct the Secretaries of Commerce and State and Assistants to the President for National Security Affairs and Economic Policy to create an effective jurisdictional dispute resolution process to reduce confusion from the overlap between USML and CCL.

C. The President should direct that control lists be examined to ensure that only the most sensitive items remain restricted and that export controls should be implemented multilaterally when possible.

D. The President should direct appropriate Cabinet Secretaries to create an integrated database for dual-use and munitions export licenses.

E. BXA should adapt its operations to export controls changing nature by providing clear and concise regulations, timely export control information, consolidating and increasing its technical resources to concentrate its expertise on nonproliferation issues, and train other nations such as those produced by the Soviet Union's collapse in the complexity of dual-use export controls to preclude WMD proliferation from these new countries.[100]

NPR recommendations would achieve limited implementation during the Clinton years. BXA continued some enforcement actions during this period as demonstrated by its February 1996 suspension of export privileges to a Norwegian firm for illegally transporting a U.S.-origin model XL020+ computer to Poland through Denmark without obtaining the requisite re-export authorization required by the 1979 EAA and Sections 774.1, 787.4(a), and 787.6 of the Export Administration Regulations (EAR) enforcing EAA.[101]

On March 25, 1996, the BXA posted the EAR's most significant revision in forty years concluding a process initiated in November 1993 and involving feedback of over 1,000 industry representatives. The revised EAR sought to simplify and clarify regulations to enhance their user-friendliness to new-to-export companies and giving companies until December 31, 1996 to start complying with EAR.[102]

A major Clinton Administration export control action which would eventually produce significant political blowback and a policy reversal was its decision to amend parts 774 and 799(A) of the EAR and transfer responsibility for administering satellite technology export controls from the State Department to Commerce. Items such as space launch vehicles and detailed spacecraft design, development, production, or manufacturing data remained subject to State Department control. However, this action gave Commerce control over commercial communication satellites, technical data provided to the launch provider including telemetry and launch vehicle parameters, and export license applications for these products were subject to full interagency review based on their consistency with U.S. foreign policy and national security interests.[103]

1998 revelations by the House Select Committee on U.S. National Security and Military Commercial Concerns with the People's Republic of China of that China had stolen design information on advanced U.S. thermonuclear weapons, ballistic missile technology; used missile launch information to improve the accuracy of Chinese launches; obtained export controlled space launch technology; proliferated this technology to other countries; and used U.S. government data to enhance its research programs in various aeronautic and astronautic fields from the Defense and Energy Departments and companies like Hughes and Loral. This produced a political firestorm between the Clinton Administration and the Republican controlled Congress.[104]

In November 1996 Clinton issued Executive Order 13026 which set restrictions on the export and foreign dissemination of computer encryption products designated as defense articles in USML Category 13 determining that their export could harm U.S. foreign and national security policy interests even if comparable products are available outside the U.S. This order went on to specify that facts and questions about the foreign availability of these encryption products could not be publicized or subject to judicial review without revealing classified information that could be detrimental to U.S. interests. The Commerce Secretary was given discretion to consider the foreign availability of comparable encryption products in deciding whether to issue export licenses or remove controls on particular products.[105]

The political blowback from the 1996 transfer of satellite technology export control technology to the State Department was reversed in March 1999 when the Clinton Administration retransferred jurisdiction over these export controls back to the State Department in adherence to the 1999 National Defense Authorization Act. Controversy over satellite export controls continues.[106]

Additional GAO reports during the Clinton Administration revealed further problems with Commerce administration of U.S. export control policymaking. A June 1994 report revealed that while Commerce and State used automated computer systems to screen export applications by ineligible or questionable parties, that they did not include numerous pertinent individuals or companies on their watchlists. This report said examples of these missing parties included: Justice Department lists of parties convicted or listed as export violation fugitives; parties listed having derogatory information on pre-licensing checks; and parties identified by intelligence reports as known or suspected weapons proliferators.[107]

Consequently, Commerce and State issued licenses to these parties without awareness of derogatory information on them; that neither of these agencies routinely share information or cooperate about names on their respective watchlists; and that each agency issues export licenses to parties on the other agencies watchlists. The report also revealed that while cooperation between State and the Customs Service is excellent cooperation between Commerce and Customs is poor.[108]

An April 1995 report covering export controls on missile-related technology to China found that Commerce had approved 19 of 33 missile technology applications worth $6.5 million between Fiscal Years (FY) 1990-1993. Report findings revealed that the export licensing and monitoring controls for missile technology and dual-use export license applications cannot ensure that U.S. exports to China are kept from sensitive end users. GAO also found that the U.S.' end-use check program monitoring license conditions is only marginally effective for Chinese exports; that Commerce's pre-license check/post-shipment verification program was inaccurate and hampered by Chinese government reluctance to cooperate; and that DOD is concerned that Commerce was not identifying and seeking interagency approval on all potential Chinese missile technology related export applications. GAO also maintained that the effectiveness of U.S. sanctions on China is unknown and that U.S. Government officials have no consensus on defining or measuring the effectiveness of proliferation sanctions on China. Commerce described other agencies descriptions of problems with its license application referrals as unsubstantiated and unfounded.[109]

A May 1997 GAO report addressed how the impending July 1, 1997 reversion of Hong Kong to Chinese suzerainty would affect sensitive U.S. technologies and affect U.S. concerns over Chinese proliferation activities. At this time Hong Kong had less restricted access to sensitive technology due to the Hong Kong Policy Act as long as it adhered to international export control standards.[110] GAO said U.S. export control policy toward Hong Kong would not change after the Chinese takeover as long as it continues protecting U.S. property and equipment and as long as Hong Kong maintains an effective export control system. The report went on to maintain that monitoring various indicators of Hong Kong's export control autonomy would be critical in assessing risk to U.S. nonproliferation interests. It went on to mention that such monitoring would not be easy considering possible changes in Hong Kong and difficulties in gauging China's intentions and behavior. Particular attentionshould be devoted to changes in the composition and volume of controlled U.S. exports to Hong Kong which could indicate Chinese efforts to obtain previously unobtainable sensitive technology including optical sensors.[111]

A September 1999 GAO report demonstrated continued need for better interagency satellite export controls coordination. This document showed that Commerce omitted legal requirements for DOD monitors, preparing technology control plans, and strictly complying with government safeguards agreements on commercial communications satellite launch campaigns for China, Russia, and Ukraine between 1989-1999. GAO demonstrated that export control regulation violations may have occurred in 14 of these campaigns due to confusion caused by shared licensing jurisdiction and insufficient clarity concerning each agency's roles and responsibilities in licensing and monitoring these exports. GAO recommended that State and DOD consult with Commerce to establish clear roles and responsibilities for all agencies and overseas posts in implementing technical safeguards agreements and U.S. exporter compliance with satellite export regulations. Commerce, however, disagreed with GAO saying that the 1996 transfer of satellite jurisdiction it received resolved this problem but that the 1999 retransfer of satellite export licensing jurisdiction to State negatively affected U.S. industry.[112]

George W. Bush Administration

The 9/11 terrorist attacks and the multiple and often controversial U.S. responses to them would be the signature event of this administration. This also affected U.S. export control policy as increased emphasis was placed on limiting financing of terrorist groups and the proliferation of weapons of mass destruction. The Bush Administration also saw continued growth in trade with China despite tension with that country over China's temporary 2001 seizure of a U.S. plane, disputes over Taiwan, and concerns over China's increasingly assertive military. U.S. exports to China went from $19.182.3 billion in 2001 to $69.732.8 billion in

2008 while U.S. Chinese imports surged from $102.278.4 billion in 2001 to $337.772.6 billion in 2008 with a trade deficit exceeding $268 billion.[113] An early example of the Bush Administration's efforts to reorient Commerce Department export control policymaking was replacing BXA with the Bureau of Industry and Security (BIS) on April 18, 2002 in order to reflect BIS activities in areas such as national, homeland, economic, and cyber security.[114]

BIS' first annual report listed multiple attributes as its guiding principles including U.S. security being its paramount concern and its credibility within government, with industry, and with the public depending on its fidelity to this principle. Where dual-use export controls are concerned, BIS stressed vigorously enforcing and administering such controls to stop delivery and proliferation of weapons of mass proliferation, halt the spread of weapons to terrorists and countries of concern, and further important U.S. foreign policy objectives.[115]

Additional BIS guiding principles include:

1. Protecting U.S. security also includes ensuring U.S. economic health and competitiveness and supporting U.S. national defense.
2. Striving to work in partnership with the private sector.
3. Working cooperatively with federal, state, and local governments.
4. Bureau activities and regulations need to be adaptable to changing global conditions and challenges.
5. Bureau rules, policies, and decisions should be stated clearly, applied consistently, and followed faithfully.
6. Decision making must be fact-based, analytically sound, and consistent with governing laws and regulations and international cooperation is critical to Bureau activities.[116]

In June 2002, BIS sought feedback from industry on reviewing then existing limits on the use of computer technology in terms of exporting and rexporting technology and software on the CCL and EAR. BIS was interested in the purpose of U.S. companies in exporting technology to develop, produce, and use computers whose speed was greater than 33,000 Millions of Theoretical Operations per second (MTOPS); the impact on U.S. economic competitiveness of foreign nationals designing and developing these products for use in the U.S., and the foreign availability of technology and software for producing, developing, and use computers with speeds exceeding 33,000 MTOPS.[117]

A year later BIS issued an interim final rule imposing a license requirement on the export and re-export of any item subject to EAR by U.S. or non-U.S. individuals designated foreign terrorist organizations pursuant to EO 13224 of September 23, 2001 which blocks property and interests of engaged in trafficking with terrorists or likely to support terrorists.[118] Additional export control actions taken by the Bush Administration BIS include a November 2005 fine of $44,000 and a five year export prohibition against Suburban Guns of Cape Town, South Africa for placing orders with U.S. companies to purchase shotgun screw chokes and related shotgun accessories which are illegal under the ECCN;[119] permitting the export or reexport of antiterrorist items listed on the CCL to U.S. individuals in Libya due to that country's efforts to dismantle its weapons of mass destruction and "renounce" terrorism;[120] and imposing a six year suspension of export privileges against a Dutch company for obtaining and exporting toxins including Aflatoxin and Staphyloccocal Enterotoxin to North Korea.[121]

Deemed exports are another complicating factor confronting U.S. export control policy. These exports are defined as the export of technology or source code (except encryption source code) having civilian and military applications to foreign nationals within the U.S. A 2007 report on deemed exports and how they affect federal export control policy making was described by a Commerce Department panel:

> Deemed exports have a significant impact on United States industry, academia and national security. If a United States commercial firm has a foreign national working in its United States-based laboratory, it may be required to obtain an export license before it can reveal information to that employee . . . if the information may also have a military application (i.e., have a 'dual-use'). Similarly, a university researcher conducting a project involving a foreign national student may be required to obtain an export license before sharing knowledge with that student relating to equipment used in a research project if that equipment might also have a military application. If compliance with the relevant licensing regulations becomes unduly burdensome, United States firms operating under such regulations are significantly handicapped when competing with firms from nations imposing less restrictive controls. The national (including 'homeland') security ramifications of Deemed Export controls are even more evident: For example

absent appropriate safeguards, biology laboratory equipment designed to produce various toxins in disease research may be used by terrorists to produce toxins for harmful purposes.[122]

This panel went on to report that the U.S. was the only nation controlling Deemed Exports and also participating in multilateral export control regimes and that other nations depend on visa processes, intelligence information, and commercial intellectual property controls instead of a formal Deemed Export licensing regime. Key panel findings pointing out Deemed Export problems included:

1. Current regulations are increasingly irrelevant to the prevailing global situation and most scientific and technological knowledge and items cannot be denied to U.S. enemies even by a perfect export control regime since they can be obtained from other sources.
2. The CCL is to all-encompassing and covers a vast spectrum of militarily less important items such as hunting rifles, police handcuffs, and radios.
3. Existing regulations are to complex and often vague. Fundamental research knowledge is not subject to Deemed Export rules but knowledge concerning laboratory equipment operation used to conduct this research may be subjected to control.
4. Many academic and industrial organizations are unaware of Deemed Export rules or figured out how to work around them. Only 900 Deemed Export license requests are submitted to the U.S. Government each year with 85% of these being approved.
5. Escaping these rules is easy. Foreign-born individuals becoming U.S. citizens and returning to their native country are not covered by Deemed Export regulations but most cases involving export violations involve U.S. citizens.
6. Criteria for assessing the potential threat that could be posed by a foreign national who is the subject of a license application and of uncertain loyalty appear superficial. The U.S. Government maintains a short list of proscribed (generally terrorist-supporting countries) but there is a longer list of countries that are consulted for Deemed Export purposes.

Matches against the Deemed Export list are based on the individual's current citizenship or legal permanent residency.[123]

Reforms recommended by the Deemed Export Advisory Committee include replacing the current licensing process with a simplified new process to enhance security and strengthen national economic competitiveness; extending BIS' educational outreach program to enhance Deemed Export parties familiarity with these rules; increasing focus on and building higher fences around technical knowledge elements having the greatest national/homeland security consequence by systematically reviewing the CCL and eliminating items and technologies with little or no such consequences; establishing a "Trusted Entities" category in academia and industry that voluntarily elect to quality for special, streamlined treatment in Deemed Export license application processing by meeting certain specified criteria; expanding potential licensees national affiliation determination by considering birth country, prior countries of residence, current citizenship, personal character and present activities to provide a more comprehensive assessment of their probable loyalties; involving outside expert science and engineering panels to conduct annual sunset reviews of technologies subject to CCL with the burden of proof resting with those seeking to add or preserve proscribed items; and increasing use of interactive, web-based self-teaching programs to enhance familiarity to those impacted by Deemed Export regulations.[124]

BIS continued receiving critical scrutiny from Commerce Department Office of Inspector General (OIG) and GAO reports during the Bush Administration. A March 31, 2004 OIG report announced that BIS regulations and policies could enable foreign nationals from countries and entities of concern to access controlled technology including approving 73% of deemed export licenses to individuals from Iran and Iraq between FY 2000-2003. This report recommended that BIS reevaluate its approval of deemed export licenses to individuals from these countries to make these approvals consistent with current deemed export control licensing policies and procedures.[125]

A 2007 report from this same organization found concerns with BIS licensing practices toward Indian exports and recommended determining why there are persistent breakdowns in BIS' process for monitoring license conditions; reviewing a sample of license applications to ensure licensing officers and countersigners are properly marking licenses for follow-up; and referring non-compliant exporters to BIS' Office of Export Enforcement.[126]

GAO assessments of BIS during the Bush Administration included a December 2006 analysis that Commerce and State have less oversight on exports of controlled information than on exports of controlled goods, that one-third of exporting companies interviewed did not have internal control plans to protect their export-controlled information which sets requirements for access to material by foreign employees and visitors, that Commerce and State did not use existing resources, including license data, to identify minimal protections for such exports, and that these agencies websites do not provide specific guidance on protecting electronic transfers of export-controlled information.[127]

During April 24, 2008 testimony before a Senate Homeland Security and Governmental Affairs Committee Subcommittee a GAO official announced that neither Commerce nor State had taken sufficient steps to ensure sufficient protection of U.S. export control interests. Specifically, she announced that Commerce and State disagree on who controls the export of particular items; that Commerce in one case claimed an item was subject to its less restrictive export requirements when the item was actually under State jurisdiction; and that neither department has assessed its security controls in recent years despite major economic and security environment changes. Commerce's license application processing times had remained stable at approximately 40 days and the number of licenses processed increased 50% between 1998-2005, but GAO could not measure the overall efficiency of Commerce's licensing process since it does not have efficiency-related measures and analyses to identify opportunities for improvement. In addition, Commerce only measures its performance in terms of how long it takes to refer an application to another agency for review and has not provided analysis of its workload or bottlenecks in its processes that could be corrected to enhance efficiency.[128]

Obama Administration

The Obama Administration came to office in 2009 as the U.S. was experiencing its worst economic climate since the Great Depression. Where international trade policy was concerned the administration continued its predecessor's policies of promoting expanded U.S. exports even though the U.S. continued experiencing international trade deficits. Bilateral trade between China and the U.S. saw U.S. exports at a level of $4.159.6

billion in January 2009 and imports at $24.743.5 billion and these fig-
ures through June 2012 saw U.S. exports increase to $8.518.7 billion
and Chinese imports at 35.919.8 billion with the U.S. trade deficit during this period going from 20.583.8 billion to $27.401.2 billion.[129]

The Obama Administration's opening year also saw the release of
another NAS report critical of U.S. export control organization and
policymaking. Continuing the conclusions of previous reports, this document found that the current export control system injures national and
homeland security and U.S. economic competitiveness; that the export
control system on the international flow of science, technology, and commerce is fundamentally broken and cannot be fixed by incremental changes
below the presidential level; that national security and economic prosperity depend on full global engagement in science, technology, and commerce, and that a new export control system can be more agile and effective while mitigating but not eliminating national security risks.[130]

Reform recommendations made by this NAS report included:

1. Presidential restructuring of the U.S. export control process
   so balancing of economic and security interests can be
   achieved more efficiently without harming
   the national technology and security base.
2. The President or National Security Advisor appointing an
   independent export license appeals panel. This organization's
   members would serve a five-ear term, act independently and
   neutrally to resolve disputes, and have no operational responsibility beyond hearing disputes and issuing opinions.
3. Presidential direction that executive authorities under AECA
   and EAA be administered to ensure U.S. scientific and technological competitiveness.
4. The President should maintain and enhance access to foreign
   source human talent to strengthen the U.S. science and technology base.
5. Streamline the visa process for credentialed short-term visitors in science and technology. Include expert vouching by
   qualified U.S. scientists in the non-immigrant visa process
   for well-known scholars and researchers.[131]

These criticisms caused the Obama Administration to start an export
control reform process. Unveiled on August 30, 2010, the proposal be-

gan by acknowledging that problems with multiple different control lists administered by multiple different departments which cause ambiguity, confusion, and jurisdictional disputes which delay clearance of license applications for months or even years. To replace this, the administration proposed creating a three tier system arranged as follows:

1. Highest tier items are those providing critical military or intelligence advantage to the U.S. and available almost exclusively to the U.S., or items that are weapons of mass destruction.
2. Middle tier items are those providing a substantial military or intelligence advantage to the U.S. and are available almost exclusively from allies or multilateral partners.
3. Lowest tier items provide significant military or intelligence advantage but are widely available.[132]

Once controlled items are assigned to a tier, a licensing policy will be as assigned to it in order to focus agency reviews on the most sensitive items. Proposed licensing policy characteristics are to involve:

1. Requiring licenses for highest tiered items to all destinations. Many second tier items will be authorized for export to allies and multilateral partners under license exemptions or general authorization. Licenses will not be required more broadly for less sensitive items.
2. On items authorized to be exported without licenses, new controls will be imposed on their re-export to prevent their diversion to unauthorized destinations.
3. Existing U.S. sanctions programs toward specific countries such as Cuba and Iran will continue.[133]

Additional proposed export control program characteristics include agencies focusing and strengthening enforcement efforts by building higher walls around the most sensitive items; implementing additional end-use assurances against diversion from foreign consignees; increasing domestic and international on-site visits and outreach; and enhancing compliance and enforcement. This reform proposal also committed the U.S. to developing a single information technology (IT) system to administer its export control system. This began with linking Defense and State to the same IT system with Commerce integration expected by 2011.[134]

A June 2012 Obama Administration "dashboard" revealed that these proposed reforms had achieved partial success in areas such as consolidating enforcement lists and in receiving public comments on revising some export control criteria. However, this document revealed that most proposals had not gone through final draft rulemaking or published rulemaking, and that the Commerce Department had not implemented its export control IT capabilities into a consolidated federal website with a public portal.[135]

The 112th Congress (2011-2012) saw two major bills introduced addressing export control reform. The Export Administration Renewal Act of 2011 (H.R. 2122) was introduced on June 3, 2011 by House Foreign Affairs Committee Chair Ileana Ros-Lehtinen (R-FL). It would renew the currently expired EAA through 2015, increase the penalty structure to make it consistent with International Economic Emergency Powers Act (IEEPA), give Commerce enhanced statutory investigative and overseas enforcement authority and allow some liberalization of USML exports except for those destined for China. On May 26, 2011 this committee's ranking member Howard Berman (D-CA) introduced the Technology Security Act of 2011 (H.R. 2004) which grants presidential authority to control exports for national security and foreign policy reasons, contends that U.S. national security requires maintaining leadership and competitiveness in manufacturing, science, and technology, and gives the President the authority to assign and maintain export licensing criteria. No significant action on these bills has occurred since their introduction.[136]

Administrative export control actions taken by Obama's BIS include proposing transferring various items such as tanks and military vehicles from USML to CCL which BIS believed would reduce the reporting costs to small exporting businesses and enable them to have greater export licensing flexibility.[137] On April 13, 2012, BIS issued a proposed rule that would remove various energy materials, explosives, incendiary agents, and propellants from USML and transfer them to CCL. The rationale presented for this liberalization included:

(i) Allowing for greater interoperability with NATO and other allies while maintaining and expanding robust controls that, in some instances, include prohibitions on exports or reexports for other countries or intended for proscribed end-users and end-uses; (ii) enhancing the U.S. defense industrial base by . . . reducing the current incentives for foreign companies to design out or avoid U.S.-origin International Traffic in Arms Regulations (ITAR)-controlled content, particularly with respect to generic, unspecified parts and components; and (iii) permitting the U.S. Government to focus its resources on controlling, monitoring, investigating, analyzing, and . . . prohibiting exports and reexports of more significant items to destinations, end users, and end uses of greater concern than NATO allies and other multi-regime partners.[138]

As of summer 2012 BIS operations were carried out by the following organizational entities whose responsibilities include:

Office of Exporter Services: Counseling exporters, conducting export control seminars, drafting and publishing EAR changes, various licensing and compliance actions, and administering license application processing and commodity actions.

Office of Nonproliferation and Treaty Compliance: Administering multilateral export control responsibilities under the Nuclear Suppliers Group and other regimes, administering unilateral U.S. foreign policy controls, enforcing industrial compliance treaties with arms control and disarmament treaties, and representing U.S. industry and security interests at multilateral arms control and disbarment deliberations.

Office of National Security and Technology Transfer Controls: Responsible for national security export and re-export controls, implements multilateral controls to restrict the spread of dual-use goods and related technologies. Responsible for U.S. export control policy for high-performance computers and encryption and administers export licensing provisions for foreign nationals under the "deemed export" technology rule while also administering EAR "short supply" provisions seeking to ensure the U.S. has sufficient domestic supplies of various commodities.

Office of Strategic Industry and Economic Security: Responsible for implementing programs supporting the U.S. defense industrial base so U.S. defense industries can meet current and future national security requirements.

Office of Technology Evaluation: Analyzes impact of export controls on U.S. competitiveness and the industrial base national defense support capability.

Office of Export Enforcement: Enforces export control and related public safety laws by focusing on violations posing the greatest threats to homeland and national security, foreign policy objectives and economic interests, and unauthorized dual-use exports for military purposes.

Office of Enforcement Analysis: Monitors and evaluates export transactions to ensure compliance with EAR, the Chemical Weapons Convention, and related laws and regulations.

Office of Antiboycott Compliance: Implementing EAR antiboycott provisions by enforcing regulations; assisting the public in antiboycott compliance; and compiling and analyzing international boycott information.[139]

During (FY) 2010 (October 1,2009-September 30, 2010), BIS processed 21,660 export license applications valued at approximately $66.2 billion representing a 6% increase over the previous year. 18,020 license applications (83%) were approved; 3,513 (16%) were returned without action; and 127 (less than 1%) were denied. The average license review processing time was 29 days. This same fiscal year saw BIS investigations convict 31 individuals and firms of export control violations as opposed to 33 violations the previous year. These convictions produced $12,298,900 in criminal fines, over $2 million in forfeitures, and over 522 months imprisonment compared to $455,409 in criminal fines, $1.5 million in forfeitures, and 886 months imprisonment the previous year.[140]
An example of one of these investigations and criminal convictions occurred on May 11, 2010 when Balli Aviation Ltd (a subsidiary of the British company Balli Group PLC) was sentenced in the U.S. District Court of the District of Columbia to pay a $2 million fine and serve a five year corporate probation period for illegally exporting Boeing 747 aircraft to Iran because these items are controlled for antiterrorism reasons.[141] During FY 2012, BIS operations were carried out by 171 employees with a budget of $101 million and the bureau is requesting $102.328 million for FY 2013.[142]

Despite these accomplishments, BIS continues receiving critical assessments from the Commerce Inspector General and GAO. During October 2011 a Commerce OIG report reviewing website security at BIS and other Commerce entities found that departmental web applications had significant security weaknesses increasing their vulnerability to cyber attacks; that these weaknesses could produce the compromise of data stored on these applications and users computers; that backend databases are improperly configured and could give attackers access to sensitive data; and that since web applications reside on insecure software they are at increased risk of being compromised.[143]

A May 2010 GAO report comparing six countries export control architectures found that Australia, Canada, Germany, Japan, and the United Kingdom had a single agency in charge of regulating arms and dual-use items and used consolidated control lists to determine which export controls apply in given cases. France was the only country examined which used multiple agencies to regulate proposed arms and dual-use exports.[144] Another report from this agency noted ongoing problems with unauthorized technology releases to foreign nationals in the U.S. Key factors involved in documenting these releases were intelligence and law enforcement sources; deemed export violations fine and suspensions; the reduced number of overseas visa applications Commerce screens; and a large number of foreign nationals in the U.S. with specialty occupation visas in high technology fields increase risks of foreign nationals gaining unauthorized access to controlled technology.[145]

This same report went on to mention that between FY 2004-2009, Commerce fined 14 U.S. companies approximately $2.3 million for making transfers of controlled technology to 25 countries; that the majority of these enforcement actions involved foreign nationals from three countries (*which the report does not name*); that Commerce screened 150 visa applications from U.S. posts overseas in FY 2009 to identify potential unlicensed deemed exports as opposed to the 54,000 visa applications they screened in 2001; and that Commerce has not implemented recommendations from GAO and other agencies on monitoring compliance with deemed export licensing conditions and using immigration data to improve deemed export enforcement.[146]

BIS was also affected by GAO's continued listing of effective protection of national security technologies as a "high risk" program in February 2011 which initially occurred in 2007. "High Risk" programs are published by GAO early in congressional sessions and highlight federal programs most vulnerable to fraud, waste, abuse, and mismanagement, or needing transformation to address economy, effectiveness, or efficiency problems. The 2011 listing particularly stressed vulnerabilities in U.S. foreign military sales programs. GAO mentioned that these weapons and their technological infrastructure are often targets for espionage, theft, and reverse engineering. While noting progress made in this area since the 2007 High Risk listing, GAO said responsible agencies needed to improve internal and interagency practices to enhance reliable shipment verification, monitoring, and administration of foreign military sales; eliminate gaps and inconsistencies in defense exports data collection systems used to monitor foreign military sales and direct commercial sales programs; development and implement specific plans to monitor, evaluate, and report routinely on outcomes for projects providing weapons, defense-critical technologies, and antiterrorism training to foreign governments; the need for the executive branch to identify measures to assess the effectiveness and sustainability of federal export control reform efforts; and the executive branch and Congress should consider re-evaluating critical technology-related programs and government review of foreign investment in U.S. companies, to ensure these programs work together to meet emerging security demands and help the military retain its technological superiority.[147]

Conclusion

BIS and its predecessor export control agencies within Commerce have achieved significant successes and failures in trying to promote U.S. dual use and high technology exports while seeking to prevent the export of technology which could be injurious to national security and foreign policy interests. Its failures have been due to a combination of bureaucratic inertia, conflicts with other agencies over the proper roles and responsibilities involved in enforcing export control laws and regulations, pressure from U.S. and foreign economic and foreign policy interests, and incredible complexity involved in keeping up with continually changing and evolving international security and technological environments. One of the agencies Commerce has to interact with in enforcing U.S. export control policy is the Defense Department whose history and programs will now be scrutinized.

Department of Defense

The Department of Defense (DOD) also plays a major role in U.S. export control policymaking. From World War II to the present numerous historical and contemporary agencies within DOD have been involved in influencing U.S. export control policies including the Defense Institute for Security Assistance Management (DISAM), Defense Security Cooperation Agency (DSCA), Defense Technology Security Administration (DTSA), Defense Threat Reduction Agency (DTRA), and various policymaking branches of the Office of the Secretary of Defense (OSD). As has been true with the Commerce Department, DOD's involvement in export control policymaking regularly involves conflicting purposes. DOD is concerning with protecting U.S. national security and foreign policy interests and technological advantage by regulating the export of equipment and technologies which could endanger U.S. national security and defense industrial base economic viability. It also seeks to promote U.S. foreign policy, national security, and economic competitiveness by promoting arms sales to allied countries around the world. Working through the contradictions involved in these objectives is a key theme in DOD export control policymaking. Working with Commerce, State, other federal departments, and defense industry, in balancing the often contradictory objectives of U.S. export control policymaking is a continual source of challenge and contention for DOD and these other agencies.[148]

World War II's approaching onset in 1941 saw policymaking initiatives seek to bring the military into the export control process. On August 1, 1941, the Roosevelt Administration created the Economic Defense Board (EDB). This entity's membership included the Vice President, who served as chair, the Secretaries of War and the Navy, and various other cabinet secretaries. Its responsibilities included developing and coordinating policies, plans, and programs to protect and strengthen U.S. international economic relations and defense. Exports, imports, acquiring and disposing materials and commodities from foreign countries and preemptive buying of products were also included in EDB's institutional mandate. An Administrator of Export Control was included as an EDB official and this organization would evolve into other wartime agencies including the Board of Economic Warfare and various postwar incarnations.[149]

Truman Administration

The modern U.S. Military Assistance Program (MAP) begins with the 1949 Mutual Defense Assistance Act. This legislation gave the President broad authority to sell or transfer U.S. military products and expertise to foreign countries if the National Military Establishment (DOD's predecessor agency) and the Joint Chiefs of Staff (JCS) determine such transfers are not detrimental to U.S. national security or if they are needed for training purposes by U.S. reserve forces. Foreign military assistance totals agreed to in this legislation totaled $1.314 billion with North Atlantic Treaty European countries receiving $1 billion of this and the remainder going to Greece, Turkey, Iran, Korea, the Philippines, and China. After DOD's 1949 establishment, these military assistance activities would be carried out by the Mutual Defense Assistance Program (MDAP) which would be operational by summer 1950.[150] An extensive scholarly corpus documents the accomplishments, failures, and controversies of U.S. military assistance programs in subsequent decades.[151]

The 1951 Mutual Security Act provided additional structural foundations for U.S. military assistance programs through DOD. Section 506(a) of this statute gave the Secretary of Defense "primary responsibility and authority" for determining country military equipment requirements, integrating military assistance with regular military procurement, supervising equipment usage and training programs, and delivering items. DOD was also given authority to determine priorities in procuring, delivering, and allocating equipment and the President was given authority to continue apportioning funds for such deliveries. This statute also centralized responsibility for U.S. economic, military, and technical foreign assistance programs in a Cabinet-level director for mutual security placed within the Executive Office of the President.[152]

Additional clarification of DOD export control authorities under the 1951 Mutual Security Act was provided in October 1952. These authorities included:

1. Determining military end-item requirements;
2. Procuring military equipment to permit its integration with service programs;
3. Supervising military item end-use by recipient countries;
4. Supervising foreign military personnel training;
5. Moving and delivering military end-items; and

6. Establishing priorities in procuring, delivering, and allocating military equipment in foreign countries.[153]

U.S. security assistance would even be used to help allies facing economic problems as evidenced by the United Kingdom receiving $360 million of military assistance in 1953 to make up for British domestic economic restraints. During the previous year, the U.S. negotiated an agreement with seven NATO countries in which these countries would pay $175 million for aircraft produced by countries such as the United Kingdom, France, Italy, Netherlands, and Belgium as part of a growing arms sales collaboration with NATO countries which sometimes produced squabbling on export controls toward the Soviet bloc.[154] The Truman Administration's concluding years would see U.S. military assistance increase from $493 million in FY 1950 to $7.0289 billion by June 30, 1953.[155]

Eisenhower Administration

The Eisenhower Administration would see U.S. defense spending transition to greater emphasis on nuclear weapons through the New Look program and congressional and administration desire to reduce foreign military aid. This resulted in U.S. military assistance for FY 1956 being reduced to $2.017 billion and congressional concern that the majority of this aid was going to countries such as Iran, Korea, and Pakistan with inordinate defense needs and insufficient capacity to absorb U.S. military assistance.[156]

U.S. and COCOM efforts to negatively impact the military ability of Communist countries such as China had less positive results. A 1953 Central Intelligence Agency (CIA) National Intelligence Estimate (NIE) mentioned that western trade controls had made it difficult for Beijing to import items like antibiotics, medical supplies, and rubber. This assessment went on to mention that Chinese ground forces had not been adversely affected by these export controls due to indigenous production and supplies from the Soviet Union which also benefitted their air and naval forces. It also said a total trade embargo would have limited effect on China's ability to sustain military operations outside Korea. A 1954 CIA NIE contended that export controls have hampered Soviet bloc military development, but that impact of these controls has been lessened by Soviet enhancement of domestic military production and prioritizing this production over civilian manufactures.[157]

1956 also saw DOD take a position of guarded support for the proposed creation of the International Atomic Energy Agency (IAEA) to regulate the peaceful development of nuclear energy while restricting the proliferation of nuclear weapons technology. Defense Secretary Charles Wilson (1890-1961) said DOD favored the IAEA's establishment due to its international character, but believed U.S. interests would be advanced by not giving IAEA responsibility for storing or protecting nuclear materials.[158]

During its second term, the Eisenhower Administration's DOD military assistance and export control saw the JCS provide military objectives and force bases for military assistance programs along with recommending material allocation priorities among recipient countries. A 1957 DOD directive gave the Assistant Secretary of Defense for International Security Affairs responsibility for directing and supervising the development, preparation, refinement, and control of military assistance programs. These programs included military equipment, training foreign personnel, mutual country weapons development, a joint NATO program for producing better weapons, facilities assistance, and financing offshore procurement.[159]

Continuing concerns over the clarity of U.S. security assistance and export control objectives within DOD resulted in the April 24, 1959 issuance of guidance on ensuring that excess military property is not sold directly or indirectly to China and Soviet bloc countries. Stipulations in this document for foreign sales of U.S. military equipment featured:

1. Including appropriate terms and conditions in sale contract.
2. Assuring that buyers are acceptable to the U.S.
3. Obtaining knowledge of buyers intended use and property destination.
4. Using measures to preclude diversion and verifying that property reached the acceptable destination designated by the buyer.[160]

Ongoing concern over the organization of U.S. military assistance programs between State and Defense lead the Eisenhower Administration to establish the President's Committee to Study the United States Military Assistance Program chaired by retired Army General William Henry Draper, Jr. (1894-1974) in November 1958. This committee issued a number of reports documenting its findings in 1959. It endorsed civilian and military aspects of foreign assistance programs and argued for enhancing funding to ensure these programs viability. The June 3, 1959 edition of this committee's report urged a sharper distinction between State program responsibilities (policy guidance) and Defense program responsibilities (policy execution). The Draper Committee was concerned about contentiousness between these two agencies in carrying out their responsibilities with State policymakers contending they had not been given sufficient opportunity to provide political and economic guidance while defense believed that State had encroached on its review of military matters. The report also recommended that military assistance be put on a three year planning basis with breakdowns for individual geographic regions and countries and budgetary guidance provided by the Bureau of the Budget. Another key report recommendation was the Secretary of Defense having clearer responsibility for implementing military assistance after funds were appropriated.[161]

Despite the Draper Report's advocacy for increased civilian and military assistance funding, overall U.S. military assistance funding during Eisenhower's second term fell from $2.892.1 million in FY 1956 to $1.877.7 million in FY 1960. While export controls were regularly discussed at Eisenhower NSC meetings, they were a source of continual frustration for administration policymakers and in relationships with allies. Eisenhower himself considered trade controls "dammed silly practices" producing laughter at a February 27, 1958 NSC meeting. All of these export control complexities and frustrations would confront the incoming Kennedy Administration and its DOD.[162]

National security issues confronting this administration intersecting with export controls included attempting to coordinate activities with allied COCOM countries, the Cuban Missile Crisis, and increasing U.S. military involvement in Vietnam. The early 1960s saw Congress leverage reductions in U.S. MAP programs and increased emphasis on civilian economic assistance. This was reflected in declining U.S. military assistance funding from $1,944.2 billion in FY 1961 to $1.269 billion in FY 1965.[163]

Kennedy Administration

Military assistance funding was increasingly targeted toward Asian countries including South Korea, Taiwan, Thailand, Turkey, and Vietnam. This stemmed from U.S. concerns about security trends in that region including Chinese explosion of an atomic bomb in 1964, Vietnam, and a deteriorating political situation in Indonesia.[164] The Cuban Missile Crisis in September-October 1962 would prove to be the most serious threat to U.S. and international security in the Cold War era as the Soviets attempted to install nuclear missiles in Cuba. The U.S. responded by placing a naval quarantine on further Soviet shipments to Cuba while also demanding the Soviets remove all Cuban missile bases and offensive weapons in that country. This U.S. demand was generally met with a reciprocal promise by the U.S. to not invade Cuba and remove its own missiles in Turkey.[165]

During the Kennedy Administration's early years, DOD played an advisory role in administering U.S. export controls. It participated actively in deliberations involving the Commerce Department's Advisory Committee on Export Policy (ACEP) and the State Department's Economic Defense Advisory Committee (EDAC) and the Secretary Defense served on a recently created Export Control Review Board (ECRB). ECRB membership included the Secretaries of Commerce, Defense, and State with Commerce given the power to refer export licensing cases with national security implications to the Board.[166]

DOD possessed a small staff in its Office of Foreign Economic Affairs which was attached to the Office of the Secretary of Defense and spoke for DOD on export control matters. It also determined departmental positions on questions addressed by ACEP and EDAC while also having access to U.S. intelligence community and armed service technical expertise and assistance. While the State Department had primary responsibility for munitions control, DOD was charged with establishing policy on distributing military aid and surplus military equipment it owned.[167]

DOD had mixed success in getting ECRB to accept its recommendations for denying export licenses for U.S. exports to other than Soviet bloc countries according to a 1962 congressional report. Between November 1959-October 1961, 49 of its license denial recommendations were approved including an application to sell two rotary wing aircraft worth $218,067 to the Soviet Union. However, between February 1960-March 1961, 26 of its license denial recommendations were rejected by ECRB and export licenses were granted including 74,733,600 pounds of cold-rolled carbon sheets worth $6,698,892 million to East Germany and the Soviet Union.[168]

As part of its broader trade embargo against Cuba, DOD issued an order on February 26, 1963 implementing National Security Action Memorandum (NSAM) 220 issued earlier that month. This edict stated that no DOD-financed cargoes will be shipped from the U.S. on foreign-flagged vessels if the vessel had called at a Cuban port on or after January 1, 1963. These provisions also applied to contracts entered into by commercial contractors involving goods they ship using foreign-flagged vessels.[169]

Johnson Administration

Concern over China's October 16, 1964 nuclear explosion and fears that its nuclear arsenal could blackmail other Asian nations lead the Johnson Administration to establish an interdepartmental Committee on Non-Proliferation. This committee sought to study ways to improve the U.S. security alliance system while also increasing nuclear support for Asian allies. There was also a desire by the Johnson Administration to enhance military support for India in order to keep it from developing nuclear weapons to deter China and from turning to the Soviet Union for support. The U.S. was unable to work out an adequate security guarantee with New Delhi and India would eventually explode a nuclear weapon on May 11, 1974.[170]

An August 11, 1965 DOD document provided guidance on how individuals and organizations involved in handling classified defense information in export trade. While acknowledging the roles played by Commerce and State in the export control process, this document mentioned that releasing Air Force, Army, or Navy material for foreign sale or production is prohibited unless these departments certify that releasing such information does not compromise information essential for safeguarding national defense. It also mentioned that disclosing classified defense information to foreign nationals or organizations acting in a non-governmental capacity is unauthorized.[171]

Later Johnson Administration export control efforts attempting to limit the spread of nuclear weapons were partially assisted by the July 1, 1968 signing of the Nuclear Nonproliferation Treaty (NPT) between the U.S., United Kingdom, and Soviet Union. NPT prohibited nuclear powers from supplying atomic weapons to nonnuclear states and these states agreed not to acquire of build such weapons. However, existing nuclear states such as China did not sign NPT at this time and potential nuclear states including India, Israel, and Pakistan did not sign it either. Ongoing controversy over Iranian and North Korean nuclear weapons programs place the NPT's long-term viability in doubt.[172]

Controversy over the Vietnam War and its inexorably rising costs resulted in further congressional and public criticism of MAP and questions over whether it was a legitimate use of taxpayer resources and advanced national interests. This was reflected in declining direct U.S. military assistance and sales between FY 1965-FY 1968 with assistance totals dropping from $1.055 billion to $400 million and sales totals declining from $1.248 billion to $1.003 billion.[173]

Export control policymaking challenges and decision-making was also reflected in Johnson Administration NSAMs. NSAM 294 on April 20, 1964 declared that U.S. policy opposed nuclear force development by other states outside of NATO's nuclear force framework. Recognizing France's desire to develop an independent nuclear force, this NSAM declared U.S. policy to not contribute to or assist French efforts to develop nuclear warhead or strategic delivery capabilities through government technology transfer, equipment sales, joint research and development activities, and industrial commercial and organizational exchanges.[174]

Reflecting the often contradictory and contentious nature of U.S. export controls toward COCOM partner, NSAM 312 on July 10, 1964 permitted the release of inertial guidance technology to West Germany to be used in navy vessels and aircraft with explicit assurance from the Germans that this technology would not be used for ballistic missiles or transferred to third parties.[175]

Nixon Administration

The Nixon Administration saw ongoing conflict between Commerce, Defense, and State over which items the U.S. could export without endangering national security. Controversy over the Vietnam War, the 1973 Arab-Israeli war, détente with the Soviet Union, and diplomatic opening to China all influenced U.S. foreign policy, international economic policy, national security policy, and export control policy during this period. Between FY 1970-1974, U.S. arms sales deliveries increased from $1.265.270 billion to $3.187.884 billion and DOD was extensively involved in seeking to promote national security interests within U.S. export control policymaking.[176]

On August 14, 1969, Nixon's NSC issued NSAM 71 directing an interagency review of U.S. policies governing foreign country access to advanced technologies vital to national security. Examples of these technologies included nuclear power reactors, ballistic missile systems, advanced computers, and other scientific and technological devices whose acquisition from the U.S. and other countries would enhance their developing or improving nuclear weapons capabilities of strategic delivery systems. This review was also directed to offer alternative recommendations for regulating the export of these technologies. This study was never produced and was cancelled. However, National Security Decision Memorandum (NSDM) 15 on May 28, 1969 urged general liberalization of East-West trade within existing legal frameworks.[177]

During March 1971, DOD also objected to the proposed $11 million sale of British computers to the Institute of High Energy Physics at Serpukhov, USSR. DOD was concerned that these computers would be misused and that this sale would seriously erode existing computer export controls. The British agreed to take safeguards to reduce potential misuse of these computers. DOD was not as confident that U.S. scientists working at Serpukhov could maintain a comprehensive monitoring schedule to monitor against potential misuse and that these scientists did not have the technical expertise to analyze potential military data garnered by the Soviets in a data dump.[178]

Illuminating insights into DOD concern over export control liberalization was provided in a June 22, 1971 letter from Defense Secretary Melvin Laird. Referring to recent decisions approving the aforementioned British computer exports and French transistor-making machinery to Poland, along with potentially forthcoming export liberalization to China Laird opined:

> My concern is that these several measures, taken together are virtually certain to weaken seriously if not destroy the existing system of security trade controls which form an important, although not always adequately recognized, element in our defense structure. In order to preserve that margin of military power required by the deterrent strategy upon which our security depends, it is not enough to maintain our Defense establishment. We must also frustrate as far as possible the build-up of forces which are or may be arrayed against us. An effective system of controls over the export to Communist countries of strategic commodities therefore contributes directly to our national security and can help keep U.S. military expenditures at a minimum . . .

In the light of this evidence, I feel compelled to express my deep uneasiness over the course we seem to be taking, not only because it appears to be based on the erroneous assumption that our controls are both ineffective and costly, but because, by approving the release of highly strategic items on an ad hoc basis, we are paving the way for the rapid dismantling of all controls. It is already clear that are Allies, who feel they can rely on the U.S. to offset whatever increased military risk may result, will treat these decisions as precedents for additional exceptions or the early removal of such items from the international embargo list altogether. In my judgment, we cannot afford thus to jeopardize our security trade controls unless as a result we will achieve tangible diplomatic and economic gains of substantial value.[179]

On March 17, 1972, Laird expressed DOD opposition to the proposed British sale of earth satellite station to China stating that approving this sale would establish another precedent weakening the U.S. negotiating position on strategic communications export controls to China and Eastern Europe. Laird also contended that if China obtained an additional earth station and eventually orbited its own satellite that it could be used for any purpose.[180]

NSDM 235 issued on October 4, 1973 emphasized U.S. policy on transferring highly enriched uranium for fueling nuclear power reactors. It stressed U.S. policy in this area as involving:

1. Reviewing future requests for supplying large quantities of highly enriched uranium on a case-by-case basis without previous presumptions of supply.
2. Requiring recipients have acceptable physical security measures in place.
3. Weighing the recipient country's position on the NPT in reviewing and deciding supply requests.
4. Considering but not requiring that fuel fabrication and reprocessing occur in the U.S. or in multinationally owned facilities as an essential supply precondition.[181]

NSDM 261 on July 22, 1974 informed China that it was prepared to negotiate an agreement with it for exporting U.S. light-water reactors and slightly enriched uranium; that it encouraged China to join the IAEA; that relevant congressional oversight committees should be notified if China expresses interest in negotiating such an agreement; and that following congressional notifications, interested U.S. companies are authorized to begin discussions with China on possible sale of light-water reactors and slightly enriched uranium fuel.[182]

Ford Administration

The Ford Administration saw continued gradual increases in U.S. arms sales deliveries going from $3.517.478 billion in FY 1975 to $5.734.897 billion in FY 1976. The administration also continued Nixon's détente policies toward the Soviet Union while also becoming increasing concerned about how U.S. exports to the Soviet bloc were enhancing Soviet military capabilities.[183] Concern over the impact of U.S. high tech exports to the Soviet bloc, lead DOD to charge the Defense Science Board with examining this topic. J. Fred Bucy, the President of Texas Instruments was chosen to chair a Task Force on this topic which issued its report in February 1976.[184] The Bucy Report proved to be a key development shaping Ford Administration DOD export control policymaking. With subcommittees focusing on airframe, jet engine, instrumentation, and solid state technologies, task force members assessed these selected technologies, their impact on U.S. strategic requirements, transfer mechanisms, and stressed that the current effectiveness of export control restrictions augment the need for export controls and make COCOM a defense necessity.[185]

The Bucy Report went on to stress that in order to preserve U.S. lead time that exports should be denied if a technology represents a revolutionary advance to the recipient nation but approved if it only represents an evolutionary advance. Additional report conclusions emphasized the following:

1. Current U.S. export control laws and COCOM provide a continuing means of protecting strategic technologies lead times.
2. Deterrents meant to discourage product diversion to military applications are not meaningful control mechanisms when applied to design and manufacturing.
3. Not having established criteria for evaluating technology transfers reinforces the clumsy case-by-case analysis of all export applications.[186]

Bucy report recommendations included placing primary export control efforts on design arrays and manufacturing information including detailed "how to" instructions on design and manufacturing processes; "keystone" manufacturing, inspection of automatic test equipment; products accompanied by sophisticated operation, application, or maintenance information; the need for companies with strategic technology to demonstrate caution to avoid unintentional know-how transfers through visits and proposals; government-to-government scientific exchanges being monitored to ensure compliance with U.S. strategic technology export restrictions; U.S. export controls should focus on protecting all key elements of superior U.S. technological positions; nations passing strategic technology to Communist countries should be restricted from receiving further U.S. origin strategic technology; U.S. export control product sales should emphasize performance capabilities; the U.S. should only release technology to non-allied, non-Communist countries only technology it is willing to transfer to Communist countries directly; and pursue actions and decisions to strengthen COCOM.[187]

Significant NSC export control decisions taken by the Ford Administration include NSDM 275 on October 10, 1974 requiring the U.S. to maintain a position in COCOM advocating Soviet return of depleted uranium tails with U-2 content exceeding 0.2%; NSDM 289 on March 24, 1975 lifting a military sales embargo on India and Pakistan as long as such sales don't promote a regional arms race and the weapons sold enhance these countries defensive capabilities; and NSDM 298 on June 14, 1975 where the U.S. agrees to a West German nuclear reactor sale to the Soviet Union if Moscow supplies the uranium for fuel and provides assurance on the peaceful uses of the reactor and the plutonium it produces.[188]

U.S. military sales also faced increasing foreign competition during the Ford Administration and DOD export control efforts also confronted increases in the quantity and technological quality of Soviet military power. From 1971 to mid-1976, French arms sales were $7.1 billion; British arms sales were $4.8 billion; and West German arms sales were $3.2 billion. This same period also saw Soviet arms sales reach approximately $17 billion making it clear that unilateral U.S. efforts to restrict these sales would not work and that multilateral agreements like COCOM were essential to regulate these sales.[189]

Enhanced Soviet military production capacity and technological capabilities was also documented in a DOD report revealing that Soviet fighter aircraft production increased by 36% between 1970-1976; that Soviet military spending increased 25% between 1972-1975; that Soviet military equipment in most areas was being modernized faster than U.S. equipment and that U.S. capabilities to offset numerical inferiority with superior technology is receiving increasing challenge; and that the closed nature of Soviet society prevents reliable determination of their objectives and forecasting their military capabilities.[190]

Continuing problems with DOD export control programs were revealed in a June 1976 GAO report. Reviewing the foreign military sales program, GAO argued DOD needed to do a better job articulating how proposed U.S. military sales would affect the regional military balance, regional military tensions, and recipient country military build-up plans. GAO also stressed that DOD must examine the recipient country's ability to effectively absorb and use these weapons; whether U.S. military interests including over-flight rights and facilities access would be supported by U.S. sales; the impact of these sales on its own military readiness; and whether substantial dependence on U.S. supply sources could enable the U.S. to better control conflict in some circumstances. This report also mentioned that DOD prefers using commercial channels as much as possible for arms sales but that 2/3 to 3/4 of all U.S. military exports pass through government channels for various reasons including the U.S. Government not being allowed to sell military equipment to private parties.[191]

Carter Administration

Despite rhetoric about combating weapons proliferation and promoting human rights, the Carter Administration saw arms sales deliveries rise from $6.971.402 billion in FY 1977 to $7.214.250 billion in FY 1980 though much of this increase was caused by the Iranian revolution and the Soviet invasion of Afghanistan.[192] In terms of DOD export control policy, efforts were made to begin implementing Bucy report recommendations. On August 26, 1977 Secretary of Defense Harold Brown issued "Interim DOD Policy Statement on Export Control of U.S. Technology" as a step in this direction. Soon after DOD released for industry comment a proposed list of critical technologies which should be subject to export control.[193]

General motivation prompting DOD in these efforts was the EAA mandating that DOD assess goods and technologies of military significance to controlled countries including Communist countries. 1977 EAA amendments require that beginning in 1979, U.S. export control policies toward individual countries are to be motivated by more than whether they are or are not Communist. DOD is legally empowered to determine which U.S. export cases it wishes to review. It can then express approval, object to proposed exports with conditions, and indicate an outright export rejection with only the President having the authority to overrule DOD's objections. The President must then report his actions to Congress and tell why he overrode DOD's objections.[194]

Bucy report implementation within DOD was carried out by the Director of Defense Research and Engineering (DDRE) which during 1977 emphasized:

1. Identifying critical technologies and products;
2. Assessing active mechanisms of technology transfer;
3. Developing simplified product control criteria; and
4. Determining the feasibility and desirability of new administrative procedures or legislation for streamlining the export control system.[195]

These efforts would culminate in the 1979 publication of the Militarily Critical Technologies List (MCTL). MCTL includes technologies DOD maintains are critical for maintaining superior U.S. military capabilities. Acquisition of these technologies by potential or real adversaries would significantly enhance their military industrial capability and be detrimental to U.S. security interests. Examples of MCTL include those covering biological, chemical, and nuclear weapons along with missile delivery systems. MCTL serves as the technical foundation for decisions on export control proposals including licensing implementation; pre-publication review of scientific papers prepared by academia, government, and industry; intelligence collection tasking; research and development planning, and international technology cooperation and transfer.

Major MCTL technological categories include: aeronautics systems; armaments and energetic materials; chemical and biological systems; directed and kinetic energy systems; electronics; ground systems; guidance, navigation, and vehicle control; information systems; information warfare; manufacturing and fabrication; marine systems; materials; nuclear systems; power systems; sensors and lasers; signature control;

space systems; and weapons effects and countermeasures.[196] MCTL would initially be published in the *Federal Register* on October 1, 1980.[197]

DOD reorganized its export control structure so export licensing and critical technologies implementation was placed under the responsibility of the Deputy Under Secretary for International Programs and Technology (IPT). Pentagon export control efforts also needed to cope with the realization of Soviet defense research and development (R&D) advances which it maintained now surpassed U.S. R&D advances. For instance, the CIA estimated annual Soviet R&D expenditures as exceeding $20 billion while annual U.S. R&D expenditures were $13 billion. DOD also mentioned that ¼ of NATO forces facing the Warsaw Pact in Europe were U.S. forces and that these forces had higher quality equipment than other NATO countries.[198]

Specific IPT program responsibility areas included: processing munitions cases, allied trade cases, and U.S. strategic trade cases; identifying critical technology on a continuing basis; managing international cooperation in research, development, and acquisition; approving data exchange agreements and information exchange projects; reviewing scientific and technological agreements, the technical implications of foreign military sales cases; and the international implications of industrial and information security policy pertaining to technology control. These responsibilities were carried out by 29 personnel who processed 2,914 licensing cases and closed 2,768 of these cases between January-October 1979 with an average processing time of 11 days. FY 1979 funding for these activities was $350,000.[199]

U.S. nonproliferation efforts and nuclear industry exports at this time were under increasing competition from foreign competitors including those from COCOM countries. An October 1977 GAO report revealed that the U.S.share of the nuclear export market fell from 85% in 1972 to 42% in 1975 with France and West Germany becoming the leading supplier of light-water reactors; Japan having a strong domestic nuclear industry and the potential to become a significant nuclear exporter; Canada becoming a major exporter of heavy-water reactors, heavy water, and uranium; and the United Kingdom being very successful in exporting nuclear fuel services.[200]

A March 1, 1979 GAO report warned that the U.S. did not have an effective policymaking structure to reconcile the conflicting goals of export control and promotion. It criticized the opacity of DOD's complex licensing system making it difficult for U.S. and COCOM exporters to request export licensing exemptions which it maintained could cause delays and injure exporters reputations for dependability. It also criticized DOD's slow pace at implementing licensing reforms announced in 1977 and contended that there remains the danger of an overloaded technical review system for applications processing.[201]

Reagan Administration

The Reagan Administration saw U.S. arms sales deliveries fluctuate from $8.951.366 billion in FY 1981 to a peak of $12.783.158 billion in FY 1983 before declining to $7.835.080 billion in FY 1989.[202] This administration was particularly concerned with rebuilding U.S. military power against the Soviet Union and seeking to reverse what it saw as excessive technology transfer to the Soviet bloc enhancing its military potential. A November 1981 CIA report mentioned Moscow's extensive attempts to obtain western weapons systems technology by illicit means including clandestine acquisition, illegal imports, and third country diversions and that they have especially sought and need equipment for their aerospace, electronics, and shipbuilding industries.[203]

This assessment went on to stress that illegal Soviet trade efforts had also targeted computers, guidance and navigation systems, sensors, and advanced manufacturing processes. It also mentioned that existing export controls have denied the Soviets very powerful computers but not kept them from illegally acquiring embargoed semiconductor production machinery. The CIA went on to argue that expanding COCOM controls would force the Soviets to make greater use of non-COCOM suppliers and illegal channels which would produce higher costs and delays but not prevent high-priority item acquisition and that comprehensive Western sanctions on new governmental and private credits would pose significant hardships on the Soviet Union since its hard currency earnings were expected to decline through the mid-1980s. Langley concluded that the main impact of Western economic sanctions would be slowing qualitative improvements in Soviet weapons systems.[204]

Concern over weaknesses in COCOM export control coverage was also expressed in DOD's FY 1983 *Annual Report to Congress*. This document decried the persistence of excessive loopholes in the international export control system; forgetting and forgiving clearcut international export control law violations and lightly punishing or absolving violators while allowing Soviet raids on the U.S. technology base to continue and increase. Consequently, this attitude has enabled the Soviets to develop new generations of smart weapons; dramatically improve their airlift capability; increase nuclear weapons accuracy; and enhance their command and control capabilities. This allows the Soviets to save billions of rubles and years of research time and enables them to avoid costly mistakes by acquiring proven technology.[205]

DOD's desire to develop a more effectual export control mechanism lead to the establishment of the Defense Technology Security Administration (DTSA) on May 10, 1985. DTSA's became DOD's lead entity for administering export control laws and regulations and retains this position after more than a quarter century. DTSA mission responsibilities include:

1. Administering DOD's Technology Security Program to ensure the international transfer of defense-related technology, goods, munitions, and services is consistent with U.S. foreign policy and national security objectives.
2. Assuring expeditious processing of export license applications consistent with national security objectives making fullest use of automation and other techniques.
3. Actively supporting U.S. Government enforcement and intelligence activities to restrain the flow of defense-related materials to potential adversaries.
4. Providing support to the Under Secretary of Defense for Policy and UnderSecretary of Defense for Research and Engineering in carrying out their responsibilities under DOD Directive 2040.2 dealing with international transfers of defense-related goods, services, technologies and munitions.[206]

DTSA's critical importance was given additional ammunition by a September 1985 CIA report on Soviet acquisition of militarily significant western technology. Key findings of this assessment included the Soviets:

1. Saving five years development time and approximately $55 million in R&D development costs by using F-18 fighter documentation to develop a new radar-guided air-to-air missile system.

2. Redirecting Soviet technical approaches in nearly one hundred projects annually for ongoing weapons systems and key military equipment resulting in improved weapons manufacturing processes.
3. Raising the technical levels of several thousand annual developmental projects involving military equipment, manufacturing or design procedures.
4. Eliminating or shortening phases of more than a thousand military work projects.[207]

This report went on to show how the Soviets use multiple legal and illegal sources to gather information about western military technologies including U.S. defense contractors, allied Eastern European intelligence services, commercial data bases such as National Aeronautics and Space Administration documents and contractor studies, other U.S. documents from the Commerce Department's National Technical Information Service, information from professional and academic applied science and technology conferences, recruited western agents, the Soviet Ministry of Foreign Trade, and science and technology oriented western universities such as Carnegie-Mellon, MIT, and Wisconsin-Madison.[208]

DTSA was successful in uncovering the Toshiba-Kongsberg scandal in which the Soviets illegally obtained an advanced and highly accurate Japanese machine tool and advanced Norwegian computer for tracking U.S. nuclear submarines. DTSA was also involved in efforts to address new threats dealing with the proliferation of weapons of mass destruction such as efforts by Iran and Iraq to acquire such weapons and advanced conventional weapons with Western technology.[209]

Between FY 1985-FY 1988 license applications reviewed by DTSA went from 3,260 to 5,479 after peaking at 9,637 in FY 1986. Dual-use products with nuclear applications and supercomputers comprise the preponderance of these reviews. Geographic breakdowns for the FY 1988 license reviews were: 3,544 for free world countries; 1,245 for the Soviet bloc and 690 for China.[210] DTSA also achieved substantive success by denying the Soviets significant access to cutting edge computer technology, microelectronics manufacturing facilities, and machine tool controller technology. It also expedited export license application reviews from an average of 90 days in 1981 to 10 days in 1987 as well as enhancing the quality of these reviews technical and policy analysis.[211]

George H.W. Bush Administration

The George H.W. Bush Administration saw tectonic changes in the international strategic landscape with the collapse of the Soviet Union and Warsaw Pact, unrest in China prompting the June 4, 1989 crushing of pro-democracy demonstrations at Tiananmen Square, and the proliferation of weapons of mass destruction capabilities to countries such as Iran and Iraq. All of these developments prompted significant changes in the architecture of U.S. and international export control regimes with DOD being heavily involved in U.S. attempts to adapt to these changes.[212]

U.S. foreign military sales deliveries during the Bush 41 Administration began at $8.359.377 billion in FY 1990 and rose to $12.118.344 billion through FY 1993.[213] The following passage aptly describes the epochal transitions affecting the global security environment and national and international export control regimes at this time:

> By the early 1990s, America's reliance on export controls and sanctions to promote nonproliferation reached its apex. The key reason why was the collapse of the Soviet Union. Without the Cold War and the prospect of global conflict, public support for continuing these restraints, began to wane. Initially, the war against Saddam Hussein and the impetus it gave to expanding existing strategic controls and sanctions, obscured this point. Besides Iraq, most American officials thought it was clear who the key trouble states were—Iran, North Korea, Syria, and Libya. Yet, without the cold war, America's allies were no longer so opposed to doing business with these nations. Ignoring this point, the United States tried to get its allies to back strengthening controls and sanctions. In the long run, this effort proved disappointing.[214]

This time period would also see the U.S. become involved with various multilateral international export control regimes such as the Missile Technology Control Regime (MTCR), Wassenaar Arrangement, and many others which will be described in Chapter 8.[215] During 1990, DTSA reorganized to meet the new challenges by a constantly changing security environment emphasized by the Soviet bloc's collapse. While recognizing ongoing security threats from Russia and China, DTSA also recognized the need for COCOM to adjust its controls to account for continuing technology advances; promote greater export control cooperation with newly independent Eastern European nations and the former Soviet Union; and assume new responsibilities for reviewing and halting sensitive exports to rogue nations such as Iran and Iraq which were emerging as security threats to the U.S. and its allies.[216]

The graphic nature of the multifaceted security threat from proliferating weapons of mass destruction was demonstrated in DOD's 1992 annual report to Congress:

> Massive Soviet arsenals, including 30,000 tactical and strategic weapons, also remain a serious concern. A loss of central control, or the proliferation of these and other weapons of mass destruction beyond the borders of the former Soviet Union, would pose great threats to world peace and stability. Today, some 15 nations have ballistic missiles—in less than a decade, as many as 20 countries may possess these systems. Nuclear, chemical, and biological weapons, as well as advanced conventional systems, can make distant conflicts a worldwide concern. Other threats, including terrorism, illegal drugs, and low-intensity conflict, can weaken the fabric of democratic societies.
>
> The uncertainty of these developments is the essence of the defense challenge in the years ahead. That uncertainty requires us to plan carefully if we are to take advantage of current opportunities for a less costly defense while preparing for the new security environment.[217]

Executive policy responses made to respond to the national security export aspects of this rapidly changing security environment by the Bush 41 Administration included National Security Directive (NSD) 24 on September 26, 1989. This document directed the U.S. to accelerate chemical weapons nonproliferation initiatives including implementing a global ban on producing, using, and storing these agents. It mentioned that the U.S. would commit to reducing its own chemical weapons stockpiles to 500 tons within eight years after an international convention enters into force, that DOD and the JCS would provide recommendations for changing military force structure and deployment to accommodate for the reduced availability of chemical weapons, and that the U.S. would expand its R&D efforts to enhance its capabilities to verify compliance with a global ban.[218]

NSD 70 on July 10, 1992 sought to minimize and reverse the spread and prevent use of weapons of mass destruction. This document recognized that countries such as North Korea, who have been of longstanding concern as developers of these weapons, are also becoming suppliers of related technologies. It also mentioned that the Soviet bloc's breakup could increase the possibility that supplies of these weapons or related technologies could proliferate if democratic and economic reforms in those countries falter. Consequently, U.S. policy will seek to strengthen international export control regimes such as COCOM and focus particular attention on areas of proliferation concern including the Korean Peninsula, Middle East, Persian Gulf, South Asia, and former Soviet bloc countries by working individually with countries in these regions to develop nonproliferation approaches appropriate to their needs.[219]

EO 12755 of March 12, 1991 further enhanced nonproliferation's importance as an export control objective by including the Secretary of Energy and Director of the Arms Control and Disarmament Agency (ACDA), along with the Secretaries of Commerce, Defense, and State, as members of the Export Administration Review Board by including "concerns about the nonproliferation of armaments" within its organizational charter.[220]

Another significant development in DOD efforts to address the potential proliferation of weapons of mass destruction from the collapsing Soviet Union was the December 12, 1991 enactment of the Nunn-Lugar Act sponsored by Senators Sam Nunn (D-GA) and Richard Lugar (R-IN). This initiative saw the United States provide selective assistance to the Soviet Union and Russian Federation in destroying, dismantling, storing, and transporting Soviet nuclear weapons. It was particularly concerned with preventing the transfer of these weapons, their components, and the technical expertise behind them to other countries and terrorist groups and contribute to their international proliferation. This statute required the President to certify to Congress that as a condition of receiving this U.S. assistance that the recipient country had to make substantial indigenous investments to dismantle or destroy these weapons; halt military modernization programs exceeding legitimate defense requirements; abandon using fissionable components in destroyed weapons in new nuclear weapons; facilitate U.S. verification of weapons destruction; comply with relevant arms control agreements; and observe internationally recognized human rights standards. Nunn-Lugar's initial budget was $400 million and the program remains in effect two decades later.[221]

Three GAO reports evaluated DOD export control performance during the Bush 41 administration. A June 1989 report examined DOD's and Commerce's role in export licensing. This assessment found that DOD recommendations significantly influenced about 1/3 of Commerce licensing decisions involving proposed exports to proscribed countries but only 4% of Commerce decisions about licensing to free world countries. DOD's input on free world license applications primarily derives from its interpretation of information contained on the license application instead of unique information it possesses. Numerous DOD recommendations approving applications are based on exporters or consignees meeting certain restrictions including no export, resale, or transfer. Between June 1987-June 1988 Commerce and DOD agreed on 90% of proposed license applications though DOD recommended conditional approval in almost half of these cases. In 71 cases, however, where DOD recommended approval Commerce denied approval based on concerns about technology diversion and DOE concerns about proscribed nuclear uses.[222]

Another June 1989 GAO report revealed that over 25 federal agencies in multiple offices and divisions collected information on foreign dual-use technology. Within DOD alone, these agencies included:

A. Air Force Foreign Technology Division
B. Air Force Office of Scientific Research—Far East
C. Army Foreign Science and Technology Center
D. Army Research Office
E. Defense Advanced Research Projects Agency
F. Defense Intelligence Agency
G. Defense Technical Information Center
H. European Office of Aerospace R&D—Air Force
I. Naval Intelligence Service Center
J. Office of Naval Research
K. Office of the Undersecretary for Acquisition[223]

A June 1990 GAO report addressed efforts by DOD, State, and Commerce to address U.S. efforts to control the transfer of nuclear capable missile technology under MTCR an international effort by western countries to regulate the spread of ballistic missile technology inaugurated in

April 1987. This report mentioned that during MTCR's first 20 months that Commerce had identified 128 applications involving 13 countries which were subject to missile technology controls. However, DTSA, which reviews applications referred to it by the State Department identified nearly 1,450 missile technology related export license applications involving over 70 countries.[224]

This report went on to mention that State, DOD, and ACDA had seven full-time employees dedicated to providing assistance on license applications and MTCR issues. GAO went on to mention there were problems with other countries adhering to MTCR guidelines, that Commerce has not always agreed with DOD's determination of items subject to MTCR controls, that two licenses approved by Commerce for export to Iraq were suspended after DOD expressed MTCR concerns, and that a DOD official said in January 1989 that he had been trying for two years to have Commerce control rocket propellant batch mixers placed under MTCR and that Commerce finally drafted export control regulations on these mixers in December 1989.[225]

Clinton Administration

Total U.S. foreign military sales deliveries during the Clinton Administration started at $11.012.232 billion in FY 1994, peaked at $16.851.181 billion in FY 1999, and declined to $12.660.254 billion in FY 2001.[226] While controversy over satellite export controls and Chinese espionage involved Clinton's Commerce, Energy, and State Departments, DOD export control efforts remained concentrated on counterproliferation.[227]

The increasing importance of counterproliferation activities in DOD's export control purview received organizational recognition with DTSA being placed under the Assistant Secretary of Defense for Nuclear Security and Counterproliferation for developing, coordinating, and overseeing implementation of DOD technology transfer policy in July 1993.[228] The Clinton Administration also announced a new missile nonproliferation policy in a September 27, 1993 presidential address at the United Nations General Assembly. Clinton announced that the U.S. would now consider approving exports of space launch vehicles and related technologies to Missile Technology Control Regime (MTCR) signatory countries. This announcement went on to declare that the U.S. would approve such exports for nations with the best nonproliferation credentials as an incentive for additional countries to sign MTCR and other nonproliferation regimes. Congress, however, was concerned about liberalizing space launch vehicle technology exports and passed a resolution expressing its concerns.[229]

DOD retained responsibility for selected denials of government contracts involving proliferation sanctions under AECA and collaborative responsibilities with State for China and weapons proliferation congressional reporting functions.[230]

The 1994 Agreed Framework Agreement with North Korea proved to be a particularly controversial attempt by the Clinton Administration to regulate weapons proliferation to this rogue regime. Signed on October 21, 1994, this agreement saw the U.S. offer Pyongyang numerous benefits in return for that regime's "promise" to freeze its nuclear weapons program. Examples of these benefits included supplying the North Koreans light water nuclear reactors and heavy oil, and allowing IAEA inspections of North Korea nuclear facilities. This agreement would ultimately fail as North Korea eventually exploded a nuclear weapon and represents another example of the difficulty involved in enforcing export controls and other non-military sanctions against an autarkic dictatorial regime unconcerned about international opinion of its activities.[231]

The Clinton Administration's first term saw the issuance of various NSC Presidential Decision Directives (PDDs) on DOD export control missions. One of these was PDD 18 on December 7, 1993 which saw Secretary of Defense Les Aspin (1938-1995) stress the need for developing new military capabilities to deal with emerging and proliferating weapons threats and developing improved non-nuclear penetrating munitions to strike underground military installations.[232]

PDD 27 in August 1994 established a Nonproliferation Arms Control and Technology Policy Working Group to coordinate arms control and nonproliferation R&D and facilitate interagency cooperation in these areas with DOD being one of the lead agencies in order to make relevant recommendations to the President.[233] PDD 34 on February 17, 1995 developed new decision-making standards on U.S. arms exports. Criteria for such exports included:

1. Consistency with international agreements and arms control initiatives.
2. Transfer's appropriateness in responding to legitimate U.S. and recipient security needs.

3. How much transfer supports U.S. strategic and foreign policy interests through increased access and influence, allied burdensharing and interoperability.
4. Impact on U.S. industry and defense industrial base in determining whether the sale is approved or not.
5. Degree of protection afforded sensitive technology and potential for unauthorized third-party transfer plus in-country diversion for unauthorized uses.
6. Risk of revealing system vulnerabilities and adversely impacting U.S. operational capabilities if system is compromised.[234]

PDD 47 on March 21, 1996 established and directed implementation of U.S. policy on stockpile safety and security concerning Comprehensive Test Ban Treaty (CTBT) monitoring and verification. Unclassified areas of cooperation approved for U.S. participation in these activities included computations, experiments, and materials, nuclear warhead safety and security, CTBT monitoring and verification in seismics, hydroacoustics, and infrasound monitoring systems, onsite inspection technologies including ground-based electromagnetic pulse technology for detecting covert underground nuclear explosions masked by chemical explosions, and techniques for detecting decoupled explosions.[235]

Significant first-term Clinton Administration DOD security export control executive orders included EO 12918 on May 26, 1994 prohibiting individuals and U.S. organizations from supplying Rwanda with arms, police equipment, or spare parts due to the internecine turmoil in that country,[236] and EO 12929 on June 3, 1994 directing DOD to identify critical components and technology items for inclusion on military command critical item lists and ensuring such items are available from reliable sources to meet peacetime, graduated mobilization, and national emergency requirements.[237]

EO 12946 on January 20, 1995 saw establishment of the President's Advisory Board on Arms Proliferation Policy within DOD whose purpose was advising the President on the proliferation of advanced conventional and strategic weapons.[238] DOD Directive 5105.31 on July 14, 1995 established the Defense Special Weapons Agency (DSWA) within DOD with export control responsibilities covering verifying technologies for monitoring and ensuring compliance with arms control treaties.[239] EO 12981 on December 5, 1995 sought to expedite license processing by having all license applications resolved or referred to the President within 90 calendar days after completed license application registration and that reviewing departments or agencies shall specify to the Secretary within 10 days of receiving a license referral from another agency if they need any additional information from the applicant to determine whether an export license will be issued.[240]

EO 13026 on November 15, 1996 saw computer encryption products designated as defense articles within USML Category 13 placed on the EAR if exporting these products could harm national security and foreign policy interests even if comparable products are available from non-U.S. sources.[241]

On September 30, 1996, GAO released a report on the U.S.-China Joint Defense Conversion Commission (JDCC). JDCC was established by DOD in cooperation with China's Minister of the Commission of Science, Technology, and Industry for National Defense (COSTIND) to promote bilateral and technical cooperation in defense conversion and maintain government-to-government contacts. JDCC met only in October 1994 and in July 1996 the Secretary of Defense informed Congress of its termination. DTSA conducted a review of 49 Chinese-proposed JDCC projects to identify potential exports of restricted items and technologies. Following its initial review, DTSA expressed concern about 23 of these projects due to the lack of technical information about these projects or the participating Chinese companies. Although none of the projects DTSA was concerned about were carried out, JDCC procedures did not require it to monitor private sector contacts. The GAO report found no evidence that U.S. controlled technology or financial transfers occurred which would enhance Chinese military modernization.[242]

However, a May 1995 GAO report expressed concern that most export licensing applications for militarily-sensitive stealth materials and technology are only reviewed by Commerce and not sent to DOD or State for more thorough review of the national security consequences of their export. For instance, between FY 1991-1994 only 15 of 166 stealth related export license applications were sent by Commerce to DOD or State for review.[243] In addition, a November 1996 GAO report determined that on September 14, 1994 Commerce had approved a McDonnell-Douglas contractor's export of machine tools to China which were shipped to the Nanchang Aircraft Company that produces aircraft and cruise missiles for the People's Liberation Army. This diversion was contrary to contractual conditions that this license only be used for civilian technologies. DOD had raised concerns about potential military diversion during the licensing process and expressed concern that these machine tools significantly heightened Chinese abilities over previous U.S. exports. Nevertheless, the sale went through.[244]

Counterproliferation remained DOD's export control policy emphasis during the Clinton Administration's second term. The 1997 Secretary of Defense annual report and *Quadrennial Security Review* stressed that DOD's technology security efforts focused on ensuring that export controls are designed and implemented to prevent nuclear, biological, and chemical (NBC) weapons proliferation and delivery and preserving U.S. military technological advantages by controlling conventional weapons and sensitive dual-use goods, services, and technologies. These documents went on to maintain that DOD's technology security policy recognized that exporting conventional weapons and related dual-use goods and technologies was not necessarily threatening or destabilizing; that such transfers could contribute to preventive defense strategy by supporting friends and allies legitimate defense requirements and their interoperability with U.S. forces; and that such exports can enhance the U.S. defense industrial base.[245]

Significant second-term Clinton security related EO's included EO 13094 on July 30, 1998 prohibiting U.S. Government departments and agencies from purchasing goods or services or contracting for such items from individuals or organizations involved in helping other countries acquire or proliferate weapons of mass destruction, EO 13159 of June 21, 2000 blocking Russian Federation property by ordering that fissile materials removed from such property not be diverted to weapons proliferation, and EO 13177 of December 4, 2000 establishing a National Commission on the Use of Offsets in Defense Trade and President's Council on the Use of Offsets in Commercial Trade to examine these practices involving industrial compensation and military sales that can affect the sale of defense articles and services.[246]

September 30, 1998 saw DSWA transition into the Defense Threat Reduction Agency (DTRA) and become the primary DOD entity responsible for maintaining the U.S. nuclear deterrent and reducing and countering threats from WMD while assisting DTSA in its export control responsibilities as a result of DOD Directive 5105.62.[247]

While the Cox Committee report on Chinese espionage at DOE labs was the hallmark event of Clinton Administration export control and technology transfer policy, DOD also faced controversy over its export control activities. This was most vividly reflected in a July 9, 1998 Senate Armed Services Committee hearing involving conflicting testimony on DOD export controls performance by former Reagan Administration DOD Undersecretary for Trade and Security Policy Stephen D. Bryen, Gary Milhollin of the Wisconsin Project for Nuclear Arms Control, and Mitchel B. Wallerstein the former Deputy Assistant Secretary of Defense for Counterproliferation Policy during the Clinton Administration's first term. Committee chair Senator Strom Thurmond (R-SC)(1902-2003) expressed his concern that current export policies on dual-use, militarily-critical technologies, and non-proliferation were inadequate to prevent WMD proliferation and preserve U.S. military technological advantages. He also expressed concern about the transfer of dual-use and military-critical technologies from State's USML to Commerce's CCL and mentioned the case of Ohio plant machine tools that produced parts for C-17 transports, B-1 bombers, F-15 fighters, and Peacekeeper ballistic missiles being sold to China without proper scrutiny by DOD and State.[248]

Stressing the critical importance of DOD involvement in export control decisionmaking, Bryen argued:

> It is extraordinarily important that strategic export decisions are reviewed by the Defense Department, and when we say that we just do not mean one little agency in the Defense Department, but we mean by all the cognizant components of the Defense Department. We need the input of the service Secretaries and the military departments. We need the input of the Defense Intelligence Agency. We need the input of the various responsible components that understand different aspects of strategic technology, the labs that work for the Defense Department, for example, in order to come to intelligent, correct decisions about strategic exports.[249]

Bryen went on to express his concerns about U.S. military force reductions, Chinese acquisition of high technology weapons giving it a long-range strike capability, and that DTSA not disappear as DOD's principal export control policymaking agency.[250] Wallerstein stressed what he saw as first term Clinton Administration export control accomplishments including strengthening IAEA and MTCR, removing weapons grade fissile material from Georgia and Kazakhstan, negotiating the Agreed Framework with North Korea, having the CIA's Nonproliferation Center review all dual-use export license applications, and bringing

Russia and the Ukraine into MTCR. He also maintained that human and economic resources are wasted by having to wide of an export control net attempting to regulate goods and technologies widely available from other countries and announced the Clinton Administration's success in creating the Wassenaar Arrangement as COCOM's international export control successor.[251]

Milhollin stressed that export controls can work citing their success in dissuading Argentina and Brazil from developing nuclear weapons and partial success in slowing down Iraqi nuclear aspirations. However, he also expressed concern about the Clinton Administration's 1996 decision to decontrol supercomputer exports and referred to Russian nuclear weapons laboratories at Arzamas and Chelyabinsk receiving U.S. supercomputers along with the Chinese Academy of Sciences which has designed Beijing's DF-5 ICBM capable of hitting the U.S., and India's Institute of Science in Bangalore which is that country's leading missile research institute. He also mentioned that India has watched China arming Pakistan, noting U.S. efforts to avoid sanctioning China for arming Islamabad, and the U.S. telling India to use restraint in testing nuclear weapons while the U.S. does not exercise restraint in satellite exports. Consequently, he believed India concludes the U.S. does not have a credible antiproliferation policy and that Commerce has a conflict of interest in export control policymaking because that agency's primary mission is trade promotion and that it should not be trusted with national security matters because it will inevitably favor trade.[252]

A June 18, 1999 DOD Inspector General (DODIG) report on the Pentagon's export licensing processes for dual-use commodities and munitions noted that DOD officials expressed general satisfaction with dual-use export license applications Commerce referred to them for review but also expressed concern over Commerce referring too few commodity classifications for review which resulted in Commerce making national security license application decisions without DOD input. The DODIG report went on to mention that DOD entities did not conduct required annual assessments of the impact of technology transfers that could provide information on proposed exports cumulative effects and that DOD is unable to ensure that the licensing process accounts for the cumulative effect of technology transfers.[253]

Other report findings included improper DTRA referral to other DOD entities of 12% of dual use and 24% of munitions license applications; the need for a classroom training and program plan for personnel reviewing export license applications; the need for DOD's Foreign Disclosure and Technical Information System (FORDTIS) to provide a better audit trail for export licensing decisions; and that DTRA had adequate procedures for monitoring foreign space launch activities. Between FY 1995-1998, DOD dual-use license applications referrals increased from 1,463 to 9,735, with an average annual agency budget of $10.3 million, and staff falling from 129 to 117.[254]

An additional 1999 report by a commission assessing federal organizational ability to combat WMD proliferation also addressed DOD export control deficiencies. It mentioned that proliferation combatting responsibilities are to diffuse and that there is no institutional means of integrating multiple separate activities below the level of Deputy Secretary. The Commission also recommended that proliferation policy responsibility should not be lumped with other policy and strategy issues but be the exclusive responsibility of an Assistant Secretary for Combating Proliferation; that DTRA's head lacks authority to set counter-proliferation R&D program priorities among military departments; that more spending needs to occur on chemical and biological defense; and the President should direct the Secretary of Defense to establish a Joint Proliferation Operations Plans Group under the Assistant Secretary of Defense for Combating Proliferation/Policy to conduct planning support for proliferation combat operations.[255]

A May 2000 GAO report noted that although DOD had taken positive steps to integrate and focus its response to the growing threat of WMD that it did not have an overarching joint counterproliferation document to present a centralized picture of how it should respond to this environment across the military operational spectrum. GAO recommended that DOD develop strategies, a management plan, and performance measures to better guide and manage its export control counterproliferation actions; include examination of departmental organization for counterproliferation in the next Quadrennial Defense Review; and devise and implement a mechanism to identify and eliminate undesirable redundancies within its counterproliferation programs.[256]

George W. Bush Administration

Wars in Afghanistan and Iraq in response to the 9/11 terrorist attacks assumed George W. Bush Administration national security policymaking priorities and this was reflected in many export controls enacted during his tenure. This included its controversial but necessary advocacy of taking preemptive action against emerging security threats including terrorism and potentially involving WMD and aggressively targeting financial assets of individuals, organizations, and states supporting terrorists and WMD proliferators.[257]

Total U.S. military sales deliveries during this administration began at $10.582.881 billion in FY 2002, peaked at $12.703.387 billion in FY 2007, and declined slightly to $12.644.688 in FY 2009.[258] Most George W. Bush Administration export control executive orders dealt with targeting terrorist and WMD proliferations financial assets and will be documented in Chapter 5. Security related EO's issued during his administration include EO 13222 continuing the episodic renewal of presidential export control authority under IEEPA; EO 13224 blocking property and prohibiting transactions with anyone supporting or threatening to support terrorism; EO 13292 exempting from declassification information assisting in developing or using weapons of mass destruction; EO 13328 establishing a commission to study whether the intelligence community is equipped to find WMD in Iraq and other countries of concern; and EO 13466 continuing legal restrictions on North Korean property and financial assets, along with Americans trading with North Korea, due to that country's ongoing efforts to develop and proliferate WMD.[259]

The Bush Administration also issued several National Security Presidential Directive (NSPDs) dealing with defense related export control activities. Although some of these remain classified, pertinent examples which are at least partially available include NSPD 19 which sought to review defense trade export policy and national security. Its objectives included retooling and realigning defense industrial links with allies to reflect the current and evolving security environment, controlling militarily critical technologies and protecting them from diversion, improving the military effectiveness of alliances and coalitions, identifying foreign market barriers impeding access to U.S. and allied cooperation, and identifying possible specific modifications and assessing the potential risks to U.S. national security and foreign policy interests posed by modifying current U.S. defense trade licensing policies and practices.[260]

NSPD 20, which remains classified, deals with counterproliferation interdiction and was issued on November 20, 2002 with its principles partially being reflected in a December 9, 2002 U.S.-Spanish seizure then release of a ship carrying Scud missiles and related cargo from North Korea to Yemen. The release of the U.S. *National Strategy to*

Combat Weapons of Mass Proliferation at this time provided further documentation of the Bush Administration's objective to seize cargo transporting WMD to rogue regimes.[261]

NSPD 41 on December 21, 2004 addressed maritime security. It stated the U.S. must use the full range of its operational maritime assets and capabilities to prevent maritime areas from being used by terrorists, criminals, and hostile states to prevent attacks against U.S. property, citizens, territory, or allies. It also called for enhanced international maritime intelligence cooperation to prevent and defeat hostile attacks on maritime assets, and improve international supply chain security.[262]

NSPD 48, the Nuclear Materials Information Program (NMIP), was issued on August 28, 2006. While remaining classified, portions of its content were described in an April 2, 2008 Senate Homeland Security and Governmental Affairs Committee hearing by DOE Intelligence and Counterintelligence Director Rolf Mowatt-Larssen. He mentioned that NMIP was an interagency effort to consolidate all source information about global nuclear materials holdings and their security status into an integrated and continuously updated information management system. This system would be accessible to federal agencies nonproliferation, counterproliferation, and antiterrorism efforts while also including a national registry to identify and track nuclear material samples held throughout the U.S.[263]

NSPD 55 dealing with dual-use export controls and NSPD 56 covering defense trade reform were both issued in January 2008 and remain classified. Key objectives of NSPD 56 included ensuring that U.S. defense trade policies and practices support the U.S. National Security Strategy. This directive mandated the State Department expedite processing of export license applications for USML controlled items; adhere to a 60 day processing goal; implement license exception for exports involving dual and third country nationals from allied partners; establish an interagency dispute mechanism; and improve the congressional notification process.[264]

The Proliferation Security Initiative (PSI) was one Bush Administration program to use defense export controls to combat WMD proliferation. Initiated by the December 2002 *National Strategy to Combat Weapons of Mass Destruction*, PSI was formally launched on May 31, 2003. It seeks to develop stronger tools for stopping this proliferation and identifies interdiction as being particularly important. PSI interdiction principles adhered to by more than 90 participating countries include:

1. Undertaking effective unilateral or multilateral measures for interdicting the transfer or transport of WMD and their delivery systems to states and non-state actors of proliferation concern.
2. Adopting streamlined procedures for rapidly exchanging relevant information on suspected proliferation activity and protecting that information's confidential character.
3. Taking specific actions supporting interdiction efforts of WMD cargoes and their delivery systems consistent with national and international laws.
4. Taking appropriate actions to stop, search, and seize such cargoes in internal waters, territorial seas, and contiguous zones.[265]

The danger of non-state actors facilitating WMD proliferation was demonstrated during 2004 when it was revealed that prominent Pakistani nuclear official Abdul Qadeer Khan began using a clandestine procurement network to supply his country's nuclear weapons program in the 1970s and that he used a similar network to supply Iran, Libya, and North Korea with materials for uranium enrichment. Pakistan's possession of nuclear weapons, its proximity to unstable countries such as Iran and Afghanistan, and ties with terrorist groups desirous of obtaining nuclear weapons reflect the serious defense export control problems involved in combating WMD proliferation.[266]

Verifying the absence or presence of WMD in countries of concern was another problem bedeviling the George W. Bush Administration. This was particularly prevalent in controversy over whether Iraq still retained WMD capabilities as controversy persisted over the failure to find such weapons during U.S. military operations in Iraq. A 2005 presidential commission report on the U.S. Government's intelligence capabilities concerning these weapons was extremely critical of U.S. intelligence capabilities in this area. Commission findings included:

1. Major failure by the U.S. Intelligence Community in assessing pre-war Iraq's WMD program capabilities and communicating these assessments to policymakers.
2. The Defense Intelligence Agency failing to authenticate sources and their reporting.

3. Overestimating Iraqi chemical warfare capabilities due to analytic flaws and insufficient quality information collected.
4. The need for enhanced capabilities to verify human source intelligence veracity.
5. Recommending that the President establish a National Counterproliferation Center with fewer than 100 personnel to manage and coordinate analysis and collection on WMD weapons throughout the Intelligence Community.[267]

DOD Directive 5105.72, issued on July 28, 2005, reinforced DTSA's authority over administering DOD security policies on international transfers of defense-related goods, services, and technologies. Key aspects of this directive included preserving critical U.S. military technological advantages; controlling and limiting transfers that could be detrimental to U.S. security interests; preventing WMD proliferation and that of related delivery mechanisms to countries and terrorists; promoting legitimate defense cooperation with foreign allies and friends; and assuring the health of the U.S. defense industrial base.[268]

DOD Instruction 2040.2, issued on July 10, 2008, provided additional guidance on dual-use technology policy stressing that U.S. export control policy in this area would place particular emphasis on the importance of interoperability with allies and coalition partners and to direct and indirect impacts on the U.S. defense industrial base. Consequently, DOD will apply export control and other technology security policies and procedures to balance economic, national security, and scientific interests with DTSA playing a key role in this review process.[269]

During an April 24, 2008 congressional hearing, DTSA Acting Director Beth McCormick testified that DTSA annually processed over 40,000 export licenses with nearly 75% of these licenses being direct commercial sales to close friends and allies. Other administration accomplishments, according to McCormick, included a 9.5% increase in munitions licenses and 11.6% increase in dual-use licenses approved since 2001; decreasing average processing time of State license referrals by 8 days and Commerce license referrals by 3 days; and average 2008 processing time for munitions reviews averaging 13 days and 12 days for dual-use reviews.[270]

Despite these accomplishments, DTSA performance flaws were still found by DODIG and GAO. A March 30, 2006 DODIG report concluded that DTSA had made some unsupported technology export decisions concerning China which could threaten U.S. ability to stop WMD proliferation, hinder regional stability, and negatively impact national security. An example of such unsupported decision making by DTSA was its failure to refer export license applications to other DOD entities if these organizations could process them thoroughly, responsively, and consistently.[271]

A September 28, 2007 DODIG report reviewed progress DOD had made in implementing DODIG export controlled related recommendations between FY 2000-2006. DODIG mentioned that 74% of their recommendations had been implemented by DTSA and other DOD components during this time period, but that further action was necessary to implement the remaining recommendations.

Examples of continuing DTSA shortcomings included insufficiently assessing the nuclear significance of a particular item in an export license application; determining whether the party in this transaction had engaged in clandestine or illegal procurement activities; assessing whether the end user had previously diverted dual-use items for proliferation purposes; failing to assess whether exporting or re-exporting this item presented an unacceptable diversion risk to nuclear explosive or nuclear fuel cycle activities; and determining the importing country's nonproliferation credentials.[272]

Notable GAO reports on Bush Administration DOD export control activities begin with a February 13, 2004 report on DTRA nonproliferation activities. This assessment acknowledged the wide range of this agency's nonproliferation activities and accomplishments, while recommending that it improve its annual performance report by comparing actual performance against planned goals, explaining why these goals were not met, and addressing how they will be met in the future.[273]

A July 28, 2006 report expressed concern about MCTL currency and the currency of the Developing Sciences Technology List (DSTL) sponsored by the DOD's Office of the Director for Defense Research and Engineering. DSTL is a compendium of internationally developed scientific and technological capabilities that have the potential to significantly enhance or degrade U.S. military capabilities five years into the future and beyond. GAO determined that MCTL and DSTL are of limited value due to inappropriate validation and generally obsolescent. Nine of twenty MCTL sections, including those covering biological warfare, communications, and weapons have not been updated for ten years despite stated program goals for quadrennial updating and DSTL has not been updated for the past five years.

DOD does not use MCTL for export control purposes or licensing decisions since the list is too broad and a similar situation applies to DSTL because many DOD components are unaware of it. DOD agreed with GAO's recommendations about determining user requirements to reassess and clarify MCTL's purposes but does not plan to take any new action to implement these recommendations.[274]

A September 19, 2007 GAO appraisal concluded that there are differences within DOD on issuing exemptions concerning the export of technical data including classified information and that these exemptions affect defense contractors, university laboratories, and federally funded research and development centers. These differences also affect DOD and State export licensing activities and GAO recommended that DOD and State resolve disagreements on exemption uses and guidelines and increase insight and oversight of certified exemptions.[275]

An October 2008 Defense Business Board task force report examining export controls best practices also recommended that the Secretary of Defense take the following steps to enhance U.S. export control rules:

1. Set a 90-day deadline for obtaining interagency agreement for annually updating USML and pay particular attention to modifying the list for dual-use and other commercially derived items.

2. Advocating counterparts at Commerce and State adopt an export control policy focusing on enforcement with appropriate critical technology controls.

3. Issuing clear policy guidance for defense sales to particular countries while ending the current transactional approach which is not transparent to the country and industry and often treats allies as foes.

4. Advocating legislative change to enhance military interoperability with allies and sustaining defense industrial base infrastructure critical capacity.

5. Working closely with the defense industry to identify items whose export is necessary and consider establishing seed money for such a program.

6. Continue streamlining DOD's export control/technology transfer organizational structure by automating standardized export reviews.[276]

Obama Administration

FY 2010 saw U.S. military sales deliveries rise to $14.078.448 billion during the Obama Administration's first year.[277] Most Obama Administration export control EO's have targeted financial assets of hostile nations and terrorist groups. Two DOD related export control EO's include 13546 of July 2, 2010 seeking to enhance the security of biological select agents and toxins (BSAT) essential to national security against unauthorized release and EO 13558 of November 9, 2010 including DOD as a member of an interagency Export Enforcement Coordination Center within the Department of Homeland Security. This entity's mission involves serving as the primary forum for executive departments and agencies to coordinate and enhance their export control enforcement efforts and identify and resolve conflicts in criminal and investigative actions involving export control violations. Additional mission responsibilities include serving as a conduit between federal law enforcement agencies and the intelligence community to exchange information about potential U.S. export control violations and coordinating law-enforcement public outreach activities about U.S. export controls.[278]

Obama Administration NSC documents are Presidential Policy Directives (PPD) and most remain classified. However, PPD 2 of November 2, 2009 directed DOD and other federal agencies to provide the NSC with a detailed implementation plan on how they would implement the *National Strategy for Countering Biological Threats* which would include budget recommendations and performance measures.[279] As mentioned earlier in this chapter, the Obama Administration has initiated an export control reform initiative seeking to consolidate several export control lists from multiple agencies into a single three tiered system of low, middle, and high priority items based on their military significance to the U.S. and international availability.[280] Rep. Berman's H.R. 2004 referenced earlier in this chapter focuses on protecting the domestic defense industrial base and giving the President flexibility to prohibit exports on national security grounds but does not provide additional export control restriction authority to DTSA or any other DOD entity.[281] Rep. Ros-Lehtinen's H.R. 2122 also did not give DOD any additional export control authority in its EAA reform proposals.[282]

DTSA currently reviews over 30,000 export license applications received annually from Commerce and State. Its organizational components include divisions covering licensing, technology, policy, international security, and space. The Licensing Division features dual-use and policy sections whose responsibilities include evaluating licenses for technical, policy, and intelligence concerns from Commerce; maintaining contact with industry on new technologies and licensing initiatives; and representing DOD in multinational export control organizations such as MTCR. Munitions Licensing Division responsibilities include receiving and evaluating licenses from State; coordinating proposed ITAR and USML changes with other agencies; and supporting State in identifying defense articles and determining AECA violations.[283]

Policy and International Security division responsibilities include technology security aspects of U.S. weapons and defense related technology transfers to allies and friends; ensuring recipient nations adequately protect these materials; reviewing and commenting on export license applications and foreign military sales to ensure their compatibility with U.S. Government policy; and developing and reviewing defense related technology security policies concerning the U.S. defense industrial base. The Assessments Division conducts end-use and end-user checks in support of proposed dual-use exports and munitions information and commodities.[284]

Space Division responsibilities include physically monitoring all aspects of satellite launches to ensure no unauthorized technology transfer occurs when a license is approved for exporting a satellite or related items for launch in a foreign country; monitoring meetings between engineers representing U.S. exporters and foreign entities where export licenses require DOD monitoring of defense services; monitoring launches conducted jointly by U.S. and foreign entities if DOD monitoring is required; and reviewing and approving technical data releases as authorized in specific licenses and technical assistance agreements.[285]

DTSA carries out these responsibilities with a staff of over 2000 whose personnel includes 50 senior engineers with unique expertise in military and dual-use systems and capabilities and 30 licensing officers along with foreign policy analysts, security specialists, and support personnel. These activities were carried out with a FY 2012 budget of $33.848 million.[286]

A May 2011 report on the Obama Administration export control initiative says DTSA contends that fundamental export control reform can only be achieved if all three phases of the administration's export control plan are implemented. It maintained that tiering controls with clear licensing guidelines, a single licensing agency, and export control licensing information system would enhance national security, protect U.S. warfighter security, facilitate cooperation with allies and prevent adversaries from accessing critical technologies.[287]

An April 2012 joint DOD and State report conducted a risk assessment of U.S. space export control policy for congress emphasizing potential problems with removing satellites and related components from USML and transferring them to CCL. This report recommended returning the export control jurisdiction status of satellites and related items to the President and that DOD should be authorized to determine whether special export controls need to be applied to U.S. companies providing technical services supporting foreign satellite or launch vehicle developments. Other report findings included other nations having fewer commercial space and space-related controls than the U.S.; many commercial satellite systems and technologies becoming less critical to national security; removing space-related items from USML without appropriate export controls on the CCL would *significantly improve* other countries military potential; exporting space-related items to allies represents a low national security risk; the U.S. should maintain strict controls on transferring non-critical space-related items to end-users and for end-uses likely to be detrimental to U.S. national interests; and that the risks due to removing space-related dual-use items from USML could be acceptably managed through CCL controls and licensing policies.[288]

Other DOD entities involved with some aspects of export control policymaking include the Defense Institute Security Assistance Management (DISAM), Defense Security Cooperation Agency (DSCA), Defense Threat Reduction Agency (DTRA), and Deputy Assistant Secretary of Defense for Manufacturing and Industrial Base Policy. DISAM is a component part of DSCA whose mission is providing professional education, research, and support to advance U.S. foreign policy through security assistance and cooperation which has existed in various incarnations since 1961.[289] DSCA was established in 1971 under control of the Undersecretary of Defense for Policy. It's responsibilities include providing security assistance including military assistance, international military education and training, and foreign military sales.[290]

Established in 1998, DTRA responsibilities include reducing the threats posed by WMD by implementing arms control treaties and executing the Cooperative Threat Reduction Program(CTRP) also known as the Nunn-Lugar Act; bridging gaps between the technical community and warfighters; and preparing for future threats by developing technologies and concepts needed to counter emerging WMD threats and enemies.[291] The Deputy Assistant Secretary of Defense for Manufacturing and Industrial Base Policy is responsible for ensuring that U.S. defense industrial base is capable of meeting national security requirements by ensuring military readiness and superiority and that export controls do not injure U.S. defense industry competitiveness or allow diversion of sensitive technologies to hostile entities.[292] It has gone through various institutional iterations in its history which arguably dates back to 1940 legislation giving the President the authority to prohibit or curtail defense exports.[293] GAO evaluation of DTSA and other DOD export control activities during the Obama Administration provides additional insights on the quality of these programs. A September 2010 report found that the total value of arms sales to Persian Gulf countries could not be determined because a State Department database also included arms transfers authorized for U.S. military units in that region. This database was unable to separate end-user authorizations or separate multiple authorizations covering the same equipment. The GAO report went on to mention that DOD and State failed to consistently document how arms transfers to these countries furthered U.S. foreign policy and national security goals and that DOD could not document its review releasing technology for 7 of 13 military sales.[294]

Conclusion

DOD has experienced success and failures in its export control initiatives as this chapter demonstrates. Like the Commerce Department, DOD faces contradictory objectives in its export control initiatives. In considering overall U.S. national security interests, DOD entities such as DSCA are primarily concerned with promoting U.S. arms sales overseas, while entities such as DTSA and DTRA seek to restrict the sales of these weapons and the proliferation of WMD to hostile nations or terrorist organizations under U.S. laws and U.S. commitments to international nonproliferation regimes.[295]

Along with dealing with different institutional export control bureaucracies and cultures within Commerce and State, DOD export control efforts involve cooperation with allied countries to prevent proliferation of WMD technology to rogue regimes such as Iran and North Korea and fighting attempts to illicitly acquire U.S. military technologies through espionage by countries such as China seeking to target U.S. defense industries such as advanced military aviation technologies and cybersecurity to bolster their own military capabilities and compensate for insufficient indigenous industrial and technological capacity.[296]

These challenges will accelerate in the future and DOD's ability to effectively promote national security interest through export controls will be affected adversely if significant defense spending cuts occur as a result of sequestration beginning in 2013. One source has said that these cuts could approach $1 trillion over ten years, terminate weapons systems, erode U.S. technological advantages, and cause serious defense industrial base damage including losing over 1,000,000 private sector jobs.[297]

The Departments of Homeland Security, Justice, and Energy are also involved in export control enforcement and their historical and contemporary activities will now be chronicled.

Notes

1. U.S. National Archives and Records Administration, *United States Government Manual*, (Washington, DC: GPO, 2011): http://www.gpo.gov/fdsys/pkg/GOVMAN-2011-10-05/xml/GOVMAN-2011-10-05-113.xml; Accessed July 12, 2012.

2. See Ibid., *Guide to Federal Records in the National Archives of the United States*, "Records of the Bureau of Foreign and Domestic Commerce RG 151," http://www.archives.gov/research/guide-fed-records/groups/151.html; and "Records of the International Trade Administration RG 489," http://www.archives.gov/research/guide-fed-records/groups/489.html; Accessed July 12, 2012.

3. See Richard T. Cupitt, *Reluctant Champions: U.S. Presidential Policy and Strategic Export Controls: Truman, Eisenhower, Bush, and Clinton*. New York: Routledge, 2000; and U.S. National Research Council, *Beyond "Fortress America": National Security Controls on Science and Technology in a Globalized World*, (Washington, DC: National Academies Press, 2009).

4. See Public Law 81-11, "Export Control Act of 1949," 63 *U.S. Statutes at Large* 7-8; U.S. Department of State, *Foreign Relations of the United States 1950: Volume IV: Central and Eastern Europe; the Soviet Union*, (herein *FRUS*), Rogers P. Churchill, Charles S. Sampson, and William Z. Slany, eds., (Wash-

ington, DC: GPO, 1980): 65-260; Michael Mastanduno, *Economic Containment: COCOM and the Politics of East-West Trade*, (Ithaca: Cornell University Press, 1992); and Tor Egil Førland, *Cold Economic Warfare: CoCom and the Forging of Strategic Export Controls, 1948-1954*, (Dordrecht: Republic of Letters Publishing, 2009).

5. U.S. Bureau of Foreign and Domestic Commerce, Department of Commerce, "Part 37-Scope of Export Control by Department of Commerce," 14 *Federal Register*, (August 31, 1949): 5389-5390.

6. See Ibid., "Exportations Requiring License and Applications for Licenses," 14 *Federal Register* (October 12, 1949): 6167-6169; Paul H. Silverstone, "The Export Control Act of 1949: Extraterritorial Enforcement," *University of Pennsylvania Law Review*, 107 (3)(January 1959): 331-362; and *FRUS, 1964-1968: Volume IX: International Development and Economic Defense Policy; Commodities*, David S. Patterson, Evan Duncan, and Carolyn B. Yee, eds., (Washington, DC: GPO, 1997): 525-528.

7. Office of International Trade, "Revision of Export Regulations," 15 *Federal Register* (May 9, 1950): 2703-2750.

8. *Code of Federal Regulations: Title 15 Commerce and Foreign Trade: Parts 300 to 799*, (Washington, DC: GPO, 2012): 661-874.

9. See Ibid., 192-874; U.S. National Research Council, *Export Control Challenges Associated With Securing the Homeland*, (Washington, DC: National Academies Press, 2012); and Joseph A. Schorl, "Clicking the 'Export' Button: Cloud Data Storage and U.S. Dual-Use Export Controls," *George Washington University Law Review*, 80 (2)(February 2012): 633-667.

10. Cupitt, 84-117.

11. See *FRUS, 1952-1954, Volume II Part I National Security Affairs*, Lisle H. Rose and Neil H. Peterson, eds., (Washington, DC: GPO, 1984): 236-237; 258-263.

12. See *FRUS, 1952-1954,Volume I Part II General Economic and Political Matters*, William Z. Slany, Editor-in-Chief, (Washington, DC: GPO, 1983): 1170-1171; and 1239. This last citation references a February 25, 1954 parliamentary statement by Prime Minister Churchill stressing the importance of healthy trade with the Soviet Union and calling for significant relaxation of East-West trade controls. See Great Britain, Parliament, House of Commons, *Hansard Parliamentary Debates*, Series 5, Volume 524, (February 25, 1954): column 587; http://hansard.millbanksystems.com/commons/1954/feb/25/foreign-ministers-conference-berlin; Accessed July 16, 2012.

13. Ibid. *FRUS*, 1184.

14. Ibid., 1191-1194.

15. Ibid., 1194-1195.

16. Department of Commerce, "Pacific States Laboratories, Inc., Et. Al.: Ordering Revoking Export Licenses and Denying Export Privileges," *Federal Register*, 19 (August 6, 1954): 4972-4974.

17. Ibid., "Italian Nova Works Et. Al.: Order Revoking Licenses and Denying Export Privileges," *Federal Register*, 20 (February 4, 1955): 775-777.

18. *FRUS, 1955-1957 Volume X: Foreign Aid and Economic Defense Policy*, John P. Glennon, Editor-in-Chief, (Washington, DC: GPO, 1989): 313-314.

19. Ibid., *Volume IX: Foreign Economic Policy; Foreign Information Program*, John Pl Glennon, Editor-in-Chief, (Washington, DC: GPO, 1987): 173

20. Ibid., *FRUS, 1958-1960 Volume IV: Foreign Economic Policy*, Glenn W. LaFantasie, ed., (Washington, DC: GPO, 1992): 724

21. Ibid., 724-725.

22. President of the United States, "Executive Order 10945: Administration of the Export Control Act of 1949," 26 *Federal Register* (May 25, 1961): 4487.

23. *FRUS, 1961-1963 Volume IX: Foreign Economic Policy*, Glenn W. LaFantasie, ed., (Washington, DC: GPO, 1995): 654.

24. Department of Commerce, "Ferrochemie S.A Order Denying Export Privileges," 26 *Federal Register* (September 27, 1961): 9092-9094.

25. Michael Mastanduno, *Economic Containment: COCOM and the Politics of East-West Trade*, (Ithaca: Cornell University Press, 1992): 113-118.

26. *FRUS, 1961-1963 Volume IX: Foreign Economic Policy*, 658-660.

27. Ibid., 671-674.

28. Ibid., 678-679.

29. Ibid., 694-695.

30. Ibid., 680-687.

31. Ibid., 711-712.

32. Ibid., 733-737.

33. *FRUS, 1964-1968 Volume IX: International Development and Economic Defense Policy; Commodities*, David S. Patterson, ed., (Washington, DC: GPO, 1997): 467.

34. Ibid., 467-474.

35. Ibid., 502.

36. Ibid., 525-528.

37. See Ibid., 516-547; Jiri Valenti, *Soviet Intervention in Czechoslovakia: Anatomy of a Decision*, (Baltimore: Johns Hopkins University Press, 1991); and U.S. Central Intelligence Agency, *Strategic Warning & the Role of Intelligence: Lessons Learned from the 1968 Soviet Invasion of Czechoslovakia*, (Washington, DC: CIA, 2010(?); http://permanent.access.gpo.gov/gpo15421/Soviet%20-%20Czech%20Invasion%20Booklet.pdf; Accessed July 20, 2012.

38. See Robert S. Litwak, *Détente and the Nixon Doctrine: American Foreign Policy and the Pursuit of Stability, 1969-1976*, (Cambridge: Cambridge University Press, 1984); Allen J. Matusow, *Nixon's Economy: Booms, Busts, Dollars, and Votes*, (Lawrence: University Press of Kansas, 1998); and Nigel Bowles, *Nixon's Business: Authority and Power in Presidential Politics*, (College Station: Texas A&M University Press, 2005).

39. *FRUS, 1969-1976 Volume IV: Foreign Assistance, International Development, Trade Policies, 1969-1972,* Bruce F. Duncombe, ed., (Washington, DC: GPO, 2002): 747-752.

40. Ibid., 756-757, 762.

41. Ibid., 779-780.

42. Ibid., 782.

43. Ibid., 821-823.

44. Ibid., 824-827.

45. Ibid., 862-863.

46. U.S. Bureau of International Commerce, Department of Commerce, "Subchapter B-Export Regulations," 36 *Federal Register* 95 (May 15, 1971): 8932-8933.

47. Ibid., 37 *Federal Register* 84 (April 29, 1972): 8659-8660

48. See Public Law 93-159, "Emergency Fuels and Fuel Allocation Act," 87 *U.S. Statutes at Large* 627; and Ibid., "Continuation of Short Supply Controls on Petroleum and Petroleum Products for the Fourth Quarter 1975," 40 *Federal Register* 191 (October 1, 1975): 45159-45162.

49. See *FRUS, 1969-1976 Volume XXXI: Foreign Economic Policy, 1973-1976,* Kenneth B. Rasmussen, ed., (Washington, DC: GPO, 2009): 643-653, 856; and U.S. National Archives and Records Service, *Public Papers of the Presidents of the United States Richard Nixon 1973,* (Washington, DC: GPO, 1975): 647-653.

50. White House, *National Security Decision Memorandum 247: U.S. Policy on the Export of Computers to Communist Countries,* (Washington, DC: National Security Council, 1974): 1-2; http://nixon.archives.gov/virtuallibrary/documents/nsdm/nsdm_247.pdf; Accessed July 23, 2012.

51. U.S. Bureau of East-West Trade, "Organization and Functions," 41 *Federal Register* 133 (July 9, 1976): 28335.

52. U.S. Bureau of East-West Trade, *Export Administration Report: 113th Report on U.S. Export Controls to the President and the Congress Semiannual: October 1975-March 1976,* (Washington, DC: U.S. Department of Commerce, 1976): 20-21, 52, 78-79, 81; http://catalog.hathitrust.org/Record/007395801; Accessed July 23, 2012.

53. U.S. General Accounting Office, *Commercial Offices Abroad Need Substantial Improvements to Assist U.S. Export Objectives,* (Washington, DC: GAO, 1972): 2, 32; www.gao.gov/assets/210/203611.pdf; Accessed July 23, 2012

54. Ibid., *Controls Over Importing and Exporting Munitions Items,* (Washington, DC: GAO, 1973): 2, 24-28; www.gao.gov/assets/210/200273.pdf>; Accessed July 23, 2012.

55. Ibid., *The Government's Role in East-West Trade-Problems and Issues,* (Washington, DC: GAO, 1976): 42-43; www.gao.gov/assets/120/116411.pdf; Accessed July 23, 2012.

56. Ibid., 43-47.

57. Ibid., 50.

58. See U.S. Constitution, Article I, Section 8; Michael J. Brenner, *Nuclear Power and Non-Proliferation: The Remaking of U.S. Policy*, (Cambridge: Cambridge University Press, 1981); and John T. Murphy and Arthur T. Downey, "National Security, Foreign Policy and Individual Rights: The Quandry of United States Export Controls," *The International and Comparative Law Quarterly*, 30 (4)(October 1981): 791-834.

59. Public Law 95-52, "Export Administration Amendments of 1977," 91 *U.S. Statutes at Large*, 235-248.

60. Murphy and Downey, 810.

61. See Ibid., 811-812; and U.S. Department of Commerce, Industry and Trade Administration, "Restriction of Exports to the Republic of South Africa and Namibia," 43 *Federal Register* 56 (February 22, 1978): 7311-7315.

62. Ibid., 799-801.

63. U.S. Department of Commerce, Industry and Trade Administration, "U.S. Trade Status with Communist Countries," (September 20, 1978): 1; http://catalog.hathitrust.org/Record/006259584; Accessed July 24, 2012.

64. U.S. National Archives and Records Service, *Public Papers of the Presidents of the United States Jimmy Carter 1978: Book II June 30-December 31, 1978*, (Washington, DC: GPO, 1979): 2264-2266.

65. See "U.S. Trade Status With Communist Countries," (March 6, 1981): 1; U.S. International Trade Administration, "Revisions to Reflect Identification and Continuation of Foreign Policy Export Controls," 45 *Federal Register* 5 (January 8, 1980): 1595-1598; and U.S. Congress, Senate Committee on Agriculture, Nutrition, and Forestry, *Embargo on Grain Sales to the Soviet Union*, (Washington, DC: GPO, 1980).

66. U.S. Federal Interagency Working Group on Hazardous Substances Export Policy, "Draft Report," 45 *Federal Register* 157 (August 12, 1980): 53754-53787.

67. "Memorandum Directing the Termination of Restrictions on United States Agricultural Sales to the Soviet Union: April 24, 1981," *Public Papers of the President Ronald Reagan 1981*, (Washington, DC: National Archives and Records Service, 1982): 383.

68. "U.S. Trade Status With Communist Countries," (September 10, 1982): 1.

69. U.S. National Security Council, "East-West Trade Controls," (July 6, 1981): 6-7; www.foia.cia.gov/Reagan/19810706.pdf; Accessed August 2, 2012.

70. Ibid., (July 9, 1981): 3-7; www.foia.cia.gov/Reagan/19810709.pdf; Accessed August 2, 2012.

71. Mastanduno, 220-265, and Alan P. Dobson, "The Reagan Administration, Economic Warfare, and Starting to Close Down the Cold War," *Diplomatic History*, 29 (3)(June 2005): 552.

72. U.S. Central Intelligence Agency, *Soviet Acquisition of Western Technology*, (Washington, DC: CIA, 1982): 1.

73. Ibid., 2-3.

74. Ibid., 3-7, 10.

75. U.S. Department of Commerce, International Trade Administration" Order Temporarily Denying Export Privileges," 47 *Federal Register* 113 (June 11, 1982): 25396-25398.

76. Ibid., "Amendment of Oil and Gas Controls to the U.S.S.R.," 47 *Federal Register* 122 (June 24, 1982): 27250-27254.

77. U.S. Department of Energy, "Unclassified Activities in Foreign Atomic Energy Programs," 47 *Federal Register* 181 (September 17, 1982): 41320-41327.

78. U.S. Nuclear Regulatory Commission, "Export and Import of Nuclear Equipment and Fuel," 49 *Federal Register* 142 (March 1, 1984): 7572-7583.

79. Ibid., 49 *Federal Register* 233 (December 3, 1984): 41791-41796.

80. U.S. National Archives and Records Administration, Office of the Federal Register, "Export Administration Bureau," (2012); https://www.federalregister.gov/agencies/export-administration-bureau; Accessed August 2, 2012.

81. Peter Swan, "A Road Map to Understanding Export Controls: National Security in a Changing Global Environment, *American Business Law Journal*, 30 (4)(February 1993): 640.

82. Public Law 100-418, "Omnibus Trade and Competitiveness Act of 1988," 102 *U.S. Statutes at Large* 1107, 1364-1366.

83. U.S. General Accounting Office, *Export-Licensing: Commerce-Defense Review of Applications to Certain Free World Nations*, (Washington, DC: GAO, 1986): 3; http://www.gao.gov/assets/150/144632.pdf; Accessed August 3, 2012.

84. Ibid., "Export Control of Commercial Goods and Technology: Statement of Allan I. Mendelowitz, National Security and International Affairs Division," (Washington, DC: GPO, 1987): 1-3; http://www.gao.gov/assets/110/101591.pdf; Accessed August 2, 2012.

85. U.S. Committee on Science, Engineering, and Public Policy, *Balancing the National Interest: U.S. National Security on Export Controls and Global Economic Competition*, (Washington, DC: National Academy Press, 1987): 4-13; http://books.nap.edu/catalog.php?record_id=987; Accessed August 2, 2012.

86. Ibid., 168-176.

87. U.S. Bureau of Export Administration, "Definition of Supercomputer," 53 *Federal Register* 233 (December 5, 1988): 48932.

88. See U.S. Congress, House Committee on Foreign Affairs, *U.S. Post-Cold War Foreign Policy*, (Washington, DC: GPO, 1993); U.S. Congress, House Committee on Science, Space, and Technology, *The Effect of Changing*

Export Controls on Cooperation in Science and Technology, (Washington, DC: GPO, 1991); Cupitt, 118-157; and Christopher Maynard, *Out of the Shadow: George H.W. Bush and the End of the Cold War*, (College Station: Texas A&M University Press, 2008).

89. U.S. Census Bureau, *Statistical Abstract of the United States 1993*, (Washington, DC: GPO, 1993): 813-816.

90. U.S. Bureau of Export Administration, "Removal of National Security Controls for Exports of Certain Prepeg Production Equipment," 56 *Federal Register* 106 (June 3, 1991): 25023-25024.

91. See President of the United States, "Chemical and Biological Weapons Proliferation: Executive Order 12735 of November 16, 1990," 55 *Federal Register* 224 (November 20, 1990): 48587; White House, "National Security Directive 53: Interagency Review and Disposition of Export Control Licenses Issued by the Department of Commerce," (Washington, DC: National Security Council, December 10, 1990): 1; http://bushlibrary.tamu.edu/research/pdfs/nsd/nsd53.pdf; Accessed August 23, 2012; and U.S. Department of State, "International Traffic in Arms Regulations," 56 *Federal Register* 203 (October 21, 1991): 53608.

92. U.S. Bureau of Export Administration, "Revisions to the Commerce Control List: Equipment Related to the Production of Chemical and Biological Weapons; Biological Agents," 57 *Federal Register* 136 (July 15, 1992): 31309-31312.

93. U.S. Committee on Science, Engineering, and Public Policy, *Finding Common Ground: U.S. Exports in a Changing Global Environment*, (Washington, DC: National Academy Press, 1991): 167-171.

94. Ibid., 181-194.

95. GAO, *Foreign Technologies: Federal Agencies Efforts to Track Developments*, (Washington, DC: GAO, 1989): 1-2, 8; http://www.gao.gov/assets/220/211477.pdf; Accessed August 6, 2012.

96. Ibid., *Arms Control: U.S. Efforts to Control the Transfer of Nuclear-Capable Missile Technology*, (Washington, DC: GAO, 1990): 1; http://www.gao.gov/assets/220/212558.pdf; Accessed August 6, 2012.

97. Ibid., 1-2, 5, 9.

98. See Cupitt, 158-209; U.S. Congress, House Select Committee on National Security and Military/Commercial Concerns With the People's Republic of China, House Report 105-851, *Report*, (Washington, DC: GPO, 1998); Alexander A. Pikayev et. al., *Russia and the U.S. Missile Technology Control Regime*, (Oxford: Oxford University Press for the International Institute of Strategic Studies, 1998); and U.S. Committee on Balancing Scientific Openness and National Security, *Balancing Scientific Openness and National Security Controls at the Nation's Nuclear Weapons Laboratories*, (Washington, DC: National Academy Press, 1999).

99. See U.S. Census Bureau, *Trade in Goods With Russia*, (2012); http://www.census.gov/foreign-trade/balance/c4621.html; Accessed August 6, 2012; Ibid., *Trade in Goods With China*, (2012); http://www.census.gov/foreign-trade/balance/c5700.html; Accessed August 6, 2012; and Imad Moosa, *The U.S.-China Trade Dispute: Facts, Figures, and Myths*, (Cheltenham: Edward Elgar Pub., 2012).

100. U.S. National Performance Review, *From Red Tape to Results: Creating a Government that Works Better & Costs Less: Department of Commerce*, (Washington, DC: Office of the Vice President, 1993): 17-23

101. U.S. Bureau of Export Administration, "Leif Kare Johansen, Constitutionsvel 21, 4085 Hundvaag, Norway; Respondent; Decision and Order," 61 *Federal Register* 32 (February 15, 1996): 5980-5981.

102. See Bureau of Export Administration, "Export Administration Regulation; Simplification of Export Administration Regulations," 61 *Federal Register* 58 (March 25, 1996): 12714-13041; and U.S. Bureau of Export Administration, *Annual Report to Congress Fiscal Year 1996*, (Washington, DC: Dept. of Commerce, 1996): I-1 to I-2; www.bis.doc/gov/news/publications/bxachap1.pdf>; Accessed August 8, 2012.

103. Ibid., "Commercial Communications Satellites and Hot Section Technology for the Development, Production or Overhaul of Commercial Aircraft Engines," 61 *Federal Register* 204 (October 21, 1996): 54540-54541.

104. See House Report 105-851, 1:ii-xxxvii; and U.S. Congress, Senate Committee on Banking, Housing, and Urban Affairs, *Export Control Issues in the Cox Report*, (Washington, DC: GPO, 2000).

105. Presidential Documents, "Executive Order 13026 of November 15, 1996: Administration of Export Controls on Encryption Products," 61 *Federal Register* 224 (November 19, 1996): 58767-58768.

106. See U.S. Bureau of Export Administration, "Removal of Commercial Communication Satellites and Related Items from the Department of Commerce's Commerce Control List for Retransfer to the Department of State's United States Munitions List," 64 *Federal Register* 52 (March 18, 1999): 13338-13340; Public Law 105-261, "Strom Thurmond National Defense Authorization Act for Fiscal Year 1999," 112 *U.S. Statutes at Large* 2174; Joan Johnson-Freese, "Alice in Licenseland: U.S. Satellite Export Controls Since 1990," *Space Policy*, 16 (3)(July 2000): 195-204; Eligar Sadeh, "Viewpoint: Bureaucratic Politics and the Case of Satellite Export Controls," *Astropolitics: The International Journal of Space Politics & Policy*, 5 (3)(2007): 289-302; and Michael J. Noble, "Export Controls and United States Space Power, *Astropolitics: The International Journal of Space Politics & Policy*, 6 (3)(2008): 251-312.

107. U.S. General Accounting Office, *Export Controls: License Screening and Compliance Procedures Need Strengthening*, (Washington, DC: GAO, 1994): 2; www.gao.gov/assets/220/219754/pdf>; Accessed August 7, 2012.

108. Ibid. 3.

109. Ibid., *Export Controls: Some Controls Over Missile-Related Technology Exports to China are Weak*, (Washington, DC: GAO, 1995): 2-4, 22; http://www.gao.gov/assets/230/221255.pdf; Accessed August 7, 2012.

110. Public Law 102-383. "United States-Hong Kong Policy Act," 106 *U.S. Statutes at Large*, 1448.

111. U.S. General Accounting Office, *Hong Kong's Reversion to China: Effective Monitoring Critical to Assessing U.S. Nonproliferation Risks*, (Washington, DC: GAO, 1997): 3; http://www.gao.gov/assets/230/224198.pdf; Accessed August 7, 2012.

112. Ibid., *Export Controls: Better Interagency Coordination Needed on Satellite Exports*, (Washington, DC: GAO, 1999): 3, 25; http://www.gao.gov/assets/230/228230.pdf; Accessed August 7, 2012.

113. See President of the United States, *Emergency Regarding Proliferation of Weapons of Mass Destruction*, House Document 107-155, (Washington, DC: GPO, 2001); U.S. Congress, Senate Committee on Banking, Housing, and Urban Affairs, *Establishing an Effective Modern Framework for Export Controls*, (Washington, DC: GPO, 2002); President of the United States, *Periodic Report on the National Emergency Caused by the Lapse of the Export Administration Act of 1979*, House Document 107-235, (Washington, DC: GPO, 2002); and U.S. Census Bureau, "Trade in Goods With China," (2012); http://www.census.gov/foreign-trade/balance/c5700.html; Accessed August 8, 2012.

114. U.S. Bureau of Industry and Security, "Industry and Security Programs; Change of Agency Names," 67 *Federal Register* 81 (April 26, 2002): 20630-29632.

115. Ibid., *Annual Report Fiscal Year 2002*, (Washington, DC: Department of Commerce, 2002): 43; http://www.bis.doc.gov/news/2003/annualreport/printableversion.pdf; Accessed August 8, 2012.

116. Ibid., 43-45.

117. Ibid., "Computer Technology and Software Eligible for Export or Reexport Under License Exception TSR (Technology and Software Under Restriction), 67 *Federal Register* 111 (June 10, 2002): 39675-39676.

118. See Ibid., "Imposition and Expansion of Controls on Designated Terrorists," 68 *Federal Register* 109 (June 6, 2003): 34192-34196; and Presidential Documents, Executive Order 13224 of September 23, 2001: Blocking Property and Prohibiting Transactions With Persons Who Commit, Threaten to Commit, or Support Terrorism," 66 *Federal Register* 186 (September 25, 2001): 49079-49083.

119. Ibid., "In the Matter of: Suburban Guns (Pty) Ltd., 119 Mail Road, Plumstead 7800, Cape Town, South Africa. Respondent," 70 *Federal Register* 219 (November 15, 2005): 69314-69316.

120. Ibid., "Establishment of New License Exception for the Export or Reexport to U.S. Persons in Libya of Certain Items Controlled for Anti-Terror-

ism Reasons Only on the Commerce Control List," 70 *Federal Register* 220 (November 16, 2005): 64932-64935.

121. Ibid., "In the Matter of MUTCO International Kelenbergweg 37 1101 EX Amsterdam, Netherlands; Respondent," 71 *Federal Register* 128 (July 5, 2006): 38133-38135.

122. U.S. Deemed Export Advisory Committee, *The Deemed Export Rule in the Era of Globalization*, (Washington, DC: Dept. of Commerce, 2007): 4-5; http://tac.bis.doc.gov/2007/deacreport.pdf>; Accessed August 8, 2012.

123. Ibid., 6-7, 15-19.

124. Ibid., 20-23.

125. U.S. Dept. of Commerce, Office of the Inspector General, *Bureau of Industry and Security: Deemed Export Controls May Not Stop the Transfer of Sensitive Technology to Foreign Nationals in the U.S.*, (Washington, DC: U.S. Dept. of Commerce OIG, 2004): ii-iv; www.oig.doc.gov/OIGPublications/IPE-16176.pdf; Accessed August 8, 2012.

126. Ibid., 27.

127. U.S. Government Accountability Office, *Export Controls: Agencies Should Assess Vulnerabilities and Improve Guidance for Protecting Export-Controlled Information at Companies*, (Washington, DC: GAO, 2006): 3; http://www.gao.gov/assets/260/254218.pdf; Accessed August 8, 2012.

128. Ann Calvaresi Barr, *Export Controls: State and Commerce Have Not Taken Basic Steps to Better Insure U.S. Interests are Protected*, (Washington, DC: GAO, 2008): 3, 8-9; http://www.gao.gov/assets/120/119838.pdf; Accessed August 8, 2012.

129. U.S. Census Bureau, "Trade in Goods With China," (2012); https://www.census.gov/foreign-trade/balance/c5700.html; Accessed August 9, 2012.

130. Committee on Science, Security, and Prosperity, *Beyond "Fortress America": National Security Controls on Science and Technology in a Globalized World*, (Washington, DC: National Academy Press, 2009): 4-5; http://books.nap.edu/catalog.php?record_id=12567; Accessed August 9, 2012.

131. Ibid., 6-12.

132. The White House, "President Obama Lays the Foundation for a New Export Control System to Strengthen National Security and the Competitiveness of Key U.S. Manufacturing and Technology Sectors," (Washington, DC: The White House, 2010): 1-4; http://www.whitehouse.gov/the-press-office/2010/08/30/president-obama-lays-foundation-a-new-export-control-system-strengthen-n; Accessed August 9, 2012.

133. Ibid.

134. Ibid.

135. U.S. Department of Commerce, *Export Control Reform "Dashboard*," (2012); http://export.gov/ecr/; Accessed August 9, 2012.

136. Ian F. Fergusson and Paul F. Kerr, *The U.S. Export Control System and the President's Reform Initiative*, (Washington, DC: Library of Congress, Congressional Research Service, 2011): 20-21

137. U.S. Bureau of Industry and Security, "Proposed Revisions to Export Administration Regulations (EAR): Control of Items the President Determines No Longer Warrant Control Under the United States Munition List (USML)," 76 *Federal Register* 136 (July 15, 2011): 41958-41985.

138. Ibid., 77 *Federal Register* 85 (May 2, 2012): 25932-25933.

139. Ibid., "BIS Program Offices," (2012); https://www.bis.doc.gov/about/programoffices.htm; Accessed August 10, 2012.

140. Ibid., *Annual Report to the Congress for Fiscal Year 2010*, (Washington, DC: Department of Commerce, 2011(?): 6, 9; https://www.bis.doc.gov/news/2011/bis_annual_report_2010.pdf; Accessed August 10, 2012.

141. Ibid., *2011 Foreign Policy Report on Export-Based Controls*, (Washington, DC: Department of Commerce, 2012): 4-5; https://www.bis.doc.gov/news/2011/2011_fpreport.pdf; Accessed August 10, 2012.

142. U.S. Department of Commerce, Office of Budget, *Bureau of Industry and Security Fiscal Year 2013 President's Submission*, (Washington, DC: U.S. Dept. of Commerce, 2012): 4, 37; http://www.osec.doc.gov/bmi/budget/fy13cbj/BIS_FY2013_Congressional%20Justification-FINAL.pdf; Accessed August 10, 2012.

143. Ibid., Office of Inspector General, *Improvements Are Needed for Effective Web Security Management*, (Washington, DC: U.S. Department of Commerce OIG, 2011): 3-4; http://www.oig.doc.gov/OIGPublications/OIG-12-002-A.pdf; Accessed August 10, 2012.

144. U.S. Government Accountability Office, *Export Controls: Observations on Selected Countries' Systems and Proposed Treaties*, (Washington, DC: GAO, 2011): 9-10; http://www.gao.gov/new.items/d10557.pdf; Accessed August 10, 2012.

145. Ibid., *Export Controls: Improvements Needed to Prevent Unauthorized Technology Releases to Foreign Nationals in the United States*, (Washington, DC: GAO, 2011): 4-5; http://www.gao.gov/assets/320/315496.pdf; Accessed August 10, 2012.

146. Ibid., 5-7.

147. Ibid., *High-Risk Series: An Update,* (Washington, DC: GAO, 2011): 107-109; www.gao.gov/new.items/d11278.pdf; Accessed August 10, 2012.

148. See U.S. Congress, House Committee on Foreign Affairs, Subcommittee on International Economic Policy and Trade, *Technology Export: Department of Defense Organization and Performance*, (Washington, DC: GPO, 1980); http://babel.hathitrust.org/cgi/pt?id=mdp.39015082336663; Accessed August 14, 2012; U.S. Department of Defense, *Selling to Allies: A Guide for U.S. Firms*, (Washington, DC: GPO, 1990); Richard A. Bitzinger, "The Globalization of the Arms Industry: The Next Proliferation Challenge," *Interna-*

tional Security, 19 (2)(Autumn 1994): 170-198; U.S. Congress, Senate Committee on Armed Services, *U.S. Export Control and Nonproliferation Policy and the Role and Responsibility of the Department of Defense*, (Washington, DC: GPO, 1998); Deborah C. Kidwell, *Public War, Private Fight?: The United States and Private Military Companies*, (Fort Leavenworth, KS: Combat Studies Institute Press, 2005); U.S. Government Accountability Office, *Defense Technologies: DOD's Critical Technology Lists Rarely Inform Export Control and Other Policy Decisions*, (Washington, DC: GAO, 2006); http://purl.access.gpo.gov/GPO/LPS73050; Accessed August 14, 2012; Jonathan A. Grant, *Rulers, Guns, and Money: The Global Arms Trade in the Age of Imperialism*, (Cambridge: Harvard University Press, 2007); and Shawn Engbrecht, *America's Covert Warriors: Inside the World of Private Military Contractors*, (Washington, DC: Potomac Books, Inc., 2010).

149. See The President, "Executive Order [8389]: Establishing the Economic Defense Board," *Federal Register*, 6 (149)(August 1, 1941): 3823-3824; and Howard Daniel, "Economic Warfare," *The Australian Quarterly*, 15 (3)(September 1943): 62-67.

150. See Public Law 81-329, "Mutual Defense Assistance Act of 1949," 63 *U.S. Statutes at Large* 714-721; and Steven L. Reardon, *History of the Office of the Secretary of Defense Volume I: The Formative Years, 1947-1950*, (Washington, DC: Historical Office, Office of the Secretary of Defense, 1984): 504-519.

151. See Lawrence S. Kaplan, *A Community of Interests: NATO and the Military Assistance Program, 1948-1951*, (Washington, DC: Historical Office, Office of the Secretary of Defense, 1980); Chester J. Pach, Jr., *Arming the Free World: The Origins of the United States Military Assistance Program, 1945-1950*, (Chapel Hill: University of North Carolina Press, 1991); *Security Assistance: U.S. and International Historical Perspectives*, Kendall G. Gott and Michael G. Brooks, eds., (Fort Leavenworth, KS: Combat Studies Institute Press, 2006); Richard L. Millett, *Searching for Sustainability: The U.S. Development of Constabulary Forces in Latin America and the Philippines*, (Fort Leavenworth, KS: Combat Studies Institute Press, 2010); and Diane E. Chido, *Civilian Skills for African Military Officers to Resolve the Infrastructure, Economic Development, and Stability Crisis in Sub-Saharan Africa*, (Carlisle, PA: U.S. Army War College, Strategic Studies Institute, 2011).

152. See Public Law 82-165, "Mutual Security Act of 1951," 65 *U.S. Statutes at Large* 373-387; and Doris M. Condit, *History of the Office of the Secretary of Defense Volume II: The Test of War, 1950-1953*, (Washington, DC: Historical Office, Office of the Secretary of Defense, 1988): 404-405.

153. U.S. Department of Defense, "Organization: Responsibilities and Relationships in International Security Affairs," 17 *Federal Register* 196 (October 7, 1952): 8961.

154. See U.S. Department of State, *FRUS, 1952-1954: Volume VI Part I, Western Europe and Canada,* William Z. Slany, ed., (Washington, DC: GPO, 1986): 865-867; Condit, 448; and Michael Mastanduno, "Trade as a Strategic Weapon: American and Alliance Export Control Policy in the Early Postwar Period," *International Organization,* 42 (1)(Winter 1988): 121-150.

155. Condit, 452.

156. See Richard M. Leighton, *History of the Office of the Secretary of Defense Volume III: Strategy, Money, and the New Look, 1953-1956,* (Washington, DC: Historical Office, Office of the Secretary of Defense, 2001): 513; and *Mutual Security Act of* 1956, House Report 84-2643, Serial 11900, (Washington, DC: GPO, 1956).

157. See U.S. Central Intelligence Agency, *Probable Effects on the Soviet Bloc of Certain Courses of Action Directed at the Internal and External Commerce of Communist China, Special Estimate (SE) 37,* (Washington, DC: Central Intelligence Agency, 1953): 6, 9; http://www.foia.cia.gov/docs/DOC_0000269301/DOC_0000269301.pdf; Accessed August 15, 2012; and Ibid., *Consequences of a Relaxation of Non-Communist Controls on Trade With the Soviet Bloc, NIE 100-3-54,* (Washington, DC: CIA, 1954): 1-2, 4; http://www.foia.cia.gov/docs/DOC_0000269320/DOC_0000269320.pdf; Accessed August 15, 2012.

158. *FRUS, 1955-1957: Volume XX: Regulations of Armaments, Atomic Energy,* David S. Patterson, ed., (Washington, DC: GPO, 1990): 346-348.

159. See Robert J. Watson, *History of the Office of the Secretary of Defense Volume IV: Into the Missile Age, 1956-1960,* (Washington, DC: Historical Office, Office of the Secretary of Defense, 1997): 658-659; and U.S. Department of Defense, *Directive 5132.03 DoD Policy and Responsibilities Relating to Security Cooperation,* (Washington, DC: DOD, 2008); www.dtic.mil/directives/corres/pdf/513203p.pdf; Accessed August 15, 2012; originally issued July 22, 1957.

160. U.S. Department of Defense, Assistance Secretary of Defense (International Security Affairs), "Delegation of Authority Regarding Strategic Security Trade Controls on Foreign Excess Personal Property," 24 *Federal Register* 81 (April 25, 1959): 3255-3256.

161. See Watson, 669-670; and Dwight D. Eisenhower Presidential Library, *U.S. President's Committee to Study the United States Military Assistance Program (Draper Committee); Records, 1958-1959,* (Abilene, KS: Dwight D. Eisenhower Presidential Library, 1977; http://eisenhower.archives.gov/research/finding_aids/pdf/US_Presidents_Committee_to_Study_US_Military_Assistance_Program.pdf; Accessed August 15, 2012.

162. See Watson, 681, Cupit, 116; and *FRUS, 1958-1960: Volume IV, Foreign Economic Policy,* Suzanne E. Koffman, Edward C. Kieffer, and Harriett Glenn W. LaFantasie, Dashiell Schwar, eds., (Washington, DC: GPO, 1992): 706.

163. See Diane B. Kunz, *Butter and Guns: America's Cold War Economic Diplomacy*, (New York: Free Press, 1997); *Foreign Relations of the United States (FRUS), 1961-1963: Volume IX: Foreign Economic Policy*, Glenn W. Lafantasie, ed., (Washington, DC: GPO, 1995): 189-191; Lawrence S. Kaplan, Ronald D. Landa, and Edward J. Drea, *History of the Office of the Secretary of Defense Volume V: The McNamara Ascendancy, 1961-1965*, (Washington, DC: Historical Office, Office of the Secretary of Defense, 2006): 428, 446.

164. See *FRUS*, 1961-1963: *IX:* 255; and Walter S. Poole, *History of the Joint Chiefs of Staff: The Joint Chiefs of Staff and National Policy Volume VIII: 1961-1964*, (Washington, DC: Office of Joint History, Office of the Chairman of the Joint Chiefs of Staff, 2011): 279-296.

165. *FRUS, 1961-1963 Volume XI: Cuban Missile Crisis and Aftermath*, David S. Patterson, ed., (Washington, DC: GPO, 1996).

166. See U.S. Congress, House Select Committee on Export Control, *Investigation and Study of the Administration, Operation, and Enforcement of the Export Control Act of 1949, and Related Acts*, House Report 87-1753 Serial 12430, (Washington, DC: GPO, 1962): 11; and President, "Executive Order 10945: Administration of the Export Control Act of 1949," 26 *Federal Register* 100 (May 25, 1961): 4487.

167. See House Report 87-1753, 12; and Sherman R. Abrahamson, "Intelligence for Economic Defense," *Studies in Intelligence*, 8 (2)(Spring 1964): 33-43.

168. House Report 87-1753, 57-58.

169. See The White House, "National Security Action Memorandum No. 220: U.S. Government Shipments by Foreign-Flagged Vessels in the Cuban Trade," (Washington, DC: The White House, February 5, 1963); http://www.jfklibrary.org/Asset-Viewer/AD4Yc0VgwEexd3-punOIoA.aspx; Accessed August 16, 2012; and U.S. Assistant Secretary of Defense (Installations and Logistics), "Department of Defense Shipments by Foreign-Flag Vessels in the Cuban Trade," 28 *Federal Register* 40 (February 27, 1963): 1797.

170. See George Perkovich, *India's Nuclear Bomb: The Impact on Global Proliferation*, (Berkeley: University of California Press, 2000); *FRUS, 1964-1968 Volume XV: South Asia,* Gabrielle S. Mallon and Louis J. Smith, eds., (Washington, DC: GPO, 2001): 451, 582-583, 596-600, 671-673, 702, 709-710; and Walter S. Poole, *History of the Joint Chiefs of Staff: The Joint Chiefs of Staff and National Policy Volume IX: 1965-1968*, (Washington, DC: Office of Joint History, Office of the Chairman of the Joint Chiefs of Staff, 2012): 214-219;

171. U.S. Air Force, "Subchapter E—Security Part 850 Safeguarding Classified Information: Miscellaneous Amendments," 30 *Federal Register* 155 (August 12, 1965): 10046-10047.

172. See Edward J. Drea, *History of the Office of the Secretary of Defense Volume VI: McNamara, Clifford, and the Burdens of Vietnam 1965-1969*, (Wash-

ington, DC: Historical Office, Office of the Secretary of Defense, 2011): 331-332; and *Reviewing the Nuclear Nonproliferation Treaty*, Henry Sokolski, ed., (Carlisle, PA: U.S. Army War College, Strategic Studies Institute, 2010), http://permanent.access.gpo.gov/gpo2502/PUB987.pdf; Accessed August 2012.

173. See Drea, 6:455, 482; and *FRUS, 1964-1968 Volume XI: Arms Control and Disarmament*, Evans Gerkas, David B. Patterson, and Carolyn B. Yee, eds., (Washington, DC: GPO, 1997): 216-224.

174. The White House, "National Security Action Memorandum 294: U.S. Nuclear and Strategic Delivery System to France," (Washington, DC: The White House, April 20, 1964); http://www.lbjlib.utexas.edu/johnson/archives.hom/nsams/nsam294.asp; Accessed August 17, 2012.

175. Ibid., "National Security Action Memorandum 312: National Policy on Release of Inertial Guidance Technology to Germany," (Washington, DC: The White House, July 10, 1964); http://www.lbjlib.utexas.edu/johnson/archives.hom/nsams/nsam312.asp; Accessed August 17, 2012.

176. See Robert S. Litwak, *Détente and the Nixon Doctrine: American Foreign Policy and the Pursuit of Stability, 1969-1976*, (Cambridge: Cambridge University Press, 1984); Gerry Argyris Andrianopolous , *Kissinger and Brzezinski: The NSC and the Struggle for U.S. National Security Policy*, (New York: St. Martin's Press, 1991); Jeremi Suri, *Henry Kissinger and the American Century*, (Cambridge: Belknap Press of Harvard University Press, 2007); and U.S. Defense Security Cooperation Agency (DSCA), *Foreign Military Sales, Foreign Military Construction Sales and Other Security Cooperation Historical Facts As of September 30, 2010*, (Washington, DC: DSCA, 2010: 2; www.dsca.mil/programs/biz-ops/factsbook/default.htm; Accessed August 20, 2012

177. See *FRUS, 1969-1976 Volume IV: Foreign Assistance, International Development, Trade Policies, 1969-1972*, Bruce F. Duncombe, ed., (Washington, DC: GPO, 2002): 909-910; and U.S. National Security Council, "National Security Decision Memorandum 15: East-West Trade," (Washington, DC: The White House, May 28, 1969): 1-2; http://www.nixonlibrary.gov/virtuallibrary/documents/nsdm/nsdm_015.pdf; Accessed August 20, 2012.

178. Ibid., 930-941.

179. Ibid., 946-947.

180. Ibid., 953-954.

181. U.S. National Security Council, "National Security Decision Memorandum 235: NSSM 150, United States Policy on Transfer of Highly Enriched Uranium for Fueling Power Reactors," (Washington, DC: The White House, October 4, 1973): 1; http://www.nixonlibrary.gov/virtuallibrary/documents/nsdm/nsdm_235.pdf; Accessed August 20, 2012.

182. Ibid., "National Security Decision Memorandum 261: Nuclear Sales to the PRC," (Washington, DC: The White House, July 22, 1974): 1; http://

www.nixonlibrary.gov/virtuallibrary/documents/nsdm/nsdm_261.pdf; Accessed August 20, 2012.

183. See DSCA, 2; and Suri.

184. Jonathan B. Bingham and Victor C. Johnson, "A Rational Approach to Export Controls," *Foreign Affairs*, 57 (4)(Spring 1979): 894-920.

185. U.S. Defense Science Board Task Force on the Export of U.S. Technology, *An Analysis of Export Control of U.S. Technology-A DOD Perspective*, (Washington, DC: DOD, 1976): xiii; www.dtic.mil/dtic/tr/fulltext/u2/a022029.pdf>; Accessed August 21, 2012

186. Ibid., xiv-xv.

187. Ibid., 4, 8, 14, 20, 22.

188. See U.S. National Security Council, "National Security Decision Memorandum 275: COCOM Position on the Return of Depleted Uranium (Tails) from the USSR," (Washington, DC: White House, October 10, 1974): 1; http://www.fordlibrarymuseum.gov/library/document/0310/nsdm275.pdf; Accessed August 21, 2012; Ibid., "National Security Decision Memorandum 289" U.S. Military Supply Policy to Pakistan and India," (Washington, DC: The White House, March 24, 1975): 1; http://www.fordlibrarymuseum.gov/library/document/0310/nsdm289.pdf; Accessed August 21, 2012; and Ibid., "National Security Decision Memorandum 298: FRG Reactor Sale to the USSR," (Washington, DC: The White House, June 14, 1975): 1; http://www.fordlibrarymuseum.gov/library/document/0310/nsdm298.pdf; Accessed August 21, 2012.

189. U.S. Department of Defense, *Annual Defense Department Report FY 1978*, (Washington, DC: DOD, 1977): 240; http://catalog.hathitrust.org/Record/006748275; Accessed August 21, 2012

190. Ibid., 263-264.

191. U.S. General Accounting Office, *Foreign Military Sales— A Growing Concern: Departments of State and Defense*, (Washington, DC: GAO, 1976): 4, 14-15; www.gao.gov/assets/120/115630.pdf>; Accessed August 21, 2012.

192. DSCA, 2.

193. U.S. Congress, House Committee on International Relations, Subcommittee on International Economic Policy and Trade, *Department of Defense Policy Statement on Export Control of United States Technology*, (Washington, DC: GPO, 1977): 1; http://catalog.hathitrust.org/Record/002943097; Accessed August 21, 2012.

194. Ibid., 3-4.

195. Ibid. 4.

196. See Public Law 96-72, "Export Administration Act of 1979," 93 *U.S. Statutes at Large* 508; U.S. Department of Agriculture, Departmental Management, *Militarily Critical Technologies List*, (n.d.); http://www.dm.usda.gov/ocpm/Security%20Guide/T1threat/Mctl.htm; Accessed August 21, 2012.

197. See U.S. Department of Defense, "Initial Militarily Critical Technologies List," 45 *Federal Register 192* (October 1, 1980): 65014-65019; and U.S. Department of Energy, "Defense Programs; List of Energy Related Militarily Critical Technologies," 45 *Federal Register* 192 (October 1, 1980): 65152-65175.

198. U.S. Congress, House Committee on Foreign Affairs, Subcommittee on International Economic Policy and Trade, *Technology Exports: Department of Defense Organization and Performance*, (Washington, DC: GPO, 1980): 1-2, 4.

199. Ibid., 6, 9, 16, 23-24.

200. GAO, *Overview of Nuclear Export Policies of Major Foreign Supplier Nations*, (Washington, DC: GAO, 1977): 4-8; http://www.gao.gov/assets/130/120163.pdf; Accessed August 22, 2012.

201. Ibid., *Export Controls: Need to Clarify Policy and Simplify Administration*, (Washington, DC: GAO, 1979): 38-39; http://www.gao.gov/assets/130/125687.pdf; Accessed August 22, 2012.

202. DSCA, 2.

203. U.S. Central Intelligence Agency, *Dependence of Soviet Military Power on Economic Relations With the West, Special National Intelligence Estimate 3/11-4-81*, (Washington, DC: CIA, 1981): 1; http://www.foia.cia.gov/docs/DOC_0000681971/DOC_0000681971.pdf; Accessed August 22, 2012.

204. Ibid., 3, 9-11

205. U.S. Department of Defense, *Annual Report to Congress Secretary of Defense: Fiscal Year 1983*, (Washington, DC: DOD, 1982): II-31; http://catalog.hathitrust.org/Record/000078603; Accessed August 22, 2012.

206. Ibid., *The Technology Security Program: A Report to the 99th Congress*, (Washington, DC: DOD, 1986): 85-120; http://www.dtic.mil/dtic/tr/fulltext/u2/a194106.pdf; Accessed August 22, 2012.

207. U.S. Central Intelligence Agency, *Soviet Acquisition of Militarily Significant Western Technology: An Update*, (Washington, DC: CIA, 1985): 8; http://www.foia.cia.gov/docs/DOC_0000500561/DOC_0000500561.pdf; Accessed August 22, 2012.

208. Ibid., 17-23.

209. "Fact Sheet: Defense Technology Security Administration," *The DISAM Journal*, 19 (3)(Spring 1997): 110.

210. U.S. General Accounting Office, *Export Licensing: Number of Applications Reviewed by the Defense Department*, (Washington, DC: GAO, 1988): 2-3; http://www.gao.gov/assets/90/88087.pdf; Accessed August 22, 2012.

211. U.S. Department of Defense, *Annual Report to Congress: Fiscal Year 1990*, (Washington, DC: DOD, 1989): 69-79.

212. See U.S. Congress, Office of Technology Assessment, *Export Controls and Nonproliferation* Policy, (Washington, DC: OTA, 1994); Peter M. Leitner, *Decontrolling Strategic Technology, 1990-1992: Creating the Military*

Threats of the 21st Century, (Lanham, MD: University Press of America, 1995); Robert L. Hutchings, *American Diplomacy and the End of the Cold War: An Insider's Account of U.S. Policy in Europe, 1989-1992*, (Washington, DC: Woodrow Wilson Center Press, 1997); and Roman Papadiuk, *The Leadership of George Bush: An Insider's View of the Forty-First President*, (College Station: Texas A&M University Press, 2009).

213. DSCA, 2.

214. Henry D. Sokolski, *Best of Intentions: America's Campaign Against Strategic Weapons Proliferation*, (Westport, CT: Praeger, 2001): 71.

215. See U.S. Congress, House Committee on Foreign Affairs, Subcommittees on Arms Control, International Security, and Science and International Economic Policy and Trade, *Missile Proliferation: The Need for Controls (MTCR)*, (Washington, DC: GPO, 1990); and Ibid., 65-71.

216. See U.S. Department of Defense, *Report of the Secretary of Defense to the President and Congress*, (Washington, DC: GPO, 1991): 6; and The *DISAM Journal*, 110.

217. Ibid., *Report of the Secretary of Defense to the President and the Congress*, (Washington, DC: GPO, 1992): vi.

218. White House, "National Security Directive 24: Chemical Weapons Control Initiatives," (Washington, DC: National Security Council, September 26, 1989): 1-4; http://bushlibrary.tamu.edu/research/pdfs/nsd/nsd24.pdf; Accessed August 23, 2012.

219. Ibid., "National Security Directive 70: United States Nonproliferation Policy," (Washington, DC: National Security Council, July 10, 1992): 1-8; http://bushlibrary.tamu.edu/research/pdfs/nsd/nsd70.pdf; Accessed August 23, 2012.

220. The President, "Administration of Export Controls: Executive Order 12755 of March 12, 1991," 56 *Federal Register* 51 (March 15, 1991): 11057.

221. See Public Law 102-228, "Conventional Forces in Europe Treaty Implementation Act," 105 *U.S. Statutes at Large* 1693-1694; and Amy F. Woolf, *Nonproliferation and Threat Reduction Assistance: U.S. Programs in the Former Soviet Union*, (Washington, DC: Library of Congress, Congressional Research Service, 2008).

222. GAO, *Export Controls: Extent of DOD Influence on Licensing Decisions*, (Washington, DC: GAO, 1989): 2-3; http://www.gao.gov/assets/150/147857.pdf; Accessed August 24, 2012

223. Ibid., *Foreign Technologies: Federal Agencies Efforts to Track Developments*, (Washington, DC: GAO, 1989): 8; http://www.gao.gov/assets/220/211477.pdf; Accessed August 24, 2012.

224. Ibid., *Arms Control: U.S. Efforts to Control the Transfer of Nuclear-Capable Missile Technology*, (Washington, DC: GAO, 1990): 1-2.

225. Ibid., 2-8

226. DSCA, 2-3.

227. See Cupitt, 158-209; and Sikolski, 91-111.

228. U.S. Department of Defense, "DOD Directive 5111.5: Assistant Secretary of Defense for Nuclear Security and Counterproliferation," 58 *Federal Register* 139 (July 22, 1993): 39365.

229. See *Public Papers of the President: William J. Clinton 1993*, (Washington, DC: National Archives, 1994): 2:1615-1616; and Sokolski, 73-74.

230. The President, "Executive Order 12851 of June 11, 1993: Administration of Proliferation Sanctions, Middle East Arms Control, and Related Congressional Reporting Responsibilities," 58 *Federal Register* 113 (June 15, 1993): 33181-33183.

231. See Jonathan D. Pollack, "The United States, North Korea, and the End of the Agreed Framework, *Naval War College Review*, 56 (3)(Summer 2003): 1-49; and Larry A. Niksch, *North Korea's Nuclear Weapons Program*, (Washington, DC: Library of Congress, Congressional Research Service, 2006)

232. White House, "Counterproliferation: Presidential Decision Directive PDD/NSC 18," (Washington, DC: The White House, December 7, 1993): http://www.fas.org/irp/offdocs/pdd18.htm; Accessed August 27, 2012.

233. Ibid., "Nonproliferation Science and Technology Strategy: Presidential Decision Directive PDD/NSC 27," (Washington, DC: The White House, August 1994); http://www.fas.org/irp/offdocs/pdd27.htm; Accessed August 27, 2012.

234. Ibid., "PDD 34: Criteria for Decisionmaking on U.S. Arms Exports," (Washington, DC: The White House, February 17, 1995); http://www.fas.org/irp/offdocs/pdd34.htm; Accessed August 27, 2012.

235. Ibid., "PDD 47: Nuclear Scientific and Technical Cooperation With Russia Related to Stockpile Safety and Security and Compehensive Test Ban Treaty (CTBT) Monitoring and Verification," (Washington, DC: The White House, March 21, 1996): 4; http://www.fas.org/irp/offdocs/pdd-pdd47.pdf>; Accessed August 27, 2012.

236. The President, "Executive Order 12918: Prohibiting Certain Transactions With Respect to Rwanda and Delegating Authority With Respect to Other United Nations Arms Embargoes," 59 *Federal Register* 103 (May 31, 1994): 28205-28206.

237. Ibid., "Executive Order 12919 of June 3, 1994: National Defense Industrial Resources Preparedness," 59 *Federal Register* 108 (June 7, 1994): 29525, 29529.

238. Ibid., "Executive Order 12946 of January 20, 1995: President's Advisory Board on Arms Proliferation Policy," 60 *Federal Register* 15 (January 24, 1995): 4829.

239. U.S. Defense Threat Reduction Agency, *Defense's Nuclear Agency, 1947-1997*, (Washington, DC: DTRA, 2002): 439-440.

240. Ibid., "Executive Order 12981 of December 5, 1995: Administration of Export Controls," 60 *Federal Register* 236 (December 8, 1995): 62981-62982.

241. Ibid., "Executive Order 13026 of November 15, 1996: Administration of Export Controls on Encryption Products," 61 *Federal Register* 224 (November 19, 1996): 58767.

242. GAO, *Defense Conversion*, (Washington, DC: GAO, 1996): 1-5; http://www.gao.gov/assets/90/85988.pdf; Accessed August 27, 2012.

243. Ibid., *Export Controls: Concerns Over Stealth-Related Exports*, (Washington, DC: GAO, 1995): 2-4, 7-8; http://www.gao.gov/assets/230/221232.pdf; Accessed August 27, 2012.

244. Ibid., *Export Controls: Sensitive Machine Tool Exports to China*, (Washington, DC: GAO, 1996): 1-12; http://www.gao.gov/assets/230/223443.pdf; Accessed August 27, 2012.

245. See U.S. Secretary of Defense, *Annual Report to the President and the Congress*, (Washington, DC: DOD, 1997): 49; and Ibid., *Report of the Quadrennial Defense Review*, (Washington, DC: DOD, 1997).

246. See The President, "Executive Order 13094 of July 28, 1998, "Proliferation of Weapons of Mass Destruction," 63 *Federal Register* 146 (July 30, 1998): 40803; Ibid., "Executive Order 13159 of June 21, 2000: Blocking Property of the Russian Federation Relating to the Disposition of Highly Enriched Uranium Extracted From Nuclear Weapons," 65 *Federal Register* 123 (June 21, 2000): 39279-39280; and Ibid., "Executive Order 13177 of December 4, 2000: National Commission on the Use of Offsets in Defense Trade and President's Council on the Use of Offsets in Commercial Trade," 65 *Federal Register* 235 (December 4, 2000): 76558-76559.

247. *Defense's Nuclear Agency, 1947-1997*, 393.

248. U.S. Congress, Senate Committee on Armed Services, *U.S. Export Control and Nonproliferation and the Role and Responsibility of the Department of Defense*, (Washington, DC: GPO, 1998): 2.

249. Ibid., 10.

250. Ibid., 11-13.

251. Ibid., 18-20.

252. Ibid., 26-29, 33.

253. U.S. Department of Defense, Office of Inspector General, *Review of the DOD Export Licensing Processes for Dual-Use Commodities and Munitions*, (Washington, DC: DODIG, 1999): ii; http://www.dodig.mil/Audit/reports/fy99/99-186.pdf; Accessed August 29, 2012.

254. Ibid., iii-v, 4.

255. U.S. Commission to Assess the Organization of the Federal Government to Combat the Proliferation of Weapons of Mass Destruction, *Report*, (Washington, DC: GPO, 1999): 37-42, 53-61.

256. GAO, *Weapons of Mass Destruction: DOD's Actions to Combat Weapons Use Should Be More Integrated and Focused*, (Washington, DC: GAO, 2000): 6-7, 24; http://www.gao.gov/assets/230/229156.pdf; Accessed August 29, 2012.

257. See President of the United States, *National Security Strategy of the United States*, (Washington, DC: The White House, 2002); 6, 14-16; and Robert G. Kaufman, *In Defense of the Bush Doctrine*, (Lexington: University Press of Kentucky, 2005).

258. DSCA, 3.

259. See President, "Executive Order 13222 of August 17, 2001: Continuation of Export Control Regulations," 66 *Federal Register* 163 (August 22, 2001): 44025-44026; Ibid., "Executive Order 13224 of September 23, 2001: Blocking Property and Prohibiting Transactions With Persons Who Commit, Threaten to Commit, or Support Terrorism," 66 *Federal Register* 186 (September 25, 2001): 49079-49083; Ibid., "Executive Order 13292 of March 25, 2003: Further Amendment to Executive Order 12954, as Amended, Classified National Security Information," 68 *Federal Register* 60 (March 28, 2003): 13521; Ibid., "Executive Order 13328 of February 6, 2004," 69 *Federal Register* 28 (February 11, 2004): 6901-6903; and Ibid., "Executive Order 13466 of June 26, 2008: Continuing Certain Restrictions with Respect to North Korea and North Korean Nationals," 73 *Federal Register* 125 (June 27, 2008): 36787-36788.

260. White House, "NSPD-19: Review of Defense Trade Export Policy and National Security: Fact Sheet," (Washington, DC: The White House, November 21, 2002): 1-2; http://www.fas.org/irp/offdocs/nspd/deftrade.html; Accessed August 31, 2012.

261. See Ibid., "NSPD-20: Counterproliferation Interdiction," (Washington, DC: The White House, 2002?; http://www.fas.org/irp/offdocs/nspd/index.html; Accessed August 31, 2012; Ibid., *National Strategy to Combat Weapons of Mass Destruction*, (Washington, DC: The White House, 2002); and Paul Kerr, "U.S. Stops, Then Releases Shipment of North Korean Missiles," *Arms Control Today* 33 (January/February 2003): 25.

262. Ibid., "National Security Presidential Directive NSPD-41: Maritime Security Policy," (Washington, DC: The White House, December 21, 2004); http://www.fas.org/irp/offdocs/nspd/nspd41.pdf; Accessed August 31, 2012.

263. U.S. Congress, Senate Committee on Homeland Security and Governmental Affairs, *Nuclear Terrorism: Assessing the Threat to the Homeland*, (Washington, DC: GPO, 2010): 385-389.

264. See Federation of American Scientists, "National Security Presidential Directives: George W. Bush Administration," (Washington, DC: FAS, 2012); http://www.fas.org/irp/offdocs/nspd/index.html; Accessed August 31, 2012; and U.S. Department of State, "D&CP-Political-Military Affairs," (Washing-

ton, DC: Department of State, 2009): 117; www.state.gov/documents/organi-zation/123563.pdf; Accessed August 31, 2012.

265. See U.S. Department of State, "Proliferation Security Initiative: State-ment of Interdiction Principles," (Washington, DC: Department of State, Sep-tember 4, 2003); http://www.state.gov/t/isn/c27726.htm; Accessed August 31, 2012; and Susan J. Koch, *Proliferation Security Initiative: Origins and Evolu-tion*, (Washington, DC: National Defense University Press, 2012).

266. See Gordon Corera, *Shopping for Bombs: Nuclear Proliferation, Glo-bal Insecurity, and the Rise and Fall of the A.Q. Khan Network*, (Oxford: Oxford University Press, 2006); and Paul K. Kerr and Mary Beth Nikitin, *Pakistan's Nuclear Weapons: Proliferation and Security Issues*, (Washington, DC: Library of Congress, Congressional Research Service, 2009): 11-12.

267. U.S. Commission on the Intelligence Capabilities of the United States Regarding Weapons of Mass Destruction, *Report*, (Washington, DC: The Com-mission, 2005): 557-577.

268. U.S. Department of Defense, "DOD Directive 5105.72: Defense Tech-nology Security Administration," (Washington, DC: Washington Headquarters Service, July 28, 2005): 1; http://www.dtic.mil/whs/directives/corres/pdf/510572p.pdf; Accessed September 5, 2012.

269. Ibid., "DOD Instruction 2040.02: International Transfers of Technol-ogy, Articles, and Services," (Washington, DC: Washington Headquarters Service, July 10, 2008): 2; http://www.dtic.mil/whs/directives/corres/pdf/204002p.pdf; Accessed September 5, 2012.

270. U.S. Congress, Senate Committee on Homeland Security and Govern-mental Affairs, Subcommittee on Oversight of Government Management, the Federal Workforce, and the District of Columbia, *Beyond Control: Reforming Export Licensing Agencies for National Security and Economic Interests*, (Wash-ington, DC: GPO, 2009): 44-45; http://purl.access.gpo.gov/GPO/LPS115037; Accessed September 5, 2012.

271. U.S. Department of Defense, Office of Inspector General, *"Export Controls: Controls Over Exports to China,"* (Washington, DC: DODIG, 2006): 4-5; http://www.dodig.mil/audit/reports/FY06/06-067.pdf; Accessed Septem-ber 5, 2012.

272. Ibid., *Followup Audit on Recommendations for Controls Over Export-ing Sensitive Technologies to Countries of Concern*, (Washington, DC: DODIG, 2007): 4, 14-15; http://www.dodig.mil/audit/reports/FY07/07-131.pdf; Ac-cessed September 5, 2012.

273. GAO, *Weapons of Mass Destruction. Defense Threat Reduction Agency Addresses Broad Range of Threats, but Performance Reporting Can Be Im-proved*, (Washington, DC: GAO, 2004): 2-3; http://www.gao.gov/assets/250/241416.pdf; Accessed September 5, 2012.

274. Ibid., *Defense Technologies: DOD's Critical Technologies Lists Rarely Inform Export Control and Other Policy Decisions*, (Washington, DC: GAO,

2006); 2-3, 21-23; http://www.gao.gov/assets/260/250929.pdf; Accessed September 5, 2012.

275. Ibid., *Defense Trade: Clarification and More Comprehensive Oversight of Export Exemptions Certified by DOD are Needed*, (Washington, DC: GAO, 2007): 2-3; http://www.gao.gov/assets/270/268269.pdf; Accessed September 5, 2012.

276. U.S. Defense Board, *Report to the Secretary of Defense: Task Force Group on Best Practices for Export Controls*, (Washington, DC: Defense Business Board, 2008): 6-8; http://dbb.defense.gov/pdf/Task_Group_on_Best_Practices_ for_Export_Controls_Final_Report.pdf; Accessed September 6, 2012.

277. DSCA, 3.

278. See The President, "Executive Order 13546 of July 2, 2010: Organizing the Security of Biological Select Agents and Toxins in the United States," 75 *Federal Register* 150 (July 8, 2010): 39439-39442; and Ibid., "Executive Order 13558 of November 9, 2010: Export Enforcement Coordination Center," 75 *Federal Register* 219 (November 15, 2010): 69573-69574.

279. See The White House, "Presidential Policy Directive 2: Implementation of the National Security Strategy for Countering Biological Threats," (Washington, DC: The White House, 2009); www.fas.org/irp/offdocs/ppd/ppd-2.pdf; Accessed September 6, 2012; and Ibid., *National Strategy for Countering Biological Threats*, (Washington, DC: NSC, 2009); http://www.whitehouse.gov/sites/default/files/National_Strategy_for_Countering_BioThreats.pdf; Accessed September 6, 2012.

280. See U.S. International Trade Administration, "President's Export Control Reform Initiative," (2012); http://export.gov/ECR/; Accessed September 6, 2012; for details on this initiative and updates on regulatory actions.

281. H.R. 2004, "Technology Security and Antiboycott Act," 112th Congress, 1st Session, (Washington, DC: GPO, May 26, 2011).

282. H.R. 2122, "Export Administration Renewal Act of 2011," 112th Congress, 1st Session, (Washington, DC: GPO, June 3, 2011).

283.

284. Ibid., "Policy Directorate," (2012); http://www.dtsa.mil/Directorates/Policy; Accessed September 6, 2012.

285. Ibid., "Space Directorate," (2012); http://www.dtsa.mil/Directorates/Space; Accessed September 6, 2012.

286. See U.S. Department of Defense, *Report on the Department of Defense's Plans to Reform the Export Control System*, (Washington, DC: DOD, 2011): 3; and Public Law 112-81, *National Defense Authorization Act for Fiscal Year 2012*, 125 *U.S. Statutes at Large*, 1298, 1782.

287. *Report on the Department of Defense's Plans to Reform the Export Control System*, 5-6.

288. U.S. Departments of Defense and State, *Report to Congress: Section 1248 of the National Defense Authorization Act for Fiscal Year 2010 (Public Law 111-84)*, (Washington, DC: DOD, 2012): iii, 1-6; http://www.defense.gov/home/features/2011/0111_nsss/docs/1248_Report_Space_Export_Control.pdf; Accessed September 6, 2012.

289. See U.S. Defense Institute for Security Assistance Management, "DISAM Mission," (2012); http://www.disam.dsca.mil/pages/disam/mission.aspx; Accessed September 7, 2012; and Ibid., *The Management of Security Assistance*, (Wright-Patterson Air Force Base, OH: Defense Institute of Security Assistance Management, 1990).

290. See *United States Government Manual* 2011, (Washington, DC: National Archives and Records Administration, 2011): 168; and "Defense Security Cooperation Agency Strategic Plan," *DISAM Journal*, 21 (2)(Winter 1998-1999): 8-37.

291. See Ibid., 169; and *Defense's Nuclear Agency, 1947-1997.*

292. See DOD, Office of Manufacturing and Industrial Base Policy, "Our Mission," (2012); < www.acq.osd.mil/mibp/about.shtml; Accessed September 7, 2012; Richard Van Atta, *Export Controls and the U.S. Industrial Base*, (Alexandria, VA: Institute for Defense Analyses, 2007); http://www.acq.osd.mil/mibp/docs/ida_study-export_controls_%20us_def_ib.pdf; Accessed September 7, 2012; "DOD Instruction 5000.60: Defense Industrial Capabilities Assessment," (Washington, DC: Washington Headquarters Service, October 15, 2009); http://www.acq.osd.mil/mibp/docs/ida_study-export_controls_%20us_def_ib.pdf; Accessed September 7, 2012.

293. Public Law 76-703, "To Expedite the Strengthening of National Defense," 54 *U.S. Statutes at Large*, 712-714.

294. GAO, *Persian Gulf: U.S. Agencies Need to Improve Licensing Data and Document Reviews of Arms Transfers for U.S. Foreign Policy and National Security Goals*, (Washington, DC: GAO, 2010): 3-4; http://www.gao.gov/assets/310/309821.pdf; Accessed September 7, 2012.

295. See Van Atta, 2-9; *The Modern Defense Industry: Political, Economic, and Technological Issues*, Richard Bitzinger, ed., (Santa Barbara: Praeger Security International, 2009); and Public Law 111-266, "Security Cooperation Act of 2010," 124 *U.S. Statutes at Large* 2797-2804.

296. See Phillip C. Saunders and Joshua K. Wiseman, *Buy, Build, or Steal: China's Quest for Advanced Military Aviation Technologies*, (Washington, DC: National Defense University Press, 2011): 3, 49; and Bryan Kekel, Patton Adams, and George Bakos, *Occupying the Information High Ground: Chinese Capabilities for Computer Network Operations and Cyber Espionage*, (Washington, DC: Prepared by Northrup Grumman Coporation for the U.S.-China Economic and Security Review Commission, 2012); http://www.uscc.gov/RFP/

2012/USCC%20Report_Chinese_CapabilitiesforComputer_Network OperationsandCyberEspionage.pdf; Accessed September 7, 2012.

297. U.S. Congress, House Committee on Armed Services, *Economic Impacts of Defense Sequestration*, (Washington, DC: GPO, 2012).

Chapter 3

Customs & Border Patrol, Justice Department, and Energy Department

U.S. Customs and Border Protection (CBP) and its predecessor agencies have been involved in export control policymaking during its historical tenure in the Treasury Department and now in the Department of Homeland Security (DHS). An early historical example of Customs involvement in export control activities was the 1789 Customs Organization Act which gave Customs the legal authority to control exports and this has evolved into the authority CBP now possesses to enforce certain provisions of U.S. export control laws and prohibit the illegal export of critical technology.[1]

Throughout its history, before and after its 2002 incorporation into DHS, Customs has been involved in various export control failures and successes including failing to effectively investigating violations of weapons brokering under the Arms Export Control Act (AECA) and various other international customs cooperation agreements.[2] Examples of historic Customs export control successes include stopping the illegal export of Condor II ballistic missile technology and components in Egypt in 1988 through the use of suspects trash investigation and telephone calls which ultimately resulted in their being sentenced to four years imprisonment; stopping shipment to Iran that year of thiyodiglicol a precursor chemical used in manufacturing mustard gas although the primary individual suspect fled the U.S., and enforcing export control regulations under the Export Administration Act (EAA), AECA, outbound provisions of the Bank Secrecy Act covering foreign financial transfers, and the Chemical Diversion and Trafficking Act seeking to regulate the export of chemicals from U.S. ports and borders.[3]

Customs was transferred from the Treasury Department and became CBP within DHS with the November 25, 2002 enactment of the Homeland Security Act.[4] CBP also collaborates with U.S. Immigration and Customs Enforcement (ICE) in enforcing various export control statutes covering topics as varied as properly licensing coal and refined petroleum products, selected semiconductor exports, smuggling goods into foreign countries, money laundering, exporting war materials, and numerous AECA provisions . Attributes of this enforcement within DHS include three enforcement datebases:

1. Treasury Enforcement Communication System-Features records containing law enforcement information including suspects, ongoing investigations, and enforcement actions.
2. Seized Asset and Case Tracking System-Captures activities associated with seizures and investigations.
3. Automated Targeting System/Anti-Terrorism-Automatically reviews electronically filed export documentation comparing it with inspector-defined criteria for high risk shipments.[5]

The presence of these databases, however, has not stopped problems from occurring in DHS export control violations as ICE and the FBI do not have a formal agreement to coordinate export control violation cases; there are often differences between DHS, Commerce, and State over whether to pursue potential export control violations; CBP's mandate and resources are more focused on preventing terrorists and terrorist weapons from entering U.S. ports; and it places more reliance on automated mechanisms to have potentially dangerous exports identified and examined by officers.[6]

CBP and ICE use the Exodus Accountability Referral System (EARS) to enforce federal export control laws. DHS personnel use this intranet resource to investigate possible export control violations by entering identifying information about parties of interest and referring them to counterpart export control offices in the Commerce, Treasury, Justice, State, and Energy Departments to determine if further investigation and enforcement action needs to be taken.[7] CBP is also involved in regulating foreign exports to the U.S. through the Container Security Initiative (CSI). Launched in 2002, CSI addresses threats to border security and maritime trade by potential terrorist use of maritime containers. CSI involves CBP stationing teams at foreign seaports to target and examine high-risk cargo before it is placed on U.S. bound vessels. During FY 2010, over 10.1 million maritime shipments were reviewed in CSI ports by CBP personnel.[8]

Additional CBP export control enforcement responsibilities include inspecting items scheduled for export at air, sea, and land ports. CBP officers check items against applicable licenses prior to shipment to ensure their compliance with export control laws and regulations. They also conduct selective physical examinations of cargo at ports and in warehouses, review shipping documents, detain questionable shipments, and seize items being exported illegally. These officers are also required by the State Department to reduce shipment quantity and dollar value from the total quantity and dollar value authorized by the exporter's license.[9]

Recent export control related actions conducted by CBP include providing Karachi, Pakistan's Port Qasim with nuclear and radiological shipping container detection equipment in May 2007 following earlier shipments of comparable equipment to Oman, Singapore, and South Korean ports.[10] On December 30, 2009, CBP agents arrested Luz Sylvia Cortez at the Reynosa/Tamaulipas border stop for attempting to smuggle into Mexico 1,996 rounds of .223 caliber ammunition, 1,408 rounds of .308 caliber ammunition, and 3,000 rounds of 7.62 caliber ammunition on charges of unlicensed export of items on the U.S. Munitions List (USML).[11]

CBP is also involved in enforcing the Obama Administration's *National Strategy For Global Supply Chain Security* issued in January 2012. This policy seeks to promote the efficient and secure movement of goods and foster supply chain resilience by promoting the efficient and timely flow of legitimate commerce and reducing supply chain vulnerability to disruption by utilizing layered defenses and adopting national security posture to changing security and operational environments. Attributes of enhanced supply chain security touching on export controls include improving verification and detection capabilities to identify goods that are not what they are represented to be and prevented from entering the supply system and protecting the supply chain and its critical nodes by limiting access to cargo, conveyances, information, and infrastructure to those possessing legitimate and relevant roles and responsibilities.[12]

In its current annual performance and accountability report, DHS mentioned that it was seeking feedback on the quality of its efforts to prevent the unauthorized acquisition or use of chemical, biological, radiological, and nuclear materials and capabilities by hostile foreign entities. This results of this survey will be published in a subsequent DHS document.[13]

Despite this effort to document the quality of its export control activities, CBP received critical scrutiny from DHS Office of Inspector General (OIG) analysis of its activities. A September 2004 OIG report revealed that CBP had failed to detect depleted uranium smuggled from Russia through Istanbul to the U.S. in a simulation done by ABC News during 2002 and that another ABC simulation successfully smuggling the same uranium during 2003 from the U.S. to Jakarta, Indonesia before being transshipped to Tanjung Pelepas, Malaysia and shipped back to the U.S. also resulted in CBP failing to detect this shipment.[14]

A June 2005 OIG report revealed that CBP did not consistently enforce federal export licensing laws and regulations for chemical and biological commodities at U.S. exit ports. It went on to mention CBP's failure to consistently document the location of State Department licenses in its Automated Export System (AES) and that such license information is necessary to determine if individual shipments are in compliance with associated license conditions. CBP is not required to document the location of State licenses in AES making it difficult for enforcement personnel at shipping ports to readily obtain license information making it difficult for CBP to enforce State licensed exports in a timely and efficient manner. A similar problem also exists for CBP enforcement of Commerce Department granted export licenses.[15]

A July 2012 Government Accountability Office (GAO) report addressed problems with monitoring exports of unmanned aerial vehicles (UAVs). This report said interagency license export determinations for UAVs take a significant amount of time to process, that there were at least seven prosecutions involving attempts to illegally export UAV technology including a 2009 case involving a Washington DC couple pleading guilty to making false statement about exporting mini-UAV autopilots to China, and enforcing export laws and regulations on UAV's is difficult due to ICE investigators losing touch with suspects outside the country and these suspects choosing not to cooperate with U.S. law enforcement officials.[16]

CBP and ICE border patrol agent personnel staffing has risen from 4,139 in Fiscal Year (FY) 1992 to 21,444 in FY 2011 and the border patrol budget has risen from $262.647 million in FY 1992 to $3.549.294 billion in FY 2011.[17] Although CBP and ICE are more focused on preventing the import of terrorists and the smuggling of terrorist equipment into the U.S., they also play a partial supportive role in enforcing U.S. export control laws by seeking to prevent the export of equipment and financial resources to hostile individuals, groups, and countries. One example of this is DHS' involvement in the Export Control and Related Border Security (EXBS) Program which also involves the State Department's Bureau of Nonproliferation. EXBS initially focused on stopping the leakage of weapons of mass destruction (WMD) from former Soviet countries including Kazakhstan, Russia, and Ukraine. It has since evolved to cover countries on potential proliferation threat smuggling routes in Eastern and Central Europe, the Balkans, South and Central Asia, the Caucasus, and countries with major transshipment hubs in the Mediterranean, Middle East, and Southeast Asia. EXBS has helped over 40 countries improve their ability to prevent and interdict shipments of dangerous items and controlled technologies. CPD uses funding from this program to provide technical assistance customized to individual countries export control requirements.[18]

Justice Department

The Justice Department (DOJ) is also involved in enforcing U.S. export control laws in various ways including investigating and prosecuting violators of relevant statutes with the lead roles in these areas played by the Federal Bureau of Investigation (FBI) and U.S. Attorneys offices. FBI investigations emphasize potential dual-use and defense export violations having a nexus with foreign counterintelligence. Some DOJ activities are carried out by its National Security Division (NSD) which was established in March 2006 by a USA Patriot Act extension.[19] NSD responsibilities include combating terrorism and other national security threats, ensuring greater coordination and unity of purpose between prosecutors, law enforcement agencies, intelligence attorneys, and the intelligence community.[20]

Key organizational components within NSD and their institutional missions include:

A. Counterterrorism Section: Designing, implementing, and enforcing law enforcement efforts, legislative initiatives, policies, and strategies for combating domestic and international terrorism.

B. Counterespionage Section: Investigating and prosecuting cases affecting national security, foreign relations, and exporting military and strategic commodities and technology.

C. Office of Intelligence: Ensuring intelligence community agencies have legal authorities to conduct intelligence operations such as those involving the Foreign Intelligence Surveillance Act.

D. Operations Section: Handling NSD intelligence operation workload and representing NSD before the Foreign Intelligence Surveillance Court.

E. Oversight Section: Overseeing intelligence community foreign intelligence, counterintelligence, and national security activities to ensure their compliance with the Constitution, statutes, and executive branch policies.

F. Litigation Section: Responsible for lowering "the wall" between intelligence and law enforcement investigations and enhancing coordination between intelligence and law enforcement personnel.[21]

The Justice Department's Bureau of Alcohol, Tobacco, Firearms, and Explosives (ATF) has also become involved in export control related operations due to a proliferation of illicit firearms sales from gun shows in the southwestern U.S. to Mexico. This has fueled that country's violent drug wars and a June 2009 GAO study revealed that 87% of firearms seized in Mexico over the past five years originated in the U.S., that 68% of these firearms were manufactured in the U.S., and that many of these firearms were high-caliber and high-powered such as the AK and AR-15 semiautomatic rifles.[22]

Major export control related statutes enforced by Justice besides AECA and International Traffic in Arms Regulations (ITAR) include the 1938 Foreign Agents Registration Act (FARA) and the 1977 Foreign Corrupt Practices Act (FCPA). FARA requires individuals acting as agents of foreign principals in a political or quasi-political capacity periodically reporting their relationship with the foreign principal along with activities, receipts, and disbursements supporting these activities.[23]

FCPA was enacted to make it illegal for certain persons and entities to pay foreign government officials to obtain or retain business. Statute anti-bribery provisions prohibit using mails or interstate commerce instrumentality to authorize payment of money or other items capable of influencing foreign officials to commit illegal actions beneficial to U.S. businesses. 1998 amendments to FCPA extended its anti-bribery provisions to foreign firms and persons making corrupt payments within U.S. territory. While FCPA has been widely used it has been criticized for meaning "what the enforcement agencies say it means" and that defendants in FCPA enforcement cases are encouraged to accept settlement proposals without testing the validity of the prosecution's enforcement theories.[24]

FCPA has been the subject of frequent congressional oversight and attempts to update it to meet domestic U.S. and even international legal standards of accountability and transparency. However, it is a problematic statute due to just cited concerns about its enforcement and because doing business to promote arms sales or economic assistance in certain countries of the world can require using bribery or other financial practices that would be considered unethical in the U.S. or other western countries.[25]

The Justice Department has been involved in investigating and prosecuting many export control violations in federal courts. On October 14, 2007, the Pittsburgh company SparesGlobal, Inc., was sentenced to pay a $40,000 fine in the Western District Court of Pennsylvania for conspiring to make false statements about an illegal 2003 export to the United Arab Emirates which ended up in Pakistan. The items concerned were restricted graphic products which could be used in nuclear reactors and ballistic missile nose cones.[26]

On January 7, 2010, Ioannis Papathanassiou of Vienna, VA plead guilty on behalf of his company Taipan Enterprises Ltd. in the Eastern District Court of Virginia for attempting to sell weapons and night vision goggles, and other military equipment to purchasers in Chile, Libya, Yemen, and other countries. Taipan was fined $15,000 for these transactions which also involved contractors in Belgium and Canada.[27]

Taiwanese national Kevin Chen and his employer Landstar Tech Company were sentenced to 42 months imprisonment and one year probation in the Southern District Court of Florida for exporting dual-use commodities to Iran possessing potential military applications. These dual-use items included 120 circular hermetic connectors and 8,500 glass-to-metal seals. Chen also attempted to obtain and export to Iran 2,000 detonators from a California company and this activity involved shipping these items to Iran through Hong Kong and Taiwan.[28] On January 5, 2011, Jesus Quintanilla was sentenced to 37 months imprisonment by the Southern District Court of Texas for straw purchasing nine AK-47 rifles and four pistols for export to a Mexican drug cartel. January 24, 2011 saw Maui's Noshir Gawadia sentenced to 32 years imprisonment by the District Court of Hawaii for communicating classified defense information to China, illegally exporting military technical data, money laundering, and other offenses. Examples of material Gawadia provided to China included a low-signature cruise missile exhaust system capable of making Chinese cruise missiles resistant to infrared missile detection and illegally communicating classified information concerning the lock-on range for infrared missiles against the B-2 bomber.[29]

On August 10, 2011 the Eastern District Court of Pennsylvania indicted six individuals with conspiring to export defense articles without a license and violating the International Emergency Economic Powers Act. These defendants were specifically charged with attempting to illegally export to Belarus defense articles such as ThOR 2 Thermal Imaging Scopes, AN/PAS-23 Min Thermal Monoculars, and L-3 x 200xp Handheld Thermal Imaging Cameras without requisite State and Commerce Department licenses. One defendant pleaded guilty on October 28, 2011 while two others plead guilty on February 29, 2012.[30]

On April 23, 2012 Huntington Beach, CA-based Sanwave International Corporation owner Jason Jian Liang was sentenced to 46 months incarceration and three years supervised release by the California Central District Court after pleading guilty to illegally exporting 63 thermal imaging digital cameras to China which were export-controlled for national security reasons. Two days later a criminal complaint against two Taiwanese nationals was unsealed in the New Jersey District court charging them with conspiring to import crystal methamphetamine from Taiwan to China and to sell F-22 fighter stealth technology, missile engine technology, and Unmanned Aerial Vehicle (UAV) technology to Chinese military and intelligence community customers.[31]

Justice has also prosecuted numerous court cases involving AECA, ITAR, or other export control related violations achieving varying degrees of success in recent decades. These cases have involved political disagreements between members of Congress and the President over U.S.

foreign and national security policy, challenges to the constitutionality of AECA and other export control statutes, and various legal technicalities which have affected government prosecution efforts. In 1982 Rep. George Crockett (D-MI)(1909-1997) and other members of Congress charged that Reagan Administration arms sales to El Salvador violated the U.S. Constitution's War Powers Clause, the War Powers Act, and Section 502B of the 1961 Foreign Assistance Act prohibiting security assistance to governments engaged in consistent human rights violations. The U.S. District Court for the District of Columbia dismissed this case because it would require judicial inquiry into sensitive military matters while also declaring that the War Powers Act's 60 day automatic termination provision was not operable because a report to Congress or a court required by this act had not been submitted by the President.[32]

In 1984 the New Jersey District Court heard a case in which the defendants were charged with violating AECA by conspiring to export radar jamming devices known as wave tube amplifiers to China. The defendants contended that the United States Munitions List (USML) description of these items was too vague because Congress designated specific items be a part of the USML and that "countermeasures" were to generic a description and that the government's charges should be dismissed as being a legal nullity. The Court ruled in favor of the defendants and dismissed the government's charges due to their excessively broad interpretation of AECA.[33]

The 1986 case *U.S. v. Reed* saw the 2nd Circuit Court of Appeals uphold a Connecticut District Court conviction of John Reed for his role as a middleman bringing together prospective buyers and sellers in an attempt to export 400,000 chemical protective suits to Iran in violation of USML which requires such exporting such items receive State Department licensing approval. The planned sale was thwarted when a prospective seller became suspicious of the purchaser's requirement that the suits not be made by Jews. This seller realized that Iran instead of Italy was the suits destination and the seller alerted the Customs Service which arrested Reed.[34]

In January 2005 the Court of Appeals for the District of Columbia affirmed the district court's ruling dismissing the indictment of Sabri Yakou charging his son with selling arms to the Iraqi Navy. In making this appeal the U.S. contended that the lower court had made three legal errors:

1. Dismissing the indictment before trial when *Federal Rules of Criminal Procedure* do not provide a summary judgment mechanism;
2. Ruling that Yakou's Lawful Permanent Resident status can change without formal administrative action by immigration officials and that he was not a "U.S. person" as defined by ITAR and subject to prosecution for arms activities; and
3. Yakou could not be indicted separately for aiding and abetting his son's alleged brokering violations.

The court rejected the Government's appeal contending the government had failed to prove Yakou was a "U.S. person" during the period alleged in the indictment since he left the U.S. in 1993 and ITAR limits extraterritorial liability for failing to register with the State Department and obtain a license before engaging in brokering activities to "U.S. persons", and that because of this Yakou could not assist his sons alleged extraterritorial violation of U.S. brokering laws.[35]

In January 2011, the Massachusetts District Court partially upheld two AECA convictions for defendants charged with illegally exporting defense items to China between 2004-2006. The defendants Zhen Zou Wou, Yufeng Wei, and their employer Chitron Electronics sought to dismiss the charges four days before trial charging that AECA gives insufficient notice of prohibited conduct, and that the government's determination that the charged items were on the USML violates the Constitution's Ex Post Facto clause. However, the Court rejected the defendant's charges in these areas and their request for a new trial.[36]

NSD carries out its responsibilities with a FY 2012 budget of $87 million and its staff consists of 359 personnel with 236 of these being attorneys. Its FY 2012 congressional budget submission requests that its budget be increased to $90 million while also noting that its workload includes increasing demands stemming from national security threats and enhanced oversight responsibilities are creating problems maintaining sufficient attorneys and support personnel staffing.[37]

Further controversy over DOJ's ability to effectively enforce firearms exports has been highlighted by the controversial Operation Fast and Furious which saw the Bureau of Alcohol, Tobacco, Firearms, and Explosives (ATF) permit licensed firearms dealers to sell weapons to illegal straw buyers in Mexico hoping this would enable tracking these weapons to Mexican drug cartel leaders, lead to their arrest, and help dismantle the cartels which would, in theory, ease the drug violence plaguing Mexico. This operation went awry resulting in the December 15, 2010 death of border patrol agent Brian Terry, producing intense criticism by congressional Republicans including House Oversight and Government Reform Committee Chair Rep. Darrell Issa (R-CA), dubious executive privilege assertions by the Obama Administration toward congressional document requests, coverup charges by Obama critics, and resulted in an unprecedented contempt of Congress citation against Attorney General Eric Holder by the House of Representatives on June 28, 2012.[38]

Fast and Furious also resulted in a Justice Department Inspector General report which was released on September 19, 2012. This document found that DOJ had insufficient control and a lack of attention to public safety in Operation Fast and Furious and a similar predecessor operation; that there was inappropriate use of cooperating Federal Firearms Licensing to advance the investigation; noted the absence of meaningful oversight by ATF headquarters; and documented the presence of significant problems coordinating Fast and Furious with other agencies such as the Drug Enforcement Administration and FBI. Report recommendations included:

1. DOJ examining ATF policies on law enforcement operations to ensure their compliance with DOJ guidelines and policies.
2. DOJ working with ATF to develop guidance on conducting enterprise investigations against gun trafficking organizations.
3. DOJ reviewing its law enforcement components policies and procedures to ensure they address concerns on overseeing sensitive and major cases including authorizing and overseeing "otherwise illegal activity" and using informants in situations where the law enforcement component has a regulatory function.[39]

The report went on to find fault with various individual ATF agents, the U.S. Attorney's Office for Arizona District, and ATF Assistant Director William McMahon, and other Justice Department officials for not considering public safety and operational effectiveness aspects of Fast and Furious. However, the report also maintained that Attorney General Holder was aware of Fast and Furious problems after late January/early February 2011 and had not reviewed weekly reports on this operation and that his staff and not highlighted these reports for his review. It also noted the poor quality and misleading responses of DOJ to congressional Fast and Furious inquiries. This failure to directly criticize Holder more directly has been noted by congressional Republicans and controversy over Fast and Furious is likely to continue.[40]

Problems with additional aspects of DOJ export control policymaking were noted in a December 2006 GAO report. This assessment revealed that neither the State nor Commerce Departments receive DOJ notification of export control criminal justice case outcomes including indictments and convictions for defense and dual-use items consequently preventing them from having the full scope of information on prosecuted companies and individuals. This information is needed by Commerce and State because indicted or convicted exporters may have their license applications and export privileges denied.

Without such criminal case outcomes, other federal export control agencies may not have a complete picture of individuals or companies seeking export licenses or illegal export activity trends.[41]

This report also revealed that during FY 2005 Justice Department data showed there were over 40 individuals or companies convicted of over 100 criminal export law violations. In contrast, State reported over $35 million in export control administrative fines and penalties and Commerce reported over $6.8 million in such administrative fines and sanctions for this same year.[42]

DOJ and its component entities have experienced success, failure, and controversy in its efforts to enforce U.S. export control laws and punish individuals and organizations violating these laws. It will continue attempting to carry out its responsibilities in these areas while coping with budgetary and personnel constraints and the increasingly sophisticated efforts of export control law violators to evade detection for their illicit activities.

Energy Department

The Department of Energy (DOE) also contributes to the U.S. export control policymaking matrix. DOEs Office of Imports and Exports, which is part of DOEs Office of Fossil Energy, regulates the export of natural gas and electric power.[43] DOEs Office of Electricity Delivery and Energy Reliability is responsible for authorizing electric energy exports and issuing permits for constructing, connecting, operating, and maintaining electric transmission facilities at international borders.[44]

DOEs National Nuclear Security Administration (NNSA), established in 2000, authorizes the export use of nuclear technology and technical data for nuclear power and special nuclear materials. NNSA accomplishes these objectives through its International Nonproliferation Export Control Program (INECP). INECP seeks to promote a strong trade control system consistent with international norms and assist U.S. efforts to detect and prevent illegal procuring of equipment, materials, and technological expertise by states and terrorist organizations seeking to develop weapons of mass destruction.[45]

This program has trained over 7,500 licensing, compliance, and enforcement officers and specializes in establishing national nonproliferation technical specialists. These individuals play key roles in applying modern risk analysis procedures to their licensing processes. INECP selects partner countries on their risk level as potential suppliers and transshippers of WMD-related assets. Its program experts work with specialists in these countries to identify and address implementation gaps in national export control systems. Examples of countries where INECP has worked include Macedonia where it has targeted areas of greatest export control vulnerability; providing instructor training to Turkey's Undersecretary of Foreign Trade, Turkish Customs, and the Turkish Atomic Energy Authority; working with Australian and Japanese trainers to provide training for Singaporean export control personnel; and working with South Korea's Ministry of Commerce, Industry, and Energy to conduct an export control seminar for over 150 Korean representatives from companies manufacturing strategic goods.[46]

NNSA programs dealing with defense nuclear nonproliferation fund programs providing policy and technical leadership to limit or prevent spreading WMD expertise, materials, and technology; advancing technologies for detecting global WMD proliferation; eliminating or securing inventories of surplus materials and infrastructure usable for nuclear weapons; and addressing the danger that hostile nations or terrorist groups may acquire WMD or weapons-usable material, dual-use production technology, or WMD production expertise. Specific NNSA programs dealing with defense nuclear nonproliferation cover Nonproliferation and Verification Research and Development, Nonproliferation and International Security, International Nuclear Materials Protection and Cooperation, Fissile Materials Disposition which seeks to dispose of surplus weapons grade fissile materials in the U.S. and Russia, and the Global Threat Reduction Initiative (GTRI) which aspires to reduce vulnerable nuclear and radiological materials at civilian sites globally.[47]

NNSA also administers the Megaports Initiative. This program collaborates with foreign customs and other law enforcement agencies, port authorities, terminal operators, and other relevant entities in partner countries to drastically enhance detection capabilities for special nuclear and other radioactive material in containerized cargo using the global maritime shipping network. Megaports helps partner countries equip their major seaports with radiation detection equipment and alarm communication systems. It also provides comprehensive training for foreign personnel, short-term maintenance coverage, and technical support for ensuring the long-term viability and sustainability of installed radiation detection systems.

Megaports also works with Homeland Security and State to counter nuclear and radiological threats to the U.S. and its partners by installing radiation portal monitors which U.S. Customs can use to scan high-risk U.S.-bound containers with minimal impact on port operations. This initiative seeks to equip 100 seaports with radiation detection systems by 2016 scanning approximately 50% of global containerized maritime cargo and over 80% of U.S.-bound container traffic. NNSA had completed 42 of 100 planned Megaports projects in 31 countries as of August 2012 spending $850 million as of December 2011.[48]

Accomplishments and shortcomings in DOE nonproliferation export control activities over the past decade have been documented by Energy Department Inspector General (IG) and Government Accountability Office (GAO) reports. A May 1999 DOE IG report revealed that DOE processes for export license applications for nuclear dual-use and munitions commodities appeared adequate. This review also expressed concern about whether there was sufficient staffing in DOE's Nuclear Transport and Supplier Policy (NTSP) Division which reviews export license applications and whether NTSP analysts had access to intelligence information needed to support their licensing activities. This assessment went on to express Commerce's concern that DOE did not always send appropriate representatives to Advisory Committee on Export Policy meetings, and that Commerce's export licensing database was unable to electronically receive images of documents supporting DOE review of export license applications.[49]

A March 2001 DOE IG report mentioned that DOE collaborated with Commerce in identifying and reviewing nuclear dual-use commodities within the Commerce Control List (CCL) and that DOE only played a minor role in developing and reviewing the USML.[50] However, an April 2004 DOE IG report found significant weaknesses in compliance with deemed exports by contractors and universities with foreign nationals access to unclassified technologies involving DOE contractor General Atomics and DOE's Ames Laboratory. This study determined that there was inconsistent application of energy export control guidance on foreign nationals having access to sensitive technologies with some hosts not being knowledgable about their deemed export control responsibilities and General Atomics having more significant foreign national access restrictions than Ames Laboratory which did not consider visual access to sensitive equipment or its use by foreign nationals as being contrary to DOE deemed export control guidelines.[51]

To correct these deficiencies, this report recommended that DOE's Director of the Office of Safety and Security Performance Assurance expedite issuing a draft document addressing training requirements for those hosting visits by foreign nationals, and ensuring that export control guidance, including deemed export guidance, is disseminated and consistently implemented throughout DOE.[52]

A March 2005 DOE IG report addressed DOE's review of chemical and biological export license applications. Its conclusions were that the DOE export licensing process was assisting in governmental efforts to deter WMD proliferation; that DOE began adding additional licensing officers with chemical and biological weapons expertise in April 2003; that agency reviews of chemical and biological license applications occurred within 30 days; and the DOE officials coordinated appropriately with other federal agencies on their review of chemical and biological export license applications. At the same time, the IG report also expressed concern with some DOE licensing officials being unable to access Commerce's export license application database.[53]

An April 2006 DOE IG report examined the agency's review of China-bound export license applications. It determined that DOE conducted reviews of all escalated export license applications it received concerning China during Fiscal Year (FY) 2004 and coordinated effectively with formal interagency entities as required by Executive Order 12981 for conducting export license reviews. Report findings also noted that DOE officials conducting license reviews needed better access to end-user review information maintained by DOE's Lawrence Livermore National Laboratory and that DOE's Deputy Administrator for Nuclear Nonproliferation should coordinate with the Director of DOE's Office of Intelligence and Counterintelligence to ensure personnel conducting export license reviews have ongoing access to Sensitive Compartmented Information Computers and be able to hand-carry Sensitive Compartmented Information documents.[54]

A March 2008 DOE IG report documented continuing problems with tracking foreign visitors to DOE facilities. Problems documented included hosts not always taking action to ensure physical access to the site or facility was promptly terminated when the visit or assignment was completed; becoming familiar with or ensuring that visitors or assignees complied with individual security plans; verifying the identity and validity of foreign nationals status information for off-site visits as required; and ensuring counterintelligence reviews were completed prior to permitting foreign nationals access to sensitive information systems and data.[55]

More specific examples of these security flaws included 12 of 23 laboratory hosts indicating their unfamiliarity with specific visitor security plans, hosts at NNSA's Headquarters office and one laboratory not always obtaining and/or validating required foreign visitor status documents such as passports and visas; hosts arranging for visitors to gain remote access to laboratory information systems; failing to obtain visitor immigration status information; failing to conduct required counterintelligence reviews prior to permitting foreign nationals to access sensitive information systems and data; and allowing some visitors to unnecessarily retain their security badges and have access to the site for two years regardless of the authorized duration of their stay.[56]

GAO has also examined NNSA export control programs and found strengths and weaknesses. A January 2007 report found DOE had improved security at hundreds of sites containing radiological sources in over 40 countries since initiating a radiological threat reduction program in 2002. However, GAO also found that the most high risk and dangerous radiological sources remained unsecured; particularly in Russia. This document went on to mention that DOE's program does not address security problems involved in transporting radiological sources between locations and that while DOE has improved its coordination with the State Department and Nuclear Regulatory Commission (NRC) on securing radiological sources globally these agencies have not efficiently integrated their regulatory development efforts. This was vividly demonstrated by DOE and NRC disagreeing over whether DOE should have transferred $5 million from its FY 2004 appropriation to NRC to strengthen international regulatory controls over radiological sources as directed the Senate Appropriations Committee.[57]

Continuing concern over DOE's ability to secure nuclear weapons assets was reflected in a March 2010 report on its plutonium disposition program. This report reviewed nearly two decades worth of efforts to dispose of surplus national security plutonium at domestic DOE facilities. It revealed ongoing delays in major construction projects including poor project and contractor oversight, disagreement with Russia about liability for work performed by U.S. contractor personnel in Russia, funding priority changes, and concern about DOE's ability to fabricate mixed oxide fuel and U.S. facilities such as Savannah River, and concerns over safety control at these facilities.[58]

Additional concern over nuclear material security was also expressed in a December 2010 GAO report. This report mentioned the laudability of the Obama Administration's nuclear material security initiative to accelerate NNSA and other U.S. nuclear material safety efforts with foreign countries. GAO went on to mention that this goal is unrealistic given the reluctance of Russia and other countries to admit weaknesses in their nuclear security programs. This assessment also asserted that the chances of securing vulnerable nuclear materials globally is exacerbated by the absence of a robust U.S. interagency implementation plan capable of clearly identifying vulnerable foreign nuclear material facilities to be addressed, assigning clear agency and program responsibilities for these locations, reviewing potential challenges and how such obstacles can be overcome, estimating time frames for completing activities at each site, and presenting estimating funding required to achieve this goal].[59]

An October 2011 GAO report described further deficiencies in the security of overseas U.S. nuclear materials. This analysis determined that DOE, NRC, and State could not fully account for overseas U.S. nuclear material subject to nuclear cooperation agreement terms because these agreements do not stipulate systematic reporting of such information and there is no U.S. policy for pursuing or obtaining such information. Neither DOE nor NRC were able to provide GAO with a current and comprehensive inventory of overseas U.S. nuclear material including the country, site, or facility.[60]

This report went on to stress that without an accurate inventory of U.S. nuclear materials such as weapon usable highly enriched uranium and separated plutonium that the U.S. has insufficient assurances concerning the location of these materials. Consequently, this makes it difficult to monitor whether partner countries are appropriately notifying the U.S. and whether the U.S. is appropriately and fully exercising approval rights for transferring, retransferring, enriching, reprocessing, and storing nuclear materials subject to agreed terms. This report expressed its concern over DOE's lack of cooperation with NRC and State on this matter including failing to visit all partner facilities holding strategic nuclear material such as U-235 every five years, not revisiting facilities failing to meet International Atomic Energy Agency (IAEA) security guidelines in a timely manner, and that relying on reported thefts of U.S. nuclear material as a security gauge is a poor program effectiveness measure when accounting processes for inventorying U.S. material at foreign facilities are limited.[61]

March 14, 2012 testimony before the Senate Homeland Security and Governmental Affairs Committee saw GAO express progress and concerns with DOE nuclear nonproliferation efforts. Positively, GAO noted that Ukraine announced in 2010 that it would ship nearly 236 pounds of highly enriched uranium and 123 tons of spent nuclear fuel to Russia by the end of 2012 and that Malaysia had enacted new export control laws to limit nuclear trafficking. In contrast, GAO noted that terrorist or countries seeking nuclear weapons could use as little as 25 kilograms of weapon-grade highly enriched uranium and 8 kilograms of plutonium to construct a nuclear weapon and that terrorists could build a crude nuclear bomb from either of these items into an improvised nuclear device capable of creating an explosion producing extreme heat, powerful shockwaves, and intense radiation which would immediately kill individuals within miles of the explosion, create radioactive fallout over thousands of square miles, and potentially produce the same force as the atomic bomb destroying Nagasaki, Japan in 1945.[62]

NNSA Defense Nonproliferation responsibilities were carried out with a FY 2012 budget of $2.295.880 billion and NNSA's FY 2013 congressional budget justification request asked for an increase to $2.458.631 billion or 7.1%. NNSA's overall budget for FY 2012 was $11 billion and it requested $11.535.586 billion for FY 2013. NNSA's current FY 2012 workforce of 1,928 carries out these multiple activities and the agency expects this workforce to be 1,922 through FY 2017.[63]

CBP, DOJ, and DOE have achieved successes and failures in their efforts to administer U.S. export control policymaking and enforce relevant statutes within existing budget and personnel appropriations. They represent yet another layer of the multifaceted historical and contemporary nature of U.S. export control policymaking. The next chapter examines how the State Department adds additional complexity to U.S. policymaking in this area with particular emphasis on its economic activities and financial transactions.

Notes

1. U.S. Customs Service, *Mission and Organization*, (Washington, DC: U.S. Customs Service, Office of the Comptroller, 1988): 1-3.

2. See Elise Keppler, "Preventing Human Rights Abuses by Regulating Arms Brokering: The U.S. Brokering Amendment to the Arms Export Control Act," *Berkeley Journal of International Law*, 19(2)(2001): 381-411; and Public Law 104-164, "Foreign Assistance Act of 1961 and Arms Export Control Act Amendments," 110 *U.S. Statutes at Large* 1421, 1437-1438.

3. U.S. Congress, House Committee on Ways and Means, Subcommittee on Oversight, *Administration and Enforcement of U.S. Export Control Programs*, (Washington, DC: GPO, 1992): 116-119, 164-167; and 414-417.

4. Public Law 107-296, "Homeland Security Act of 2002," 116 *U.S. Statutes at Large* 2135-2321.

5. See U.S. Customs and Border Protection (CBP), *Summary of Laws and Regulations Enforced by CBP*, (Washington, DC: CBP, n.d.); http://www.cbp.gov/xp/cgov/trade/legal/summary_laws_enforced/; Accessed September 18, 2012; and U.S. Government Accountability Office (GAO), *Export Controls: Challenges Exist in Enforcement of an Inherently Complex System*, (Washington, DC: GAO, 2006): 22; http://www.gao.gov/new.items/d07265.pdf; Accessed September 17, 2012.

6. Ibid., 14-21.

7. U.S. Department of Homeland Security, *Privacy Impact Assessment for the Exodus Accountability Referral System (EARS)*, (Washington, DC: DHS, 2010): 2-4; http://www.dhs.gov/xlibrary/assets/privacy/privacy_pia_ice_ears.pdf; Accessed September 17, 2012.

8. See CBP, *Container Security Initiative Fact Sheet*, (Washington, DC: CBP, 2011): 1; http://www.cbp.gov/linkhandler/cgov/trade/cargo_security/csi/csi_factsheet_2011.ctt/csi_factsheet_2011.pdf; Accessed September 18, 2012; and U.S. Department of Homeland Security, Office of Inspector General, *CBP's Container Security Initiative Has Proactive Management But Future Direction is Uncertain: Letter Report,* (Washington, DC: DHS OIG, 2010); http://purl.fdlp.gov/GPO/gpo12206; Accessed September 18, 2012.

9. GAO, *Export Controls: Challenges Exist in Enforcement of an Inherently Complex System*, (Washington, DC: GAO, 2006): 8; www.gao.gov/assets/260/254812.pdf; Accessed September 21, 2012.

10. CBP, "Secure Freight Initiative Begins Data Transmission for Radiation Scanning in Pakistan," (Washington, DC: CBP, May 2, 2007); http://www.cbp.gov/xp/cgov/newsroom/news_releases/archives/2007_news_releases/052007/05022007.xml; Accessed September 18, 2012.

11. Ibid., "CBP Officers Arrest Woman on Alien Smuggling Charges, Seize 6,486 Rounds of High Powered Ammunition," (Washington, DC: CBP, December 31, 2009); http://www.cbp.gov/xp/cgov/newsroom/news_releases/archives/2009_news_releases/dec_2009/12312009_6.xml; Accessed September 18, 2012.

12. The President, *National Strategy for Global Supply Chain Security*, (Washington, DC: The White House, 2012): 1-3; http://www.whitehouse.gov/sites/default/files/national_strategy_for_global_supply_chain_security.pdf; Accessed September 18, 2012.

13. U.S. Department of Homeland Security, *Annual Performance Report: Fiscal Years 2011-2013 Appendix A: Measure Descriptions and Data Collection Methodologies*, (Washington, DC: DHS, 2012); 8; www.dhs.gov/xlibrary/assets/mgmt/cfo_apr_fy2011_appa.pdf; Accessed September 18, 2012.

14. U.S. Department of Homeland Security, Office of Inspector General (DHS OIG), *Effectiveness of Customs and Border Protection's Procedures to Detect Uranium In Two Smuggling Incidents*, (Washington, DC: DHS OIG, 2004): 2; www.oig.dhs.gov/assets/Mgmt/OIG-04-40.pdf; Accessed September 18, 2012.

15. Ibid., *Review of Controls Over the Export of Chemical and Biological Commodities (Redacted)*, (Washington, DC: DHS OIG, 2005): 2; http://www.oig.dhs.gov/assets/Mgmt/OIGr_05-21_Jun05.pdf; Accessed September 18, 2012. Detailed portions of this report remain redacted seven years later.

16. U.S. Government Accountability Office, *Nonproliferation: Agencies Could Improve Information Sharing and End-Use Monitoring on Unmanned Aerial Vehicle Exports*, (Washington, DC: GAO, 2012): 32-33; http://www.gao.gov/assets/600/593131.pdf; Accessed September 19, 2012.

17. See CBP, "United States Border Patrol: Border Patrol Agent Staffing by Fiscal Year (Oct. 1st through Sept. 30th), (Washington, DC: DHS, 2011): 1; http://www.cbp.gov/linkhandler/cgov/border_security/border_patrol/usbp_statistics/staffing_92_10.ctt/staffing_92_11.pdf; Accessed September 19, 2012; and Ibid., "United States Border Patrol: Enacted Border Patrol Program Budget by Fiscal Year (Dollars in Thousands)," (Washington, DC: DHS, 2011): 1; http://www.cbp.gov/linkhandler/cgov/border_security/border_patrol/usbp_statistics/budget_stats.ctt/budget_stats.pdf; Accessed September 19, 2012.

18. Ibid., "Export Control and Related Border Security (EXBS) Program Overview," (Washington, DC: DHS, 2008): 1; http://www.cbp.gov/xp/cgov/

border_security/international_operations/international_training/exbs.xml; Accessed September 19, 2012.

19. See Public Law 109-177, "USA PATRIOT Improvement and Reauthorization Act," 120 *U.S. Statutes at Large* 191, 247-250; and *Export Controls: Challenges Exist in Enforcement of an Inherently Complex System*, 8, 20.

20. U.S. Department of Justice, National Security Division, "About the Division," (Washington, DC: USDOJ, n.d.): 1; http://www.justice.gov/nsd/about-nsd.html; Accessed September 20, 2012.

21. Ibid., "Sections and Offices, http://www.justice.gov/nsd/list-view.html; Accessed September 20, 2012.

22. GAO, *Efforts to Combat Arms Trafficking to Mexico*, (Washington, DC: GAO, 2009): 3; www.gao.gov/assets/300/291223.pdf; Accessed September 21, 2012.

23. See Public Law 75-583, "To Acquire the Registration of Certain Persons Employed by Agencies to Disseminate Propaganda in the United States and for Other Purposes," 52 *U.S. Statutes at Large*, 631-633; and U.S. Department of Justice, "Foreign Agents Registration Act, " www.fara.gov/; Accessed September 20, 2012 provides detailed reporting and documentation of individuals and organizations lobbying for foreign countries and governments which can involve advocating for or against particular U.S. Government export control policies.

24. See Public Law 95-213, "Foreign Corrupt Practices Act," 91 *U.S. Statutes at Large* 1494-1500; Public Law 105-366, "International Anti-Bribery and Fair Competition Act," 112 *U.S. Statutes at Large* 3302-3312; and Mike Koehler, "The Façade of FCPA Enforcement," *Georgetown Journal of International Law*, 41 (4)(2010): 907-1009.

25. See U.S. Congress, House Committee on Interstate and Foreign Commerce, Subcommittee on Oversight and Investigations, *Foreign Corrupt Practices Act*, (Washington, DC: GPO, 1979); U.S. Congress, House Committee on Energy and Commerce, Subcommittee on Telecommunications, Consumer Protection, and Finance, *Foreign Corrupt Practices Act-Oversight*, (Washington, DC: GPO, 1982); U.S. Congress, House Committee on Foreign Affairs, Subcommittee on International Economic Policy and Trade, *The Foreign Trade Practices Act,* (Washington, DC: GPO, 1985); U.S. Congress, House Committee on Commerce, Subcommittee on Finance and Hazardous Materials, *The International Anti-Bribery and Fair Competition Act of 1998,* (Washington, DC: GPO, 1999); U.S. Department of State, *Fighting Global Corruption: Business Risk Management Information for Global Businesses and Organizations Navigating the International Anticorruption Environment*, (Washington, DC: Department of State, 2000); Rajib Sanyal, "Determinants of Bribery in International Business: The Cultural and Economic Factors," *Journal of Business Ethics*, 59 (1/2)(June 2005): 139-145; Professor Mike Koehler, Assistant Professor, Southern Illinois University School of Law, FCPA Professor: A Forum

Devoted to the Foreign Corrupt Practices Act; www.fcpaprofessor.com/; Accessed September 20, 2012.

26. U.S. Department of Justice, National Security Division, *Summary of Major U.S. Export Enforcement, Economic Espionage, Trade Secret and Embargo-Related Criminal Cases (January 2007 to the present: updated September 6, 2012*, (Washington, DC: U.S. Department of Justice, 2012): 74; www.justice.gov/nsd/docs/export-case-fact-sheet.pdf; Accessed September 21, 2012.

27. Ibid., 49.

28. Ibid., 46.

29. Ibid., 36-39.

30. Ibid., 26.

31. Ibid., 10.

32. *Crockett v. Reagan*, 558 F. Supp. 893 (1982).

33. *U.S. v. Da Chuan Zeng et. al.* 590 F. Supp. 274 (1984).

34. *U.S. v. Reed*, 790 F.2d 208 (1986).

35. *U.S. v. Yakou*, 428 F.3d 241 (2005).

36. *U.S. v. Zhen Zou Wu, Chitron Corporation*, 668 F. Supp. 2d 298 (2011).

37. U.S. Department of Justice, Justice Management Division, *Department of Justice FY 2013 Congressional Budget Submission: National Security Division (NSD)*, (Washington, DC: U.S. Department of Justice, 2012): 1-2; http://www.justice.gov/jmd/2013summary/pdf/fy13-nsd-bud-summary.pdf; Accessed September 26, 2012.

38. See U.S. Congress, House Committee on Government Oversight and Reform, *Operation Fast and Furious: Reckless Decisions, Tragic Outcomes*, (Washington, DC: GPO, 2011); Ibid., *Operation Fast and Furious: The Other Side of the Border*, (Washington, DC: GPO, 2012); Katie Pavlich, *Fast and Furious: Barack Obama's Bloodiest Scandal and Its Shameless Coverup*, (Washington, DC: Regnery Pub., 2012); and *Congressional Record*, 158 (99)(June 28, 2012): H4420-4421.

39. U.S. Department of Justice, Office of the Inspector General, *A Review of ATF's Operation Fast and Furious and Related Matters*, (Washington, DC: OIG, 2012): 419-430; http://www.justice.gov/oig/reports/2012/s1209.pdf; Accessed September 26, 2012.

40. See Ibid., 431-471; and U.S. Congress, House Committee on Government Oversight and Reform, *IG Report: The Department of Justice's Office of the Inspector General Examines the Failures of Operation Fast and Furious*, (Washington, DC: GPO, 2012); . http://purl.fdlp.gov/GPO/gpo31471; Accessed January 30, 2013.

41. *Export Controls: Challenges Exist in Enforcement of an Inherently Complex System*, (Washington, DC: GAO, 2006): 3.

42. Ibid., 6.

43. U.S. International Trade Administration, *Export Licenses,* (Washington, DC: ITA, 2011): 1; http://export.gov/regulation/eg_main_018219.asp; Accessed September 26, 2012.

44. Ibid., *Electricity Imports/Exports-International Electricity Regulation,* (Washington, DC: ITA, 2009); 1; http://export.gov/regulation/eg_main_018222.asp; Accessed September 26, 2012.

45. See Public Law 106-65, "National Defense Authorization Act, for Fiscal Year 2000," 113 *U.S. Statutes at Large,* 512, 953-971; and U.S. Nuclear Nonproliferation Administration, Office of Global Security Engagement and Cooperation, *International Nonproliferation Export Control Program,* (Washington, DC: NNSA, 2008): 1; http://nnsa.energy.gov/sites/default/files/nnsa/inlinefiles/INECP_Brochure.pdf; Accessed September 26, 2012.

46. Ibid., 2-11.

47. U.S. Department of Energy, Chief Financial Officer, *Department of Energy FY 2013 Congressional Budget Request: Budget Highlights,* (Washington, DC: DOE, 2012): 61-62; http://www.cfo.doe.gov/budget/13budget/Content/Highlights.pdf; Accessed September 28, 2012.

48. See U.S. Department of Energy, National Nuclear Security Administration, *Office of the Second Line of Defense: Megaports Initiative,* (Washington, DC: NNSA, 2010): 2; http://nnsa.energy.gov/sites/default/files/nnsa/inlinefiles/singlepages_9-15-2010.pdf; Accessed December 18, 2012; and U.S. General Accountability Office, *Combating Nuclear Smuggling: Megaports Initiative Faces Funding and Sustainability Challenges,* (Washington, DC: GAO, 2012): 9-10; http://www.gao.gov/assets/650/649759.pdf; Accessed December 18, 2012.

49. U.S. Department of Energy, Office of Inspector General (DOE IG), *The Department of Energy's Export Licensing Process For Dual-Use and Munitions Commodities,* (Washington, DC: DOE IG, 1999): 3-4; http://energy.gov/sites/prod/files/igprod/documents/CalendarYear1999/ig-0445.pdf; Accessed September 28, 2012.

50. Ibid., *Inspection of the Department of Energy's Role in the Commerce Control List and the U.S. Munitions List,* (Washington, DC: DOE IG, 2001): 3-6; http://energy.gov/sites/prod/files/igprod/documents/CalendarYear2001/inso0103.pdf; Accessed September 28, 2012.

51. Ibid., *Contractor Compliance With Deemed Export Controls,* (Washington, DC: DOE IG, 2004): 1-2; http://energy.gov/sites/prod/files/igprod/documents/CalendarYear2004/ig-0645.pdf; Accessed September 28, 2012.

52. Ibid., 4.

53. Ibid., *The Department of Energy's Review of Chemical and Biological Export License Applications,* (Washington, DC: DOE IG 2005; 1-2; http://energy.gov/sites/prod/files/igprod/documents/CalendarYear2005/ig-0682.pdf; Accessed September 28, 2012.

54. See Ibid., *The Department of Energy's Review of Export License Applications for China,* (Washington, DC: DOE IG, 2006); 3-5; http://energy.gov/sites/prod/files/igprod/documents/CalendarYear2006/IG-0723.pdf; Accessed September 28, 2012; and The President, "Executive Order 12981 of December 5, 1995: Administration of Export Controls," 60 *Federal Register* 236 (December 8, 1995): 62981-62985.

55. Ibid., *The Department's Unclassified Foreign Visits and Assignments Program,* (Washington, DC: DOE IG, 2008): 1; http://energy.gov/sites/prod/files/igprod/documents/IG-0791.pdf; Accessed September 28, 2012.

56. Ibid., 3-5.

57. GAO, *Nuclear Nonproliferation: DOE's International Radiological Threat Reduction Program Needs to Focus Future Efforts on Securing the Highest Priority Radiological Sources,* (Washington, DC: GAO, 2007); 5-7; http://www.gao.gov/assets/260/256110.pdf; Accessed October 1, 2012.

58. Ibid., *Nuclear Nonproliferation: DOE Needs to Address Uncertainties with and Strengthen Independent Safety Oversight of Its Plutonium Disposition Program,* (Washington, DC: GAO, 2010); 4-5, 38; http://www.gao.gov/assets/310/302279.pdf; Accessed October 1, 2012.

59. Ibid., *Nuclear Nonproliferation: Comprehensive U.S. Planning and Better Foreign Cooperation Needed to Secure Vulnerable Nuclear Materials Worldwide,* (Washington, DC: GAO, 2010): 38; http://www.gao.gov/assets/320/313961.pdf; Accessed October 1, 2012.

60. Ibid., *Nuclear Nonproliferation: U.S. Agencies Have Limited Ability to Account for, Monitor, and Evaluate Security of U.S. Nuclear Material Overseas,* (Washington, DC: GAO, 2011): 8; http://www.gao.gov/assets/330/323043.pdf; Accessed October 1, 2012.

61. Ibid., 34-35.

62. Ibid., *Nuclear Nonproliferation: Further Actions Needed by U.S. Agencies to Secure Vulnerable Nuclear and Radiological Materials,* (Washington, DC: GAO, 2012): 5, 1; http://www.gao.gov/assets/590/589345.pdf; Accessed October 1, 2012.

63. See U.S. Department of Energy, Office of Chief Financial Officer, *Department of Energy FY 2013: Congressional Budget Request Budget Highlights,* (Washington, DC: DOE, 2012): 54; http://www.cfo.doe.gov/budget/13budget/Content/Highlights.pdf; Accessed October 1, 2012; and Ibid., *Department of Energy FY 2013 Congressional Budget Request National Nuclear Security Administration: Office of the Administrator Weapons Activities Defense Nuclear Nonproliferation Naval Reactors,* (Washington, DC: DOE, 2012): 1:9; http://www.cfo.doe.gov/budget/13budget/Content/Volume1.pdf; Accessed October 1, 2012.

Chapter 4

The State Department and Export Controls

The Department of State (State Department) is another U.S. agency playing a critical role in administering U.S. export control policy. This agency first became involved in regulating arms exports with the passage of the 1935 Neutrality Act out of concern that the U.S. could find itself unwittingly drawn into an armed conflict with other countries. Provisions of this legislation included imposing an embargo on trading arms and war material with parties at war and declaring that Americans traveling on ships owned by warring countries did so at their own risk.[1]

This legislation enabled the President to establish a legal basis for instituting a general arms export control system. It established an inter-agency National Munitions Control Board (MCB) chaired by the Secretary of State whose membership also included the Secretaries of Commerce, Navy, Treasury and War. MCB responsibilities included administering Neutrality Act export control provisions; requiring all individuals engaging in manufacturing, exporting, or importing arms to register with the Secretary of State; authorizing this official to promote rules and regulations for administering and enforcing arms export controls; authorizing the President to designate a list of articles subject to these controls; and establishing universal licensing requirements for all arms imports and exports.[2]

On September 19, 1935 this board was established in the State Department under the leadership of Joseph C. Green (1887-1978) and held its first meeting on September 24. A key result of this first meeting was determining a list of items to be classified as arms, ammunition, and war implements; authorizing the chair to recommend this list to the President; and prescribing permanent records on manufacturing for exporting and importing arms, ammunition, and war implements that must be maintained by individuals legally required to register this information under the Neutrality Act.[3]

Six categories of weapons and war supplies (United States Munitions List-USML) were established by the MCB with samples of these materials in each category including:

> Category 1—Rifles, machine guns, automatic rifles, ammunition exceeding .22 caliber;
>
> Category 2—War vessels including aircraft carriers and submarines;
>
> Category 3—Aircraft; aerial gun mounts; bomb racks; and torpedo carriers;
>
> Category 4—Revolvers and automatic pistols using higher than .22 caliber ammunition;
>
> Category 5—Assembled or dismantled aircraft besides those in Category 3; propellers; fuselages; wings, and aircraft engines;
>
> Category 6—Flame throwers, mustard gas, and other chemical weapons.[4]

These classifications would be called the International Traffic in Arms Regulations (ITAR) and became effective on November 29, 1935 when MCB began issuing licenses to exporters. The value of these licenses rose from $27.9 million in 1935 to $873.1 million in 1940. ITAR was incorporated into Title 22 Parts 120-130 of the Code of Federal Regulations (CFR) which is published annually by the National Archives and Records Administration.[5]

An additional factor affecting the development of governmental export control policy during this time period was the efforts of the Curtiss-Wright aviation company to expand its sales internationally by exporting planes to Bolivia which was involved in a war with Paraguay during this time period. The League of Nations asked the U.S. to help end the fighting and the Roosevelt Administration responded by asking Congress to pass legislation empowering the President prohibit arms sales to these countries. Congress complied with Roosevelt's request and the U.S. proceeded to order an arms sales embargo on these two countries.

Curtiss-Wright continued smuggling weapons to this region and was caught and charged with violating presidential orders. The company sued the U.S. charging that this congressional legislation was an unconstitutional delegation of legislative power to the President and a federal district court judge agreed with the company. The Roosevelt Administration appealed to the Supreme Court contending that Congress had historically given the President broad discretionary power to act in international affairs. In December 1936, the Supreme Court ruled in favor of the government saying the President and executive branch had broad powers to conduct foreign policy which the legislative branch did not. Curtiss-Wright pleaded guilty in February 1940 and ended up paying fines of nearly $250,000.[6]

World War II saw MCB go through many institutional evolutions including being lumped into other State Department divisions such as passports, visas, and immigration. This emerging Cold War international security environment saw additional evolutions to ITAR with January 1954 revisions expanding definition of "article" to include "components, parts, accessories, and related attachments" into existing arms, armaments, and war implements classification. These changes would ultimately culminate in the 1954 Mutual Security Act.[7] Congress enacted this legislation establishing many objectives of U.S. military assistance principles including promoting U.S. national security interests, preventing the proliferation of weapons of mass destruction; and regulating and reducing the amount of arms and military forces with sufficient safeguards to protect complying nations against violations or evasions of these restrictions by other countries. Section 414 of this statute directed the President to regulate the export and imports of arms, ammunition, and technical data and to require individuals engaged in exporting, importing, and manufacturing defense items to register with the U.S. Government. The State Department's Office of Munitions Controls (OMC) was designated for these purposes.[8]

The growing economic and political influence of the civilian aerospace industry saw these entities raise concerns over civil aviation aircraft and equipment being included on the Munitions List of restricted export items. Consequently, ITAR was changed on June 1, 1959 when civil aircraft and avionics including commercial radar, communications, and navigation equipment were removed from this list and placed under Commerce Department administered export control regulations.[9]

COCOM Origins

Another important early Cold War development of export controls involving the U.S. and its western allies was the 1950 establishment of the Coordinating Committee (COCOM). This saw these countries establish a strategic trade control system which sought to restrict Communist countries from receiving equipment and technology which could enhance their military strength. This Paris-based organization's membership consisted of every NATO nation except Iceland and also included Japan. U.S. participation in COCOM was authorized by the 1951 Mutual Defense Assistance Control Act (Battle Act) and U.S. positions and actions within COCOM were taken by the State Department in coordination with the Commerce and Defense Departments and the Atomic Energy Commission.

COCOM actions focused on a list of commodities and technologies whose export was embargoed. Member countries were prohibited from licensing export of these items to Communist countries without unanimous COCOM approval. As this organization developed and evolved over subsequent decades, the U.S. tended to favor more reswtrictive export controls than partner countries who would regularly seek to reduce embargo coverage scope which would often increase strains within COCOM.[10]

Background to Foreign Military Sales Act
PL 90-629 Including Legislative History

Controversy over U.S. arms sales to undeveloped countries became particularly heated during congressional debate over the annual 1967 foreign assistance legislation. This contentiousness stemmed from several factors including U.S. arms sales to foreign countries being made through direct commercial arrangements and bilateral government contact. Approximately 2/3 of these sales were with cash with the remainder being on credit with developed countries being the primary recipient. Less developed nations could purchase arms on credit with governmental backing. The Defense Department's (DOD) military assistance credit account was the primary source of this line of credit. A revolving fund financed some loans directly and other loans for such sales were backed by the Export-Import Bank (Eximbank) and private banks. Countries receiving Eximbank loans were designated by the Pentagon but their identity was not disclosed to Eximbank and these loans became known as Country-X loans.

A January 1967 Senate Foreign Relations Committee staff study revealed the scope of these sales as exceeding $2 billion by 1967 and that the military assistance credit account was large enough to finance over $1 billion in additional arms sales at any time. All of this caused many congressional policymakers to object to Country-X program secrecy which they believed promoted regional arms races and diverted developing country capital from essential economic development programs. Passage of this legislation that year resulted in Congress imposing multiple restrictions on overseas weapons sales including ending DOD's military assistance credit account as of June 30, 1968. As consideration of this legislation began in 1968, the Johnson Administration separated the arms sales provision of annual foreign assistance legislation and submitted it as a separate piece of legislation.[11]

This administration then introduced H.R. 15681 to consolidate and revise foreign assistance legislation concerning reimbursable military exports on February 29, 1968 by House Foreign Affairs Committee Chair Representative Thomas Morgan (1906-1995) (D-PA).[12] Hearings on this legislation and its Senate companion S. 1872 were held by the Senate Foreign Relations Committee on June 12, July 14, and July 26, 1967. General foreign assistance topics addressed in these series of hearings included the Vietnam War and the use of multilateral aid agencies in distributing U.S. foreign assistance. Additional military assistance topics debated and discussed included whether U.S. economic assistance is a harbinger of potential military intervention; whether U.S. military assistance exacerbates regional and international conflict; if military equipment should be sold on credit, and numerous other topics.[13]

The House reported this legislation without amendment on July 3, 1968. In its report the committee emphasized that foreign military sales and assistance were important in fulfilling U.S. policy and that arms shipments should be controlled to discourage sales to countries which may seek this material for prestige, to reduce arms competition, and prevent spending that would divert a country's finite resources. This document also recognized that the U.S. had little control on arms sales since other countries participated in this market, that it was in the U.S.' interest to assist the internal security of developing countries so they could develop free institutions, and that having a controlled military sales program to replace grants of aid would be shortsighted.[14]

Additional floor amendments added to this legislation included limiting arms sales to less developed countries, military dictators, and countries seizing U.S. vessels in international waters; to recipients transferring such weapons to third parties; and selling missiles and jet aircraft to less developed countries except for allies like Iran, Israel, South Korea, and Taiwan unless the President considered such sales critical to U.S. security and reported it to Congress within 30 days. This legislation passed the House 312-29 on September 10.[15]

The Senate Foreign Relations Committee reported this legislation on October 9, 1968 without amendments. At least five committee members, including Chair William Fulbright (1905-1995)(D-AR), reportedly opposed the legislation and other committee members opposed to the legislation including Frank Church (1924-1984) (D-ID); and Wayne Morse (1900-1974)(D-OR) were campaigning for reelection and were away from Washington. The committee report recommending approval of this legislation was filed by Senator John Sparkman (1899-1985) (D-AL) and four other committee members and approved by the Senate October 10, 1968 by voice vote and sent to the President.[16]

Johnson signed this legislation on October 22, 1968. The statute stressed the need for international defense cooperation by the United States and its allies declaring:

> [I]t remains the policy of the United States to facilitate the common defense by entering into international arrangements with friendly countries which further the objective of applying agreed resources of each country to programs and projects of cooperative exchange of data, research, development, production, procurement, and logistics support to achieve specific national defense requirements and objectives of mutual concern.[17]

Specific provisions of this legislation included the Secretary of State, with presidential direction, being responsible for U.S. foreign military, economic, and food assistance and integrating these sales with other U.S. foreign policy objectives. Defense articles were to be sold to friendly countries for internal security, legitimate self-defense, and to allow these countries to participate in regional or collective arrangements consistent with the United Nations Charter to maintain and restore international peace and security. Recipient countries were required to pay for weapons from Defense Department stocks at their current market value within 120 days of delivery; that credit sales are authorized to eligible countries and international organizations as long as payment at market price occurs within ten years; that military sales may not exceed $296 million in Fiscal Year 1969; that the EximBank may not finance military sales to less developed countries after June 30, 1968; that the President transmit semiannual reports to Congress on such sales to less developed countries as well as forecasts of anticipated future sales and credit extensions.[18]

Challenges to U.S. export control policies toward Communist countries occurred throughout the 1960s. Some of this was due to controversy over the Vietnam War and the early beginnings of détente with the Soviet Union. These challenges were accelerated within COCOM by the desire of Western European countries to increase their trade with the Soviet bloc countries. Between 1961-1971 the value of exceptions granted to COCOM embargo exports rose from $3.4 million to over $75 million and the number of exceptions cases processed through COCOM increased from 142 to 635 per year during this time period.[19]

Debate over these exceptions could heighten strains within COCOM and tensions in the bilateral relationship between member countries. An example of this occurred in late 1969 between the U.S. and France. The French wanted to sell Poland a silicon transistor production line and the contract for this deal also included machines and transistor production technology that would be used in communications equipment which could be used for military applications that would be beneficial to Poland the Soviet Union. The transistor portion of this contract was valued at $2 million but was part of an overall joint Franco-Polish industrial venture whose value was $50 million. The Defense Department recommended the U.S. objecting to the French request based on the potential military potential of this technology and that recommendation became policy.[20]

Export Administration Act

The desire to ease export controls on commercial items with military potential was reflected with congressional passage in 1969 of the Export Administration Act (EAA). This act explicitly limited the export of goods and technology to those items that would be injurious to the United States.[21] Earlier evidence of U.S. easing national security controls came with the October 22, 1968 issuance of Executive Order 11432 which saw responsibility for controlling firearms and war implements transferred from the State Department to the Treasury Department with these being incorporated into ITAR.[22]

The State Department established the Bureau of Politico-Military Affairs on September 18, 1969 to strengthen its role in formulating international security policy, supervising security assistance and foreign military sales programs, and directing the issuance of arms control export licenses. This bureau's director was initially designated by the Secretary of State with rank equivalent to an Assistant Secretary of State. The Director would become a Presidential appointee, subject to Senate confirmation, and an Assistant Secretary of State on April 14, 1986. Within the Bureau of Politico-Military Affairs, the Director of the Office of Munitions Control (OMC) was given the authority held by the President to exercise the authority given in Section 414 of the 1954 Mutual Security Act to administer departmental export munition control responsibilities.[23]

The next major military export controls legislation which remains the general foundation for contemporary State Department and commercial military sales is the 1976 International Security Assistance and Arms Export Control Act (AECA).[24] This legislation sought to regulate commercial arms sales and the dangers they might promote military conflict while also seeking to enhance the U.S.' leverage over its arms export customers. Its passage came with considerable concern over the growing volume of U.S. arms sales with particular emphasis on Mideast countries such as Iran and Saudi Arabia who wanted to purchase Maverick air-to-air missiles and F-16 jet fighter planes.[25]

One section of this legislation declared U.S. policy should demonstrate global leadership in reducing international weapons trade, lessening the possible outbreak of regional conflict, and the burden of armaments. It went on to maintain that the President should initiate multilateral discussions among leading arms suppliers and purchasers and other countries to control the international arms trade. Congress particularly stressed its desire that the President should work actively with all nations to control the international sale and distribution of conventional weapons of mass destruction and encourage regional arms control agreements.[26]

Additional provisions of this statute imposed extensive reporting requirements detailing the estimated amount of arms sales to individual countries and how they would further U.S. foreign and national security policy interests and analysis of the relationships between expected arms sales to these countries and how such sales would relate to that country's arms control efforts and impact regional stability.[27] Additional reporting requirements in this statute required OMC to notify Congress of applications to export major defense equipment exceeding $14 million or defense articles and services exceeding $50 million before issuing licenses to these exporters. This law also made it illegal to export weapons without a license or making untrue or materially misleading statements in license applications with potential sanctions for such illegality including goods forfeiture, prohibition from obtaining future export licenses, and fines up to $1 million and maximum imprisonment of ten years.[28]

U.S. Munitions List and International Traffic in Arms Regulations

Section 38 of this statute also granted presidential authority to designate items considered as defense articles and services and promote regulations for importing and exporting these articles and services. These items are known as the United States Munitions List (USML) and can be found in Title 22 Part 121 of the Code of Federal Regulations which is part of ITAR.[29]

As mentioned earlier ITAR covers Title 22 Parts 120-130 of the Code of Federal Regulations (CFR). These are the regulations the State Department uses to enforce ITAR and their topical areas broken down by part with detailed subpart headings include:

- Part 120 Purpose and Definitions
- Part 121 United States Munitions List
- Part 122 Registration of Manufacturers and Exporters
- Part 123 Licenses for Exporting Defense Articles
- Part 124 Agreements, Off-shore Procurement, and Other Defense Services
- Part 125 Licenses for Exporting Technical Data and Other Classified Defense Articles
- Part 126 General Policies and Provisions
- Part 127 Violations and Penalties
- Part 128 Administrative Procedures
- Part 129 Broker Registration and Licensing
- Part 130 Political Contributions, Fees, and Commissions

ITAR regulations totaled 166 pages in the CFR as of April 2012.[30]

A detailed breakdown of USML, including parts reserved for potential future regulatory activity, includes the following itemization:

Part 121.1 featuring the following categories of weapons:

Category 1—Firearms, Close Assault Weapons and Combat Shotguns, e.g., fully automatic firearms to .50 caliber inclusive (12.7 mm), combat shotguns, silencers, and mufflers;

Category 2—Guns and Armament e.g., Guns over .50 caliber (12.7 mm) not limited to howitzers, mortars, cannons, and recoilless rifles, flame throwers; and kinetic energy weapons systems specifically designed or modified for destroying or mission-aborting targets;

Category 3—Ammunition/Ordnance e.g., guidance and control components including cartridge cases, bullets, or shells;

Category 4—Launch Vehicles, Guided Missiles, Ballistic Missiles, Rockets, Torpedoes, Bombs, and Mines e.g., missile and space launch vehicle powerplants, military explosive excavating devices, and non-nuclear rockets for warheads and guided missiles;

Category 5—Explosives and Energetic Materials, Propellants, Incendiary Agents, and Their Constituents e.g., specifically formatted fuels for aircraft, missile, and naval applications consisting of solid, liquid, or gaseous substances or mixtures of substances;

Category 6—Vessels of War and Special Naval Equipment e.g., warships, amphibious warfare vehicles, unarmored patrol craft, turrets and gun mounts, harbor entrance detection equipment, and naval nuclear propulsion plants;

Category 7—Tanks and Military Vehicles e.g., military railway trains, bridge launching vehicles, and amphibious vehicles;

Category 8—Aircraft and Associated Equipment e.g., helicopters, non-explosive balloons, drones, military aircraft engines, launching and recovery systems; and inertial navigation systems;

Category 9—Military Training Equipment and Training e.g., simulation devices, battle management simulation equipment, and components and software for training purposes;

Category 10—Protective Personnel Equipment and Shelters e.g., body armor, anti-gravity suits, diving suits, goggles, visors, shelters designed to protect against ballistic shock and weapons of mass destruction attack;

Category 11—Military Electronics e.g., electronic control equipment including active and passive countermeasures, command, control, and communications systems, and intelligence, surveillance, and reconnaissance systems;

Category 12—Fire Control, Range Finder, Optical and Guidance and Control Equipment e.g., fire control systems; gun and missile tracking guidance systems; and lasers;

Category 13—Auxiliary Military Equipment e.g., cameras and specialized processing equipment, Military Information Security Assurance systems and equipment, military cryptanalytic systems, and structural materials such as carbon and metal matrix composites;

Category 14—Toxicological Agents Including Chemical Agents, Biological Agents and Associated Equipment e.g., nerve agents, sulfur mustards, nitrogen mustards, defoliants, and equipment for detecting and preventing use of these agents;

Category 15—Spacecraft Systems and Associated Equipment e.g., remote sensing satellites, ground control stations for spacecraft and satellite telemetry, tracking, and control; and Global Positioning System (GPS) receiving equipment designed for military use;

Category 16—Nuclear Weapons, Design and Testing Related Items e.g., materials used to carry out and evaluate nuclear weapons tests, nuclear radiation detection and measurement devices with military applications

Category 17—Classified Articles, Technical Data, and Defense Services not Otherwise Mentioned;

Category 18—Directed Energy Weapons e.g., laser systems, particle beam systems; high-power radio frequency systems,

Category 19—Reserved;

Category 20—Submersible Vessels, Oceanographic, and Associated Equipment, e.g., swimmer delivery vehicles designated or modified for military purposes;

Category 21—Miscellaneous Articles e.g., anything not already listed in USML.[31]

Carter Administration

The Carter Administration came to power in 1977 with an acute concern over how U.S. arms exports might influence international conflicts and sought to address its concerns through various regulatory actions. A June 1977 ITAR amendment prohibited individuals leaving the U.S. from taking more than three weapons and accompanying ammunition with them without a license. This regulation was enacted because it was primarily used by non-U.S. citizens based on the concern that these weapons could be exported to countries where U.S. firearms are not licensed for export and that such transfers could take place multiple times per year and not promote U.S. foreign and national security policy objectives.[32]

An August 25, 1977 rule sought to strengthen the State Department's ability to impose civil penalties on those violating U.S. arms export laws. Authorities received by the department under this order included the ability to revoke, suspend, or amend export licenses without notice if this would benefit international peace and U.S. national interests and the authority to debar individuals from participating in the export license process if they have violated applicable federal laws and regulations.[33]

The late 1970s also saw the continued conflict between advocates of expanding U.S. exports of defense sensitive goods and technologies and those advocating continued restrictions on the exports of these technologies out of concern that they would benefit the Soviet Union and other U.S. enemies. The 1979 Export Administration Act (EAA) attempted to balance these concerns by minimizing uncertainty in U.S. export control policies and encouraging trade with all countries the U.S. has diplomatic relations with except where the President determines such trade is detrimental to U.S. national interests. It required the Commerce Department to maintain a commodities control list describing licensing administrations for exporting strategic goods and technologies. Another provision of this act confronted the emerging problem of state-sponsored terrorism by requiring a specific license to export critical goods and technologies to countries with documented records of supporting international terrorism.[34]

However, this time period also saw increasing concern over what was seen as a diminishing U.S. technological advantage in strategic technologies facilitated by significant Soviet bloc technological and espionage breakthroughs which enabled these countries to enhance their military technological capabilities with reduced research, development, and financial costs.[35] These concerns were reflected in a 1976 Defense Science Board report and a hearing that same year by the Senate Governmental Affairs Committee. The report recommended that U.S. export control should focus on specific product performance capabilities instead of commercial specifications; that the U.S. should only release technologies to non-allied, non-Communist countries technology it is willing to transfer to Communist countries directly; that U.S. actions and decisions should work to strengthen COCOM; and that key elements of revolutionary technology advances should only be released to COCOM nations and that if these nations transfer it to Communist countries they should be prohibited from receiving strategic technology.[36]

This report also introduced the concept of "militarily critical technologies" which sought to encourage export licensing authorities such as the State Department to focus on technologies most likely to deliver cutting edge equipment and information and on the military significance of equipment and expertise slated for potential export.[37] Some of these recommendations were incorporated into two 1977 EAA amendments which stressed restricting state promotion of terrorism, extending jurisdiction over reexports by the overseas subsidiaries of U.S. companies, and requiring export licenses to be granted for goods available without restriction from non-U.S. sources in significant quantities and of comparable quality to goods for which licenses were sought. An important piece of companion export control legislation enacted during 1977 is the International Emergency Economic Powers Act (IEEPA) giving the President the authority to regulate commerce in response national security threats by declaring a national emergency in response to unusual and extraordinary threats to the U.S. from these sources.[38]

Selected State Department Export Control Sanctions

OMC and its successor entities within the State Department maintain a busy schedule seeking to enforce U.S. military sale laws and punishing violators of those laws. In 1978, it initiated debarment proceedings against Olin Corporation for violating 22 CFR 127 of ITAR enforcing the Arms Export Control Act and provisions of Section 414 of the 1954 Mutual Security Act. Olin was debarred from defense export articles and technical data for 60 days except for exports to foreign governments under direct procurement contracts.[39]

During 1992, Japan Aviation Electronics Industry Limited (JAE) was charged with AECA and ITAR violations by transferring or causing defense articles, including gyroscopes, be transferred to Iran without State Department permission between 1984-1987. As part of the settlement, JAE agreed to pay a $5 million civil fine, received a one year debarment, and had to cooperate with the State Department to address its concerns about its noncompliance with AECA and ITAR.[40]

During 2010, charges were brought against XE Services LLC for committing 288 AECA and ITAR violations between 2005-2009 by engaging in unauthorized contacts with South Sudanese insurgent leaders. Specific charges included not being unable to account for 113 weapons in Iraq; failing to provide biographical information on defense force personnel assisting them from countries such as Canada, Kuwait, and Niger; providing unauthorized military training to individuals from Columbia and the Philippines; not ensuring that biometric data for Afghan nationals had been properly collected or vetted by the U.S. Government; and giving five unauthorized firearms to Jordan's King Abdullah during an official 2005 visit to the United States. Consequently XE Services was forced to pay $42 million in fines and take remedial compliance measures if it desires to continue having an export license, and that this consent agreement remains in effect for four years.[41]

Reagan Administration

The Reagan Administration's advent in 1981 witnessed renewed expressions of international U.S. assertiveness through the beginning of increased defense spending. It also witnessed the U.S. efforts to balance Soviet power by continuing a geopolitical balancing with China begun during the Nixon Administration. An example of this was reflected when ITAR was revised in late 1981 to remove China from the list of countries denied licenses and other State Department approvals for U.S. Munitions List exports. Arms exporters could now export military material to China on a case-by-case basis following a standard review process.[42]

The increasing influence of high technology military applications was reflected in a January 14, 1983 State Department rule proposing OMC gain export jurisdiction over very high speed integrated semiconductors specifically designed for military applications and possessing high-speed signal and image processing capability. This rule as adopted on June 23, 1983.[43]

Significant ITAR revisions also occurred during the Reagan Administration administration in the form of clarifying terminology; codifying OMC licensing policies and procedures; introducing new licensing requirement exemptions; establishing distribution agreement procedures; relaxing selected prior approval requirments; and strengthening controls by closing loopholes and improving enforceability. Specific examples of these changes include requiring Americans engaging in supplying defense services to foreign persons to register with OMC just like companies manufacturing and exporting defense articles and regularizing arrangements for warehousing and distributing materials abroad.[44]

Tension between the U.S. and allied countries and the desire of companies in allied countries to have greater independence in exporting came to head during the Reagan Administration with the Toshiba-Kongsberg affair in 1987. During the 1980s, the Japanese company Toshiba's subsidiary Toshiba Machine Company sold propeller milling machinery to the Soviet Union through Norway's Kongsberg company in violation of COCOM rules. This drastically increased the quietness of Soviet submarines and reduced Soviet research and development expenditures while enhancing the difficulty of U.S. submarines in detecting and tracking Soviet submarines in their often tense Cold War undersea rivalry.[45]

When this sale was revealed in 1985 it caused extensive political blowback in the U.S. with numerous investigations and congressional committee hearings.[46] Congress responded by enacting the Multilateral Export Control Enhancement Act (MECA) of 1988 as part of gigantic international trade legislation enacted that year. Specific provisions of this statute required the President to apply sanctions for two to five years against individuals violating COCOM munitions list rules if the violation substantially enhanced Soviet and East bloc technologies in submarine or antisubmarine warfare, ballistic or antiballistic missile technology, strategic aircraft, command, control, communications, and intelligence, or other critical technologies determined by the President and National Security Council to adversely impact the strategic military force balance.[47]

Toshiba/Kongsberg was sanctioned for three years by this legislation. Additional provisions of this legislation including extending such sanctions beyond the violating company to its subsidiaries, dependents, and predecessor and successor agencies and giving the Attorney General the civil authority to seek compensation from the violator and foreign government with jurisdiction over the violator. Congress specified that such compensation should cover U.S. and allied research, development, and procurement costs to counteract the technological advances the Soviets gained by this acquisition and the costs of restoring U.S. military preparedness. While such litigation would not be practical, the fact that it was included in this legislation reflects the deep anger by Congress and the Reagan Administration toward Toshiba and its affiliates.[48]

Such deficiencies in State Department munitions control activities were part of the often contradictory nature of U.S. export control policy between Commerce and State and the failure of both of these departments, at various times, to exercise due diligence in their export applications reviews. This was reflected in a September 1987 General Accounting Office (GAO)(later Government Accountability Office) assessment of the arms export licensing review process. Document findings included:

1. OMC approved about 90% of license applications it acted upon during Fiscal Year 1986 with 80% of these being acted on in less than a month; however;

2. Export license application data were not routinely checked for accuracy or veracity; OMC rarely requested U.S. embassies assistance in verifying the legitimacy of purchasers or other foreign parties to the sale; OMC did not use readily available information about exporters or others involved in commercial sales transactions who might need closer scrutiny; and OMC did not use U.S. Customs or Commerce listings of individuals and companies previously convicted of export law violations or denied export privileges;

3. OMC facilities and automated capabilities are insufficient for storing and quickly retrieving historical data useful in license application reviews including detailed data on prior export licenses cited by license applicants as precedents; and that the license application review process has been primarily manual instead of automated;

4. OMC procedures and systems are inadequate to ensure compliance with some administrative and reporting requirements including over 40% of export license applications sampled not containing information on political contributions and agents fees; and

5. OMC's caseload increasing from 26,000 in 1977 to over 49,000 in 1986, with an expected increase of over 52,000 in 1987 while its staff has remained at 30 during this period

with only 10 of these individuals authorized to approve licenses.[49]

George H.W. Bush Administration

The first Bush Administration witnessed epochal changes in U.S. foreign
and national security policy as well as events in its export control policies
which affected the State Department and other agencies. These events
included the collapse of the Soviet Union and its Eastern European satellite countries with many of these countries eventually becoming part of
the western alliance and the rise of the proliferation of weapons of mass
destruction as an international security concern. This last factor was most
vividly demonstrated by Iraq's attempts to develop an arsenal of these
weapons and by its August 1990 invasion of Kuwait which resulted in an
international military coalition driving the Iraqis from Kuwait during the
1991 Persian Gulf War. Controversy over the extent of Iraqi efforts to
develop these weapons would rage for the next two decades.[50]

These revolutionary events would also impact U.S. export control
policy and further complicate the relationship between those favoring
expansion of U.S. exports of sensitive technologies to promote the expansion of the U.S. international economic competiveness and those concerned with given advanced technologies to emerging hostile powers like
Iran and Iraq. An example of this tension was the Reagan Administration
receiving a June 1988 request from a Maryland company for an advisory
opinion on an export license for 500,000 to a 1,000,000 injectors for
atropine (an antidote for tabin and sarin nerve gases) for the Iraqi Army.
Stephen Bryen, a Defense Department official in charge of the Defense
Technology and Security Administration, told Congress in September
1990 that Iraq was the only country in the Mideast with nerve agents and
that it had used chemical weapons which would allow it to increase its
chemical weapons arsenal. Bryen went on to mention that it took him
three months to persuade State and Defense Department officials to oppose this company's export license application and that this company
eventually sold 400,000 injector atrophine kits to the U.S. Army in September 1990 to counteract the potential threat from Iraqi chemical
weapons.[51]

Consequently, the first Bush Administration would seek to transition
U.S. export control policies from stopping communism to promoting
antiproliferation measures. This policy shift had been given intellectual

sustenance by a 1987 National Academy of Sciences report which concluded U.S. export controls were not "rational, credible, or predictable;" that existing licensing and enforcement processes produced "conflict, confusion, and unbalanced policy;" and that subsequent export controls should focus on key technologies.[52]

The Bush Administration began transitioning to massive liberalization of arms export controls in February 1990. At this time officials from the Commerce, Defense, and State Departments told the International Economic Policy Subcommittee of the House Foreign Affairs Committee that they desired to expedite consideration of export applications and reduce the list of goods, including computers, whose sale to Eastern Europe had been restricted. In addition, OMC changed its name to the Office of Defense Trade Controls (ODTC) on January 8, 1990 and began reporting to the Under Secretary of State for International Affairs.[53]

These initiatives, however, would be overshadowed by Iraqi aggression against Kuwait in August 1990 and U.S. efforts to assemble and lead an international force to expel the Iraqis from Kuwait in the first quarter of 1991. On September 30, 1990 President Bush issued Executive Order (EO) 12730 which declared that unrestricted foreign access to U.S. goods, technology, and technical data, and the boycott practices of foreign nations and that these circumstances represented an unusual and extraordinary threat to U.S. national security, foreign policy, and economy. In response, this order sought to extend preexisting provisions of the expired 1979 EAA and that existing export control authorities possessed by the President and his delegates under AECA Section 38(e) remained in effect.[54]

Concern over the growing danger of the proliferation of mass destruction weapons lead to the Bush Administration's imposition of foreign policy controls on the export of dual-use equipment (having civilian and military applications) on technologies that can be used to produce chemical or biological warfare agents and technical data that can be used to produce the equipment for using these agents. Examples of equipment covered in this directive included pumps or valves designed to be vapor leak proof; thermometers of other chemical processing sensors encased in nickel alloy; toxic gas monitoring systems; biological agents detection or assay systems; and biohazard containment equipment.[55]

Following consultation with the Defense and Commerce Departments, the State Department determined in May 1991 that certain inertial navigation systems should be transferred to the Commerce Department for export control purposes and that this would be reflected in relevant USML sections.[56]

Yugoslavia's disintegration and descent into civil war during the early 1990s resulted in U.S. suspension of the ability of U.S. government agencies or companies to export defense articles or services to this country.[57] Continuing evidence of U.S. willingness to liberalize exports of sensitive technology was reflected in a September 16, 1991 *Federal Register* proposed rule announcing that certain kinds of lasers and image intensification and infrared equipment would be removed from USML Category XII.[58] Changing assessments of U.S. geopolitical, economic, and national security interests later in 1991 saw the State Department formally remove Chile, Czechoslovakia, East Germany (now part of a reunified Germany), Hungary, Poland, and South Yemen from ITAR sections prohibiting the export of arms to these countries. Some existing ITAR sanctions against South Africa were also eased as part this edict.[59]

During this period, the State Department also sought to improve the quality of its defense trade regulatory activities by establishing the Defense Trade Advisory Group (DTAG) on February 28, 1992. DTAG consists of up to sixty members appointed by the Assistant Secretary of State for Politico-Military Affairs and its membership consists of representatives from the U.S. defense industry, professional associations, academic and foundation personnel, and include appropriate military and technical experts. Its primary objectives include advising the Bureau of Politico-Military Affairs on its support for and regulation of commercial defense trade while reducing impediments to legitimate exports and protecting and advancing foreign policy and national security interests in accordance with AECA. Additional DTAG responsibilities include providing advice on commercial defense trade and technology transfer policy issues; regulatory and licensing procedures applicable to defense articles, services, and technical data; USML technical issues; and questions about carrying our AECA and ITAR.[60]

An additional significant example of U.S. export control liberalization during the first Bush Administration was the decision to remove most commercial Global Positioning Satellites (GPS) from the USML list unless such movement would jeopardize U.S. national security.[61]

Overall, the George H.W. Bush Administration achieved mixed results in its export control initiatives. Previous illustrations demonstrate that significant liberalization began in U.S. export control polices during this administration. It also sought to make weapons nonproliferation a key emphasis of U.S. national security policy as demonstrated by the 1991 *National Security Strategy of the United States* which favored augmenting existing export control regimes and expanding their membership while also developing new nonproliferation initiatives and strengthening export controls on sensitive technologies.[62] Although widespread international political and commercial consensus existed on the danger of exporting sensitive technologies to countries such as Iraq, Iran, North Korea, Serbia, and Syria, there was greater disagreement on specific controls to apply to these states including Iran. Additionally, key supplier states including Japan and the U.S. disagreed over whether China and the emerging Russian Federation were proliferation dangers.[63]

U.S. Government Evaluations of State Department Export Control Actions

Congressional oversight agencies such as GAO and congressional committees have and continue having divergent assessments on the effectiveness of State Department export control efforts. A 1983 GAO assessment was critical of four federal export control actions taken during the early 1980s under the EAA. These included 1981 controls of oil and natural gas exports to the Soviet Union in response to the December 13, 1981 martial law declaration in Poland; 1981 and 1982 export controls on Libya; and relaxing export controls on South Africa during 1981 and 1982. GAO revealed that formal contact with businesses on the impact of these actions on their interests did not take place; that businesses advised the Administration that the availability of alternative oil and natural gas suppliers to the Soviets consequently restricting the effectiveness of these export controls; that limited time for public comment on proposed export controls was allowed; that it was difficult to remove export controls once they were imposed; and that it was very difficult to quantify the adverse impact of export controls on U.S. companies reputations as reliable suppliers and concomitant adverse trade pattern structural changes.[64]

A previously cited 1987 GAO report recommended that the Secretary of State require OMC to use readily available information on parties involved in arms exports to help identify license applications requiring closer scrutiny, developing procedures and criteria for requesting U.S. embassies help in verifying license application information; and ensuring export compliance with verification and reporting requirements.[65]

A 1991 GAO report analyzed the quality of U.S. and international efforts to ban chemical weapons. This report found that in 1988 the Customs Service discovered that a precursor chemical used in mustard gas was illegally shipped to Iran and Iraq and that due to a lack of resources and agents to identify and deal with potentially toxic chemicals that this agency had essentially conducted no spot checks of dockside chemical containers to ensure their compliance with U.S. export control laws. This report also revealed that the State Department only reviews limited chemical export license applications, documented communication problems between the Customs Service and Commerce Department, and referenced a July 1991 congressional committee report recommending creation of a new federal agency with responsibility for administering all export licenses including munitions, dual-use, and nuclear items.[66]

Clinton Administration

The Clinton Administration came to office desirous of improving the U.S. economic position and its international economic competitiveness with particular emphasis on China's growing economic clout and the U.S. desire to enhance its penetration into this burgeoning market for U.S. exports. An assessment of historical U.S. export control policy described this administration's mindset on these issues as it began its tenure and the seeming convergence of viewpoints between policymaking officials and commercial interests desirous of expanding U.S. exports:

> For any administration, developing presidential policy to implement its grand strategy is not about choosing between national security and economic prosperity but how to achieve both. Regarding export controls, the Clinton   Administration followed the lead of its predecessors: Officials tended to see military security and economic prosperity as competing objectives. The demise of the Soviet Union and its associated military threat, however, offered President Clinton an opportunity to devise a grand strategy that could alter the fundamental relationship between those objectives. For U.S. commercial interests, the end of the Cold War paved the way for a radical reformation of export controls. If the United States removed the bulk of the controls, with market reforms in the former Soviet bloc already under way, leading U.S. manufacturers saw an unparalleled opening for new sales. With the election of President Clinton, many industry leaders perceived this as the most propitious moment to act. Consequently, industry lobbyists intensified their campaign to relax and streamline export controls.[67]

The dual desire to combat the proliferation of weapons of mass destruction and significantly expand U.S. export markets to advance U.S. security interests was reflected in the Clinton Administration's February 1995 *National Security Strategy of Engagement and Enlargement.* This document maintained that stemming the proliferation of weapons of mass destruction and their missile delivery systems was a critical United States priority and among the most important criteria in judging U.S. bilateral relationships with other countries. It also went on to maintain that the U.S. would seek to expand membership in the Missile Technology Control Regime (MTCR) to prevent the further spread of ballistic missile technology.[68]

This presidential document went on to emphasize that promoting U.S. prosperity at home and abroad was a central national security policy component; that U.S. exports would be boosted by reforming an obsolete licensing system by significantly liberalizing export licensing controls for computers, supercomputers, and telecommunications equipment; and expanding U.S. company access to international markets through bilateral, multilateral, and regional agreements with particular emphasis on Pacific Rim countries.[69]

The Clinton Administration's eight years would see considerable liberalization on the export control front and particular controversy over its decisions to license the exports of sensitive satellite technology to China given that country's increasing military power and the belief of many that it threatens or will eventually threaten U.S. national security. An early instance of Clinton's efforts to liberalize export licensing requirements was a July 22, 1993 document increasing license validity from three to four years and creating new exemptions from licensing requirements including exports under approved manufacturing or technical assistance agreements; spare parts valued at $500 or less; intra-company component transfers being sent abroad for assembly; temporary imports for repair and servicing; and items previously licenses for temporary export to trade shows.[70]

September 10, 1993 saw the Clinton Administration amend ITAR by moving remote sensing satellites, selected ground stations controlling these satellites, and relevant component parts and accessories from these satellites into USML Category 15 in an effort to reduce burdens on exporters by consolidating all spacecraft controlled under USML and giving the Commerce Department greater control over exports of these items.[71] The 1994 end of the South Africa's apartheid government resulted in an August 17, 1994 ITAR amendment enabling that country to import defense articles and services from the U.S.[72]

The growing influence of computer technology, including encryption, in U.S. national security and international trade policy was reflected in a September 2, 1994 ITAR amendment. This action gave U.S. encryption manufacturers the authority to ship products covered by USML Category 13(b)(1) directly to customers in approved countries without obtaining individual licenses for each end user. Exporters were now required to submit a proposed arrangement detailing specific items to be shipped and proposed end users and end use and countries to which these items are destined. Once ODTC approves this arrangement, exporters are permitted to ship specified products to end users in these countries based on a single license.[73]

1994 also saw the dissolution of COCOM which had served as the west's principal mechanism for restricting the export of sensitive technologies to the Soviet bloc. This event occurred with the concurrence of member countries and this organization was replaced by the Wassenaar Arrangement on Export Controls for Conventional Arms and Dual-Use Goods and Technologies (Wassenaar Arrangement) in September 1996. This organization and its 33 member countries places particular emphasis on exporting sensitive items to countries of concern such as Iran, Iraq, Libya, and North Korea.[74]

Thawing post-Cold War relations with the Russian Federation lead to the May 3, 1996 decision that it was no longer U.S. policy to deny licenses, other approvals, exports and imports of defense articles and services, destined for or originating in Russia with items on USML being reviewed on a case-by-case basis.[75] The evolving security situation in the former Yugoslavia saw ITAR amended on July 12, 1996 to allow U.S. arms exports to Bosnia and Herzegovina, Croatia, the Former Yugoslav Republic of Macedonia, and Slovenia while maintaining these sanctions on Serbia and Montenegro.[76]

1996 would also see significant liberalization in U.S. satellite export control policy which would eventually prove particularly controversial because it involved China. ITAR was amended on November 15, 1996 when hot-section technologies associated with commercial aircraft engines and commercial communications satellites were removed from USML and transferred to the Commerce Control List (CCL) which are administered by the Department of Commerce and has much more liberal licensing requirements than USML.[77]

A few days later, Clinton issued Executive Order 13026 moving encryption controls that had been designated as defense articles in USML Article 13 moved to the CCL unless it is determined that exporting them would harm U.S. national security and foreign policy interests.[78]

Growing Concern With China and Cox Report

Increasing exports of sensitive technology began to attract expanding concern from Congress due to uncertainty over China's long-term geopolitical aspirations and its attitudes toward U.S. security interests in the Asia-Pacific. Some of these concerns about China were reflected in the findings of a 1995 GAO report. This document found that between 1990-1993 the State Department had approved 48 of 85 missile technology export license applications to China worth approximately $523.5 million dollars and that the President had waived applicable sanctions to allow these exports. This document went on to maintain that export licensing controls for missile technology and dual-use export license applications could not ensure that U.S. exports to China are kept from sensitive end users; that the U.S. end-use check program monitoring license conditions has only been marginally effective for Chinese exports; that the State Department's Blue Lantern Chinese end-use check program is minimal and rarely monitors the end use of Chinese licensed missile technology exports; and that there is no consensus among U.S. government officials to assess the effectiveness of sanctions on China to prevent it from proliferating missile exports to other countries.[79]

These concerns and growing evidence of Chinese espionage at U.S. nuclear weapons laboratories lead the House of Representatives to create a select committee to investigate Chinese efforts to acquire cutting edge missile and national security technology from the U.S. Government and from private sector contractors such as Loral and Hughes. Chaired by Rep. Christopher Cox (R-CA), this committee's three volume report was released in 1998 and made a number of findings including:

1. China stealing design information on the U.S.' most advanced thermonuclear weapons;
2. Next generation PRC thermonuclear weapons would exploit stolen U.S. design information;
3. Chinese penetration of national weapons laboratories has occurred over several decades;

4. Security at U.S. nuclear weapons laboratories does not meet minimal standards;
5. U.S. satellite manufacturers transferred missile design information and technology to China without obtaining legally required licenses;
6. These technology transfers improved the design and reliability of Chinese rockets;
7. Foreign brokers and satellite and space launch insurance industry underwriters have obtained controlled U.S. space and missile-related technology outside of the system applying to U.S. satellite manufacturers.
8. U.S. technologies stolen by China have been proliferated to countries such as Iran, North Korea, Pakistan, and Saudi Arabia.[80]

This espionage was confirmed by other government reports and intelligence agency assessments. 1998 congressional legislation (Public Law 105-261) banned cooperative nuclear weapons stockpile stewardship activities with China and restored jurisdiction over commercial satellite sales to China to the State Department. Additional congressional committee investigations issued reports critical of Justice Department handling of the espionage investigations and Section 3146 of the 2000 National Defense Authorization Act (Public Law 106-65) required background checks on foreign visitors to national laboratories and imposed a moratorium on visits to these facilities by visitors from sensitive countries such as China until the Energy Department's Director of Counterintelligence, the FBI Director, and Director of Central Intelligence issued certifications about foreign visitors program security measures. Congress would eventually establish the National Nuclear Security Administration (NNSA) within the Energy Department to provide enhanced security at U.S. nuclear laboratories.[81]

As part of the blowback from Cox Report findings, commercial communications satellites were returned to the USML in March 1999 less than a year after the Clinton Administration initially removed them from the USML.[82] A final significant Clinton Administration ITAR amendment was implementing export controls initiated at the NATO Ministerial on May 24, 2000 in Florence, Italy. These reforms applied to NATO allies, Japan, and Australia and sought to streamline the export control licensing process; produce closer industrial links between U.S. and allied defense suppliers; promote interoperability with allies and friends in promoting trans-Atlantic defense industrial cooperation; and permit transferring technical data without a license to support procuring defense articles from defense firms within these NATO countries, Japan, and Australia.[83]

Clinton Administration export control policies, as applied to the State Department, achieved significant gains in expanding U.S. exports and liberalizing the nation's export control regime. It was less successful in promoting antiproliferation activities and failed miserably in protecting sensitive U.S. technologies from reaching hostile or potentially hostile forces such as China and transnational terrorist groups. The competition between promoting national security and expanding U.S. export trade would continue during the George W. Bush Administration.[84]

George W. Bush Administration

The George W. Bush Administration came to office after a contentious election and during its first months State Department policymaking on the export control front was essentially dormant. This changed with the horrific 9/11 terrorist attacks and the administration's responses with controversial military interventions in Iraq and Afghanistan. Targeting nations and groups supporting terrorism and weapons proliferation would become key components of Bush Administration foreign and national security policy and export controls would become key parts of the administration's antiterrorism strategy.[85]

The USA PATRIOT act was the government's first major statutory response to the 9/11 terrorist attacks. Its provisions provided the Treasury Department with expanded powers to track and seize the financial assets of those supporting terrorism; authorized the State Department to pay financial rewards to those assisting U.S. antiterrorism efforts, expanded penalties to those shipping or transporting biological weapons, and authorized establishing the infrastructure to more effectively track foreign terrorist financial assets.[86]

Ongoing concern over the quality of the U.S.' export licensing process and complaints about this process from the export industry were reflected in a December 2001 GAO report. This document pointed our numerous factors reducing this process' efficiency and causing delays including:

1. The State Department not establishing formal guidelines for determining the agencies and offices needed to review license applications;
2. This department lacking procedures to monitor license flow applications through the review process, an absence of guidelines on how long reviews should take, no requirements justifying lengthy reviews, no systematic checks on application progress; and hundreds of applications being lost and thousands delayed during Fiscal Year 2000 since no substantive review occurred;
3. While the State Department has hired new officers to decrease processing time, the planned business processing system upgrade must ensure a controlled and timely application flow and implementing an application tracking process mechanism.[87]

Missile technology proliferation was another export control issues of increasing concern during the Clinton and Bush Administration and it was also addressed in an October 2001 GAO report. This report revealed that the Commerce and State Departments had not clearly established which of them possessed jurisdiction for the approximately 25% of items the U.S. has agreed to control as part of its MTCR commitments; that one department claims jurisdiction over items not explicitly appearing on its export control list but appearing on the other department's list; that both departments disagree over how to determine which items should be controlled by Commerce or controlled by State; that interdepartmental consultations have been ineffective in determining which items are only subject to one department's jurisdiction; and that while it's generally illegal for State to authorize exporting missile technology and other items on USML to China it can be possible to export similar technology and items under the Commerce Department.[88]

The Bush Administration sought to balance its antiterrorism policies, export promotion policies, and overall U.S. export control policies through a variety or actions during its two terms. One area of activity was dealing with export control activities affecting U.S. universities and commercial companies since many of them conduct technology transfer and research collaboration with foreign counterparts and technology centers whose content may intersect with and even be in conflict with national export control policy. In March 2002, ITAR was amended to establish an exemption for accredited U.S. higher educational institutions from obtaining a license for permanently exporting, temporarily exporting, and temporarily importing most articles intended for exclusively fundamental research purposes under USML Category XV(a) or (e) covering space technology. Despite this amendment problems still exist with university compliance with U.S. export control statutes due to the large number of foreign students conducting science/technology research at U.S. universities, the failure of the State and Commerce Departments to conduct systematic assessments of risk vulnerability at these universities, and that these institutions believe that State and Commerce Department training in helping them follow export controls laws and regulations is insufficient.[89]

As part of its counterterrorism emphasis of identifying and seeking to sanction countries not supporting cooperating with its antiterrorism efforts and fulfilling AECA Section 40A requirements, the Bush Administration announced on May 15, 2002 that these countries were: Cuba, Iran, Iraq, Libya, North Korea, Sudan, and Syria.[90] Later that year, ITAR was revised to incorporate directed energy weapons into USML Category 18. These weapons were defined as items used to burn out receivers, disable electro-optic sensors, or intercept missiles.[91]

Organizational structural changes are common to many organizations as they seek to enhance their operating efficiency or respond to external pressures for better quality performance. This occurred in State Department export control policymaking when the ODTC became the Directorate of Defense Trade Controls (DDTC) on January 20, 2003. New organizational officials within DDTC were Deputy Assistant Secretary for Defense Trade Controls; Managing Director of Defense Trade Controls; Director, Office of Defense Trade Controls Licensing; Director, Office of Defense Trade Controls Compliance, and Director, Office of Defense Trade Controls Policy.[92]

A positive assessment of State Department progress in processing export licenses for biological and chemical commodities was made by the department's Office of Inspector General (OIG) in April 2005. In a review of 55 cases, OIG determined that DDTC adhered to its export licensing process; that it followed established export licensing policies and procedures for biological and chemical commodities; that it screened all license applications to determine that the application, commodity, country, and intended user were eligible to receive an export license; that DDTC tracked interagency and interagency referrals to ensure it received their responses in a timely manner and accepted respondents recommendations; and that DDTC personnel conclusions were fully supported by file documentation.[93]

The increasing hostility of Venezuelan President Hugo Chavez's government toward the United States and South American allies such as Colombia and its refusal to cooperate with U.S. antiterrorism programs, resulted in AECA section 38 being invoked to prohibit the export of defense articles and services to this country.[94]

An October 2006 State OIG report on DDTC licensing of sensitive technology exports to China and Hong Kong presented a more mixed appraisal. This report sought to determine if DDTC executed licensing policies by following established policies and procedures and reviewed the Blue Lantern end-use monitoring program. OIG found that while DDTC followed policies and procedures prior to issuing a license there were instances when its end-use checks, conducted before or after license issues, resulted in unfavorable determinations. This means that DDTC found derogatory, incomplete, or inaccurate information in the license application or violations of export control policies and procedures. Out of 12 end-use checks for Hong Kong during Fiscal Year (FY) 2004, three resulted in unfavorable findings with one participant possibly receiving the item before the license application was approved. In the other two unfavorable finding cases, a company received technical data without required DDTC registration and the DDTC's Licensing Division denied a license because the alleged end user was not the end user.[95]

Consequently, OIG expanded the scope of its investigation to review all 132 postlicense end-use checks DDTC completed during FY 2004 because such checks cover militarily sensitive items exported before DDTC conducted its indepth review. DDTC reported 19 unfavorable checks, including seven cases where their alleged recipient did not order the items and these particular cases included items such as aircraft C-130 cargo spare parts and gyroscopes. OIG also determined that DDTC did not have performance measures detailing how it planned to reduce and eliminate unfavorable end-use checks and recommended that DDTC establish such performance measures within 60 days of report issuance detailing benchmarks and timeframes for eliminating unfavorable postlicense end-use checks.[96]

An additional ITAR amendment reflecting the evolving nature of space industry technology was issued on July 17, 2007. This document sought to alter one of the performance characteristics defining radiation-hardened microelectronic circuits in USML Category 15. Specifics of this order emphasize that any microelectronic circuit specially designed, developed, configured, adapted, or modified for military or space application be incorporated into the USML and remain subject to ITAR licensing requirements.[97]

Testifying before Congress on April 24, 2008, the State Department's Acting Assistant Secretary for Political-Military Affairs Stephen D. Mull described Bush Administration accomplishments and challenges in administering U.S. defense trade control laws. He began by stating DDTC views its mission as giving allies what they need to fight with us during wartime, protecting our technology and capabilities from falling into hostile hands, and working with the defense industrial base to help them have the opportunity to be successful in a competitive global marketplace.[98]

Mull went on to mention that these three missions are often in conflict with each other but that DDTC works to carry out its responsibilities as conscientiously as possible. He went on to mention that the number of defense goods export applications had risen from 44,000 in FY 1998 to 79,000 in FY 2007 representing nearly $100 billion in defense trade. This application caseload increase produced a standing case log of 10,000 cases in FY 2007 with many of them being unresolved for over 60 days and as long as 100 days. At the time of his congressional testimony, Mull maintained that the case log had been reduced to 3,500 cases and that DDTC was in the process of instituting major reforms to achieve this improvement including closer consultation with the Commerce and Defense Departments, the business community, and Congress. He also stressed that President Bush had signed Presidential Directive 56 on January 22, 2008 giving DDTC the authority to institute business process reforms including a 60 day deadline for executing licensing decisions with regular monitoring; that there were fewer licensing restrictions on third-country nationals with whom there are pre-existing licensing arrangements; increased cooperation with the Justice Department has produced increased successful prosecutions of those violating U.S. procedures; the use of greater electronic applications processing; and negotiating treaties with trusted partners such as Australia and the United Kingdom to expedite defense exports to these countries.[99]

The Bush years also saw concern over proliferation of sensitive technologies to countries such as those mentioned in the beginning of this section and analysis of how it and Congress responded to these matters is reflected in a variety of literature and these same issues were passed on to the Obama Administration in 2009 which continues grappling with them.[100]

Obama Administration

The Obama Administration came to power in the aftermath of a severe global financial downturn which continues till the present. This administration continued making technical adjustments to ITAR to accommodate emerging technological and military developments. This was demonstrated by an August 6, 2009 ITAR amendment allowing individuals travelling to foreign countries where they need to wear body armor for personal safety such as Afghanistan and Iraq to be exempt from restrictions. Additional conditions of this exemption is that individuals using this body armor may not re-export it to foreign nationals, transfer ownership, or export it to countries where importing it would violate that country's laws.[101]

A key theme in any discussion of U.S. export control policy has been tension between those favoring liberalizing U.S. export control laws to promote international trade and augment the U.S.' export market and those advocating a more restrictive export control market to maintain the U.S.' national security position. This chapter has demonstrated numerous government reviews documenting problems with how the State Department administers its U.S. export control responsibilities. Each year, GAO issues an annual "High-Risk" report documenting government programs it believes at risk of abuse, waste, fraud, and mismanagement. The February 2013 edition of this report included "Ensuring the Effective Protection of Technologies Critical to U.S. National Security Interests" as one of its "High-Risk" programs making it the sixth consecutive time this was included on this list.[102]

GAO noted that the State Department and other agencies involved in this area of activity had reduced the time for issuing guidelines in commodity jurisdiction cases from 118 days in 2002 to 36 days as of July 2010 and that the Defense Department had improved its system of identifying military-critical technologies and coordinated with Commerce and State to establish guidance for developing and maintaining this system. Ongoing deficiencies noted in this assessment include:

1. Defense, Homeland Security, and State needing to improve internal and interagency practices for facilitating reliable ship-

ment verification, monitoring, and administering the foreign military sales program;

2. Agencies needing to eliminate gaps and inconsistencies in defense data exports collection systems used to monitor foreign military sales and direct commercial sales programs; and

3. Defense and State needing to develop and implement specific plans to monitor, evaluate, and report routinely on outcomes for projects providing weapons; defense critical technologies; and training to foreign governments to help them respond to global terrorism.[103]

The multiple agencies involved in administering U.S. export control policies have hampered the efficiency and effectiveness of these programs. A May 2010 GAO study on the arms export control practices of Australia, Canada, Germany, Japan, and the United Kingdom revealed that a single agency in each of these countries is responsible for regulating sales of arms and dual-use items and uses consolidated control lists to determine which export controls apply in individual cases. These responsibilities are handled within Australia by the Defence Export Control Office within the Australian Department of Defence; in Canada by the Export Controls Division within the Department of Foreign Affairs and International Trade; in Germany by the Federal Office of Economics and Export Control within the Ministry of Economics and Technology; and in the United Kingdom by the Export Control Organization within the Department for Business, Innovation, and Skills.[104]

2009-2011 Export Control Reform Proposals

Concern over these export control inefficiencies and security lapses has produced a renewed emphasis on streamlining and reforming the U.S. export control regime by the Obama Administration and Congress. On August 13, 2009 President Obama announced the beginning of a comprehensive review of the U.S. export control system which was followed in an April 20, 2010 speech by Secretary of Defense Robert Gates proposing a four-part approach to establish:

1. A single export control licensing agency for both dual-use and munitions exports;

2. A unified control list;
3. A single enforcement coordination agency; and
4. A single integrated information technology system including a single database of sanctioned and denied parties.[105]

An additional element of the Administration's export control reform was creating a revised and simplified USML consisting of seven categories:

A. Equipment, Assemblies and Components;
B. Test, Inspection, and Production Equipment;
C. Materials;
D. Software;
E. Technology;
F. Defense Services; and
G. Manufacturing and Production Authorizations.[106]

Specific administration plans for implementing these proposals included a multifaceted project involving the three phases. Phase I would see attempts to harmonize the CCL with USML and establish a tiered control structure allowing items to cascade from tier to tier as technology evolves. Control agencies would develop standardized licensing processes in this phase and an "Enforcement Fusion Center" would be established to synchronize enforcement and a single electronic gateway to access the licensing system. Phase II envisions implementing a harmonized licensing system with two identically structured tiered control lists. This could potentially permit reducing the amount of licenses required by the system; moving certain items from USML to CCL with congressional notifications retained; and consulting with multiple control regime partners on adding or removing multilateral controls on certain items. A new export system would begin in Phase III and feature a single licensing agency, two harmonized tiered control lists would be merged with review and updating mechanisms; a single licensing and enforcement IT systems, would become an operational and an Export Enforcement Coordination Center (EETC) was established by Executive Order on November 9, 2010 within the Department of Homeland Security.[107]

Continuing concern over the impact of U.S. space exports on national security was also reflected in Section 1248 of the 2010 National Defense Authorization Act requiring the Defense and State Departments to review U.S. space export control policy and include a risk assessment of removing commercial communication satellites and other components from USML. An interim May 2011 report by these departments maintained that removing commercial communication satellites from USML and transferred to CCL could be done with certain conditions without unacceptable national security risk.[108] ITAR was also updated on May 24, 2011 to permit the sale of certain weapons to Libyan insurgents fighting to overthrow Muammar Gaddafi's government in Libya.[109] 2010 Iran sanctions legislation saw an increase in the maximum fines that could be imposed for violating Section 38(c) of AECA concerning exports to Iran from $10,000 to $1,000,000 while also seeking to harmonize criminal penalties for exporting defense articles and services to this country.[110]

The House Foreign Affairs Committee held a May 12, 2011 hearing on this export control reform legislation. Committee chair Rep. Ileana Ros-Lehtinen (R-FL) criticized the scope and pace of the administration's proposed reforms maintaining that "a compelling case has not been made for the wholesale restructuring of our current system" while also expressing concern that proposed reforms would stretch existing export control system and personnel to a "breaking point." Such Republican skepticism toward Obama Administration policies in this and other areas and concerns over federal budgetary constraints make passage of significant export control reforms doubtful.[111]

On May 26, 2011 this committee's ranking member Rep. Howard Berman (D-CA) introduced H.R. 2004 "The Technology Security and Anti-Boycott Act" which seeks to comprehensively rewrite U.S. dual-use controls and give the President liberal and flexible authority to deploy controls to counteract current and future national security threats.[112] On June 3, 2011, Ros-Lehtinen introduced H.R. 2122 "The Export Administration Renewal Act of 2011" which would renew the currently expired EAA through 2015, amend other provisions of this act, amend AECA to permit differential control over USML parts and components, and increase the penalty structure consistent with existing IEEPA penalties. These proposals also stand against a background in which the 1979 EAA amendments expired in August 2001 and have seen the President use IEEPA as the statutory basis for U.S. export control policy since subsequent presidential administrations and congresses have been unable to agree on extensions to EAA or comprehensive export control reform.[113]

DDTC Statistics and License
and Enforcement Actions

DDTC is part of the State Department's Bureau of Political-Military Affairs and its consists of four offices: Management, Policy, Licensing, and Compliance. This latter office is responsible for administering internal civil enforcement actions, including charging letters and consent agreements, policies of denial, debarments, transition exceptions, and reinstatements to those violating munition export control laws. It also supports investigations and criminal enforcement actions conducted by Immigration and Customs Enforcement (ICE) and the Federal Bureau of Investigation (FBI). DDTC's budget for FY 2010 was $12.2 million; its staff was 81; it completed action on 82,094 export license applications, and its FY 2012 budget request is $11.3 million.[114]

Its website www.pmddtc.state.gov/ provides a variety of metrics and analytical reports on its activities. In July 2011 it received 6,622 cases; closed 6,545 cases; and had 4,006 cases open at the end of the month; and its average case processing time was 18 calendar days.[115] Numerous other publicly available reports on agency activities include congressional notification requests covering agreements involving the overseas manufacture of significant military equipment; a license for firearms exports exceeding $1 million; information on proposed exports of major defense equipment greater than $14 million ($25 million if involving NATO member countries, Australia, Japan, and New Zealand); and any other proposed exports of defense articles, services, and technical data exceeding $50 million ($100 million if involving the aforementioned countries).[116]

Additional congressionally required reports from DDTC include end-user reports from AECA Section 2778 describing the end-use of defense articles and services and related technical data exported with geographic and commodity type breakdowns through commercial channels and subject to State Department license approval as part of the Blue Lantern monitoring program which increased from 413 investigations in FY 2003 to 774 in FY 2009.[117] Another noteworthy DDTC information resource are Annual Military Assistance reports filed under AECA Section 655 covering the aggregate dollar value and quantity of defense articles and services authorized as direct commercial sales to each foreign country though they do not cover articles and service provided by the Defense Department's Foreign Military Sales program.[118]

Section 655 reports provide detailed breakdowns of commercial U.S. arms sales to individual counties broken down by USML category. For instance, the FY 2010 report reveals that 3,844,838 commercial military items and services with an authorized value of $2,774,097,786 were sold to Afghanistan. Key USML category breakdowns included Category III (Ammunition and Ordnance) featuring 3,700,163 items with an authorized value of $1,169,590; Category VIII (Aircraft and Equipment) featuring 13,896 items whose authorized value was $55,594,760; Category XI (Military Electronics) featuring 20,361 items whose authorized value was $9,436,444 and Category XII (Auxiliary Military Equipment e.g., cameras, concealment and deception equipment) featuring 44,187 items and an authorized value of $971,283,350.[119]

DDTC's website also provides information about its electronic license application system DTRADE, registration procedures, commodity jurisdiction information, the text of regulations and laws it enforces as well as the text of proposed regulations published in the *Federal Register*, Frequently Asked Questions, a list or individuals and organizations legally barred from commercial arms sales with accompanying *Federal Register* citations, country policy and embargo information, organizational structure information including the names and phone numbers of key personnel, and the text of defense trade treaties and implementation documents with Australia and the United Kingdom.[120]

It also features a link to a February 2011 Justice Department document detailing major federal export enforcement and embargo criminal prosecutions from 2007 to present including a February 1, 2011 indictment of Iranian citizen Milad Jafari who was charged with illegally exporting and attempting to export specialized metals from the U.S. to companies in Turkey to several Iranian entities that have been involved in ballistic missile activities. Another example of a recent federal prosecutorial action in this area was the January 27, 2011 sentencing of Yufueing Wei to three years in prison in Massachusetts for conspiring to illegally export to China military electronics components and sensitive electronics used in military phased array radar, electronic warfare, and missile systems. Wei's employer Chitron Electronics was fined $15.5 million.[121]

During 2012 DDTC received 85,188 export licensing cases, closed 86,314 of these cases, its monthly range of cases open at the end of the month ranged from a low of 3,525 in December 2012 to a high of 4,316 in July 2012, and its average case processing time fluctuated from 18-20 calendar days throughout this year.[122]

Conclusion

This chapter demonstrates that DDTC and its historical twentieth century predecessor agencies have experienced numerous successes and failures in attempting to regulate the export of defense articles and services to other countries. These successes and failures have occurred due to a multifaceted and multiagency legal and regulatory regime which has created often duplicative laws and regulations governing U.S. export control policy. This situation is exacerbated by the multiple congressional committees having jurisdiction over agencies having export control enforcement authorities and by conflict between agencies responsible for enforcing U.S. export control laws and regulations including the Commerce, State, and Defense Departments and conflict between these agencies and defense export industries and their association representatives.

Obama Administration proposals to streamline U.S. export control practices and policies may seem designed to enhance the quality of these programs. Their passage is unlikely in a severely constrained federal budgetary environment and in a highly contentious political environment between the Administration and congressional Republicans controlling the House of Representatives who are highly suspicious of any Obama Administration foreign policy initiative which can be portrayed as jeopardizing national security. This situation has been further exacerbated by the administration's controversial "Fast and Furious" program which allowed the export of guns to Mexican drug trafficking cartels and the September 11, 2012 bombing of the U.S. consulate in Benghazi, Libya.

Consequently, the status quo is likely to remain the norm in U.S. export control policy for the foreseeable future, despite the urgent need for significant reform and streamlining of an enormously complicated and bureaucratically dysfunctional process that does not assist U.S. export promotion or advance U.S. national security.[123]

Notes

1. See Public Law 74-479, "Neutrality Act," 49 *U.S. Statutes at Large,* 1081-1085; and Stuart L. Weiss, "American Foreign Policy and Presidential Power: The Neutrality Act of 1935," *Journal of Politics,* 30 (3)(July 1968):

672-695. This legislation was also influenced by the Senate Special Committee Investigating the Munitions Industry (Nye Committee) chaired by Senator Gerald Nye (1892-1971) (R-ND) hearings U.S. Congress, Senate Special Committee Investigating the Munitions Industry, *Hearings* 40 Pts, (Washington, DC: GPO, 1935-1936).

2. Joseph P. Smaldone, "U.S. Commercial Arms Exports: Policy, Process, and Patterns," In *Marketing Security Assistance: New Perspectives on Arms Sales*, David J. Louscher and Michael D. Salamone, eds., (Lexington, MA: Lexington Books, 1987): 185.

3. See Ibid., p. 186; and *First Annual Report of the National Munitions Control Board For the Year Ending November 30, 1936*, House Document 75-10, Serial 10126, (Washington, DC: GPO, 1937): 1.

4. Ibid., 5-6.

5. See *Sixth Annual Report of the National Munitions Control Board for the Year Ended December 31, 1940*, House Document 77-127, Serial 10581, (Washington, DC: GPO, 1941): 73; and Smaldone, 186.

6. See "United States v. Curtiss-Wright Export Corp. 1936," in *Judging Executive Power: Sixteen Supreme Court Cases That Have Shaped the American Presidency,* Richard J. Ellis, ed., (Lanham, MD: Rowman and Littlefield Publishers, 2009): 87-94; and 299 *U.S. 304.*

7. Smaldone, 187.

8. See Public Law 83-665, "Mutual Security Act of 1954," 68 *U.S. Statutes at Large,* 832-833, 848; U.S. Congress, House Committee on International Regulations and Library of Congress, Congressional Research Service, *Administration of Export Controls*, (Washington, DC: GPO, 1976); and *Foreign Relations of the United States, 1955-1957 Volume X: Foreign Aid and Economic Defense Policy,* John P. Glennon, Editor in Chief, (Washington, DC: GPO, 1989): 17-25, 118-119.

9. Smaldone, 188.

10. A large corpus of literature exists on COCOM including Frank M. Cain, "Exporting the Cold War: British Responses to the U.S.A's Establishment of COCOM: 1947-1951," *Journal of Contemporary History*, 29 (3)(July 1994): 501-522; U.S. Department of State, *Foreign Relations of the United States, 1969-1976 Volume IV: Foreign Assistance, International Development, Trade Policies, 1969-1972*, Bruce F. Duncombe, ed., (Washington, DC: GPO, 2002): 960-961; Public Law 82-213, "Mutual Defense Assistance Control Act of 1951," 65 *U.S. Statutes at Large,* 644-647; Tor Egil Førland, *Cold Economic Warfare: CoCom and the Forging of Strategic Export Controls, 1948-1954,* (Dordrecht: Republic of Letters Publishing, 2009); and James K. Libbey, "CoCom, Comecon, and the Economic Cold War," *Russian History*, 37 (2)(2010): 133-152.

11. See Public Law 90-137, "Foreign Assistance Act of 1967, 81 *U.S. Statutes at Large* 455-458; U.S. Congress, Senate Committee on Foreign Rela-

tions, "*Arms Sales and Foreign Policy: Staff Study*, (Washington, DC: GPO, 1967); and "Congress Approves Separate Arms Sales Measure," *Congressional Quarterly Almanac 90th Congress 2nd Session*, 52 (1968): 523-524.

12. *Congressional Record*, 114 (4)(February 29, 1968): 4759.

13. U.S. Congress, Senate Committee on Foreign Relations, *Foreign Military Sales: Hearing, Ninetieth Congress, Second Session, on S. 3093 to Consolidate and Revise Foreign Assistance Legislation Relating to Reimbursable Military Exports*, (Washington, DC: GPO, 1968).

14. "Foreign Military Sales Act," House Report 90-1641 (Serial 12795-4); (Washington, DC: GPO, 1968).

15. *Congressional Record*, 114 (20) (September 10, 1968): 26216-26231.

16. See *Congressional Quarterly Almanac*, 52 (1968): 524-25; and "Foreign Military Sales Act," Senate Report 90-1632 (Serial 12792-5); (Washington, DC: GPO, 1968).

17. "Foreign Military Sales Act", Public Law 90-629, 82 *U.S. Statutes at Large*, 1321.

18. Ibid., 1320-1328.

19. *Foreign Relations of the United States, 1969-1976: Volume IV: Foreign Assistance, International Development, and Trade Policies, 1969-1972*, 964.

20. Ibid., 914-915, 917.

21. "Export Administration Act of 1969," Public Law 91-184, 83 *U.S. Statutes at Large*, 841-847.

22. "Executive Order 11432 Control of Arms Imports," 33 *Federal Register* 208, (October 24, 1968): 15701.

23. See U.S. Department of State, Office of the Historian, "Assistant Secretaries of State for Politico-Military Affairs," (n.d.): 1; http://history.state.gov/departmenthistory/people/principalofficers/assistant-secretary-for-politico-military-affairs; Accessed July 26, 2011; and "Department of State Bureau of Politico-Military Affairs, Director, Office of Munitions Control: Redelegation of Authority," 35 *Federal Register* 63 (April 1, 1970): 5423-5424.

24. See Public Law 94-329, "International Security Assistance and Arms Export Control Act of 1976," 90 *U.S. Statutes at Large*, 729-769; and Smaldone, 189.

25. "Congress Declines to Block Arms Sales," *CQ Almanac,* 32 (1976): 253-256. For additional background information and debate on this legislation see U.S. Congress, House Committee on International Relations, "*International Security Assistance and Arms Export Control Act of 1976*," (Washington, DC: GPO, 1976); http://catalog.hathitrust.org/Record/003220332; Accessed July 27, 2011; and Ibid., *The Arms Export Control Act*, (Washington, DC: GPO, 1976); http://catalog.hathitrust.org/Record/003220393; Accessed July 27, 2011.

26. Public Law 94-329, 90 *U.S. Statutes at Large*, 734.

27. Ibid., 739.

28. See Peter Swan, "A Road Map to Understanding Export Controls: National Security in a Changing Global Environment," *American Business Law Journal*, 30 (4)(February 1993): 616; and Ibid. .

29. Public Law 94-329, 90 *U.S. Statutes at Large,* 744.

30. U.S. National Archives and Records Administration, *Code of Federal Regulations Title 22 Foreign Relations: Parts 1-299*, (Washington, DC: National Archives and Records Administration, 2012): 461-626.

31. Ibid., 471-495.

32. "Licenses for Export of Firearms," 42 *Federal Register* 124 (June 28, 1977): 32770.

33. "Administrative Remedies and Procedures," 42 *Federal Register* 165 (August 25, 1977): 42851-42856.

34. See Jere W. Morehead and David A. Dismuke, "Export Control Policies and National Security: Protecting U.S. Interests in the New Millenium," *Texas International Law Journal*, 34 (2)(Spring 1999): 173-186; and Public Law 96-72, "Export Administration Act of 1979," 93 *U.S. Statutes at Large* 503-536.

35. Swan, 618.

36. See U.S. Congress, Senate Committee on Governmental Affairs, Permanent Subcommittee on Investigations, *Transfers of Technology and the Dresser Industries Export Licensing Actions*, (Washington, DC: GPO, 1976); http://catalog.hathitrust.org/Record/002948072; Accessed July 27, 2011; and U.S. Defense Science Board, *An Analysis of the Export Control of U.S. Technology*, (Washington, DC: Defense Science Board, 1976): 21-22.

37. Swan, 619.

38. See Public Law 95-52, "Export Administration Amendments of 1977," 91 *U.S. Statutes at Large*, 235, 241; and Public Law 95-223, "International Emergency Economic Powers Act," 91 *U.S. Statutes at Large*, 1625-1629.

39. U.S. Department of State, Directorate of Defense Trade Controls, "Consent Agreement 1978: Olin Corporation," http://www.pmddtc.state.gov/compliance/consent_agreements/OlinCorp.htm>;Accessed July 27, 2011.

40. Ibid., "Consent Agreements 1992: Japan Aviation Electronics Industry Ltd.," http://www.pmddtc.state.gov/compliance/consent_agreements/OlinCorp.htm; Accessed July 27, 2011.

41. Ibid., "Consent Agreements 2010: XE Services LLC," http://www.pmddtc.state.gov/compliance/consent_agreements/XeServicesLLC.html; Accessed July 27, 2011.

42. "Revision of Controls on Exports of Munitions List Articles to the People's Republic of China," 46 *Federal Register* 239 (December 14, 1981): 60820.

43. See "Amendment of the International Traffic in Arms Regulations (ITAR)-U.S. Munitions List," 48 *Federal Register* 10 (January 14, 1983): 1758;

and "Amendment of the International Traffic in Arms Regulations (ITAR)-U.S. Munitions List," 48 *Federal Register* 122 (June 23, 1983): 28633.

44. See Smaldone, 197-198; and "Revision of the International Traffic in Arms Regulations," 49 *Federal Register* 236 (December 6, 1984): 47682-47712.

45. Swan, 640.

46. See U.S. Congress, Senate Committee on Banking, Housing, and Urban Affairs, Subcommittee on International Finance and Monetary Policy, *Toshiba-Kongsberg Technology Diversion Case*, (Washington, DC: GPO, 1987); and U.S. Congress, House Committee on Ways and Means, Subcommittee on Trade, *Legislation to Prohibit the Importation of Products Made by Toshiba Corp. and Kongsberg Vaapenfabrik Co.*, (Washington, DC: GPO, 1987).

47. "Omnibus Trade and Competitiveness Act of 1988," Public Law 100-418, 102 *U.S. Statutes at Large* 1107, 1364-1366.

48. Ibid., 1367-1369.

49. U.S. Government Accountability Office, *Arms Exports: Licensing Review for Exporting Military Items Can Be Improved*, (Washington, DC: GAO, 1987): 2; http://archive.gao.gov/d29t5/133904.pdf; Accessed August 5, 2011.

50. Assessments of these events include Lawrence Friedman and Efraim Karsh, *The Gulf Conflict, 1990-1991: Diplomacy and War in the New World Order*, (Princeton: Princeton University Press, 1993); Philip Zelikow and Condoleezza Rice, *Germany Unified and Europe Transformed: A Study in Statecraft*, (Cambridge: Harvard University Press, 1995); Arthur I. Cyr, *After the Cold War: American Foreign Policy, Europe, and Asia*, (New York: New York University Press, 1997); U.S. Congress, Senate Select Committee on Intelligence, *Report of the Select Committee on Intelligence on the U.S. Intelligence Community's Prewar Intelligence Assessments on Iraq Together With Additional Views*, (Washington, DC: GPO, 2004); and Graham S. Pearson, *The Search for Iraq's Weapons of Mass Destruction: Inspection, Verification, and Non-Proliferation*, (Houndsmill, UK: Palgrave Macmillan, 2005).

51. See Richard T. Cupitt, *Truman, Eisenhower, Bush, and Clinton Reluctant Champions: U.S. Presidential Policy and Strategic Export Controls*, (London: Routledge, 2000): 118-119; and U.S. Congress, House Committee on Government Operations, Subcommittee on Commerce, Consumer, and Monetary Affairs, *U.S. Government Controls on Sales to Iraq*, (Washington, DC: GPO, 1991): 34-37.

52. See Cupitt, 120; and Panel on the Impact of National Security Controls on International Technology Transfer, *Balancing the National Interest: U.S. National Security Export Controls and Global Economic Competition*, (Washington, DC: National Academy Press, 1987): 152, 161.

53. See John R. Cranford, "Administration Eases Stand on High-Tech Exports," *CQ Weekly*, (February 24, 1990): 575; and "Amendments to the International Traffic in Arms Regulations Part II," 58 *Federal Register* 139 (July 22, 1993): 39280-39281.

54. "Continuation of Export Control Regulations Executive Order 12730 of September 30, 1990," 55 *Federal Register* 192 (October 2, 1990): 40373. For an example of the trade boycott of Arab countries on Israel and U.S. efforts to combat this, see U.S. Congress, Senate Committee on Banking, Housing, and Urban Affairs, Subcommittee on International Finance, *Arab Boycott*, (Washington, DC: GPO, 1977).

55. "Imposition of Foreign Policy Controls on Equipment and Technical Data Related to the Production of Chemical and Biological Weapons," 56 *Federal Register* 49 (March 13, 1991): 10760-10761.

56. "Bureau of Politico-Military Affairs; Amendment to the International Traffic in Arms Regulations (ITAR)," 56 *Federal Register* 97 (May 20, 1991): 20320.

57. "Suspension of Munitions Export Licenses to Yugoslavia," 56 *Federal Register* 139 (July 19, 1991): 33322.

58. "Bureau of Politico-Military Affairs Amendments to the International Traffic in Arms Regulations," 56 *Federal Register* 179, (September 16, 1991): 46753.

59. "International Traffic in Arms Regulations; Amendments," 56 *Federal Register* 208 (October 29, 1991): 55630.

60. U.S. Department of State, Bureau of Politico-Military Affairs, "Defense Trade Advisory Group Terms of Reference," (2006) www.pmddtc.state.gov/DTAG/documents/reference_terms_06.pdf; 1-2; Accessed August 3, 2011.

61. "Amendment to the International Traffic in Arms Regulations (ITAR)," 57 *Federal Register* 175 (September 9, 1992): 41077.

62. President of the United States, *National Security Strategy of the United States*, (Washington, DC: The White House, 1991): 15-16.

63. Cupitt, 157.

64. "Statement of Allan I. Mendolowitz, Associate Director, National Security and International Affairs Division, Before the Senate Committee on Foreign Relations on Foreign Policy Export Controls," (Washington, DC: GAO, 1983): 1-12; < http://archive.gao.gov/d40t12/121773.pdf > ; Accessed August 3, 2011.

65. U.S. General Accounting Office, *Arms Exports: Licensing Reviews for Exporting Military Items Can Be Improved*, (Washington, DC: GAO, 1987): 4; http://archive.gao.gov/d29t5/133904.pdf> ; Accessed August 3, 2011.

66. See Ibid., *Arms Control: U.S. and International Efforts to Ban Chemical Weapons*, (Washington, DC: GAO, 1991): 11-13, 15; http://archive.gao.gov/t2pbat7/114972.pdf; Accessed August 3, 2011; and U.S. Congress, House Committee on Government Operations, *Strengthening the Export Licensing System: First Report*, House Report 102-137, (Washington, DC: GAO, 1991).

67. See Cupitt, 159-160; and Duncan L. Clark and Robert J. Johnston, "U.S. Dual-Use Exports to China, Chinese Behavior, and the Israel Factor: Effective Controls?," *Asian Survey*, 39 (2)(March/April 1999): 199-213.

68. See President of the United States, *A National Security Strategy of Engagement and Enlargement*, (Washington, DC: The White House, 1995): 13; Seema Gahlaut and Victor Zaborsky, "Do Export Control Regimes Have Members They Really Need?," *Comparative Strategy*, 23 (1)(January-March 2004): 73-91; and Dinshaw Mistry, *Containing Missile Proliferation: Strategic Technology, Security Regimes, and International Cooperation in Arms Control*, (Seattle: University of Washington Press, 2003).

69. See *A National Security Strategy of Engagement and Enlargement*, 19-21; U.S. Congress, Senate Committee on Governmental Affairs, Subcommittee on Federal Services, Post Office, and Civil Service, *A Review of Arms Export Licensing*, (Washington, DC: GPO, 1994); and U.S. Congress, House Committee on International Relations, Subcommittee on International Economic Policy and Trade, *Issues in Export Control*, (Washington, DC: GPO, 1995).

70. "Amendment to the International Traffic in Arms Regulations Part II," 58 *Federal Register*, 139 (July 22, 1993): 39280.

71. "Amendment to the International Traffic in Arms Regulations (ITAR)," 58 *Federal Register*, 174 (September 10, 1993): 47636.

72. "Amendment to the International Traffic in Arms Regulations" 59 *Federal Register* 158 (August 17, 1994): 42158.

73. See "Amendment to the International Traffic in Arms Regulations" 59 *Federal Register* 170 (September 2, 1994): 45631-45622; and J. Terrence Stender, "Too Many Secrets: Challenges to the Control of Strong Crypto and the National Security Perspective," *Case Western Reserve Journal of International Law*, 30 (1)(Winter 1998): 287-337.

74. See U.S. Congress, House Select Committee on U.S. National Security and Military Commercial Concerns With the People's Republic of China, House Document 105-851, (Washington, DC: GPO, 1998): 3:2-4; U.S. Congress, Senate Committee on Governmental Affairs, *The Wassenaar Arrangement and the Future of Multilateral Export Controls*, (Washington, DC: GPO, 2000); and *Non-Proliferation Export Controls: Origins, Challenges, and Proposals for Stengthening*, Daniel Joyner, ed., (Burlington, VT: Ashgate, 2006).

75. See "Amendment to the List of Proscribed Items," 61 *Federal Register* 87 (May 3, 1996): 19841; and Office of International Affairs, National Research Council, *Dual-Use Technologies and Export Administration in the Post-Cold War Era: Documents from a Joint Program of the National Academy of Sciences and the Russian Academy of Sciences*, (Washington, DC: National Academy Press, 1994).

76. "Amendment to the International Traffic in Arms Regulations," 61 *Federal Register* 135 (July 12, 1996): 36625.

77. See "Removal of Commercial Communications Satellites and Hot Section Technology from State's USML for Transfer to Commerce's CCL," 61 *Federal Register* 215 (November 5, 1996): 56894-56896; Frank Reynolds, *Managing Exports: Navigating the Complex Rules, Controls, Barriers, and Laws*,

(Hoboken, NJ: J. Wiley, 2003); and Matthew D. Burris, "Tilting at Windmills?: The Counterposing Policy Interest Driving The U.S. Commercial Satellite Export Control Reform Debate," *Air Force Law Review*, 66 (2010): 255-329.

78. "Executive Order 13026 of November 15, 1996: Administration of Export Controls on Encryption Products," 61 *Federal Register* 224 (November 19, 1996): 58767-58768.

79. U.S. General Accounting Office, *Export Controls: Some Controls Over Missile-Related Technology Exports to China are Weak*," (Washington, DC: GAO, 1995): 2-4; www.gao.gov/archive/1995/ns95082.pdf; Accessed August 4, 2011.

80. See U.S. Congress, House Select Committee on U.S. National Security and Military Commercial Concerns With the People's Republic of China, House Document 105-851, 1:i-xxxvii; Kenneth G. Weiss, "Space Dragon: Long March, Missile Proliferation, and Sanctions," *Comparative Strategy*, 18 (4)(October-December 1999): 335-359; and U.S. Congress, Senate Committee on Banking, Housing, and Urban Affairs, *Export Control Issues in the Cox Report*, (Washington, DC: GPO, 2000).

81. See Shirley A. Kan, *China: Suspected Acquisition of U.S. Nuclear Weapons Secrets*, (Washington, DC: Library of Congress, Congressional Research Service, 2000): 4-19; Public Law 106-65, "National Defense Authorization for Fiscal Year 2000, 113 *U.S. Statutes at Large* 953-971; and Public Law 105-261, "Strom Thurmond National Defense Authorization Act for 1999," 112 *U.S. Statutes at Large*, 2174.

82. See "Amendments to the International Traffic in Arms Regulations (ITAR): Control of Commercial Communications Satellites on the United States Munitions List," 64 *Federal Register* 54 (March 22, 1999): 13679; "Amendments to the International Traffic in Arms Regulations," 63 *Federal Register* 68 (April 9, 1998): 17329-17330; U.S. Congress, House Committee on International Relations, *Munitions List Export Licensing Issues*, (Washington, DC: GPO, 2000), http://purl.access.gpo.gov/GPO/LPS8616>; Accessed August 5, 2011.

83. "Amendments to the International Traffic in Arms Regulation: NATO Countries, Australia and Japan," 65 *Federal Register* 141 (July 21, 2000): 45282-45286.

84. See Cupitt, 201-209; Condoleezza Rice, "Promoting the National Interest, *Foreign Affairs*, 79(1)(January/February 2000): 45-62; and Ronald J. Sievert, "Urgent Message to Congress—Nuclear Triggers to Libya, Missile Guidance to China, Air Defense to Iraq, Arms Suppliers to the World: Has the Time Arrived to Overhaul the U.S. Export Regime?—The Case for Immediate Reform of our Outdated, Ineffective, and Self-Defeating Export Control System," *Texas International Law Journal*, 37 (1)(Winter 2002): 89-109.

85. See Stanley A. Erickson, "Economic and Technological Trends Affecting Nuclear Nonproliferation," *Nonproliferation Review*, 8 (2)(Summer 2001): 40-54; and President of the United States, "Continuation of Export Control Regulations," House Document 107-114, (Washington, DC: GPO, 2001); http://purl.access.gpo.gov/GPO/LPS15157>; Accessed August 5, 2011.

86. Public Law 107-56, "Uniting and Strengthening America by Providing Appropriate Tools Required to Intercept and Obstruct Terrorism (USA Patriot Act) Act of 2001," 115 *U.S. Statues at Large* 296-320, 364, 386, 389-390.

87. U.S. General Accounting Office, *Export Controls: Reengineering Business Processes Can Improve Efficiency of State Department License Reviews*, (Washington, DC: GAO, 2001): 1-2; http://purl.access.gpo.gov/GPO/LPS44344>; Accessed August 5, 2011.

88. Ibid., *Export Controls: Clarification of Jurisdiction for Missile Technology Items Needed*, (Washington, DC: GAO, 2001): 2; http://purl.access.gpo.gov/GPO/LPS46638; Accessed August 5, 2011.

89. See "International Traffic in Arms Regulations; Exemptions for U.S. Institutions of Higher Learning," 67 *Federal Register* 61 (March 29, 2002): 15099; Genevieve Johanna Knezo, *Counter Terrorism: Impacts on Research, Development, and Higher Education*, (Hauppauge, NY: Novinka Books, 2002); U.S. Department of State and the Broadcasting Board of Governors Office of Inspector General, *Review of Export Controls for Foreign Persons Employed at Companies and Universities*, (Washington, DC: Department of State, 2004); http://oig.state.gov/documents/organization/104036.pdf; Accessed August 5, 2011; and U.S. Government Accountability Office, *Export Controls: Agencies Should Assess Vulnerabilities and Improve Guidance for Protecting Export-Controlled Information at Universities*, (Washington, DC: GAO, 2006): 3-4; http://purl.access.gpo.gov/GPO/LPS77457; Accessed August 5, 2011.

90. "Determination and Certification Under Section 40A of the Arms Export Control Act," 67 *Federal Register* 99 (May 22, 2002): 36062.

91. See "Amendment to the International Traffic in Arms Regulations; United States Munitions List," 67 *Federal Register* 182 (September 19, 2002): 58984-58985; Doug Beason, *The E-Bomb: How America's New Directed Energy Weapons Will Change the Way Future Wars Will Be Fought*, (Cambridge, MA: Da Capo Press, 2005); and U.S. Defense Science Board, *Defense Science Board Task Force on Directed Energy Weapons*, (Washington, DC: Office of the Undersecretary of Defense for Acquisition, Technology, and Logistics, 2007); http://purl.access.gpo.gov/GPO/LPS91811; Accessed August 5, 2011.

92. "Bureau of Political-Military Affairs; Amendment to the International Traffic in Arms Regulations," 68 *Federal Register* 31 (February 14, 2003): 7417-7418.

93. U.S. Department of State and the Broadcasting Board of Governors Office of Inspector General, *Report of Audit: Export Licensing of Chemical and Biological Commodities,* (Washington, DC: Department of State, 2005): 7;

http://oig.state.gov/documents/organization/126942.pdf>; Accessed August 5, 2011.

94. See "Bureau of Political-Military Affairs: Revocation of Defense Export Licenses to Venezuela," 71 *Federal Register* 159 (August 17, 2006): 47554, Ibid., *A Review of U.S. Policy Toward Venezuela November 2001-April 2002*, (Washington, DC: Department of State, 2002); <http://oig.state.gov/documents/organization/13682.pdf>; Accessed August 5, 2011; U.S. Congress, House Committee on International Relations, Subcommittee on the Western Hemisphere, *Democracy in Venezuela*, (Washington, DC: GPO, 2006); <http://purl.access.gpo.gov/GPO/LPS72914>; Accessed August 5, 2011; and U.S. Congress, House Committee on International Relations, Subcommittee on International Terrorism and Nonproliferation, *Venezuela: Terrorism Hub of South America?*, (Washington, DC: GPO, 2006); <http://purl.access.gpo.gov/GPO/LPS74890>; Accessed August 5, 2011.

95. U.S. Department of State and Broadcasting Board of Governors Office of Inspector General, *Review of Export Controls,* (Washington, DC: Department of State, 2006): 1-2; <http://oig.state.gov/documents/organization/104037.pdf>; Accessed August 5, 2011.

96. Ibid., 2.

97. "Amendment to the International Traffic in Arms Regulations: United States Munitions List," 72 *Federal Register* 136 (July 17, 2007): 39010.

98. U.S. Congress, Senate Committee on Homeland Security and Governmental Affairs, Subcommittee on Oversight of Government Management, the Federal Workforce, and the District of Columbia, *Beyond Control: Reforming Export Licensing Agencies for National Security and Economic Interests*, (Washington, DC: GPO, 2009): 5; http://purl.access.gpo.gov/GPO/LPS115037; Accessed August 5, 2011.

99. See Ibid., 5-6; and U.S. Department of State, "D&CP-Political-Military Affairs: Resource Summary," (n.d.): 117-118; <www.state.gov/documents/organization/123563.pdf; Accessed August 5, 2011.

100. See U.S. Congress, Senate Committee on Governmental Affairs, Subcommittee on International Security, Proliferation, and Federal Services, *Russia and China: Non-Proliferation Concerns and Export Controls*, (Washington, DC: GPO, U.S. Congress, House Committee on Foreign Affairs, Subcommittee on Terrorism, Nonproliferation, and Trade, *Export Controls: Are We Protecting Security and Facilitating Exports?*, (Washington, DC: GPO, 2007); U.S. National Research Council, *Beyond "Fortress America": National Security Controls on Science and Technology in a Globalized World*, (Washington, DC: National Academies Press, 2009); and U.S. Congress, House Committee on Foreign Affairs, *Nuclear Cooperation and Non-Proliferation after Khan and Iran: Are Asking Enough of Current and Future Agreements?*, (Washington, DC: GPO, 2010).

101. "Amendment to the International Traffic in Arms Regulations: Temporary Export Exemption for Body Armor," 74 *Federal Register* 150 (August 6, 2009): 39312-39213.

102. U.S. Government Accountability Office, "High-Risk Series: An Update," (Washington, DC: GAO, 2013): 192; http://www.gao.gov/assets/660/652133.pdf; Accessed March 4, 2013. From p. 232.

103. Ibid., 193.

104. Ibid., *Export Controls: Observations on Selected Countries' Systems and Proposed Treaties*, (Washington, DC: GAO, 2010): 8-9; www.gao.gov/new.items/d10557.pdf; Accessed August 8, 2011.

105. See Ian F. Ferguson and Paul K. Kerr, *The U.S. Export Control System and the President's Reform Initiative*, (Washington, DC: Library of Congress, Congressional Research Service, 2011): 1-2. A more detailed overview of Obama Administration export control initiatives can be found at http://export.gov/ecr/>; Accessed August 9, 2011.

106. "Revisions to the United States Munitions List," 75 *Federal Register* 237 (December 10, 2010): 76935, 76937.

107. See Ferguson and Kerr, 10; and "Executive Order 13558 of November 9, 2010: Export Enforcement Coordination Center," 75 *Federal Register* 219, (November 15, 2010): 69573-69574.

108. See Public Law 111-84, "National Defense Authorization Act for Fiscal Year 2010," 123 *U.S. Statutes at Large* 2546-2547; Fergusson and Kerr, 15; and U.S. Departments of Defense and State, *Report to Congress: Section 1248 of the National Defense Authorization Act for Fiscal Year 2010 (Public Law 111-84) Risk Assessment of United States Space Export Control Policy*, (Washington, DC: Departments of Defense and State, 2011); http://www.defense.gov/home/features/2011/0111_nsss/docs/1248_Report_Space_Export_Control.pdf; Accessed January 29, 2013.

109. "Amendment to the International Traffic in Arms Regulations: Libya," 76 *Federal Register* 100 (May 24, 2011): 30001.

110. Public Law 111-95, "Comprehensive Iran Sanctions, Accountability, and Divestment Act of 2010," 124 *U.S. Statutes at Large*, 1337.

111. U.S. Congress, House Committee on Foreign Affairs. *Export Controls, Arms Sales, and Reform: Balancing U.S. Interests, Part I,* (Washington, DC: GPO, 2011): 2.

112. H.R. 2004, 112th Congress, 1st Session, "Technology Security and Anti-Boycott Act," (2011): 18.

113. See H.R. 2122, 112th Congress, 1st Session, "Export Administration Renewal Act of 2011," and Ferguson and Kerr, 2-3, 20-22.

114. Fergusson and Kerr, 6-7.

115. U.S. Department of State, Directorate of Defense Trade Controls, "License Processing Times," (2011): 1; <http://www.pmddtc.state.gov/metrics/index.html>; Accessed August 9, 2011.

116. Ibid., "Directorate of Defense Trade Controls: Congressional Notifi-cations, (2011): 1; www.pmddtc.state.gov/reports/intro_conghotify.html; Accessed August 9, 2011.

117. Ibid., "End-Use Monitoring of Defense Articles and Defense Services Commercial Exports FY 2009," (2010): 4; www.pmddtc.state.gov/reports/documents/End_Use_FY_2009.pdf; Accessed August 9, 2011.

118. Ibid., "Section 655 Annual Military Assistance Reports," (2011): 1; http://www.pmddtc.state.gov/reports/655_intro.html; Accessed August 9, 2011.

119. Ibid., "Unclassified Report by the Department of State Pursuant to Section 655 of the Foreign Assistance Act, As Amended Direct Commercial Sales Authorizations for Fiscal Year 2010, (2010): 1; www.pmddtc.state.gov/report/documents/rpt655_FY10.pdf; Accessed August 9, 2011.

120. Ibid., www.pmddtc.state.gov/; Accessed August 9, 2011.

121. Ibid., and U.S. Department of Justice, National Security Division, "Summary of Major U.S. Export Enforcement and Embargo Criminal Prosecutions: 2007 to the Present,: (Washington, DC: U.S. Dept. of Justice, National Security Division, February 2011): 1-2; www.pmddtc.state.gov/compliance/documents/OngoingExportCaseFactSheet.pdf; Accessed August 9, 2011.

122. U.S. Department of State, Directorate of Defense Trade Controls, *License Processing Times*, (2013); 1; http://www.pmddtc.state.gov/metrics/; Accessed January 3, 2013.

123. See Burris (2010); Stephen Rademaker, "The Role of Export Controls in Non-Proliferation Strategy," *International Affairs: A Russian Journal of World Politics, Diplomacy, & International Relations*, 50 (6)(December 2004): 29-33; Michael J. Noble, "Export Controls and United States Space Power," *Astropolitics*, 6 (3)(2008): 251-312; Dean Cheng, "Export Controls and the Hard Case of China," (Washington, DC: Heritage Foundation, 2010): http://www.heritage.org/Research/Reports/2010/12/Export-Controls-and-the-Hard-Case-of-China>; Accessed August 10, 2011; Mark Bromley and Paul Holton, "The International Arms Trade: Difficult to Define, Measure, and Control," *Arms Control Today*, 40 (6)(July-August 2010): 8-14; and U.S. Congress, House Committee on Foreign Affairs, Subcommittee on Terrorism, Nonproliferation and Trade, *Transshipment and Diversion: Are U.S. Trading Partners Doing Enough to Prevent the Spread of Dangerous Technologies?*, (Washington, DC: GPO, 2010); http://purl.fdlp.gov/GPO/gpo2627; for divergent assessments on the complicated present and future of U.S. defense export controls. For information on Operation Fast and Furious see U.S. Congress, House Committee on Oversight and Government Reform, *Operation Fast and Furious: The Other Side of the Border*, (Washington, DC: GPO, 2012); http://purl.fdlp.gov/GPO/gpo19478; Accessed January 29, 2013.

Chapter 5

Treasury Department

Monitoring financial aspects of export control and the international transfer of money between countries and transnational organizations is a major factor in U.S. and international export control policymaking. The U.S. Treasury Department plays multiple roles in this area and its Office of Foreign Assets Control (OFAC) is the primary player involved in this aspect of U.S. policymaking.

Throughout its history the U.S. has periodically sought to use export controls such as trade embargoes to economically punish offending nations or groups with mixed results. During the War of 1812, President James Madison (1751-1836) ordered a prohibition on exports with Britain. The embargo proved to be extremely unpopular in New England which had long-standing trading relationships with British North America and the British isles and ultimately proved ineffective.[1] During World War I, the Trading with the Enemy Act (TEA) was enacted in 1917 which sought to prevent providing materials to benefit other countries warfighting capabilities including military supplies, clothing and food, and financial assets including trade and credit.[2]

The Treasury Department has always played a key role in administering U.S. international economic policy and World War II's outbreak increased U.S. desires to use its significant international economic leverage to punish those perpetrating this conflict. On April 10, 1940 Executive Order (EO) 8389 established the Office of Foreign Funds Control (OFFC) within Treasury under TEA authority. OFFC received the authority to administer wartime import controls over enemy assets including freezing Danish and Norwegian financial assets in the U.S., restrict trade with these German occupied countries, administered the Proclaimed List of Certain Blocked Nationals ("Black List"), and took censuses of foreign-owned assets in the U.S. and U.S.-owned assets overseas.[3]

OFFC functions were transferred to Treasury's Office of Alien Property in July 10, 1947 before being transferred to the Division of Foreign Assets Control within the Office of International Finance on December 17, 1950 to administer controls over Chinese and North Korean financial assets frozen following Chinese intervention in the Korean War.[4] The modern organization of the Treasury Department's export control responsibilities begins with the October 15, 1962 establishment of the Office of Foreign Assets Control (OFAC) by Treasury Department order.[5]

OFAC responsibilities include administering and enforcing economic and trade sanctions based on U.S. foreign policy and national security goals against targeted foreign countries and regimes, terrorists, international narcotics traffickers, those proliferating weapons of mass destruction (WMD), and other threats to the U.S. economy, foreign policy, and national security. OFAC acts under presidential national emergency powers such as the International Emergency Economic Powers Act (IEEPA) and authority granted by specific legislation to impose transaction controls and freeze assets under U.S. jurisdiction. Many of these sanctions are based on United Nations and other international mandates, are multilateral in scope, and involve close cooperation with allied governments Other U.S. legislation enforced by OPAC includes TEA, the 1996 Antiterrorism and Effective Death Penalty Act, the 2001 USA PATRIOT Act, and legislation targeting countries such as Cuba, Iran, North Korea, and Syria.[6]

The quality of OFAC policies has achieved mixed success and their level of legal propriety has been the subject of controversy and critical analysis. Some analyses contend that financial sanctions against countries are more likely to be effective if done multilaterally instead of unilaterally by countries such as the U.S. There is also debate over whether economic sanctions targeting the financial interests of countries or groups promoting terrorism or seeking to acquire WMD is effective. Legal criticisms of sanctions levied by OFAC contend that such sanctions deprive targeted individuals or organizations of due process by labeling them as supporters of terrorism, that appealing these designations requires targeted parties to directly appeal to OPAC without having the right to review OFAC gathered evidence and that courts have generally sided with OFAC actions pursuant to the Administrative Procedures Act and deferred to executive branch foreign and national security policy decisions. The costs of sanctions on U.S. companies and industries must also be considered as globalization makes it easier for foreign competitors to enter trading and financial markets closed off by U.S. sanctions.[7]

OFAC has imposed selected economic sanctions against foreign countries and terrorists in the decades preceding the 1990s although its use of such sanctions has accelerated considerably since the mid-1990s. On February 5, 1965, OFAC adopted regulations prohibiting transactions involving shipments between various foreign Communist countries and individuals within the U.S. if such items are on the Commerce Department's Commodity Control List.[8] On August 14, 1969, OFAC allowed U.S. citizens possessing valid passports traveling to China to conduct routine financial transactions such as acquiring items for living expenses, purchasing certain goods to import to the U.S., and journalists working in China were given permission to transmit news-related items to the U.S. These liberalizations did not cover transactions blocked by existing export control regulations.[9]

Enforcing the Cuban Trade Embargo has been a significant OFAC responsibility since 1963. This policy has undergone various modifications in its history and July 1974 amendments to it prohibited unlicensed U.S. nationals from purchasing, transporting, or dealing in Cuban origin commodities outside the U.S. This action also allowed U.S. educational and research institutions to import Cuban origin books and related materials on an exchange basis and allowed scholars holding U.S. passports to travel to Cuba for study and research purposes.[10] The 1975 collapse of the South Vietnamese government to communist North Vietnam represented the end of America's controversial involvement in that conflict. It also saw the U.S. block financial assets of South Vietnam and Cambodia from being used by the newly unified Vietnamese government.[11]

On November 4, 1979, Iranian-supported terrorists seized control of the U.S. Embassy in Tehran precipitating a hostage crisis that would last until the diplomatic personnel were released on January 20, 1981. It also heralded the beginning of diplomatic enmity and the first round of U.S. sanctions against Tehran for its policies which have continued until the present despite the presence of loopholes in these sanctions for commodities such as tobacco. OFAC responded by freezing Iranian assets in the U.S. and implementing EO 12170 on November 14, 1979. Penalties for violating this order included up to a $10,000 fine for individual violators and $50,000 fine and up to ten years imprisonment for any corporate violator.[12]

OFAC also begin regularly publishing a list of Specially Designated Nationals (SDN)'s listing individuals and organizations whose property is blocked due to violating U.S. laws on conducting business with prohibited individuals, countries, and organizations in December 1986 due to their activities in areas such as narcotics trafficking, terrorism promotion, and proliferating weapons of mass destruction. U.S. individuals and financial institutions and nonbank subsidiaries are prohibited from dealing with SDN individuals and institutions unless authorized by OFAC.[13] The SDN list is 545 pages long as of October 4, 2012, consists of thousands of proscribed individuals and organizations, and is a critical reference source for understanding U.S. economic sanctions and export control policies because it also includes categories of export violations such as aircraft and vessels.

Examples of entries from the current SDN, their charged offense, and relevant U.S. administrative law provisions from the Code of Federal Regulations (CFR) include:

- 3MG (a.k.a. Mizan Machine Manufacturing Group), Box 16595-365, Tehran, Iran [NPWMD]. NPWMD refers to a violator of Weapons of Mass Destruction Proliferations Sanctions Regulations 31 CFR Part 544.
- 101 Days Campaign (a.k.a. Charity Coalition; . . . P.O. Box 136301, Jeddah 21313, Saudia Arabia [SDGT]. SDGT refers to a violator of Global Terrorism Sanctions Regulations 31 CFR Part 594.
- AA Trading FZCO, P.O. Box 37089, Dubai, United Arab Emirates [SDNTK]. SDNTK refers to a violator of Foreign Narcotics Kingpin Sanctions Regulations 31 CFR Part 598.
- ALCO (a.k.a. Beijing Alite Technologies Co., Ltd.,12A Beisanhuan Zhong Road, P.O. Box 342, Beijing, China; and all other locations worldwide [NPWMD].[14]

The emergence of Islamist terrorist movements such as Al Qaeda and the Taliban would cause the U.S. to place increased emphasis on using OFAC authorities to target the financial infrastructure of terrorist groups as an arsenal of U.S. export control policy. The 1996 Antiterrorism & Effective Death Penalty Act expanded U.S. power to prevent individuals in the U.S. and subject to U.S. jurisdiction from giving material support or resources to foreign organizations engaging in terrorist activities. Provisions of this statute gave the Treasury Department authority to require U.S. financial institutions holding or controlling assets of foreign organizations involved in supporting terrorism to block all financial transactions involving these assets; penalize individuals or organizations assisting or attempting to materially assist foreign terrorist organizations with up to 10 years imprisonment and civil penalties of $50,000 per violation; granted presidential authority to use covert and overt means to disrupt, dismantle, and destroy international terrorist infrastructures; and prohibit economic and military assistance to countries providing assistance to terrorism supporting states and not fully cooperating with U.S. antiterrorism efforts as determined by the State Department.[15]

Legislation passed that same year saw Congress enact further nonproliferation and antiterrorism sanctions against Iran and Libya whose financial provisions included restricting annual investments of over $40 million to help those countries petroleum industries and directing the Export-Import Bank to not provide financial assistance to individuals sanctioned for violating this act.[16] On July 4, 1999, President Clinton signed (EO) 13129 declaring Afghanistan's sheltering of Osama bin Laden (1957-2011) and Al Qaeda constituted a national emergency and an extraordinary threat to U.S. foreign policy and national security. Provisions of this EO allowed seizing Taliban property and interests in the U.S. while cutting off financial, material, and technological support for Taliban assets in the U.S.; prohibiting U.S. exports to Taliban-controlled territory in Afghanistan; and prohibiting U.S. imports of Taliban products, services, and technologies. This EO would be reaffirmed by President Bush on September 23, 2001.[17]

The 2001 USA Patriot Act, enacted in response to the 9/11 terrorist attacks, also included expanded Treasury Department powers to attempt to restrict terrorist financial assets and access to capital. This statute helped harmonize U.S. anti-money laundering laws with the United States Munitions List and Export Administration Regulations and strengthened Treasury Department data collection on financial transactions such as exporting monetary instruments involving potential terrorist activity.[18]

Both the George W. Bush and Obama Administrations sought to make increased use of OFAC to initiate financial sanctions against international terrorists and WMD proliferators. These efforts sought to overcome a historic lack of concern with terrorist financing by the U.S. Government. A 2004 terrorist financing assessment by 9/11 Commission staff revealed that terrorist financing and not been a priority for domestic and foreign intelligence collection. The National Security Council (NSC) considered terrorist financing important in U.S. attempts to disrupt Al Qaeda but other federal agencies failed to participate to NSC's satisfaction and there was little interagency strategic planning or coordination. Consequently, responsibility for this was dispersed among multiple agencies such as the CIA and FBI each working independently. OFAC lacked comprehensive access to actionable intelligence to search out, designate, and freeze Al Qaeda assets and the indifference of high-level Treasury policymakers stymied its efforts. The U.S. had some success with persuading the United Nations to economically sanction Al Qaeda but had mixed results with persuading Saudi Arabia and this helped produce a steady and secure cash flow for Al Qaeda on September 11, 2001.[19]

This report went on to argue that the U.S. had achieved significant progress in monitoring terrorist financing but that the nature and extent of Al Qaeda fund-raising and money movement make intelligence collection extremely difficult. Al Qaeda uses a complex variety of ways to collect and move small amounts of money internationally through Islamic "charities", various non-governmental organizations, and the Hawala system which are not readily subject to international financial regulatory scrutiny. Consequently, there are limits as to what governmental agencies like OFAC and the commercial financial industry can do to fully track and stop terrorist financing sources.[20]

During the Bush Administration, OFAC carried out its responsibilities with 144 employees administering 28 programs. Besides the Washington, DC headquarters office, OFAC had 10 divisions with offices in Miami, Mexico City, Bogota, and a soon to be opened office in Manama, Bahrain. Its enforcement division provided liaison with the law enforcement community while the international programs and foreign terrorist divisions emphasized narcotics and terrorism programs and preparing evidentiary material to support its designation process best exemplified by the SDN list. The civil penalties division stressed expanding civil penalty enforcement process transparency by developing an automated system to report enforcement actions. The compliance division was in the process of building new customer service capabilities with a top-flight automated telephone system, enhanced hot-line capabilities, and improved Web-based forms to allow public transmission of detailed live transaction data for real-time analysis and response. It also used EO 13382 on June 28, 2005 to block the property and financial interests of individuals and organizations designated as seeking to proliferate, promote, and transport WMD.[21]

The Obama Administration has made significant use of OFAC to enforce U.S. economic sanctions against WMD proliferating and terrorist supporting regimes and organizations. EO 13590 on November 20, 2011 imposed sanctions on individuals and organizations providing goods, services, technologies, and other means of support to Iran's energy and petrochemical sectors. This EO also directed the Federal Reserve and Treasury Department to prohibit U.S. financial institutions from making loans to individuals sanctioned under this order for more than $10 million unless the person was engaged in activities relieving human suffering and blocked all property and property interests held by individuals doing business with Iranian entities.[22]

EO 13599 on February 5, 2012 sought to block Iranian government property and the property of Iranian financial institutions including the Central Bank of Iran.[23] EO 13608 on May 1, 2012 imposed sanctions on individuals and organizations attempting to evade existing U.S. economic and financial sanctions on Syria including suspending their immigration into the U.S.[24] EO 13611 of May 16, 2012 blocked the property of individuals and organizations of anyone threatening the stability of the U.S.-backed government in Yemen or providing those providing material support to insurgent organizations such as Al Qaeda in the Arabian Peninsula threatening that government under IEEPA provisions.[25]

Concern over the large volume of weapons usable fissile material in Russian Federation territory continuing to constitute a serious threat to U.S. foreign policy and national security resulted in the June 25, 2012 issuance of EO 13617. This edict directed that all Russian property and property interests dealing with existing Highly Enriched Uranium Agreements within the U.S. that come with possession or control of U.S. persons, including foreign branches, are blocked and may not be transferred, paid, exported, withdrawn, or otherwise dealt with.[26]

Ongoing efforts to "tighten the screws" on Iran were reflected in EO 13622 on July 30, 2012. This document authorized the Treasury Department to impose financial penalties on foreign financial institutions knowingly doing business with the National Iranian Oil Company, and purchasing or acquiring Iranian petroleum or petrochemical products. It also authorized the Federal Reserve Board to revoke the authority of individual financial dealers and financial institutions as sanctioned dealers of U.S. Government debt instruments; prohibit foreign exchange transactions subject to U.S. jurisdiction; prohibit credit or payment transfers between U.S. financial institutions and foreign individuals or institutions with property blocked by the U.S.; and gives the Treasury Department authority to impose sanctions on individuals or organizations materially assisting or providing financial or technological support to the Central Bank of Iran and to Iranian Government purchases of U.S. bank notes and precious metals.[27]

OFAC's increasing involvement and importance in administering U.S. export control policy has achieved successes and failures. Consequently, its performance has received increased scrutiny from Treasury Department Inspector General (TIG) and Government Accountability Office (GAO) since the late 1990s. An April 26, 2002 TIG report revealed OFAC was limited in its ability to monitor financial institution compliance with foreign sanction requirements due to legislative restrictions. OFAC primarily relies on authority derived from TEA and IEEPA which do not give it authority to randomly monitor financial institution compliance with foreign sanction requirements. Consequently, it cannot monitor or examine financial institution compliance with these sanctions unless it is informed that a prohibited transaction occurred.[28]

Further constraint on OFAC includes the Right to Financial Privacy Act (RFPA) which generally does not allow financial institution regulators to share financial records of institutions they supervise with OFAC because it is not a bank supervisory agency. Consequently, OFAC must rely on financial institution regulators examinations to monitor financial institution compliance with foreign sanctions which may not provide sufficient assurance that these financial institutions are complying with foreign sanction requirements. Such testing involving testing individual financial transactions rarely occurs in determining foreign sanction compliance and is critical in determining whether a prohibited transaction occurred.

This report went on to add that OFAC generally followed its guidance for processing blocked and rejected financial transactions and issuing penalties. However, there were also instances where procedures were not established, databases not updated, and guidance not followed. TIG also recommended OFAC inform Congress of these legislative deficiencies and amend RFPA to give it bank regulator authority.[29]

A March 2, 2007 TIG report revealed serious deficiencies in OFAC completing civil penalty case enforcement. Between Fiscal Years (FY) 2002-2005, OFAC's Civil Penalties Division took enforcement action against some 3,800 violators collecting $10.32 million in civil penalties. However, because of a five year statute of limitations on imposing penalties, this division failed to complete enforcement actions for 295 cases during this period totaling potential fines of $3.87 million. This report also noted that OFAC had insufficient resources to address the number of sanctions programs and violations it was responsible for which increased from 21 to 29 during this period, that OFAC managers ability to monitor and handle these penalty cases was constrained by insufficient, accurate, and reliable case status and disposition information, and that administrative law judges were not always available to conduct required hearings.[30]

A September 20, 2007 TIG report announced that OFAC had concluded Memorandums of Understanding (MOU) in April 2006 with federal banking authorities to ensure financial institution compliance with OFAC sanctions. The report revealed that OFAC had not sought additional legislative authority in this regard since it believes its legal authority is sufficient despite these changes recommended by TIG in its 2002 report. TIG acknowledged these OFAC MOU's needed time to mature while expressing concern that RFPA information restriction exchanges may continue hampering OPAC's ability to fulfill its responsibilities.[31]

On November 14, 2007, TIG released a report on OFAC's SDN list and its contribution to the National Counterterrorism Center's (NCTC) ability to electronically access this information and check SDN names against the Terrorist Identities Datamart Environment (TIDE). TIG determined that SDN was working well at this time but said OFAC should regularly reassess if addition processes or measures are necessary to provide terrorism information to NCTC. Treasury does not have a specific process to nominate individuals to the consolidated terrorist watchlist. However, individuals added to SDN are electronically sent to NCTC to be checked against TIDE for possible inclusion in that database.[32]

OFAC was not the only Treasury Department agency experiencing deficiencies in administering U.S. international criminal statutes. A May 15, 2008 TIG report on the Office of Thrift Supervision (OTS) examined 95 thrift institutions between 2004-2006 to determine their evaluations of Banking Secrecy Act (BSA) and USA Patriot Act compliance. TIG found that in 82 of the 95 thrifts examined that OTS examiners did not evaluate if significance compliance program elements had been implemented by the thrifts. Examiners frequently accepted claims that because thrifts and policies and procedures in place for certain BSA and Patriot Act programs that these measures were up to standard without determining how well or poorly these policies and procedures were implemented. Sometimes examiners did not understand the Patriot Act added updated provisions to BSA and that this produced limited reviews of potential money laundering or other activities posing potential risks to the thrift. Some of these thrifts were also found to be deficient in sharing information with federal law enforcement agencies investigating money laundering or terrorist activity, verifying customers identities, and conducting due diligence on customer activities.[33]

Problematic federal enforcement of terrorist financing and money laundering was revealed by an April 9, 2008 TIG report. This document identified 12 organizations with BSA responsibilities including Treasury's Financial Crimes Enforcement Center, the Internal Revenue Service, the Office of the Comptroller of the Currency, OTS, Federal Deposit Insurance Corporation, Federal Reserve System, National Credit Union Administration, Securities and Exchange Commission, Commodity Futures Trading Commission, and the FBI. The report also identified 80 Treasury compliance information sharing MOU's as of October 1, 2007 to improve interagency BSA compliance information while acknowledging it is difficult to determine the effectiveness of these MOU's. This administrative overlap and lack of reporting to Treasury by some of these organizations makes effective BSA enforcement highly problematic.[34]

This same time period also produced another TIG report denouncing Treasury's failure to provide Congress with a critical report on foreign industrial acquisition strategies and industrial espionage activities. Section 721(k) of the 1950 Defense Production Act required quadrennial reports on these strategies and activities be submitted to Congress within one year of this section's enactment while also authorizing presidential suspension or prohibition of acquisitions that might threaten national security.[35]

TIG revealed that this report was prepared by an interagency Treasury working group in 1994. However, it was not prepared in 1998 and 2002, because Treasury Department officials did not believe they were responsible for preparing this report. This report was also not prepared because the CIA quit subscribing to a commercial database used in compiling material for the 1994 report. This report was prepared in 2006 and in 2007 Congress enacted the Foreign Investment and National Security Act (FINSA) assigning the Treasury Department's Committee on Foreign Investment in the United States (CFIUS) with annual responsibility for preparing this report which includes documentation of foreign espionage activities in U.S. industries.[36]

A September 2010 TIG report analyzed the quality of OFAC's documentary reviews of potential sanctions violations. This report examined OFAC's review in the Federal Reserve Bank of New York's (FRB-NY) Fedwire Integrity Pilot Program. Between 2004 and 2006 FRB-NY periodically compared name samples from OFAC's SDN list against a moving history of Fedwire transactions to determine if depository institutions appropriately blocked transactions against selected SDNs. FRB-NY searched 8 samples of 10 SDNs selected from a subset of 198 SDNs provided by OFAC. FRB-NY searches produced 305 transactions containing a potential match with an SDN list for a total value exceeding $11 million. While, FRB-NY believed the overwhelming majority of financial institutions were properly screening for SDN list names, it did not have customer data to make a final determination.[37]

This report went on to assert that OFAC failed to provide TIG with sufficient documentation to support the activities and analysis it used to reach its conclusion that the vast majority of Fedwire institutions properly screened their transactions to determine compliance with OFAC sanctions. Between November 2007-March 2008, OFAC did not give TIG the criteria used to select the subset of SDN names provided to FRB-NY, the results of what was done with potential suspicious transactions identified by FRB-NY, and OFAC did not supply written policies or procedures for reviewing potentially suspicious transactions. Additionally, OFAC officials told TIG that they believed Fedwire should be treated as sensitive and that public disclosure of the program would harm the government without giving a rationale other than business proprietary information. TIG also cited OFAC for marking certain documents as Sensitive But Unclassified (SBU) without placing this marking on other documents containing the exact information.[38]

TIG program reform recommendations included OFAC establishing policies and procedures for reviewing referrals of potential OFAC sanctions violations including documenting research and conclusions derived from its analysis; informing TIG of report sensitivity levels and of specific information that cannot be disclosed; periodically reassessing with FRB-NY whether Fedwire should be restarted; consulting with Treasury's

Office of Intelligence and Analysis to determine Fedwire's appropriate sensitivity level based on Treasury Security Manual (TSM) criteria; and appropriately marking and securing program documentation based TSM criteria.[39]

Between 1979-2009, GAO produced six different reports detailing deficiencies in OFAC activities. An October 4, 1979 report found that OFAC had improperly blocked over $6 million in Defense Department funds which DOD had used to circumvent the Arab oil embargo and supply petroleum to South Vietnam.[40] The following year GAO found Treasury needed to get better information and more closely monitor foreign assets blocked under emergency economic authority. This report went on to mention that Treasury administrators do not require asset-holders to systematically report blocked assets which makes it impossible to determine the value of these assets, properly account for these assets, and give assurances that they are properly managed.[41]

A November 2003 GAO analysis said the U.S. should do a better job analyzing terrorists use of alternative financing systems for moving funds such as contraband cigarettes, counterfeit goods, illicit drugs, charitable organizations that launder money, informal banking systems such as Hawala, bulk cash, and precious stones and metals which cannot be monitored by traditional banking systems.[42]

In September 2004, GAO reported that U.S. Government agencies and financial institutions desiring to recover foreign regimes assets face numerous challenges. These include potentially being unable to obtain accurate and complete information on targeted entities such as spelling of names, addresses, and birth dates. The domestic legal systems of some foreign countries do not allow governments to freeze targeted assets and can prohibit asset transfers to newly constituted governments. OFAC's ability to monitor financial institution's compliance with its regulations is limited since it does not have supervisory authority over these institutions and is dependent on financial institution regulators to monitor institutional compliance with OFAC regulations.[43]

A November 2007 GAO analysis revealed that loosening Cuban embargo rules had produced significant increases in U.S. exports to Cuba; tightened travel by restricting the frequency with which U.S. residents could visit Cuban family members from once a year to once every three years; that OFAC officials were unable to show data on allocations for Cuban embargo enforcement activities; that the percentage of total embargo violations from Cuba penalties fell from 70% in 2000-2005 to

29% in 2006; and that declining international and domestic U.S. support for the embargo against Havanna hindered its effectiveness.[44]

During September 2009, GAO issued a report critiquing Treasury's Office of Terrorism and Financial Intelligence (TFI) management policies and procedures. This analysis asserted that TFI had enhanced its financial intelligence against terrorism and WMD proliferation. It went on to suggest that TFI cooperation with other agencies could be improved; that these other agencies had different perceptions about the collaborative quality of international multilateral export control forums; that there needs to be clearly documented policies and procedures to facilitate multilateral collaboration; and that TFI strategic management needs to implement a comprehensive strategic workforce planning process so it has the workforce to meet emerging national security threats.[45]

As of October 2012, OFAC had taken enforcement actions against 11 companies producing penalties and settlements of $623,405,923.[46] One example of these actions included fining ING Bank N.V. $619 million on June 12, 2012 for violating provisions of U.S. laws covering Cuban Assets Control Regulations and sanctions against Burma, Sudan, Libya, and Iran. These sanctions violations involved ING commercial banking offices in Belgium, Curacao, Cuba, and the Netherlands and did not involve the company's U.S. insurance or banking operations.[47] On October 19, 2012, OFAC fined Savannah, GA medical supply company Brasseler USA $18,900 for violating Iranian Transactions Regulations three times between 2006-2009. The specific nature of these violations included Brasseler concealing the identities of its Iranian customers with the awareness of its management staff; demonstrating reckless disregard for U.S. sanctions requirements; and not having a compliance program in place when these violations occurred. Brasseler cooperated with OFAC in his case which limited the total of its fine.[48]

OFAC powers give it the authority to issue criminal penalties ranging from $50,000 to $10 million and imprisonment from 10-30 years for willful violations of export control laws. Civil penalties range from $250,000 or twice the amount of each underlying transaction to $1,075,000.[49]

OFAC's budget is part of the Treasury Department's Office of Terrorism and Financial Intelligence (TFI). Its FY 2012 budget was $100 million and it received $102,117,000 from the House Appropriations Committee in its report on the Treasury Department's FY 2013 budget although this could be changed by the Senate Appropriations Committee.[50] TFI carried out its multiple responsibilities with 418 staff during FY 2012 and its FY 2013 congressional budget request asked for funding for 417 staff which is down from its 429 staff during FY 2011.[51]

The Treasury Department has achieved successes and failures in its efforts to enforce financial sanctions against hostile international governments and transnational organizations promoting drug trafficking, proliferation of weapons of mass destruction, and terrorism. Its activities have increased in recent years as the U.S. has sought to place increasing financial pressure on nations and organizations it deems antagonistic to U.S. foreign policy and national security interests. These nations and organizations respond by seeking to elude the reach of U.S. financial laws and regulations while the U.S. continually enacts and enforces laws and regulations in order to place increasing financial pressure on antagonistic nations and organizations.

Legislation creating these laws and the funding and oversight of federal agencies administering U.S. export control policymaking is carried out by the U.S. Congress and multiple congressional committees. Their role will be examined in the next chapter.

Notes

1. See "Prohibition of Exports," *American State Papers Foreign Relations 03 No. 259* (Washington, DC: Gales and Seaton, 1832): 620-21; and Reginald C. Stuart, "Special Interests and National Authority in Foreign Policy: American-British Provincial Links During the Embargo and the War of 1812," *Diplomatic History*, 8 (4)(October 1984): 311-328.

2. Public Law 65-91, "An Act to Define, Regulate, and Punish Trading With the Enemy, and for Other Purposes," 40 *U.S. Statutes at Large* 411-426.

3. See "Executive Order," 5 *Federal Register* (April 12, 1940): 1400-1401; and U.S. National Archives and Records Administration, "Records of the Office of Foreign Assets Control," (Washington, DC: National Archives, 1995); http://www.archives.gov/research/guide-fed-records/groups/265.html; Accessed October 5, 2012.

4. See Ibid., and "Title 31: Money and Finance: Treasury Chapter V-Foreign Assets Control, Department of the Treasury," 15 *Federal Register* 245 (December 19, 1950): 9040-9055.

5. Ibid. "Records of the Office of Foreign Assets Control".

6. See U.S. Department of the Treasury, "Terrorism and Financial Intelligence Office of Foreign Assets Control (OFAC): Mission," (Washington,

DC: OFAC, 2012): 1; http://www.treasury.gov/about/organizational-structure/offices/Pages/Office-of-Foreign-Assets-Control.aspx; Accessed October 5, 2012; and Ibid., "Resource Center: United States Statutes," (2012): 1-2; http://www.treasury.gov/resource-center/sanctions/Pages/statutes-links.aspx; Accessed October 5, 2012.

7. See U.S. Congressional Budget Office, *Domestic Costs of Sanctions on Foreign Commerce*, (Washington, DC: CBO, 1999); Lance Davis and Stanley Engerman, "History Lessons Sanctions: Neither War nor Peace," *Journal of Economic Perspectives*, 17 (2)(Spring 2003): 187-197; Stephen D. Collins, "Dissuading State Support of Terrorism: Strikes or Sanctions? (An Analysis of Dissuasion Measures Employed Against Libya)," *Studies in Conflict and Terrorism*, 27 (1)(2004): 1-18; Dingli Shen, "Can Sanctions Stop Proliferation?," *The Washington Quarterly*, 31 (3)(Summer 2008): 89-100; Vanessa Ortblad, "Criminal Prosecution in Sheep's Clothing: The Punitive Effects of OFAC Freezing Sanctions," *The Journal of Criminal Law and Criminology*, 98 (4)(Summer 2008): 1439-1466; Wesley J.L. Anderson, *Disrupting Threat Finances: Using Financial Information to Disrupt Terrorist Organizations*, (Hurlburt Field, FL: Joint Special Operations University Press, 2008); and Jeffrey N. Davenport, "Freezing Terrorist Finance in its Tracks: The Fourth Amendment, Due Process, and the Office of Foreign Assets Control After Kindhearts V. Geithner," *Syracuse Law Review*, 61 (2)(2010): 173-201.

8. U.S. Department of the Treasury, Office of Foreign Assets Control, "Regulations Prohibiting Transactions Involving the Shipment of Certain Merchandise Between Foreign Countries," 30 *Federal Register* 25 (February 6, 1965): 1284.

9. Ibid., "Certain Transactions Incident to Travel to and Inland Mainland China," 34 *Federal Register* 156 (August 15, 1969): 13277.

10. See U.S. Department of the Treasury, "Cuban Asset Control Regulations: Control of Financial and Commercial Transactions Involving Cuba of Nationals Thereof," 28 *Federal Register* (July 9, 1963): 974; and Ibid., "Cuban Assets Control Regulations," 39 *Federal Register* 133 (July 10, 1974): 25317-25319.

11. Ibid., "Blocking Extended to Vietnam," 40 *Federal Register* 86 (May 2, 1975): 9202-9203.

12. See Ibid., "Iranian Assets Control Regulations," 44 *Federal Register* 222 (November 15, 1979): 65956-65958; and Esfandyar Batmanghelidj, "Sanctions, Smuggling, and the Cigarette: The Granting of Iran OFAC Licenses to Big Tobacco," *Iranian Studies*, 45 (3)(May 2012): 395-415.

13. See Ibid., "List of Specially Designated Nationals," 51 *Federal Register* 237 (December 10, 1986): 44549; U.S. Department of the Treasury, Office of Inspector General (TIG), *Foreign Assets Control: OFAC Should Have Better and More Timely Documented its Review of Potential Sanctions Violations*, (Washington, DC: TIG, 2010): 8; http://www.treasury.gov/about/organiza-

tional-structure/ig/Documents/OIG10045%20%28Fedwire%29-Not%20SBU%20%282%29.pdf; Accessed October 23, 2012.

14. Ibid., "Specially Designated Nations and Blocked Persons List," (October 4, 2012): 1, 40; www.treasury.gov/ofac/downloads/t11sdn.pdf; Accessed October 8, 2012.

15. Public Law 104-132, "Antiterrorism and Effective Death Penalty Act of 1996," 110 *U.S. Statutes at Large* 1214-1215, 1247-1248, 1250, 1255-1258.

16. Public Law 104-172, "Iran and Libya Sanctions Act of 1996," 110 *U.S. Statutes at Large* 1541-1551.

17. See "Executive Order 13129 of July 4, 1999: Blocking Property and Prohibiting Transactions With the Taliban," 64 *Federal Register* 129 (July 7, 1999): 36759-36761; and "Executive Order 13224 of September 23, 2001: Blocking Property and Prohibiting Transactions With Persons Who Commit, Threaten to Commit, or Support Terrorism," 66 *Federal Register* 186 (September 25, 2001): 49079-49083.

18. See Public Law 107-56, "USA Patriot Act," 115 *U.S. Statutes at Large* 292, 308-309, 330-331, Charles Doyle, *USA Patriot Act: A Legal Analysis*, (Washington, DC: Library of Congress, Congressional Research Service, 2002); and Ray Banoun, Derrick Cephas, and Larry Fruchtman, "USA Patriot Act and Other Recent Money Laundering Developments Have Broad Impact on Financial Institutions," *Journal of Taxation and Regulation of Financial Institutions*, 15 (March/April 2002): 17

19. John Roth, Douglas Greenburg, and Serena Wille, *Monograph on Terrorist Financing: Staff Report to the Commission*, (Washington, DC: U.S. National Commission on Terrorist Attacks Upon the United States, 2004): 4-6; http://govinfo.library.unt.edu/911/staff_statements/911_TerrFin_Monograph.pdf; Accessed October 9, 2012.

20. See Ibid., 13-16; Robert Looney, "Hawala: The Terrorists Informal Financial Mechanism," *Middle East Policy*, 10 (1)(Spring 2003): 164-167; U.S. Department of Justice, Executive Office of for United States Attorneys, "Terrorist Financing," *U.S. Attorneys Bulletin*, 51 (4)(July 2003); Mark Basile, "Going to the Source: Why Al Qaeda's Financial Network is Likely to Withstand the Current War on Terrorist Financing," *Studies in Conflict & Terrorism*, 27 (3)(2004): 169-185; Robert Feldman, "Fund Transfers-African Terrorists Blend Old and New: Hawala and Satellite Telecommunications," *Small Wars and Insurgencies*, 17 (3)(September 2006): 356-366; and U.S. Congress, Senate Committee on Homeland Security and Governmental Affairs, Permanent Subcommittee on Investigations, *U.S. Vulnerabilities to Money Laundering, Drugs, and Terrorist Financing: HSBC Case History: Majority and Minority Staff Report*, (Washington, DC: GPO, 2012); http://www.hsgac.senate.gov/subcommittees/investigations/hearings/us-vulnerabilities-to-money-laundering-drugs-and-terrorist-financing-hsbc-case-history; Accessed October 9, 2012.

21. See U.S. Congress, House Committee on Financial Services, Subcommittee on Oversight and Investigations, *Oversight of the Department of Treasury*, (Washington, DC: GPO, 2004): 26-28; Presidential Documents, "Executive Order 13382 of June 28, 2005: Blocking Property of Weapons of Mass Destruction Proliferators and Their Supporters," 70 *Federal Register* 126 (July 1, 2005): 38567-38570; and U.S. Congress, House Committee on Financial Services, Subcommittee on Oversight and Investigations, *Weapons of Mass Destruction: Stopping the Funding—The OFAC Role*, (Washington, DC: GPO, 2006): 6-8.

22. Presidential Documents, "Executive Order 13590 of November 20, 2011: Authorizing the Imposition of Certain Sanctions With Respect to the Provision of Goods, Services, Technology, or Support for Iran's Energy and Petrochemical Sectors," 76 *Federal Register* 226 (November 23, 2011): 72609-72612.

23. Ibid., "Executive Order 13599 of February 5, 2012: Blocking Property of the Government of Iran and Iranian Financial Institutions," 77 *Federal Register* 26 (February 8, 2012): 6659-6662.

24. Ibid., "Executive Order 13608 of May 1, 2012: Prohibiting Certain Transactions With and Suspending Entry Into the United States of Foreign Sanctions Evaders With Respect to Iran and Syria," 77 *Federal Register* 86 (May 3, 2012): 24609-24611.

25. See Ibid., "Executive Order 13611 of May 16, 2012: Blocking Property of Persons Threatening the Peace, Security, or Stability of Yemen," 77 *Federal Register* 97 (May 18, 2012): 29533-29535; and W. Andrew Terrill, *The Conflicts in Yemen and U.S. National Security*, (Carlisle, PA: U.S. Army War College, Strategic Studies Institute, 2011).

26. Ibid., "Executive Order 13617 of June 25, 2012: Blocking Property of the Russian Federation Relating to the Disposition of Highly Enriched Uranium Extracted from Nuclear Weapons," 77 *Federal Register* 124 (June 27, 2012): 38459-38461.

27. Ibid., "Executive Order 13622: Authorizing Additional Sanctions With Respect to Iran," 77 *Federal Register* 149 (August 2, 2012): 45897-45902.

28. U.S. Department of the Treasury, Office of Inspector General, *Foreign Assets Control: OFAC's Ability to Monitor Financial Institution Compliance is Limited Due to Legislative Impairments*, (Washington, DC: TIG, 2002): 2; http://www.treasury.gov/about/organizational-structure/ig/Documents/oig02082.pdf; Accessed October 10, 2012.

29. See Ibid., 3; and Public Law 95-630, "Right to Financial Privacy Act," 92 *U.S. Statutes at Large* 3698.

30. Ibid., *Foreign Assets Control: Hundreds of OFAC Civil Penalty Cases Expired Before Enforcement Action Could be Completed*, (Washington, DC: TIG, 2007): 2; http://www.treasury.gov/about/organizational-structure/ig/Documents/oig07032.pdf; Accessed October 10, 2012.

31. Ibid., *Financial Assets Control: Actions Have Been Taken to Better Ensure Financial Institution Compliance With OFAC Sanction Programs, But Their Effectiveness Cannot Yet Be Determined*, (Washington, DC: TIG, 2007): 2-3, 7-8; http://www.treasury.gov/about/organizational-structure/ig/Documents/ OFAC%20Final%20Report%209-20-07.pdf; Accessed October 10, 2012.

32. Ibid., *Combating Terrorism: Treasury Provides Terrorism Information for Consolidated Watchlist Purposes Through Its Specially Designated Nationals List*, (Washington, DC: TIG, 2007): 2-3, 7-8; http://www.treasury.gov/ about/organizational-structure/ig/Documents/oig08022.pdf; Accessed October 10, 2012.

33. See Ibid., *Terrorist Financing/Money Laundering: OTS Examinations of Thrifts for Bank Secrecy Act and Patriot Act Compliance Were Often Limited*, (Washington, DC: TIG, 2008): 2-3; http://www.treasury.gov/about/organizational-structure/ig/Documents/oig08034.pdf; Accessed October 10, 2012; and Public Law 91-508, "Currency and Foreign Transactions Reporting Act," 84 *U.S. Statutes at Large* 1118-1124.

34. Ibid., *Terrorist Financing/Money Laundering: Responsibility for Bank Secrecy Act is Spread Across Many Organizations*, (Washington, DC: TIG, 2008): 2-13; http://www.treasury.gov/about/organizational-structure/ig/Documents/oig08030.pdf; Accessed October 10, 2012.

35. See Public Law 81-774, "Defense Production Act of 1950," 64 *U.S. Statutes at Large*, 798-822; and Public Law 102-558, "Defense Production Act Amendments of 1992," 106 *U.S. Statutes at Large* 4219-4220.

36. See U.S. Department of the Treasury, Office of the Inspector General, *Foreign Investments: Review of Treasury's Failure To Provide Congress Required Quadrennial Reports in 1998 and 2002 on Foreign Acquisitions and Industrial Espionage Activity Involving U.S. Critical Technology Companies*, (Washington, DC: TIG, 2008): 2-15; http://www.treasury.gov/about/organizational-structure/ig/Documents/oig08031.pdf; Accessed October 10, 2012; Public Law 110-49, "Foreign Investment and National Security Act of 2007," 121 *U.S. Statutes at Large* 246-260; and U.S. Department of the Treasury, Committee on Foreign Investment in the United States, *Annual Report to Congress: CY 2010*, (Washington, DC: CFIUS, 2011); http://www.treasury.gov/ resource-center/international/foreign-investment/Documents/2011%20CFIUS% 20Annual%20Report%20FINAL%20PUBLIC.pdf; Accessed October 10, 2012.

37. U.S. Department of the Treasury, Office of the Inspector General, *Foreign Assets: OFAC Should Have Better and More Timely Documented Its Review of Potential Sanctions Violations*, (Washington, DC: TIG, 2010): 1;

38. Ibid., 1-5

39. Ibid., 5.

40. U.S. General Accounting Office, *Improper Blocking of U.S. Funds by Office of Foreign Assets Control*, (Washington, DC: GAO, 1979); http:// www.gao.gov/assets/130/127865.pdf; Accessed October 23, 2012.

41. Ibid., *Treasury Should Keep Better Track of Blocked Foreign Assets*, (Washington, DC: GAO, 1980): i-ii; http://www.gao.gov/assets/140/130936.pdf; Accessed October 23, 2012.

42. Ibid., *U.S. Should Systematically Assess Terrorists Use of Alternative Financial Systems*, (Washington, DC: GAO, 2003): 3-5; http://www.gao.gov/assets/250/240616.pdf; Accessed October 23, 2012.

43. Ibid., *U.S. Faces Challenges in Recovering Assets, Has Financial Mechanisms*, (Washington, DC: GAO, 2004): 3; http://www.gao.gov/assets/250/244163.pdf; Accessed October 23, 2012.

44. Ibid., *Competing Priorities Enforcing Cuban Embargo*, (Washington, DC: GAO, 2007): 3-9; http://www.gao.gov/assets/270/269849.pdf; Accessed October 23, 2012.

45. Ibid., *Treasury's Office of Terrorism and Financial Intelligence Could More Effectively Manage Its Mission*, (Washington, DC: GAO, 2009): 30-31; http://www.gao.gov/assets/300/295922.pdf; Accessed October 23, 2012.

46. U.S. Department of the Treasury, Office of Foreign Assets Control, *Civil Penalties and Enforcement Information: 2012 Enforcement Information*, (Washington, DC: OFAC, 2012); 1-2; http://www.treasury.gov/resource-center/sanctions/CivPen/Pages/civpen-index2.aspx; Accessed October 23, 2012.

47. Ibid., *Enforcement Information for June 12, 2012*, (Washington, DC: OFAC, 2012): 1-2; http://www.treasury.gov/resource-center/sanctions/CivPen/Documents/06122012_ing.pdf; Accessed October 23, 2012.

48. Ibid., *Enforcement Information for October 19, 2012*, (Washington, DC: OFAC, 2012): 1; http://www.treasury.gov/resource-center/sanctions/CivPen/Documents/20121019_brasseler.pdf; Accessed October 23, 2012.

49. Ibid., *Frequently Asked Questions and Answers*, (Washington, DC: OFAC, 2007); 5; http://www.treasury.gov/resource-center/faqs/Sanctions/Pages/answer.aspx; Accessed October 23, 2012.

50. U.S. Congress, House Committee on Appropriations, *Financial Services and General Government Appropriations Bill, 2013*, House Report 112-550, (Washington, DC: GPO, 2012): 8.

51. U.S. Department of the Treasury, *Departmental Offices-S&E FY 2013 President's Budget Submission*, (Washington, DC: Department of the Treasury, 2012): DO-3; http://www.treasury.gov/about/budget-performance/Documents/2%20-%20FY%202013%20DO%20SE%20CJ.pdf; Accessed October 23, 2012.

Chapter 6

Congress and Export Controls

Any examination of U.S. export control history must scrutinize the role played by Congress and its multiple oversight committees. Congress is responsible for approving new laws dealing with export control programs, revising existing laws, funding these programs, and conducting oversight of their performance. Over several decades a staggering number of congressional committees and their subcommittees have become involved in U.S. export control policymaking and oversight complicating governmental policymaking in this area and understanding of this topic. Numerous factors influence congressional activity in this area including genuine national security and international trade concerns by members of Congress preventing WMD proliferation and aiding hostile governments or terrorist organizations, the desire of congressional lawmakers to assist constituent businesses in dealing with the export control complexities posed by federal laws and regulations and the confusing mass of agencies involved in administering export control policy, and the desire of these same lawmakers to score political points against agencies or presidential administrations they believe are not promoting the export goals of companies in their constituencies or advancing what they regard as overall U.S. foreign and national security policy interests.[1]

Understanding the magnitude of Congress' role in U.S. export control policymaking requires specific understanding of the variety of congressional congressional committees whose oversight encompasses agencies dealing with this topic. During the 112th Congress (2011-2012) the following congressional committees and their subcommittees had at least partial involvement with export control policymaking:

1. House and Senate Appropriations Committees
2. House Armed Services Committee
3. House Financial Services Committee
4. House Foreign Affairs Committee
5. House Homeland Security Committee
6. House Judiciary Committee
7. House Select Committee on Intelligence
8. House Ways & Means Committee
9. Senate Armed Services Committee
10. Senate Banking, Housing, and Urban Affairs Committee
11. Senate Finance Committee
12. Senate Foreign Relations Committee
13. Senate Homeland Security and Governmental Affairs Committee
14. Senate Judiciary Committee
15. Senate Select Committee on Intelligence.[2]

A significant component of congressional oversight responsibilities includes mandating agencies report to Congress on their activities in certain areas. This occurs through the preparation of often lengthy written reports prepared at various frequencies describing how these agencies carry out laws or portions of laws enacted by Congress. The vast majority of these reports are publicly accessible.[3] Examples of some of these congressionally mandated export control oriented reports, as of January 2012, include presidential reports on missile proliferation and proposed nuclear exports to non-nuclear-weapon states failing to meet International Atomic Energy Safeguards, the Commerce Department's Bureau of Industry and Security annual report, a Defense Department report on furnishing nuclear test monitoring equipment to foreign countries, a State Department report on exports to foreign space launch vehicle programs, and a Treasury Department report on Kuwaiti assets control regulations.[4]

Congress has sought to influence export control policymaking through enacting laws. The 1949 Export Control Act served as the foundation for postwar legal activity in this area and legislative intent was expressed in the congressional committee report on this legislation. This document stressed that postwar export controls were retained to reduce inflationary effects of abnormal foreign demands on U.S. supplies; recognized that export controls over non-military items be consistent with U.S. foreign and national security policy objectives; called for the creation of advisory panels to examine export controls effect on small businesses; recognized that export controls must be flexible to meet U.S. export as well as national security requirements; provided administrative powers permitting investigating, subpoenas, and requiring testimony under oath; and also noted the dangers of the U.S. becoming dependent on foreign suppliers of critical materials such as petroleum.[5]

Congress sought to strengthen export controls by passing the Mutual Defense Assistance Control Act or Battle Act in October 1951. Named for its sponsor Rep. Laurie Battle (D-AL)(1912-2000), this legislation declared it to be U.S. policy to embargo shipments of arms, military supplies, atomic energy materials, petroleum, and strategically valuable transportation materials to the Soviet Union and its allies in order to increase U.S. national security. The Senate vote and debate approving this legislation on August 28, 1951 was 55-16 with 25 Senators not voting revealed conflicting attitudes on export controls which remain present six decades later. Legislation supporters, including Senator John Sparkman (D-AL)(1899-1985) argued it would centralize export control enforcement in a single agency; that the U.S. could not assist countries shipping prohibited items to the Soviet Union; gives the free world the flexibility to barter with the Soviet Union for strategic items; strives for cooperative trade between the U.S. and other free world countries; and strengthened existing Western European embargos on strategic exports to the Soviet bloc. Legislation opponents like Senator James Kem (R-MO)(1890-1965) asserted that Western Europe resented U.S. attempts to restrict its trade with the Soviet bloc; that the President should have the flexibility to continue providing aid to the Soviet bloc if halting it would be detrimental to U.S. security; and opposed American taxpayer supported goods shipped to Western Europe being sold as military goods to the Soviet bloc.[6]

While debating and ultimately enacting the 1954 Mutual Security Act which sought to standardize U.S. military assistance objectives, Congress was in ongoing negotiation with the Eisenhower Administration on the effectiveness of U.S. export controls and on possible enhancements which could be made to these controls. Testifying before the House Foreign Affairs Committee on February 16, 1954 Foreign Operations Administration Assistant Deputy Director for Mutual Defense Control Kenneth R. Hansen (1923-1981) stressed that U.S. trade controls on illegal products were having increasing impact on the Soviet bloc by drastically increasing the prices for illegally purchased goods, that the number of rejected export licenses had increased, and that there had been a decline in East-West trade since before the Korean War. Representative John Vorys (R-OH)(1896-1958) stressed his hope that U.S. foreign aid programs would eventually be ended and that this would also end the necessity of economic defense assistance while increasing opportunities for trading peaceful goods.[7]

Rep. Edna Kelly (D-NY)(1906-1997) described the Mutual Security Act as implementing U.S. foreign policy and representing the cost of collective security. She went on to stress the military assistance components of this legislation while also emphasizing how mutual security was enhanced by promoting direct economic and commodity assistance to recipient nations. She also expressed pleasure that this law gave the President enhanced flexibility in allocating security assistance and tightened controls on military shipments into and out of the U.S. while also criticizing the Eisenhower Administration's decision to alter the Battle Act's strategic control list; and contending that the administration should not succumb to foreign pressure to admit China to the United Nations.[8]

Eisenhower Administration Battle Act liberalization, while received favorably by allies such as the British, incurred the displeasure of some members in Congress who thought it showed excessive favoritism toward the Soviet bloc. One of these upset members of Congress was Senator John McClellan (D-AR)(1896-1977) who chaired the Senate Government Operations Committee's Permanent Subcommittee on Investigations. McClellan claimed he received damaging information about increased strategic exports to the Soviet bloc following Battle Act controls liberalization. His subcommittee held public hearings on February 15 and March 29, 1956 on this subject. One witness was Defense Department (DOD) machine tools specialist John Williams who contended, under questioning from committee members such as John Kennedy (D-MA)(1917-1963) and Joseph McCarthy (R-WI)(1908-1957), that liberalized export controls allowed machine tools with primarily military applications to be exported and that such tools enabled the Soviets to surpass U.S. arms production.[9]

The Eisenhower Administration was put on the defensive by these developments and former Foreign Operations Administration Director Harold Stassen (1907-2001) maintained this liberalization had occurred to preserve the western alliance and had done no real harm to U.S. security. McClellan's committee requested additional information about the controls and the U.S. role in the multilateral export control system

COCOM. Administration officials refused to provide this information by invoking national security and executive privilege. Eventually, general statistical information on this trade was released, but technical descriptions of controlled list items were withheld. 10

The committee filed a report on its investigation on July 18, 1956 denouncing the Administration for disregarding congressional intent in liberalizing so many items and withholding from Americans information that foreign nations receiving U.S. aid were helping Communist countries arm themselves. Committee recommendations included the need for Congress to receive current and complete information on export controls administration on whether Battle Act legislative intent was being fulfilled; that proposed removal of export control list items be submitted to congressional armed services, foreign relations, and government operations committees for review; that DOD play a more active role in proposed export control revisions; and that careful attention be paid to the qualifications of administration staff charged with reviewing export control or decontrol decisions. 11

Senator Karl Mundt (R-ND)(1900-1974) and George Bender (R-OH)(1896-1961), both staunch anticommunists, issued a minority report blasting the majority's conclusions. They accused their colleagues of producing a distorted and simplistic picture of East-West trade. Their appraisal defended the Eisenhower Administration's voluntarily testifying before the committee; lambasted the report for failing to recognize what they saw as the administration's strong position on trade with Soviet bloc countries; maintained that there are limits on how much multilateral control can be exerted on trade with the Soviet bloc; failing to provide Deputy Director for Mutual Defense Assistance Control Admiral Walter Delany additional opportunity to testify before the committee concluded its investigation; and regretting that allied nations were not as realistic as the U.S. in restricting strategic shipments to the Soviet bloc. 12

Congressional deference to executive branch export control policymaking continued in the early 1960s. A House Select Export Controls committee chaired by Rep. Paul Kitchen (D-NC)(1908-1993) believed a total embargo on U.S. trade with communist countries should be the primary goal of U.S. export controls. This committee passed export control legislation in 1962 authorizing the President to consider the economic significance of unrestricted material exports; determining whether such exports would adversely affect U.S. military security; giving the President the power to deny export licenses to any nation or nations threatening U.S. national security; and determining if such exports significantly enhance the economic and military potential of nations in a way detrimental to U.S. security. A 1962 Senate Banking and Currency Committee report on export controls also called for continuing expansive presidential export control authority.[13]

Congressional support for broad presidential export control authority lessened as the 1960s progressed due to increasing disenchantment with Vietnam War developments. Congressional concern over arms sales, their impact on relationships with allied nations, and an increasing belief that they promoted conflict between developing countries was reflected in a 1967 Senate Foreign Relations Committee study. This document recommended that the U.S. needed to reappraise the sufficiency of arms sale policy control and legislative oversight; that the State Department's Munitions Control Office should have to compile a quarterly list of commercial and governmental arms exports; that DOD should give full accounting of public funds used in the annual military assistance credit account; that Congress should examine the military sales program's decision making to determine if federal agencies, including the Agency for International Development, are meeting their legal responsibilities, and that the U.S. should play a leadership role in organizing regional conventional weapons "free zones" that would be free of sophisticated offensive and defensive weapons such as missiles, supersonic fighter jets, and tanks from regions such as Latin America and Africa.[14]

This increasing congressional desire to assert itself on export control issues and restrict military sales culminated with the 1968 Arms Export Control Act (AECA). This legislation passed the House 312-29 on September 10, 1968 and was approved by voice vote in the Senate on October 10. Speaking in favor of AECA, Rep. Clarence Long (D-MD)(1908-1994) stressed that the U.S. was the biggest arms seller in the world selling $11-12 billion worth of weapons in recent years and declared:

> I think the record shows we need this type of legislation to protect us against the State Department, which seems to be determined to sell arms anywhere for various purposes, either to get exchange, or power, or influence, or for some other purpose.[15]

AECA was signed by the President on Oct. 22, 1968 and its provisions included directing recipient countries to pay for weapons from Defense Department stocks at current market value and requiring the

President to report to Congress semiannually on arms sales to developing countries including forecasts of anticipated future sales.[16]

Congressional assertion of its influence and desire to liberalize trade laws occurred with 1969 passage of the Export Administration Act (EAA). Members of Congress became increasingly concerned that U.S. export controls were weakening the economic competitiveness of export oriented companies. This concern was demonstrated by declines in the U.S. international balance of payments during the 1960s. In 1960, the U.S. trade surplus was $3.508 billion which rose to $6.022 billion by 1964. However, the U.S. trade surplus had declined to $91 million by 1969 and would become a trade deficit for every year since then except 1973.[17]

Concern over the lack of competitiveness of U.S. export industries with their international competitors in having access to the Soviet bloc market and inconsistencies in U.S. and allied countries export controls toward the Soviet bloc played a significant role in producing EAA's more liberalized export control provisions. These concerns were reflected by in comments made by Rep. Garry Brown (R-MI)(1923-1998) in a congressional committee report on this legislation. Brown noted that the 1949 Export Control Act occurred when U.S. friends and allies saw no reason to protect or promote their Soviet trade and were content to support U.S. trade restriction policies. He went on to add that times had changed contending:

> Straight extension of the Export Control Act is economically unrealistic because it limits and restricts trade by our domestic exporters to Soviet bloc nations without in any way controlling the receipt [of] Soviet bloc nations of the very same goods as commodities from other sources . . . and, we have been advised by witnesses appearing before the committee that there are many items on our prohibited trade list which could make no significant strategic contribution to Soviet bloc nations. . . . It is not only unrealistic but it is unwise for us to extend the authority of an act, the substantial impact of which is the penalizing of our exporters and the prevention of trade which would help us improve our disgraceful balance of trade and payments position.[18]

Further concern over the effectiveness of U.S. export controls and their impact on the competitive status of U.S. export trade was reflected during 1969 congressional hearings on this topic. This hearing noted that U.S. extension of foreign aid to allied countries after World War II was contingent on their adhering to U.S. export control laws toward the Soviet bloc and that Europeans did not believe that denying trade with the Soviet bloc would end Communism or derail Communist countries economic development. One witness noted that the rise of multinational corporations made it more difficult to regulate and control the issuance of export licenses while another witness noted that his company's attempts to export an agricultural insecticide plant to the Soviet Union took five months to receive Commerce Department license application approval and that the Soviets became so frustrated with this licensing delay that they bought a similar plant from Japan two months before the U.S. firm received its export license.[19]

Upon its enactment later that year, EAA sought to encourage trade with all countries the U.S. had diplomatic and trade relations with unless the President determined such trade was against the national interest; restricted exports of goods and technologies that would significantly enhance the military potential or hostile nations; exercise vigilance over how exports impact U.S. national security; coordinate export controls in cooperation with countries the U.S. has defense treaty commitments with; use domestic economic resources and trade potential to enhance sound national economic growth and stability consistent with foreign and national security policy objectives; oppose restrictive trade practices or boycotts supported by hostile foreign countries; and encourage U.S. export oriented businesses to refuse to take part in such boycotts targeting U.S-alllied countries.[20]

Congressional influence was also apparent in 1977 enactment of the International Economic Emergency Powers Act (IEEPA) giving the President expanded authority to investigate, regulate, or prohibit various activities for national emergency reasons including:

1. Investigating, regulating, compelling, notifying, and prohibiting foreign exchange transactions and transfers involving foreign countries or nationals;
2. Declaring why these actions must be taken against national security threats to U.S. economic prosperity, foreign policy, or national security and reporting to Congress every six months to explain these actions.[21]

This statute was enacted to update the 1917 Trading With the Enemy Act (TEA). Insightful comments on congress' desire to update TEA, along with often conflicting congressional and presidential administration interpretations of this and other export control laws, occur in the transcripts of committee hearings reviewing IEEPA. On April 26, 1977 Rep. Jonathan Bingham (D-NY)(1914-1986) asked the State Department's Assistant Secretary of State for Economic and Business Affairs Julius Katz what national emergency facing the U.S. warranted using TEA powers. Katz responds and the following exchange occurs:

Katz: It continues to be the emergency involving the threat of Communist aggression which was declared in 1950 at the time of the aggression in Korea?

Bingham: Are you serious?

Katz: That is the national emergency, Mr. Chairman, and it continues.

Bingham: The emergency is the emergency that existed in 1950?

Katz: It has not been terminated.

Bingham: I am asking you for the facts. What is the national emergency that the country confronts today?

Katz: No President since that time has seen fit to terminate that emergency. I think that some of the precise circumstances have changed, but I think the general situation remains unchanged. The need for controls against North Korea has remained unchanged. . . .[22]

A 1979 *Foreign Affairs* article by Bingham, who chaired the House Foreign Affairs Subcommittee on International Economic Policy and Trade, contains interesting analysis of some congressional assessment on export controls diminishing returns over a protracted time period:

Trade embargoes are typically justified at first as a device to deny resources to an offending regime, both to limit its capabilities and with the ultimate hope of bringing the regime down. However, the fact that embargoes invariably remain in effect long after the regime in question is firmly ensconced in power indicates that the real purpose has become—or always was—the basically symbolic one of dissociating the United States from the regime and expressing disapproval of its behavior. Because embargoes serve these symbolic purposes, both internationally and domestically, it is difficult to lift them without seeming to send an unwanted signal. This alone suggests that trade embargoes are too insensitive to changes in another country's behavior to be a very Appropriate tool for influencing that behavior.[23]

Congress also sought to work its influence on U.S. export control laws during the Reagan Administration's early years. A particularly vivid example of this was its efforts to end the Carter Administration's grain embargo imposed on the Soviet Union following its 1979 invasion of Afghanistan. This move proved particularly unpopular with farm belt congressional delegations reflecting vociferous opposition to this from farmers benefitting from U.S. agricultural exports. Senator David Pryor (D-AR) questioned Secretary of Agriculture Bob Bergland on whether the government had considered creating a mechanism protecting farmers from future market disruptions such as embargoes. Senator Rudy Boschwitz (R-MN) criticized Berglund for continuing to supply the Soviet Army with meat and continuing to comply with a contract to send Moscow six million tons of grain the following year. This congressional opposition and other agricultural trading countries increasing their exports to the Soviet Union doomed this attempt at export controls.[24]

The Reagan Administration's early years also saw one congressional attempt to enhance the efficiency of federal export control policymaking. On August 18, 1982 Rep. Robin Beard (R-TN)(1939-2007) introduced H.R. 7015 the Office of Strategic Trade Act of 1982. This legislation sought to create an Office of Strategic Trade as an independent executive agency. Elements of this office included an Operations Division, Compliance Division, COCOM Division, Licensing Division, and General Counsel's Office. Beard also sought for this office's Director to issue various kinds of licenses and prohibit imposing export controls on goods or technology for foreign policy or national security reasons if the President determines there is sufficient evidence showing comparable goods are available from foreign sources in significant quantities and the absence of such controls would not injure U.S. foreign policy of national security.[25]

Beard's legislation also sought to establish a National Security Control Agency within the Office of the Under Secretary of Defense for Policy to help carry out Defense Department (DOD) national security export control policies; required (DOD) to report annually to Congress on actions taken on national security export controls; and required the office's director to appoint technical advisory committees to assist DOD and other federal agencies in carrying out national security export control policy. This legislation only attracted six cosponsors and died at the end of the 97th Congress.[26]

Congressional displeasure with allied countries lack of effective export controls was revealed with the Toshiba-Kongsberg affair during the Reagan Administration. This scandal saw the Japanese company's Toshiba's subsidiary machine company sell propeller milling machinery to the Soviet Union through the Norwegian Kongsberg company violating COCOM export control rules. This sale drastically increased the quietness of Soviet submarines, reduced Soviet research and development costs; and enhanced the difficulty of U.S. submarines in detecting and tracking Soviet submarines. Congress would ultimately respond by enacting the Multilateral Export Control Enhancement Act in 1988 whose provisions included requiring the President to apply sanctions of two to five years against individuals violating COCOM munitions list rules if the violation substantially enhanced Soviet bloc technologies in submarine or antisubmarine warfare and related ballistic missile technologies.[27]

Senator Alan Dixon (D-IL), commenting on the problems inherent in enforcing multilateral export controls and global technology diffusion stressed:

> The United States no longer has a monopoly on high technology. We have to work together with our allies on a joint control regime, one that is creditable and workable. If we are to prevent future diversions of this type, we must work jointly with our allies on a control regime that makes sense for them and us. Without that kind of joint action, the Soviets will be able to get whatever technology they need. This case is a powerful illustration to the allies of the cost of lax enforcement of export controls. I hope the American Government will be able to make good use of it in encouraging the allies to beef up their enforcement efforts. It is also a powerful illustration to our own Government of the perils of not taking foreign availability considerations seriously enough in making export control policy. I hope our own officials take the lesson to heart.[28]

Senator Jake Garn (R-UT) emphasized the serious military consequences of the diversion of submarine technology to the Soviet Union, asked a DOD witness how much it would cause for the U.S. to make up for this technological diversion at a time of prospective defense spending cuts, also stressed frustration with Japan's limited defense spending and anger at Tokyo's decision to only suspend Toshiba trading privileges with the Soviet Union for one year, and recommended enacting legislation banning Toshiba products from the U.S. He went on to express his anger with the following rhetorical flourish:

> Let me put it as bluntly as I can. We have a company who has endangered the security of their own country as well as ours and our Western allies, and I don't care how many indictments they have, it isn't sufficient and we ought to start hitting them in the pocket book and really hurt Toshiba and let the word go out that we are not going to continue to spend defense dollars for these diversionary purposes while our allies, so-called allies Japan and Western Europe, continue to subsidize exports to this country, reduce employment in this country, hurt our profit picture and all of the things that go with that trade deficit and continue to handle it with tokenism.[29]

Congressional involvement in drafting the 1996 Antiterrorism and Effective Death Penalty Act saw the initial incorporation of targeting terrorist group finances and linking U.S. foreign assistance to countries degree of cooperation with U.S. antiterrorism policies as House Judiciary Committee Chair Rep. Henry Hyde (R-IL)(1924-2007) noted on April 18, 1996:

> This bill provides for an open designation process of what is a foreign terrorist organization. It denies those terrorist organizations the ability to raise money in this country. It provides authority to the State Department to deny entrance visas to members of those designated foreign terrorist organizations. It provides a fair and even process to deport alien terrorists. It denies assistance to foreign countries that do not cooperate with us in our antiterrorism efforts.[30]

Congress also sought to put its inprint on export control policymaking and restricting terrorism financing in the aftermath of the 9/11 terrorist attacks. The biggest early demonstration of this was 2001's USA Patriot Act. Provisions of this act included tracking and seizing terrorist financial assets; prohibiting facilitating the design, development, or production of weapons of mass destruction; including smuggling and export control violations involving items on USML and EAR into U.S. anti-money laundering statutes; enhancing Treasury Department data collection on financial transactions such as exporting monetary instruments involving potential terrorist activity; and prohibiting restricted individuals from possessing, shipping, or receiving biological agents in foreign or interstate trade.[31]

During October 25, 2001 Senate debate on this legislation many Senators, including Sam Brownback (R-KS), John Kerry (D-MA), and Arlen Specter (R-PA)(1930-2012) commented positively on these antiterrorism financing provisions. Their comments noted that, once passed, this legislation would make it possible to capture those committing acts of terrorism along with those financing them; enhance the ability to track money laundering through hawala financial institutions supporting Al Qaeda; lessen financial account secrecy for those assisting terrorists; ensuring foreign financial institutions maintain adequate records on foreign terrorist organizations and their membership or individuals engaged in money laundering or other financial crimes; and making this information readily available to U.S. financial regulation and law enforcement personnel.[32]

The Iran Freedom Support Act was signed by President Bush on September 30, 2006. Key characteristics of this statute included permitting the President to investigate imposing sanctions against individuals investing in Iran and imposing sanctions against individuals, nations, and organizations knowingly transporting materials and technologies facilitating Iranian attempts to acquire weapons of mass destruction.[33]

Legislation supporters such as Rep. Ileana Ros-Lehtinen (R-FL) presented their case maintaining:

> This bill provides a comprehensive approach, providing U.S. officials with strong leverage to secure cooperation from our allies in order to counter The Iranian threat. The sanctions under title II of this bill seek to target the Iranian regime where it is most vulnerable: Its energy sector. Knowledgeable experts agree that for Iran, a fuel importer, sanctions could be crippling. Thus, Mr. Speaker, this bill is not an alternative to diplomacy, but rather complimentary to our multilateral efforts. We cannot afford to wait any longer as the potential consequences of further inaction could be catastrophic.[34]

Critics of this legislation such as Rep. Maurice Hinchey (D-NY) argued the legislation was contrary to Iranian and U.S. national interests; that it reminded him of President George W. Bush's Axis of Evil remarks in a State of the Union address; that the U.S. has had an excessively aggressive and overbearing attitude to Iran for over 50 years; and claimed that the U.S. needed to engage Iran in a more objective, serious, filial, and friendly manner.[35]

Congressional fingerprints were also involved in 2011 legislation designating Iran's financial sector as a money laundering concern due to

Tehran's pursuit of nuclear weapons and supporting terrorism; giving the President power to freeze Iranian financial institution assets; and other actions seeking to weaken Iran's petroleum industry.[36] This legislation received broad bipartisan support from Senators such as John Hoeven (R-ND), Mark Kirk (R-IL), and Robert Menendez (D-NJ). Justifications for this legislation cited by these and other Senators during December 1, 2011 debate included Iranian Central Bank attempts to evade international sanctions on Iran by that institution aiding its government's efforts to acquire nuclear weapons; Iran's attempt to assassinate the Saudi Ambassador to the U.S.; recent Iranian sacking of the British Embassy in Tehran; the need to penalize U.S. and other U.S. companies doing business with Iran; and the desire to drastically weaken Iran's economically and strategically important petroleum industry.[37]

The Obama Administration sought to introduce legislation to streamline the export control system and process beginning in March 2012 which has already been covered in Chapter 2.[38] However, legislative initiatives to implement or negotiate on these proposed reforms has been very limited. On May 26, 2011 Rep. Howard Berman (D-CA) introduced H.R. 2004 The Technology Security Act of 2011 to permit presidential authority to control exports for national security and foreign policy reasons; promote U.S. leadership and competitiveness in manufacturing, science, and technology for national security, and foreign policy reasons, and give the President authority to assign and intain export licensing criteria.[39]

June 3, 2011 saw House Foreign Affairs Committee Chair Ros-Lehtinen introduce H.R. 2122 the Export Administration Renewal Act to reauthorize the expired EAA through 2015; increase the export control penalty structure to make it consistent with IEEPA; provide the Commerce Department enhanced investigative and overseas export enforcement authority; and permit liberalization of some United States Munitions List (USML) exports except for those destined for China. No significant action was taken on these bills during the 112th Congress.[40]

Conclusion

Congressional legislation, debate, oversight, lack of oversight, and funding authority has created and sustained the complex byzantine and labyrinthine U.S. export control regime. This process has occurred over several decades, created deeply entrenched bureaucratic and political interests in the executive and legislative branches, and makes reforming this system incredibly difficult, if not impossible, due to the involvement of so many oversight committees, the shifting and spasmodic interest held toward this subject by Representatives and Senators, and by the variety of opinions held on international trade and national security oriented trade by private sector companies represented by congressional members.

A 1989 assessment of the relationship between the executive branch and Congress over export control policymaking remains valid nearly a quarter century later:

> Certain patterns have emerged over forty years of U.S. export controls. First, the lawmaking process often reveals a clash of executive and congressional interests. Although policy differences have existed between agencies and within Congress (especially of late), the executive has generally presented a unified front in expressing statutory preferences distinct from those of the congressional majority. Contrary to the congressional emphasis on making the export control system more efficient and accountable, and its use as a tool of general foreign policy acceptable, the executive has stressed the need to use export controls to further its national security and foreign policy goals. Moreover, during the lawmaking process, the executive has been able to prevail on Congress to modify legislation so that executive authority and flexibility would not be significantly altered.[41]

This assessment goes on to contend that although executive departments and agencies have divergent export control policy attitudes, they are better able to unite around a legislative strategy and pursue that strategy than congressional members seeking to change that policy. This cohesion is particularly enhanced if given clear White House direction. These factors, including partisan influence, help create more unified executive branch export control policymaking than congressional policymaking, which is augmented by the executive branch's historic and constitutional responsibility for protecting U.S. national security, furthering U.S. foreign policy interests, and possessing superior export control administration technical experience and expertise than Congress.[42]

Congress will continue attempting to influence export control policymaking through its oversight responsibilities and funding authorities. The U.S.' heavily constrained fiscal environment, the unwillingness of the executive branch and congressional oversight committees to surrender export control jurisdictional activity, and continuing partisan enmity between the Obama Administration and a Republican controlled House of Representatives, even after the 2012 presidential election, is not likely to produce significant progress in reforming U.S. export control laws for the foreseeable future.

Notes

1. See *U.S. Constitution*, Article 1, Sections 8-9 for relevant congressional oversight and funding powers; Jonathan B. Bingham and Victor C. Johnson, " A Rational Approach to Export Controls," *Foreign Affairs*, 57 (4)(Spring 1979): 894-920; William J. Long, *U.S. Export Control Policy: Executive Autonomy vs. Congressional Reform*, (New York: Columbia University Press, 1989); and Wendy J. Schiller, "Trade Politics in the American Congress: A Study of the Interaction of Political Geography and Interest Group Behavior," *Political Geography*, 18 (7)(1999): 769-789.

2. See U.S. Congress, House Committee on Appropriations, *Semiannual Report of Committee Activities*, House Report 112-145, (Washington, DC: GPO, 2011): 6-8; Ibid., House Committee on Armed Services, *First Semiannual Report of the Activities of the Committee on Armed Services*, House Report 112-123, (Washington, DC: GPO, 2011): 18, 46, 69; Ibid., House Committee on Financial Services, *First Semiannual Report on the Activities of the Committee on Financial Services*, House Report 112-121; (Washington, DC: GPO, 2011): 39-61, 114, 119-121, 123; Ibid., House Foreign Affairs Committee, *Legislative Review and Oversight Activities*, House Report 112-126, (Washington, DC: GPO, 2011): 4, 8-18; Ibid., House Committee on Homeland Security, *Report on Legislative and Oversight Activities*, House Report 112-127, (Washington, DC: GPO, 2011): 3-8, 65-78; Ibid., House Committee on the Judiciary, *First Semiannual Report on the Activities of the Committee on the Judiciary*, House Report 112-119, (Washington, DC: GPO, 2011): 2, 11-14; Ibid., House Permanent Select Committee on Intelligence, *Semiannual Report of the Activity of the House Permanent Select Committee on Intelligence*, House Report 112-134; (Washington, DC: GPO, 2011): 19-20; Ibid., House Committee on Ways and Means, *Report on the Legislative and Oversight Activities*, House Report 112-130; (Washington, DC: GPO, 2011): 11-12; 19; Ibid., Senate Committee on Appropriations, *Subcommittee Jurisdiction by Program*, Senate Print 110-11, (Washington, DC: GPO, 2007); Ibid., Senate Committee on Armed Services, *Report of the Activities*, Senate Report 112-2, (Washington, DC: GPO, 2011): 1, 26-30; Ibid., Senate Banking, Housing, and Urban Affairs Committee, *Report on the Activities of the Committee on Banking, Housing, and Urban Affairs*, Senate Report 112-7, (Washington, DC: GPO, 2011): 7-8; Ibid., Sen-

ate Finance Committee, *Report on the Activities of the Committee on Finance*, Senate Report 112-11; (Washington, DC: GPO, 2011): 1, 13-14; Ibid., Senate Committee on Foreign Relations, *Membership and Jurisdiction of Subcommittees*, Senate Print 111-3, (Washington, DC: GPO, 2009); Ibid., Senate Committee on Homeland Security and Governmental Affairs, *Rules and Procedures*, Senate Print 112-11, (Washington, DC: GPO, 2011): 31-36; Ibid., Senate Committee on the Judiciary, *Report of the Activities of the Committee on the Judiciary*, Senate Print 112-5, (Washington, DC: GPO, 2011): 1, 12; and Ibid., Senate Permanent Select Committee on Intelligence, *Report of the Select Committee on Intelligence*, Senate Report 112-3.(Washington, DC: GPO, 2011): 12-37.

3. See U.S. Congress, *Reports to Be Made to Congress: Communication From the Clerk, U.S. House of Representatives*, House Document 112-79, (Washington, DC: GPO, 2012). For the voluminous scholarly literature on this topic see also Joel D. Aberbach, *Keeping a Watchful Eye: The Politics of Congressional Oversight,*" (Washington, DC: Brookings Institution, 1990); Jonathan G. Pray, "Congressional Reporting Requirements: Testing the Limits of Oversight Power, *University of Colorado Law Review* 76 (1) (Winter 2005): 297-325; Richard F. Grimmett, *Arms Sales: Congressional Review Process*, (Washington, DC: Library of Congress, Congressional Research Service, 2007); and Lee Mordecai, *Congress vs the Bureaucracy: Muzzling Agency Public Relations*, (Norman: University of Oklahoma Press, 2011).

4. *Reports to Be Made to Congress*, 18-19, 51, 61, 145, 154.

5. U.S. Congress, Senate Committee on Banking and Currency, *Export Control Act of 1949: Report to Accompany S. 548*, Senate Report 81-31, (Washington, DC: GPO, 1949): 2-10.

6. *Congressional Record,* 97 (9)(August 28, 1951): 10719-10720, 10738, 10740, 10746.

7. U.S. Congress, House Committee on Foreign Affairs, Subcommittee on Foreign Economic Policy, *East-West Trade*, (Washington, DC: GPO, 1954): 20, 30, 36.

8. *Congressional Record* 100 (12)(August 20, 1954): 15666-15667.

9. See Richard T. Cupitt, *Reluctant Champions: Truman, Eisenhower, Bush, and Clinton: U.S. Presidential Policy and Strategic Export Controls*, (New York: Routledge, 2000): 111; and U.S. Congress, Senate Committee on Government Operations, Permanent Subcommittee on Investigations, *East-West Trade Pts. 1-3*, (Washington, DC: GPO, 1956): 56-71, 75-79.

10. Cupitt, 112-113.

11. U.S. Congress, Senate Committee on Government Operations, Permanent Subcommittee on Investigations, *East-West Trade: Report Together With Minority Views*, Senate Report 84-2621, Serial 11890 (Washington, DC: GPO, 1956): 48-49.

12. Ibid., 50-58.

13. See Long, 25; and U.S. Congress, House Select Committee on Export Control, *Investigation and Study of the Administration, Operation and Enforcement of the Export Control Act of 1949, and Related Acts*, House Report 87-1753, Serial 12430 (Washington, DC: GPO, 1962); and U.S. Congress, Senate Committee on Banking and Currency, *Extension of Export Control Act of 1949*, Senate Report 87-1576, Serial 12417 (Washington, DC: GPO, 1962): 4-5.

14. U.S. Congress, Senate Committee on Foreign Relations, *Arms Sales and Foreign Policy*, (Washington, DC: GPO, 1967): 12-13.

15. See *Congressional Record*, 114 (20)(September 10, 1968): 26227; Ibid., 114 (20)(October 10, 1968): 30403-30405; and Peter K. Tompa, "The Arms Export Control Act and Congressional Codetermination Over Arms Sales", *American University International Journal of International Law and Policy*, 1 (1)(Summer 1986): 291-33

16. Public Law 90-629, "Foreign Military Sales Act," 82 *U.S. Statutes at Large* 1320-1328

17. U.S. Census Bureau, "U.S. Trade in Goods and Services-Balance of Payments (BOP) Basis 1960 thru 2011," (Washington, DC: U.S. Census Bureau, 2012); 1; http://www.census.gov/foreign-trade/statistics/historical/gands.txt; Accessed November 6, 2012.

18. U.S. Congress, House Committee on Banking and Currency, *Export Control Act Extension: Report Together With Supplemental Views To Accompany H.R. 4293*, House Report 91-524, Serial 12837-3, (Washington, DC: GPO, 1969): 17-18.

19. Ibid., Subcommittee on International Trade, *To Extend and Amend the Export Control Act of 1949*, (Washington, DC: GPO, 1969): 4-5, 10-11, 31.

20. Public Law 91-184, "U.S. Export Administration Act of 1969," 83 *U.S. Statutes at Large*, 842-844

21. Public Law 95-223, "With Respect to the President in Time of War of National Emergency," 91 *U.S. Statutes at Large* 1625-1628.

22. U.S. Congress, House Committee on International Relations, Subcommittee on International Economic Policy and Trade, *Emergency Controls on International Economic Transactions*, (Washington, DC: GPO, 1977): 110; http://catalog.hathitrust.org/Record/002939966; Accessed November 6, 2012.

23. Bingham and Johnson, "A Rational Approach to Export Controls," *Foreign Affairs*, 57 (4)(Spring 1979): 908.

24. See U.S. Congress, Senate Committee on Agriculture, Nutrition, and Forestry, *Embargo on Grain Sales to the Soviet Union*, (Washington, DC: GPO, 1980); Joseph Hajda, "The Soviet Grain Embargo," *Survival*, 22 (6)(December 1980): 53-58; and Robert L. Paarlberg, "Lessons of the Grain Embargo," *Foreign Affairs* , 59 (1)(Fall 1980): 144-162.

25. H.R. 7015, *Office of Strategic Trade Act of 1982*, (Washington, DC: GPO, 1982).

26. *Bill Summary & Status 97th Congress (1981-1982) H.R. 7015 CRS Summary*, (Washington, DC: Library of Congress, Congressional Research Service, 1982): 3-4; http://thomas.loc.gov/cgi-bin/bdquery/D?d097:183:./temp/ ~bdlm1A:@@@D&summ2=m&|/home/LegislativeData.php?n=BSS;c=97|; Accessed November 7, 2012.

27. See U.S. Congress, Senate Committee on Banking, Housing, and Urban Affairs, Subcommittee on International Finance and Monetary Policy, *Toshiba-Kongsberg Technology Diversion Case*, (Washington, DC: GPO, 1987); and Public Law 100-418, "Omnibus Trade and Competitiveness Act of 1988, 102 *U.S. Statutes at Large* 1107, 1364-1366.

28. *Toshiba-Kongsberg Technology Diversion Case*, 10.

29. Ibid., 22, 25.

30. See Public Law 104-132, "Antiterrorism and Effective Death Penalty Act of 1996," 110 *U.S. Statutes at Large* 1214-1215, 1247-1248, 1250, 1255-1258; and *Congressional Record* 142 (50)(April 18, 1996): H3603.

31. Public Law 107-56, "USA Patriot Act," 115 *U.S. Statutes at Large* 292, 308-309, 330-331.

32. See *Congressional Record* 147 (144)(October 25, 2001): S11018, 11027-11028, 11044, 11046; and U.S. Congress, Senate Committee on Governmental Affairs, Permanent Subcommittee on Investigations, *Role of U.S. Correspondent Banking in International Money Laundering*, 5 vols. (Washington, DC: GPO, 2001).

33. Public Law 109-293, "Iran Freedom Support Act," 120 *U.S. Statutes at Large* 1344-1350.

34. *Congressional Record,* 152 (124)(September 28, 2006): H7697.

35. Ibid., H7704.

36. Public Law 112-81, "National Defense Authorization Act for Fiscal Year 2012," 125 *U.S. Statutes at Large*, 1647-1649.

37. *Congressional Record*, 157 (183) (December 1, 2011): S8105-S8138.

38. U.S. Department of Commerce, *President's Export Control Reform Initiative*, (Washington, DC: Department of Commerce, 2012); http://export.gov/ ECR/; Accessed November 7, 2012.

39. *Congressional Record*, 157 (74)(May 26, 2011): H3753.

40. Ibid., 157 (79)(June 3, 2011): H4034.

41. Long, 102.

42. Ibid.

Chapter 7

Nongovernment Organizations and Export Controls

Our attention now turns to how nongovernment organizations (NGOs) have sought and continue seeking to influence U.S. export control policymaking. Export oriented U.S. companies have taken various positions on federal export control policies and have taken optimal advantage of their constitutional right to "petition the government for redress" in their efforts to enhance their business interests and promote their visions of how export controls influence national security. Efforts of businesses to use this constitutional right have received significant scrutiny.[1]

NGOs have been involved in influencing all areas of U.S. export control policymaking including being involved in congressional investigative efforts, lobbying presidential administrations and congressional power brokers to intervene on their behalf, and seeking to gain competitive advantages against their domestic and international competitors. Testifying before the McClellan Committee on February 15, 1956, Rhodesian businessman Ronald Prain denied knowledge that any of his company's copper shipped to Great Britain was transshipped to the Soviet Union but admitted that copper shipped from Chile could go to the Soviet Union and he was unaware that the Soviet bloc was receiving copper from western sources.[2]

Business and NGOs were also involved in lobbying for and against various provisions of the U.S. export control policy regime between the Eisenhower and Ford Administrations on issues such as the Cuban Trade Embargo, the 1968 Arms Export Control Act, trading with Communist countries such as the Soviet Union and China, and constantly complaining about the complexity of U.S. export controls including onerous licensing requirements.[3]

Recognition of changes in the international trade environment in the late 1960s and concern that U.S. export controls such as the 1949 Export Control Act no longer reflected this reality was reflected in a June 5, 1969 letter from the Electronic Industries Association to Rep. Thomas Ashley (D-OH)(1923-2010) who chaired the House Banking and Currency Committee's International Trade Subcommittee. This letter emphasized:

> The world trade situation is undergoing such change that a decision to regulate U.S. exports by simply extending the present law is, in our view, inappropriate. The present law is twenty years old and is the product of a time when the world climate was significantly different. Year by year, as competition in international trade has become more intensive, the impact of the present law has been to impair the capability of U.S. exporters to claim for the United States a fair share of the trade in peaceful goods which has been steadily growing between companies in Eastern Europe and companies in Western Europe, plus Japan. However, if time or other considerations make extension of the present law unavoidable, this Association suggests that such extension be for one year only, or at most, for two years, and that during this time the Congress undertake further intensive review of all aspects of this important matter.[4]

Continuing criticism of the burdensome nature of U.S. export controls was expressed on March 11, 1976 by Alan Spurney from the Joint High-Technology Industries' Group on Export Administration. He mentioned that these industries supported export controls essential for U.S. national security and foreign policy interests while adding that administration of such controls impeded commercial activity and prevented U.S. business and industry from timely and profitable performance. Spurney went on to contend that existing law should be strengthened to simplify federal agency procedures; yield more equitable results for private business; facilitate efforts to trade with Soviet bloc countries; and that high-tech businesses abilities to maintain profit margins are hindered by poorly defined and partially hidden government policies.[5]

He was particularly vociferous in his criticism of U.S. export licensing policy which foreign competitors view as one of their top selling advantages. For instance, he maintained that it can take four to five months to obtain a license for a previously approved commodity, to a previously approved end user, for a previously approved end use, while competitors from allied countries can obtain processed licenses for identical items within six weeks. Spurney went on to propose that a maximum period of 60 days be allowed to approve or deny an export license, subject to one 60-day extension, with the application receiving automatic approval after 120 days.[6]

The Carter Administration's grain export embargo against the Soviet Union for its 1979 invasion of Afghanistan received scathing criticism from the agribusiness community. American Farm Bureau Federation Assistant Director Bruce Hawley told a Senate committee hearing on July 29, 1982, that in 1970 the U.S. controlled nearly 95% of the world soybean and soybean products export market with that percentage of control declining to 59% in 1981. Hawley attributed this decline to events such as the grain embargo and to federal actions which have created international belief that the U.S. is an unreliable agricultural trading partner.[7]

Donald E. Henderson, a Madison County, IN grain farmer serving as the Indiana Farm Bureau's director of national affairs, supported passage of legislation which he believed would enhance U.S. agricultural credibility by meeting its ability to fulfill national sales commitments and counter an international belief that the U.S. would use food as a foreign policy weapon making it an unreliable supplier. A National Corn Growers analysis of the Soviet grain embargo prepared for this congressional committee included the following estimates of direct economic costs and losses for the following domestic economic sectors:

1. Inland transportation-$120-$175 million
2. Reduced value of ocean shipping-$240-$365 million
3. Balance of Payment losses of up to $2.5 billion from lost exports and up to $1.9 billion from U.S. grain exports for 1980 and most of 1981.
4. Direct U.S. Government costs of $1.5 billion for acquiring additional commodities, and $1 billion for interest, storing, and handling from owningthese commodities; and
5. Additional $375 million in target price payments to wheat farmers.[8]

A series of 1983 congressional hearings also saw business organizations express concern over the impact of the 1977 Foreign Corrupt Practices Act (FCPA) on their ability to gain access to some international export markets. Testifying on April 25, 1983 on behalf of the National Association of Manufacturers, Harris Corporation Vice President Joseph Creighton noted that his company, which manufactured electronics, communications, and information processing systems equipment, had not seen an increase in its export growth since 1976 despite expanded marketing efforts. Creighton went on to maintain that FCPA strongly contributed to this decline because it and other U.S. laws signal foreign customers and distributors that the U.S. is judging them and their practices, indicating that the U.S. intends to apply its own laws extraterritorially and control economic activities within these countries, and that this is offensive to these foreign customers.[9]

Creighton went on to urge reform of FCPA advocating:

FCPA is basically unfair to corporate employees. As a corporate general counsel, who must constantly advise my firms and its employees, I am especially concerned about this inherent unfairness. The current law is unfair particularly to persons who must make sales in remote countries without benefit of on-the-spot legal advice and with little ability to investigate facts or time to investigate them or to make decisions. It is even more unfair to their superiors who, under most interpretations of the act, are said to be responsible for controlling overseas activities, not only by the corporate employees, but also controlling the individual dealers who are independent and who the American company really has no legal right to control.[10]

NGOs also expressed their concern over the security of loans made by U.S. banks and international financial institutions such as the International Monetary Fund to unreliable and potentially hostile foreign governments who have proven unable to repay these loans. During the 99th Congress (1985-1986), S. 812, The Financial Export Control Act was introduced Senator Jake Garn (R-UT) which sought to amend the 1979 Export Administration Act to make it U.S. policy to use export controls to restrict capital exports, credit extension, or transferring financial resources to countries subject to national security export controls.

Although this legislation did not pass, it received an ideologically interesting cross-section of support. Howard Ruff of the Free the Eagle Citizen's Lobby urged its passage arguing that there is no control over banks wanting to lend money to hostile countries; that there need to be prohibitions on loans for military and high technology equipment; that any bank loans to hostile countries should not receive U.S. taxpayer guarantees; that Cuba, Nicaragua, and Poland have defaulted on loans they received from private banks; and that Soviet client states have used such loans to assist Communist countries in their political activities such as East Germany giving $84 million in cash and credits to Nicaragua.

This legislation was also supported by the AFL-CIO whose Economic Research Department Deputy Director Henry Schechter argued that financial assistance should not be extended to countries violating human rights and suppressing free and independent trade unions.[11]

The 1989-1991 collapse of the Soviet bloc brought further advocacy for liberalized export controls from NGOs including the business and academic communities. Testifying before the House Science Committee on May 16, 1990, U.S. Council for International Business Senior Vice President for Policy and Programs Ronnie Goldberg, maintained that COCOM was essential to maintaining U.S. national security interests and that if it collapsed the competitive disadvantage of U.S. technology exporters, in comparison with their European and Japanese counterparts, would become even greater at a time of expanding Eastern European markets.[12]

However, Goldberg also expressed concern that the U.S. still maintained unilateral export controls and reexport controls and also criticized the delays in U.S. licensing approval which was competitively injurious to U.S. companies in relationship to their COCOM competitors. He also expressed concern about Bush Administration export control emphasis on maintaining the existing Militarily Critical Technologies List (MCTL) asserting:

> We're troubled, frankly, at the suggestion in the administration proposals that the militarily critical technologies list will be "a vital guide in building this new core technologies list." Those of us who have followed the progress of the critical technologies exercise since 1976, . . . will understand our concern on basing the U.S. contribution to a new core technology exercise on the MCTL may prove simply impracticable. Should the U.S. embark on this new exercise, intending to base its participation mainly on the MCTL, it would face in our view, at least two very serious practical problems.

First, it is unlikely that agreement on core technology could be reached within the ambitious time frame set by the administration and dictated by the pace of events, . . . and secondly, we think there would be great difficulty in producing proposals for a core list acceptable to our COCOM allies. We know that there are very great differences in the views between our government and the governments of our COCOM allies on what constitutes a critical technology in the military sense.

We believe, . . . that the U.S. must be at least willing to consider a fundamentally new concept and set of criteria for core technologies.[13]

The Sisphyean effort to promote U.S. international economic competitiveness, reform export control structures, and protect national security continued its protracted saga throughout the 1990s as NGOs expressed their perspectives and frustrations. On July 31, 1996, the Senate Banking Committee held a hearing on H.R. 361, the Export Administration Act of 1996 introduced by Rep. Toby Roth (R-WI) which sought to place emphasis on imposing export controls to restrict the export of weapons of mass destruction. American Electronics Association President William T. Archey supported provisions of this legislation requiring export controls to be multilateral with strict discipline against unilateral application; restricting truly sensitive choke-point technologies through international negotiation and input from business; consolidating routine export licensing authority in the Commerce Department; clearly telling exporters what goods are controlled, to whom they are controlled, and the circumstances in which export control licenses can be issued; and conducting an annual controlled products review binding the Administration to decontrol prospective exports when evidence of their ineffectiveness, foreign availability, and economic impact is clear.[14]

Archey also expressed concern that this legislation would codify a recent executive order authorizing five agencies instead of two to review any export license application regardless of the product's significance; that frivolous lawsuits against companies would increase from other companies seeking to charge their competitors with violating antiboycott laws; that increasing company fines for export control violations from $10,000 to $250,000 doesn't make sense; and that antiterrorism sections of this proposed legislation would place decontrolled products back under export control listing.[15]

Representing the Association for Manufacturing Technology, Thomas T. Connelly urged approval of this legislation and improving its foreign availability provisons. He went on justify his organization's support for H.R. 361 by mentioning a 1994 cable received from China's Chengdu Aircraft Corporation by Cincinnati Milacron which was the U.S.' largest machine tool producer at the time. In this cable Chengdu revealed that because of their difficulty in obtaining export licenses for American products, as opposed to not having such problems with European and Japanese governments, they were not inviting American companies to China for technical discussions or planning visits to United States manufacturers for possible future purchases.[16]

During this same hearing Chemical Manufacturers Association spokesman Richard H. Burgess supported many aspects of H.R. 361 but also urged enhancements to this legislation. These improvements included opposing provisions allowing for lawsuits against companies allegedly violating antiboycott laws; opposing giving the State Department unlimited authority to limit international agreements, and also expressing concern that it may force U.S. chemical companies to follow stricter export mixture rules than their foreign competitors.[17]

1996 also saw Congress pass the Economic Espionage Act due to increasing concerns over the need to protect proprietary economic information. This statute affects corporations and universities by establishing federal criminal penalties for stealing and making unauthorized copies of trade secrets to benefit a foreign government or agent while also authorizing wiretaps and other communication intercepts to investigate illicit trade secret usage.[18]

The increasing influence of computer technology and Clinton Administration attempts to impose export controls on encryption technology also incurred the concern of high technology companies at this time. During a March 8, 1997 House International Relations Committee hearing, Sun Microsystems Network Security Products Group General Manager Humphrey Polanen criticized Clinton efforts to control encryption exports with the following assessment:

> [W]e believe that the government's plan to control the export of strong cryptography does not really lead to an effective policy of protecting the national security interests, nor protecting the availability of this technology. . . . You can easily buy it today, you can import it, you can buy it abroad, so by restricting exports, you are not really accomplishing anything except the ability of our industry to take advantage of the burgeoning market for strong cryptography which we believe

will be about $60 billion in only a few years, and we cannot play on a level playing field with the proposed Administration's policy.[19]

This hearing also addressed conflicts between Internet commerce and personal privacy with Center for Democracy and Technology Executive Director Jerry Berman stressing how technology was impacting business and personal freedom as reflected in the following statement:

> I do not see the debate as a debate between security and privacy but a debate between two views of how we have security on the Internet. It is, . . . instructive that the business community is not coming to Congress and saying, in order for us to do business on the Internet, we need more police. They are coming in and saying, law enforcement is one thing, but if you want to protect us from the hackers, the security, the financial transactions, our information that is on the Net, we need encryption, we need technical means of protecting against crime around the world, because law enforcement stops at the border.

> Privacy advocates are saying the same thing from the other side, which says the fourth amendment stops at our border. We don't know how the fourth amendment will work in this global environment. We could use unlimited encryption in the United States, but when we get out on the information network, how are these systems going to work?[20]

NGO experts were also heavily involved in helping Congress conduct oversight over 1998 revelations of Loral-Hughes' satellite exports to China uncovered by the Cox Committee. Henry Sokolski of the Nonproliferation Policy Executive Center warned that technology transfer standards had become laxer during the 1990s and that China was very interested in U.S. ballistic missile defense development. Gary Milhollin of the Wisconsin Project on Nuclear Arms Control warned that U.S. export control liberalization enabled China to transfer ballistic missile technology to Iran and Pakistan without seriously worrying about losing its most powerful revenue source of U.S. satellite contracts. He also contended that China no longer exports complete missiles but that it engages in piecemeal releases of missile components which are harder to track.[21]

Milhollin went on to describe the contradictory standards the Commerce and State Departments use to define missile technology within satellites:

The State Department defines missile-related technology as technology even if it's embedded in a satellite. So even if a satellite has missile items in it, under the rules in the State Department, it's still sanctioned if the recipient is guilty of missile proliferation behavior. In the Commerce Department, as you might expect, things are defined differently. A missile-related item loses its character, under the Commerce Department view, once it is embedded in a satellite. So even if the recipient of the satellite is selling—is proliferating—missile technology to Iran and Pakistan, the Commerce Department wouldn't block the export of the satellite under its rules.[22]

Air War College International Security Studies Professor Joan Johnson-Freese noted contradictory export control expectations between China and various Western countries. She contended that rules applying in Western countries do not apply in Beijing; that China's bureaucracy was far more complex than the U.S.', and that the U.S. should do everything it could to promote China's commercial space industry to incentivize positive Chinese behavior in international missile nonproliferation activities.[23]

The multifaceted changes in U.S. security policy during the George W. Bush Administration also caused continuing frustration by U.S. export industries toward cumbersome export licensing procedures. During July 26, 2007 congressional testimony Lowell Defense Trade, LLC Managing Director Will Lowell stressed that the U.S. export control statutory system was sound. However, he expressed concern that the Government Accountability Office has designated export controls as a high risk government management matter; that licensing delays injure the commercial interests of U.S. and allied country companies by negatively affecting compliance with laws and regulations; that the U.S. export control system needs to be administered more efficiently to strengthen international compliance with it; that there has been no systematic evaluation of Commerce and State export controls in the post 9/11 environment; and stressing inconsistencies in licensing regulations such as requiring government approval to transfer a commercial communications satellite to a foreign individual but not requiring a license for transferring biological weapons to foreign individuals, or harbor entrance detection equipment or other munitions list controlled items to terrorist groups.[24]

Aerospace Industries Association of America President John W. Douglass also emphasized problems in distinguishing between military and civilian items in export licensing. Douglass was particularly concerned that the current licensing system created industries among U.S. international competitors such as in the space business because Washington has put commercial products on the U.S. Munitions List. He went on to stress that an effective export control system should include the following attributes:

1. Accurately identifies and safeguards sensitive and militarily critical technologies;
2. Enhances U.S. technological leadership and global industrial competitiveness through more responsive and efficient regulatory management;
3. Facilitates defense trade and technological exchange with allies and trusted partners;
4. Supports a strong U.S. technology industrial base and highly-skilled workforce; and
5. Promotes greater multilateral cooperation with our friends and allies on export controls.[25]

A February 24, 2008 report from the Center for Strategic and International Studies examining the impact of export controls on the U.S. space industrial base reached the following conclusions:

1. The overall health of top tier space manufacturers is satisfactory but there are areas of concern within the industry's broader health.
2. The U.S. space industrial base is largely dependent on the defense national security budget.
3. The U.S. does not control the proliferation of rapidly emerging foreign space capabilities.
4. Current export control policy has not prevented the rise of foreign space capabilities preventing the grand strategic intent of space export controls from being achieved.
5. U.S. space leadership benefits significantly from access to foreign innovation and human capital but that access is becoming increasingly difficult.
6. Current export control policy constricts U.S. engagement and partnership with the international space community and feeds growing separation between the U.S. space community and its international counterparts.

7. Some export control laws conflict with U.S. National Space
   Policy which seeks to encourage international cooperation
   on mutually beneficial space activities.
8. A U.S. export control policy protecting sensitive space security capabilities is important there is unanimous agreement
   that the export control process can be improved without harming national security.[26]

Further NGO criticism of U.S. export controls occurred during an
April 24, 2008 Senate Homeland Security and Governmental Affairs
Committee hearing. National Foreign Trade Council President William
A. Reinsch emphasized that export businesses contend delay and uncertainty in decision-making and repetitive licensing requirements in weapons are the systems biggest problems. Reinsch also stressed that failing
to keep the Commerce Control List current by removing widely available lower level items produces a constantly increasing number of applications that enhances bureaucratic processing burdens and that the government makes the best export control decisions when invested
stakeholders covering foreign policy, national security, commerce, nonproliferation, and energy sectors are involved in the process. He also
criticized the State Department for resisting transparency and information sharing with other agencies on licensing decisions.[27]

Daniel B. Poneman of the Scowcroft Group acknowledged that federal export control architecture was still structured for the Cold War era
and did not account for technological globalization and the increasing
overseas availability of technology the U.S. seeks to control. He went on
to stress that protecting the sources of U.S. and allied military superiority should be the primary U.S. export control policymaking objective,
and that the Export Administration Act needs to rewritten and emphasize
multilateral instead of unilateral controls.[28]

Coalition For Employment Through Exports, Inc., President Edmund
B. Rice argued the problems in dual-use licensing further weakens the
effectiveness of U.S. export controls:

[B]oth the Executive Branch and the Congress, is having difficulty in
adjusting U.S. policy and export controls to global forces, . . . Dual-
use technologies diffuse. There is almost nothing on the dual-use control list that is U.S.-only sourced. Almost everything now can be pur-

chased globally. There is a growing disparity between the U.S. and other government's policies on export controls, leading the United States to increasingly move toward unilateral controls, as the previous witnesses have also mentioned. And military capability increasingly depends on commercial technology, which is changing the make-up of the defense industrial base and the responsibility of the export control systems to take that into account in their licensing decisions and policies.[29]

The academic community also plays a significant role as an NGO seeking to influence U.S. export control policy while also promoting scientific research and commercial offshoots. Testifying before the House Science Committee on February 25, 2009, Massachusetts Institute of Technology Vice President for Research and Associate Provost Claude R. Canizares referenced the Reagan Administration's National Security Decision Directive 189 of September 21, 1985 stressing that results of fundamental science and technology research be published and shared as widely as possible.[30]

Canizares went on to stress that by 2000 nearly a quarter of U.S. science and engineering workers were foreign nationals with 2/3 of post-doctoral researchers in the U.S. being international. He also noted how export controls can inhibit academic research by emphasizing:

> For universities, the primary area of concern regarding export controls involves restrictions on the sharing of technical information about controlled items with non-U.S. persons within the United States often referred to as deemed exports. The scope of regulated technologies is broad and includes many that are available outside the U.S. as my colleagues have already mentioned.

> Despite a Presidential directive protecting fundamental research, export controls continue to inhibit, retard, or eliminate university research projects. . . .[31]

The open information dissemination and exchange environment of universities allows for the use and potential misuse of sensitive information. A 2011 Federal Bureau of Investigation (FBI) report reveals that foreign government adversaries and foreign commercial competitors may use U.S. universities to

1. Steal technical information or products
2. Bypass expensive research and development
3. Recruit individuals for espionage
4. Exploit the student visa program for improper purposes
5. Spread false information for political or other reasons.

Such individuals or organizations may achieve these goals by various methods including: computer intrusions; collecting sensitive research; using students or visiting professors to collect information; spotting and recruiting students or professors; sending unsolicited email or invitations; sending spies for language and cultural training and to establish credentials; and funding or establishing university programs.[32]

An example of academic abuse of U.S. export laws occurred in 2008 when University of Tennessee Electrical Engineering Professor John Reece Roth was convicted on 18 counts of conspiracy, fraud, and Arms Export Control Act violations. Roth ignored university warnings concerning restrictions on his research and employed a Chinese and Iranian student to help him with plasma research while working on a classified U.S. Air Force project stipulating that no foreign nationals could work on it. Roth traveled to China with his laptop containing export restricted information and had a sensitive paper mailed to him from a Chinese professor's email account. Roth claimed his research was "fundamental" and not sensitive but the jury disagreed. He was sentenced to four years imprisonment and Atmospheric Glow Technologies, the company he set up to commercialize plasma research and the lab where the Air Force project was researched, pled guilty to 10 counts of exporting defense-related materials.[33]

Many research intensive universities have officials responsible for providing guidance on export control matters to their faculty and staff. One of these officials interviewed stressed the positive intent of the U.S. export control system in enforcing U.S. foreign policy and national security. The regulations are not perfect and their weaknesses include infrequent updating, not accounting for technological change, and complicated and lengthy regulations. This official went on to emphasize that International Traffic in Arms Regulations (ITAR) is an area of concern due to the minimal amount of data required for a deemed export to occur; faulted export control regulations for not providing guidance on what is due diligence in terms of securing controlled data; noted that export controls do not apply to most University activities due to exclusions within the regulations, projects subject to these regulations only comprise about 5% of the total research budget, that deemed exports are a problem and that university professors should ensure that confidential data is not introduced into student projects.[34]

Additional observations from this individual, noted that university corporate research sponsors don't recognize that the university has exclusions and allowances that do not apply to industry; that companies lack knowledge of the university environment; and the mission of universities has changed dramatically in recent years becoming almost like a research arm to industry partners. This has not only export control implications but other laws also come into play such as the 1996 Economic Espionage Act. Furthermore, he stressed that some students at his university are subject to sanctions from OFAC, that OFAC and State do not provide timely answers and are not transparent when export licenses are filed. He is unaware if his state's congressional delegation is familiar with export control regulations and how they impact the University. He praised Indiana Senators for their assistance in university applications.[35]

He went on to emphasize that not enough is known yet about the Obama Administration's proposed export control reforms. There are positives of dealing with one regulatory licensing agency and a review of technologies and "sunsetting" some older technologies is important but the reforms don't appear to make the regulations more simple or less complicated. The licensing process needs to be more transparent. Finally, he emphasized that his university is only one of a few that accepts terms and conditions that include publication restrictions, making the project results subject to export control regulations. Due to this as well as other university-related functions, 3 individuals have varying degrees of export control responsibilities including reviewing material agreements, research contracts, faculty outreach, travel reviews, field shipping questions, performing jurisdiction reviews of intellectual property, engaged in the visa system (H-1B and citizens from OFAC countries), and managing and auditing technology control plans. He acknowledged that export controls will always be in direct conflict with the academic enterprise. It is most difficult when faculty wish to receive funding for cutting edge research that is subject to the export control laws and also wish to have an open, academic, and multinational lab group.[36]

Concern over how export and restrictive immigration policies can have negative impacts was expressed in a congressional hearing by American Institute of Aeronautics and Astronautics (AIAA) Executive Director Major General Robert S. Dickman. After expressing concern that the

U.S. was training highly skilled foreign students but couldn't employ them due to security regulations, he noted that U.S. taxpayers were subsidizing development of a technical workforce building systems that was taking business away from U.S. companies and threatening national security. Dickman also mentioned his concerns that AIAA papers had to comply with ITAR opining:

> Each year AIAA administers about 25 technical conferences across the whole spectrum of aerospace. In 2008 over 5,300 technical papers were published in our conference proceedings. Every one of these conferences has a requirement that all papers comply with ITAR. How much collaboration, how much information wasn't exchanged because of that limitation? On the one hand you could say that the authors were appropriately protecting information important to our national security, and in many cases, I am sure that was correct. On the other hand, we weren't getting insight into what is being done overseas. When our companies can't sell to overseas manufacturers, we will lose understanding of what else is in those foreign systems. When a company or individual is reluctant to even discuss the design of a simple component in a spacecraft and enter into technical dialogue with an international colleague because of the very real criminal penalties associated with ITAR, we lose a source of information that simply isn't available in any other way.[37]

Besides congressional testimony, NGOs participate in seeking to influence U.S. export control policy through the rulemaking process. This allows interested individuals and organizations to comment on proposed federal agency rules published by these agencies in the *Federal Register*. Public participation in this process has been expanded by the readily accessible availability of the electronic rulemaking portal regulations.gov/ . These public comments can influence federal agencies to revise or drop proposed regulations depending on the nature and extent of these comments.[38]

Export oriented companies have commented on proposed federal export control regulations since the *Federal Register* started publishing federal regulations in 1936. The Obama Administration's proposed export control reform agenda introduced in 2010 has already produced significant NGO comment on its provisions which are publicly accessible. The July 15, 2011 *Federal Register* saw the Bureau of Industry and Security (BIS) propose 28 pages worth of proposed revisions of United States

Munitions List (USML) items no longer needed to be included in Export Administration Regulations (EAR).[39]

In September 12, 2011 comments on these proposed changes, Continental Tire commended Commerce's intent to reform the U.S. export control system and bring these export controls in line with contemporary realities. However, Continental also expressed concern that these proposed rules did not sufficiently advance the government's intent to erect higher walls around fewer products. Continental went on to maintain:

> [T]hat the proposed rules would have a number of unintended consequences, such as continuing to make it expensive and difficult for the U.S. military to obtain the sorts of commercially available parts and components that are available for consumer and commercial vehicles around the globe. Indeed, foreign militaries would continue to enjoy greater access to these commercial parts and components than the U.S. military. The proposed rules would also leave unnecessary compliance burdens in place for companies like Continental.[40]

Continental went on to assert that current U.S. export controls regulating military parts and components severely limited their ability to contribute commercially available technologies to producing next generation U.S. military vehicles; repairing, modernizing, and upgrading existing U.S. military vehicles; and even have limited opportunity to provide commercially available technologies to the U.S. Government. They went on to argue:

> It is time to bring U.S. export controls fully up-to-date and focus on militarily significant technologies. In addition, the U.S. military deserves access to commercially available automotive parts and components and the benefits of commercial pricing on par with what is available on passenger cars, commercial trucks, construction vehicles, trash trucks, and foreign militaries. This is not just an export control issue; it is an opportunity to provide better access and pricing to the U.S. military on commercially available technologies, and ultimately, to better serve the U.S. warfighter.[41]

Commenting on these same BIS proposed regulations the following day, the Association Connecting Electronic Industries (IPC), whose membership emphasizes areas of the electronic interconnect industry including design, printed board manufacturing, and printed board assembly expressed various concerns about these proposed rules. IPC stressed that the rule's proposed definition of "specially designed" failed to clarify printed board regulation and printed board designs in export controlled items. Their comments went on to stress that such ambiguous rules for printed boards could enable a U.S. adversary to gain access to these boards during manufacturing and sabotage defense systems and that hostile nations could use printed board designs to militarize commercial items.[42]

On November 7, 2011, BIS published additional proposed regulations on aircraft and related items which the Obama Administration determined no longer required USML control.[43] The American Association of Exporters and Importers (AAEI) posted comments on these proposed regulations on December 22, 2011. In their comments, AAEI mentioned that the proposed Export Control Classification Number (ECCN) 9A610.h covered "canopies," but did not clarify whether it covered other types of windows or transparencies including door windows, cabin windows, or lenses; regardless of their special characteristics such as ballistic protection or electromagnetic interference. AAEI also expressed their concern over the 29 calendar days it took BIS to review licenses which was contrasted with metrics posted on BIS' website claiming its average processing time ranged between 16 and 27 calendar days with their average November 2011 processing time being 18 calendar days. AAEI emphasized the importance of exporters having license processing predictability so they can plan production and delivery.[44]

Besides seeking to influence administration policy on exporting weapons and related technologies, NGO's also attempt to influence the U.S.' increasing use of financial sanctions as a mechanism for punishing undesirable behavior by individuals, countries, and transnational organizations. Following passage of the Comprehensive Iran Sanctions, Accountability, and Divestment Act (CISADA) in 2010, the Obama Administration issued proposed regulations for implementing this legislation on April 29, 2011 about the status of U.S. banks correspondent accounts with foreign banks and whether foreign financial institutions had contributed to Iranian efforts to promote terrorism or acquire weapons of mass destruction.[45]

These proposed CISADA regulations received positive and critical evaluations by American and European financial analysts. On June 1, 2011, The American Bankers Association (ABA) said it appreciated the government's need to take actions to protect against terrorist activities and weapons of mass destruction. ABA went on to express its concern that 30 days was an inadequate time frame for financial institutions to respond to the administration's proposal; that increasing rules imposed by the Dodd-Frank Act would make it harder for community banks to survive independently due to added data collection burdens; that information provided by banks to the Financial Crimes Enforcement Network and federal government needs to be collected more efficiently and effectively; and that such federal information collecting activity needs to be taken in ways that don't alienate businesses or discourage foreign individuals and companies from doing business with the U.S.[46]

ABA went on to assert that Section 311 of the USA Patriot Act already covers foreign correspondent reporting and that Section 314(a) of this legislation already contains faster and more institutionally focused reporting processes to identify sanctions targets including government-to-government requests. ABA also stressed the value of central banks approaching other central banks to urge these countries to adopt and implement similar sanctions against offending individuals and institutions while being careful to not inundate foreign correspondents with a proliferation of reporting requests.[47]

On May 31, 2011, the European Banking Federation (EBF) was very critical of these proposed regulations which they complained highlighted what they saw as CISADA's "deeply questionable extraterritorial character" and violated fundamental political and legal relationship principles between friendly nations. Specific EBF expressed concerns included:

1. Adding significant compliance burdens to banks conducting legitimate business with an Iranian linked financial institution through licensed transactions and clearing such as the British Treasury providing a British bank a license to process transactions as part of the Dubai clearing system if they have a United Arab Emirates branch;
2. Non-U.S. banks approached by U.S. banks under this proposal rule could face conflicts with national banking privacy law and European Union and national data protection rules;
3. Providing details of all transactions within 30 days would be very burdensome for large banking groups with multiple cross-jurisdictional operations;
4. Threshold amounts for other transfers to correspondent accounts should be set with individual banks not having to be at

risk determining what "significant" means in assessing financial transfers; and

5. Non-U.S. bank certifications should not be required to be stated by a single individual but by the bank as an institution to prevent the risk of individual legal liability.[48]

The Clearing House, the U.S. oldest banking association and payments company, also urged that these proposed CISADA regulations be modified by increasing the time U.S. banks have to comply with these transactional details from 30 to 90 days and saying that a foreign bank's failure to respond to a U.S. inquiry will not require a U.S. bank to close the correspondent account.[49]

Conclusion

NGOs have achieved both success and failure in influencing U.S. Government export control policy. Their motivations in trying to influence this policy range from promoting their business' financial interests, desiring to gain lucrative government contracts and access to emerging export markets, enhancing U.S. national security, promoting the expansion of scientific knowledge and technological expertise, and seeking to evade or defy federal export control policymaking. These organizations must interact with a wide variety of federal agencies depending on the areas of export control policymaking they wish to influence and will use their congressional representatives as a way of gaining leverage with these agencies.

These NGOs must also interact with a variety of international export control regimes which have appeared in the post-Cold War world in efforts to stop the spread of weapons of mass destruction and other threats to global economic and international security. The next chapter will examine the historic and contemporary development of these international government organizations.

Notes

1. See *U.S. Constitution, First Amendment, Clause Six*; Stephen A. Higginson, "A Short History of the Right to Petition Government for the Redress of Grievances, *Yale Law Journal*, 96 (1)(November 1986): 142-166; and Charles S. Mack, *Business, Politics, and the Practice of Government Regulations*, (Westport, CT: Quorum Books, 1997).

2. U.S. Congress, Senate Committee on Government Operations, Permanent Subcommittee on Investigations, *East-West Trade*, (Washington, DC: GPO, 1956): 86-91.

3. See Joseph C. Brada and Larry J. Wipf, "The Impact of U.S. Trade Controls on Exports to the Soviet Bloc," *Southern Economic Journal*, 41 (1)(July 1974): 47-56; David Dent and Carol O' Brien, "The Politics of the U.S. Trade Embargo of Cuba, 1959-1977, *Towson State Journal of International Affairs*, 12 (1)(1977): 43-60; Karen M. Hayworth, "The Arms Export Control Act: Proposals to Improve Observance of American Arms Law," *New York University Journal of Law and International Politics*, 12 (1)(Spring 1979): 135-158; U.S. Department of State, *Foreign Relations of the United States, 1961-1963 Volume IX: Foreign Economic Policy*, Glenn W. LaFantasie, ed., (Washington, DC: GPO, 1995): 729-732, Ibid., *FRUS, 1961-1963 Volume X: Cuba, January 1961-September 1962*, David S. Patterson, ed., (Washington, DC: GPO, 1997): 703-705; Kailai Huang, "American Business and the China Trade Embargo in the 1950s," *Essays in Economic and Business History*, 19 (2001): 33-48; and *FRUS, 1973-1976, Volume XXXI, Foreign Economic Policy*, Edward C. Keefer, ed., (Washington, DC: GPO, 2009): 643-646.

4. U.S. Congress, House Committee on Banking and Currency, Subcommittee on International Trade, *To Extend and Amend the Export Control Act of 1949*, (Washington, DC: GPO, 1969): 431-432.

5. U.S. Congress, House Committee on International Relations, *Export Licensing of Advanced Technology: A Review*, (Washington, DC: GPO, 1976): 104-105.

6. Ibid., 106-107.

7. U.S. Congress, Senate Committee on Banking, Housing, and Urban Affairs, Subcommittee on International Finance and Monetary Policy, *Agricultural Embargoes and the Sanctity of Contracts*, (Washington, DC: GPO, 1982): 16.

8. Ibid., 18, 40.

9. U.S. Congress, House Committee on Foreign Affairs, Subcommittee on International Economic Policy and Trade, *The Foreign Trade Practices Act*, (Washington, DC: GPO, 1985): 76-78.

10. Ibid., 80.

11. U.S. Congress, Senate Committee on Banking, Housing, and Urban Affairs, *Controls on the Export of Capital From the United States*, (Washington, DC: GPO, 1986): 61-63, 193.

12. U.S. Congress, House Committee on Science, Space, and Technology, *The Effect of Changing Export Controls on Cooperation in Science and Technology*, (Washington, DC: GPO, 1991): 111.

13. Ibid., 112.

14. Ibid., Senate Committee on Banking, Housing, and Urban Affairs, Subcommittee on International Finance, *The Export Administration Act of 1996 [H.R. 361]*, (Washington, DC: GPO, 1997): 26.

15. Ibid. 26-27.

16. Ibid., 28.

17. Ibid., 30-31.

18. See Public Law 104-294, "Economic Espionage Act of 1996," 110 *U.S. Statutes at Large*, 3488-3513; and U.S. Congress, Senate Permanent Select Committee on Intelligence and Senate Committee on the Judiciary, Subcommittee on Terrorism, Technology, and Government Information, *Economic Espionage*, (Washington, DC: GPO, 1996).

19. Ibid., U.S. Congress, House Committee on International Relations, Subcommittee on International Economic Policy and Trade, *Encryption: Individual Right to Privacy Vs. National Security*, (Washington, DC: GPO, 1998): 31.

20. Ibid., 32.

21. U.S. Congress, House Committee on National Security and House Committee on International Relations, *United States Policy Regarding the Export of Satellites to China*, (Washington, DC: GPO, 1999): 13, 15.

22. Ibid., 16.

23. Ibid., 19, 22.

24. Ibid., House Committee on Foreign Affairs, Subcommittee on Terrorism, Nonproliferation, and Trade, *Exports Controls: Are We Protecting Security and Facilitating Exports?*, (Washington, DC: GPO, 2007): 75-76.

25. Ibid., 79-81.

26. Center for Strategic and International Studies, *Briefing of the Working Group on the Health of the U.S. Space Industrial Base and the Impact of Export Controls*, (Washington, DC: CSIS, February 2008); 7-10; http://csis.org/files/media/csis/pubs/021908_csis_spaceindustryitar_final.pdf; Accessed November 19, 2012.

27. U.S. Congress, Senate Committee on Homeland Security and Governmental Affairs, Subcommittee on Oversight of Government Management, the Federal Workforce, and the District of Columbia Subcommittee, *Beyond Control: Reforming Export Licensing Agencies for National Security and Economic Interests*, (Washington, DC: GPO, 2009): 22-23. Reinsch served as the Commerce Department's Undersecretary for Export Administration during the Clinton Administration.

28. Ibid. 26.

29. Ibid., 28.

30. President of the United States, *National Policy on the Transfer of Scientific, Technological, and Engineering Information (NSDD-189)*, (Washington, DC: The White House, 1985); http://www.fas.org/irp/offdocs/nsdd/nsdd-189.htm; Accessed November 19, 2012.

31. U.S. Congress, House Committee on Science and Technology, *Impacts of U.S. Export Control Policies on Science and Technology Activities and Competitiveness*, (Washington, DC: GPO, 2009): 39-40. The increasing presence of foreign workers in the U.S. science and engineering workforce continues to the present. See Wan-Ying Chang and Lynn M. Milan, *International Mobility and Employment Characteristics Among Recent Recipients of U.S. Doctorates*, (Washington, DC: National Science Foundation, 2012); http://www.nsf.gov/statistics/infbrief/nsf13300/nsf13300.pdf; Accessed November 19, 2012.

32. U.S. Department of Justice, Federal Bureau of Investigation, *Higher Education and National Security: The Targeting of Sensitive, Proprietary and Classified Information on Campuses of Higher Education*, (Washington, DC: FBI, 2011): 1; http://www.fbi.gov/about-us/investigate/counterintelligence/higher-education-national-security; Accessed November 28, 2012.

33. Ibid., 3.

34. Interview with Michael Reckowsky, Research Security Administrator, Purdue University, November 28, 2012.

35. Ibid.

36. Ibid.

37. *Impacts of U.S. Export Control Policies on Science and Technology Activities and Competitiveness*, 44.

38. See David L. Weimer, "The Puzzle of Private Rulemaking: Expertise, Flexibility, and Blame Avoidance in U.S. Regulation," *Public Administration Review*, 66 (4)(July/August 2006): 569-582; and David Eduardo Cavazos, "Citizens and Bureaucracy: Electronic Participation in Regulatory Processes," *Electronic Government*, 8 (1)(2010): 59-72.

39. U.S. Department of Commerce, Bureau of Industry and Security, "Proposed Revisions to the Export Administration Regulations (EAR): Control of Items the President Determines No Longer Warrant Control Under the United States Munitions List (USML), 76 *Federal Register* 136 (July 15, 2011): 41958-41985.

40. Miles & Stockbridge, P.C. "Re: Continental Tire and Continental Automotive Comments on Proposed Revisions to the EAR Parts and Components of Military Vehicles Docket No: 110310188-1335-01; BIS-2011-0015; (September 12, 2011); 1; http://www.regulations.gov/#!documentDetail;D=BIS-2011-0015-0004; Accessed November 20, 2012.

41. Ibid., 2, 4.

42. Association Connecting Electronic Industries, "Re: Proposed Revisions to the Export Administration Regulations (EAR): Control of Items the President Determines No Longer Warrant Control Under the United States Munitions List (USML) . . . ," (September 13, 2011): 2-3; http://www.regulations.gov /#!documentDetail;D=BIS-2011-0015-0031; Accessed November 20, 2012.

43. U.S. Department of Commerce, Bureau of Industry and Security, "Revisions to the Export Administration Regulations (EAR): Control of Aircraft and Related Items the President Determines No Longer Warrant Control Under the United States Munitions List (USML), 76 *Federal Register* 215 (November 7, 2011): 68675-68690.

44. American Association of Exporters and Importers, "Comments on Proposed Regulations to the Ear: Control of Aircraft and Related Items the President Determines No Longer Warrant Control Under the USML," (December 22, 2011): 2-3; http://www.regulations.gov/#!documentDetail;D=BIS-2011-0033-0016; Accessed November 20, 2012.

45. U.S. Department of the Treasury, Financial Crimes Enforcement Network, "Financial Crimes Enforcement Network: Comprehensive Iran Sanctions, Accountability, and Divestment Act of 2010 ("CISADA") Reporting Requirements Under Section 104 (e)," 76 *Federal Register* 84 (May 2, 2011): 24410-24421.

46. American Bankers Association, "Attention: CISADA Reporting Requirements under Section 104(e), RIN 1506-AB12," June 1, 2011; 2; http://www.regulations.gov/#!documentDetail;D=FINCEN-2011-0002-0007; Accessed November 21, 2012.

47. Ibid., 3-4.

48. European Banking Federation, "EBF Comments on the FinCEN Notice of Proposed Rulemaking (NPR) Implementing the Reporting Requirements under Section 104(c) of the Comprehensive Iran Sanctions, Accountability and Divestment Act (CISADA); May 31, 2011; 1-3; http://www.regulations.gov/#! documentDetail;D=FINCEN-2011-0002-0005; Accessed November 21, 2012.

49. The Clearing House, "CISADA Reporting Requirements Under Section 104(e);" May 26, 2011; 2; http://www.regulations.gov/#!document Detail;D=FINCEN-2011-0002-0003; Accessed November 21, 2012.

Chapter 8

International Government Organizations

The globalized interconnectivity of international trade and international security means that international government organizations (IGOs) must play a role in promoting and enforcing export controls. The U.S. has been involved in many of these organizations and frequently plays a leading role in sculpting and providing financial support for their activities. During the Cold War era, the Coordinating Committee (COCOM) was the principal international export control regime involving the U.S. and other western democracies as they sought to prevent the export of militarily sensitive goods and technologies to the Soviet bloc.[1]

The Soviet bloc's collapse between 1989-1991 ended the principal reason for COCOM's existence and this organization concluded its work in 1994. However, the emergence of a new multipolar world did not mean that export controls were unecessary. The diffusion of weapons of mass destruction (WMD) and delivery mechanisms such as ballistic missiles and space launch capabilities to rogue regimes such as Iran, Iraq, and North Korea does not always require possession of the most advanced technology. The sometimes irresponsible behavior of nuclear states such as China, North Korea, and the Russian Federation in exporting these technologies to rogue governments or even terrorist groups poses new challenges for international export control policymakers. In an effort to address these concerns, the U.S. has become involved in a variety of multilateral export control regimes which seek to create a balance between promoting legitimate trade, scientific advancement and technology transfer, and preventing the proliferation of weapons of mass destruction and conventional weapons systems to irresponsible international stakeholders and volatile regions.[2]

These regimes derive their international legal authorization from United Nations (UN) Security Council Resolution 1540 of April 28, 2004. This document declared that proliferating Weapons of Mass Destruction (WMD) and their delivery mechanisms constitutes a threat to international peace and security under Chapter 7 of the UN Charter. 1540 imposes theoretically binding obligations on all states to adopt legislation preventing proliferation of these weapons and delivery mechanisms while also establishing appropriate domestic controls to prevent their illicit trafficking and encouraging international cooperation on such efforts . This resolution was reaffirmed with Resolution 1673 of April 27, 2006, Resolution 1810 of April 25, 2008, and Resolution 1977 of April, 20, 2011.[3] This chapter seeks to provide brief historical background on these export controls IGOs and their activities while noting varying degrees of U.S. involvement in these organizations.

Australia Group

The Australia Group (AG) is an informal forum of countries started in 1985 desiring to harmonize export controls to ensure that exports do not contribute to developing chemical or biological weapons. AG's 40 participating countries seek to ensure that national export control measures adhere to their international obligations under the Biological and Toxin Weapons Convention (BWC) and the Chemical Weapons Convention (CWC).[4]

Participating countries have licensing measures for over 63 chemical weapons precursors with participants requiring licenses to export: dual-use chemical manufacturing facilities, equipment, and related technology; plant pathogens; animal pathogens; biological agents; and dual-use biological equipment and related technology. These items form the basis for AG's Common Control Lists which are adjusted regularly to ensure their continued effectiveness and group members meet on a regular basis to ensure their measures comply with BWC, CWC, and United Nations Security Council Resolution 1540 requiring countries to prohibit WMD exports.[5]

During AG's annual meeting in Paris in June 2012, members expressed their concern with the ongoing violence in Syria noting that it remains of ongoing proliferation concern due to its active biological and chemical weapons programs. AG participants also expressed concern over Syria's use of third country front companies to shield its efforts to obtain items on the Common Control Lists and dual-use items for proliferation purposes. The group also agreed increased vigilance was needed on dual-use exports to Syria and that exports to Syria needed to be subject to exceptional scrutiny.[6]

Biological and Toxin Weapons Convention

The Biological and Toxin Weapons Convention (BWC) was influenced by the 1925 Geneva Convention prohibiting bacteriological and gas weapons and signed simultaneously in London, Washington, and Moscow on April 10, 1972 and entered into force on March 26, 1975. It bans developing, producing, stockpiling, acquiring, and retaining microbial and other biological agents or toxins in quantities without justification for prophylactic, peaceful, and protective purposes. Its prohibitions also encompass weapons, equipment, or mechanisms for delivering these agents or toxins in armed conflict. 171 countries have signed BWC as of June 2005, there are 23 non-signatory countries, and some countries place various reservations on their signatures.[7]

Between 1980-2011, BWC has held seven review conferences in Geneva. A paper prepared by New Zealand, Norway, and Switzerland for the 2011 conference expressed concern over confidence-building measures (CBMs) of participating states documenting their adherence to arms control, disarmament, and nonproliferation agreements. This report mentioned that only one country produced a statutorily mandated report on its public compliance with these agreements. It went on to mention that other countries use CBMs in more formal and less public ways such as submitting information on biological defense facilities and programs and comparing them with what was declared in previous submissions. These states use different bilateral and multilateral standards to determine whether their CBMs are in compliance with BWC.

This report recommended that participating states submit their CBM measures into a more streamlined and interactive format instead of a series of static PDF files, that they be prepared in all official United Nations languages instead of the host country's language, and that these submissions be made publicly accessible because restricting access to CBM returns risk enhancing public suspicion instead of confidence among civil society stakeholders.[8]

Chemical Weapons Convention

The Chemical Weapons Convention (CWC) historical origins date from the 1899 Hague Convention declaring a desire to prohibit the use of chemicals in projectiles. It received renewed emphasis with the 1925 Geneva Convention and in 1990 the U.S. and Soviet Union signed a bilateral agreement committing themselves to not producing chemical weapons, to begin destroying these weapons in 1992, and to limit their chemical weapons stockpiles to 5,000 tons each by 2002. Various international negotiations ensued and the CWC entered into force on April 29, 1997.

The Organization for the Prohibition of Chemical Weapons (OPCW) is responsible for implementing CWC provisions. Review conferences were held in 2003 and 2008 on implementing this agreement which currently includes 188 countries. Countries not signing or ratifying CWC include Angola, Egypt, North Korea, Somalia, South Sudan, and Syria.[9]

CWC's ratification by the U.S. Senate was challenging. Opponents charged that it was unenforceable; that it would be difficult to verify; that countries suspected of having chemical weapons including Iraq and Libya were unlikely to join and would not suffer consequences for failing to join; that the treaty did not cover nonstate actors such as terrorist groups, and that it would impose intrusive regulatory burdens on the U.S. chemical industry including onsite inspections. Proponents contended CWC would enhance U.S. national security, significantly reduce the threat of chemical warfare, and that it would isolate and punish nonadherents by restricting their ability to import or export prohibited chemicals. After considerable political maneuvering, the Senate ratified CWC 74-26 on April 24, 1997.[10]

OPCW contains provisions on chemical weapons possession, chemical weapons production facilities, national implementation measures, assistance and protection against chemical weapons, dispute settlement provisions, and vague and weak enforcement measures. The lack of explicit enforcement measures is a critical problem with this and other international export control agreements due to the reluctance of United Nations member states to punish offenders using biological chemical weapons in areas such as Afghanistan, Chechnya, Iraq, Laos, and elsewhere.[11]

Container Security Initiative

The Container Security Initiative (CSI) was established in January 2002 by the U.S. Customs and Border Protection (CBP) and became permanent with the *Security and Accountability for Every Port (SAFE Port) Act* in 2006. CSI operates in 58 ports in Africa, Asia, Europe, Latin and Central America, and the Middle East and prescreens 80% of all maritime containerized cargo imported into the U.S. Specific CSI objectives include:

1. Identifying high risk containers by using automated targeting tools to detect containers posing potential terrorism risk based on advanced information and strategic intelligence.
2. Prescreening and evaluating containers prior to shipment. Such screening and evaluation occurs as early as possible in the supply chain such as the departure port.
3. Using technology to pre-screen high-risk containers ensures that screening can be done rapidly and not slow down trade movement. Such technology includes large-scale x-ray and gamma ray machines and radiation detection devices.[12]

CSI is supported by the World Customs Organization (WCO), European Union, and G8 countries. During Fiscal Year 2010 more than 10.1 million maritime shipments were reviewed in CSI ports before arriving in U.S. seaports for an average of 27,600 per day. Shipping companies are also required to provide 24 hours advance notice of manifest data for all U.S. bound cargo containers.[13]

Examples of CSI successes include the November 26, 2012 collaboration with the Consumer Product Safety Commission to seize 24,000 toys with a value of nearly $220,000 due to their containing excess amounts of lead from the Jacksonville, FL port.[14] CSI areas needing improvement were noted in a February 2010 Department of Homeland Security Inspector General report. Enhancements recommend in this document included:

1. Identifying minimum essential elements for including in every local port standard operating procedures; and
2. Making sure CSI's strategic plan addresses other CBP maritime security program objectives such as examining the pos-

sibility of moving from a risk-based approach to 100% scanning of all cargo containers bound for U.S. ports.[15]

An October 2012 Government Accountability Office (GAO) report expressed concern that CSI was not cooperating with the Energy Department's National Nuclear Security Administration's Megaports Program to establish radiation detection equipment for weapons of mass destruction and illicit drugs at foreign seaports, train foreign personnel, and create sustainability programs to help these countries operate and maintain this equipment. GAO also expressed concern about the Obama Administration's proposed Fiscal Year 2013 budget reducing Megaports budget by 85%.[16]

Additional GAO assessments of CSI have addressed matters such as supply chain security and cargo targeting and the need for better performance reporting and sustainability plans to further enhance cooperation with major drug ransiting countries.[17]

European Union

European Union (EU) export controls are the closest thing there is to a unified international export control regime. Established by EU Council Regulation EC 428/2009 on May 5, 2009, this document is the latest iteration of European Economic Community regulation 2603/69 establishing European export control standards on December 20, 1969.[18] These regulations set unified EU wide standards while also giving member nations some degree of individual flexibility in establishing export controls. Categories covered in these EU-wide controls include: scope, export authorization and authorization for brokering services, updating dual-use item lists, customs procedures, administrative cooperation, and control measures.[19]

Specific categories of dual use items covered by EU export control regulations, while implementing internationally agreed dual-use controls from the Australia Group, and other international export control regimes, include:

Category 0 Nuclear materials, facilities, and equipment
Category 1 Special materials and related equipment
Category 2 Materials Processing
Category 3 Electronics

Category 4 Computers
Category 5 Telecommunications and "information security"
Category 6 Sensors and Lasers
Category 7 Navigation and avionics
Category 8 Marine
Category 9 Aerospace and Propulsion.[20]

The EU has six general export authorizations (GEA) categories covered by geographic destinations and export types to non-EU countries including:

EU0001   Australia, Canada, Japan, New Zealand, Norway, and United States
EU0002   Export of certain dual-use items to certain destinations
EU0003   Export after repair/replacement
EU0004   Temporary export for exhibition or fair
EU0005   Telecommunications
EU0006   Chemicals

National general export authorizations may be issued by individual EU member countries provided they do not conflict with existing GEAs and to not cover any items listed in Annex 2G to Regulation 428/2009 such as natural and depleted uranium, special fissile materials, animal, human, and plant pathogens, and space launch vehicles. France, Germany, Italy, Sweden, the Netherlands, and the United Kingdom have NGA authorizations which are posted in host country official journals.[21]

These policies are subject to judicial review by the European Court of Justice. A December 17, 2008 European Council draft document sought to prioritize combating WMD as an EU objective. This work recommended increasing efforts to fight intangible transfers of WMD-related knowledge and know-how; enhancing efforts to fight transfers of pertinent, technologies, goods, and equipment; taking preventative and punitive action against proliferation financing; augmenting efforts to combat trafficking in WMD substances and strengthening systems for intercepting proliferation flows; restarting European discussion on taking punitive action against proliferation; and drafting a risk and threat evaluation document.[22]

On July 26, 2010, the EU imposed various sanctions on Iran for that country's efforts to acquire WMD include imposing various export and import restrictions targeting Tehran's financial, transport, and energy sectors along with freezing funds of individuals and organizations seeking to enhance Iran's ability to acquire WMD. The EU's overall export controls sanctions program covers arms embargoes, economic and financial sanctions, and travel restrictions is administered through the EU's Common Foreign and Security Policy.[23] A June 30, 2011 EU Green Paper proposing enhancements to the EU's export control regime sought public comment on existing features of this regime and desirable features of future EU export controls. Examples of questions presented by this solicitation include:

1. What is the importance of dual-use exports for your business? What are the associated costs of compliance? Please provide figures.
2. What is the impact of the foreign availability of certain controlled items on the competitiveness of EU dual-use exports?
3. How would you rate the current EU export control system as compared to the export control systems of third countries?
4. Have you encountered any problems due to differences in the application of export controls across EU member states? What was the nature of these problems?
5. What is the time needed to obtain an individual or global license?
6. How would you rate the quality of the EU control list? Is it updated regularly enough?
7. What are your views concerning a possible new EU export control model based on a network of existing licensing authorities operating under more common rules?
8. What type of information would customs authorities need to properly enforce export controls at EU borders?[24]

The EU Parliament's International Trade committee adopted a draft report on export control legislation on March 2, 2012, the legislation passed in its second reading on March 29, 2012, it was signed on April 16, 2012, and published in the EU's *Official Journal* on May 16, 2012. The effectiveness or ineffectiveness of these controls will be determined over time.[25]

International Atomic Energy Agency

The International Atomic Energy Agency (IAEA) is a United Nations affiliated agency located in Vienna. Its overall mission is ostensibly promoting safe, secure, and peaceful uses of nuclear technology and engaging in global efforts to stop the spread of nuclear weapons. Its performance in this latter area can be characterized as an absolute failure given historic and ongoing nuclear proliferation involving groups such as the Aga Khan network, countries as diverse as Iran, North Korea, Pakistan, Syria, and others and the IAEA's abject failure to stop such proliferation and punish those engaged in this proliferation due to a variety of reasons such as managerial ineptitude and political favoritism shown by IAEA personnel toward proliferant individuals and regimes.[26]

Missile Technology Control Regime

The Missile Technology Control Regime (MTCR) is an informal and voluntary association of 34 countries seeking to promote the nonproliferation of unmanned delivery systems capable of delivering WMD and coordinating national export licensing efforts intended to prevent their proliferation. MTCR was established in 1987 by Canada, France, Germany, Italy, Japan, the United Kingdom, and United States. This regime strives to achieve success through common export policy guidelines and holds international meetings on a regular basis. Member countries take their decisions by consensus and regularly exchange information about national export licensing procedures. Particular emphasis is placed on voluntarily introducing export licensing measures on rocket and other unmanned aerial vehicle delivery systems and related equipment, material, and technology.[27]

Guidelines used by MTCR for regulating sensitive missile-relevant transfers include the missile and space program capabilities and objectives of recipient states; the transfer's significance in terms for its potential delivery of WMD through mechanisms other than manned aircraft; the transfer's applicability to relevant multilateral agreements; the risk of controlled items falling into the hands of terrorist groups or individuals; sponsoring governments making sure that items transferred and their byproducts are not re-transferred without host government consent; and the exporter of their items needing to be aware of their compatibility with national export controls.[28]

MTCR has prepared detailed equipment, software, and technology documentation for the missile technology control exports it seeks to regulate covering categories such as: propulsion components and equipment; propellants, chemicals, and propellant production; instrumentation, navigation, and direction finding; flight control; computers; avionics; stealth; and nuclear effects protection.[29]

As a voluntary organization, MTCR depends on member cooperation to ensure its success. One assessment contends MTCR has been successful in keeping regional powers from gaining access to complete missiles but has experienced only modest success in keeping them from acquiring the technology to build such missiles due to the absence of enforcement and verification mechanisms, not offering incentives to prevent WMD proliferation, and insufficient legal barriers for proliferant countries.[30]

MTCR's 2011 plenary meeting in Buenos Aires saw members exchange information and express concerns about ongoing developments in the Middle East, Northeast Asia, and South Asia with particular emphasis on Iran and North Korea; expressed its determination to implement United Nations Security Council resolutions such as 1874 (2009) and 1929 (2010) dealing with WMD nonproliferation; noted that MTCR's outgoing chair Brazil had conducted outreach with Belarus, China, India, Kazakhstan, and Thailand; and that incoming chair Argentina pledged to continue this outreach while increasing MTCR transparency and gaining additional members.[31]

Nuclear Suppliers Group

The Nuclear Suppliers Group (NSG) is a group of nuclear supplying countries seeking to promote nuclear weapons nonproliferation by implementing guidelines for nuclear exports and nuclear related exports with particular emphasis on adhering to the 1968 Nuclear Nonproliferation Treaty (NPT). NSG was established following India's 1974 nuclear explosion and its current membership consists of 46 countries representing a variety of cultures and political systems including Argentina, Australia, China, Kazakhstan, the Russian Federation, and the United States.[32]

NSG issues guidelines for transferring nuclear equipment, materials, and technology for peaceful purposes. Provisions within these guidelines stress:

1. Making maximum use of the international commercial market and other mechanisms for nuclear fuel services without undermining the global fuel market.
2. Prohibiting the transfer of nuclear explosives only with formal governmental assurance from recipients that such explosions would not occur.
3. Suppliers of trigger technology should ensure that non-nuclear states receiving this technology adhere to IAEA safeguards on peaceful uses of nuclear materials.
4. Suppliers should exercise restraint in transferring facilities, equipment, supplies, and technology to countries in noncompliance with NPT provisions;
5. Support the highest possible levels of physical security on these items; and
6. Suppliers should maintain regular contact with nuclear material recipients on handling of these materials.[33]

NSG activities are carried out by annual plenary meetings, a consultative group whose responsibilities include consensually developing and revising group guidelines on nuclear supply and related technical annexes, Licensing and Export Enforcement Experts Meetings, and working groups of dedicated technical experts discussing NSG control lists.[34]

NSG held its most recent annual meeting in Seattle on June 21-22, 2012. Activities at this meeting included exchanging positive and negative information on nuclear nonproliferation with particular emphasis on Iranian and North Korean developments while desiring peaceful solutions to these problems; emphasizing the importance of keeping export control lists current due to continually changing technological developments; discussing ongoing developments of the 2008 Civil Nuclear Cooperation Agreement with India and NSG's relationship with India; and stressing the value of nuclear industry engagement with NSG and efforts for enhancing such activity.[35]

The NSG is an example of an organization started with good intentions which has proven ineffective in its efforts to stop the proliferation of nuclear weapons technologies. This is due to the conflicting economic, political, and strategic interests of its member states and technical disagreements on topics such as fuel supply assurances and voluntary export control guidelines. NSG's utopian objective of stopping the proliferation of these weapons no longer adheres to international strategic realities and scientific and technological diffusion as demonstrated by the nearly global proliferation of this technology.[36]

Proliferation Security Initiative

The Proliferation Security Initiative (PSI) is a U.S.-led international initiative seeking to stop WMD trafficking, their delivery systems, and related materials to and from states and transnational organizations of proliferation concern. PSI's documentary foundation began with the Bush Administration's December 2002 release of the *National Strategy to Combat Weapons of Mass Destruction* which emphasized expanding international cooperation to combat WMD proliferation.[37]

PSI's formal launch was on May 31, 2003 as this strategy sought to create more robust tools to stop global proliferation and explicitly identified interdiction as the area of greatest focus.[38] 103 countries participated in PSI as of November 20, 2012 with China and India being the largest non-participants.[39]

PSI provisions include bilateral ship boarding agreements between the U.S. and select participating countries and overall principles adopted by these countries include:

1. Adopting streamlined procedures for rapidly exchanging relevant information concerning suspected proliferation activity, protecting confidential information provided by other states, dedicating appropriate resources and efforts to interdiction operations and capabilities; and maximizing participants interdiction efforts coordination.
2. Reviewing and strengthening relevant national legal authorities to accomplish interdiction efforts and working to strengthen international legal frameworks in these efforts.
3. Not transporting or assisting in transporting cargoes of concern to states or non-state actors of proliferation concern. Seriously considering providing consent, under appropriate circumstances, to other states boarding, searching, and seizing nationally flagged vessels suspected of carrying WMD cargoes.
4. Allowing other states to seize aircraft suspected of carrying WMD cargoes to land in their countries for inspection and

confiscation and denying national airspace access for these planes.[40]

PSI has experienced some level of success due to the U.S. ceding some of its authority to other participating countries, giving these countries the freedom to determine "innocent passage" in international maritime law according to their national legal standards and interpretation of international law, by affirming the validity of national territorial waters and placing responsibility on individual countries for enforcing PSI within their littoral waters, and presenting PSI participation as being supplemental to existing bilateral agreements and commitments these countries have with the U.S.[41]

Two different public policy research institute reports have evaluated PSI. A 2009 report by the National Institute for Public Policy stressed that PSI had been "extraordinarily successful" judging by the extent of its international support; counterproliferation capacity building; training exercises cooperation; intelligence sharing law enforcement; and actual interdictions. This document went on to stress that PSI should work on expanding its membership to underrepresented areas of Africa and South America; that participating governments should make annual dedicated budget appropriations to PSI instead of regular non-dedicated appropriations; and that there needs to be more training to combat nuclear terrorism and conventional weapons smuggling.[42]

A June 2012 report from the European Union's Non-Proliferation Consortium stressed that PSI can be described as being successful in seeking to strengthen national and collective capacities to interdict WMD related materials. This report went on to stress that problems with this program include:

1. Certain significant global actors such as China, Egypt, India, Indonesia, and Pakistan are not involved in PSI.
2. There are gaps in the national legislation of PSI participants and international legal frameworks.
3. Capacity-building activities within PSI are irregular.
4. Civilian law enforcement officers are insufficiently involved in PSI exercises creating the impression that PSI fails to provide states with the most needed tools. PSI should focus its exercises on scenarios for interdicting dual-use civilian trade

goods would make better use of civilian law enforcement expertise in fulfilling PSI objectives.

5. PSI has failed to develop effectiveness assessment measures and needs to expand its outreach to make public opinion more informed about its operations.[43]

South Eastern European Clearinghouse for the Control of Small Arms and Light Weapons (SEESAC)

The South Eastern European Clearinghouse for the Control of Small Arms and Light Weapons (SEESAC) was established on May 8, 2002 by the United Nations Development Program (UNDP) and is located in UNDP's Belgrade office. Its purpose is strengthening national and regional security stakeholders capacities to control and reduce small arms proliferation and misuse and contribute to enhancing southeastern European development, security, and stability. SEESAC members include southeastern European countries such as Bulgaria, Greece, Serbia, Slovenia, the Former Yugoslav Republic of Macedonia, European Union countries, NATO, the United States, World Bank, and other international government organizations.[44]

Key activities engaged in by SEESAC member countries include weapons destruction, weapons collection and awareness raising, storage upgrades and storage management training, marking, tracing, and registering legally used weapons by civilians and governments, and arms export control. SEESAC has destroyed over 250,000 weapons concentrated in the former Yugoslavia's countries; collaborated with the Croatian Interior Ministry in collecting 14,621 weapons, 564,434 bullets, and 190 kg of explosives between May 2010-August 2011; helped Bosnia and Herzegovina, Croatia, and Montenegro upgrade their weapons storage facilities; and sought to harmonize firearms marking, registration, and tracing for consistency with international standards.[45]

SEESAC arms export control activities involve publishing over 30 comprehensive national and 3 regional reports containing information on relevant legislation and actual arms exports and imports data; organizing regular information exchange meetings on arms export control practices; and organizing parliamentary arms control forums where regional legislators responsible for arms control oversight can meet.[46] The 2010 edition of SEESAC's regional arms export report revealed that arms exports to EU countries increased 107.5% of 2009 with the biggest recipients of these exports being in Bosnia and Herzegovina and Serbia. Weapons categories receiving the most traffic include smooth-bore weapons of less than 20 mm caliber, ammunition and fuse setting devices, ground vehicles and components, energetic materials and related substances, aircraft including lighter than air vehicles, and armored or protective equipment.[47]

Like all other international export control regimes, SEESAC's success or lack of success depends on the willing participation and support of its member countries.

UN Small Arms Treaty

The United Nations Small Arms Treaty or Arms Trade Treaty (ATT) is an emerging and controversial effort to regulate the international conventional weapons trade to prevent the proliferation of these armaments. Initial efforts to develop ATT began at the United Nations in 2006 and over subsequent years countries have worked to develop this document which seeks to implement some kind of regulation on what is seen as an unregulated international weapons market.[48]

On November 2, 2009, the UN General Assembly approved a draft version of this treaty 153-1 with 20 abstentions. Reversing the Bush Administration's opposition to ATT, the Obama Administration supported the treaty with Zimbabwe being the only opponent. Countries abstaining on this vote included China, India, Iran, Pakistan, Russia, Syria, and Venezuela.[49]

The Obama Administration justified its support for ATT stressing that conventional arms transfers are a crucial U.S. national security concern, that it already has a rigorous and existing arms transfer control system, that it hopes the ATT continues its consensus based approach to international member participation, that ATT only covers international conventional weapons transfers and not domestic weapons transfers or possession, contended that the U.S. will oppose any effort to address internal transfers or provisions conflicting with the U.S. Constitution or national U.S. law, and that the U.S. wants a treaty capable of significant impeding conventional weapons trade and making sure that such trade is conducted lawfully, transparently, and accountability.[50]

International negotiators met in New York to conduct further work on ATT between July 2-27, 2012 but were unable to reach agreement though the UN General Assembly may convene another ATT conference in March 2013. An August 1, 2012 draft version of ATT referred to the inherent right of states to individual or self-defense and said states respect the legitimate interests of other states in acquiring conventional weapons for self-defense, peacekeeping operations, and arms exports, but was silent about non-state individual and organizational ownership and possession of such weapons. This version also seeks to prohibit countries from transferring conventional arms within the treaty scope if it violates international agreements it participates in, that individual countries will adopt detailed national measures and policies to support this action, and keep detailed records of its ATT related activities.[51]

ATT has received a frosty U.S. reception from some sections of Congress who are concerned that it infringes on national sovereignty, constitutional Second Amendment rights, and would be ineffective in regulating weapons sales by countries and organizations hostile to the U.S. On March 19, 2012, Senator Jerry Moran (R-KS) introduced S. 2205 to prohibit giving the State Department funding to negotiate this treaty based on concern that it restricts U.S. citizens Second Amendment Rights. This legislation had been sponsored by 21 Senators as of December 12, 2012.[52]

More detailed criticism of ATT was expressed in a July 18, 2012 speech by Senator James Inhofe (R-OK). He stressed his concerns about infringing on Second Amendment rights and covering arms transfer transports within national territory; argued that law-abiding nations such as the United States will restrict their arms sales in the name of the treaty while corrupt nations like Russia and Syria will violate the treaty while they are rhetorically endorsing it; criticized its lack of stringent enforcement mechanisms; maintained that selling weapons to U.S. allies like Israel, South Korea, and Taiwan would be regarded as undermining peace and security according to ATT; that U.S. international arms sales are already regulated under the Arms Export Control Act; and that a bipartisan group of 51 Senators have already signed a letter opposing ATT to President Obama and Secretary of State Clinton mentioning these and other concerns.[53]

A June 29, 2012 letter expressing similar concerns about ATT was sent to Obama and Clinton by a bipartisan group 130 Representatives including House Foreign Affairs Committee Chair Ileana Ros-Lehtinen

(R-FL).[54] This agreement is not likely to be ratified by the U.S. Senate given this level of congressional opposition and the presence of existing conventional arms transfer agreements.

Wassenaar Arrangement

The Wassenaar Arrangement on Export Controls for Conventional Arms and Dual-Use Goods and Technologies (WA) was established following the Cold War in 1993-1994 as COCOM member countries realized that an East-West focus was no longer the best basis for export controls. WA was established on December 19, 1995 in Wassenaar, the Netherlands with an emphasis on dealing with regional and international security and stability concerning spreading conventional weapons and dual-use technologies.[55]

Aspiring WA members must meet the following admission criteria conducted by existing members:

1. Whether they produce/export arms and industrial equipment respectively;
2. Whether they take WA Control lists as a reference in their national export controls;
3. Whether their nonproliferation policies and appropriate national policies, including: adherence to non-proliferation policies, control lists, and international export control regime guidelines such as the Australia Group, MTCR, NSG, and international WMD conventions such as the CWC; and
4. Adhere to fully effective export controls.[56]

WA contains 41 countries as of December 2012 including the United States, Russia, and other mostly European and anglospheric countries.[57] Member states hold annual meetings in Vienna and reach decisions by consensus with implementation of these decisions carried out by national export control policymaking entities. At its December 2001 meeting, WA committed to preventing terrorist groups and individuals from acquiring conventional weapons and dual-use goods and technologies. They also produce guidelines on conventional arms export control transfers covering areas such as best practice guidelines for exporting small arms and light weapons; characteristics of effective arms brokering legislation; best practices for implementing intangible transfer of technology controls; and elements for controlling conventional arms transfers between third countries.[58]

WA held its 2011 annual meeting in Vienna on December 13-14, 2011. This meeting's plenary statement noted members ongoing work to make existing control lists better understood and more user-friendly for licensing authorities and exporters while ensuring the detection and denial of undesirable exports. This statement noted that WA is open to states in compliance with agreed export controls criteria though doubt exists about WA's overall effectiveness due to actors having no trouble finding conventional arms and member states not having sufficient mechanisms for restricting illicit arms traffic.[59]

World Customs Organization

The World Customs Organization (WCO) is based in Brussels and was established in 1947, adopted its current name in 1994, and consists of 179 members globally. Besides facilitating international trade, organizational objectives include harmonizing and simplifying customs systems and procedures, supporting member compliance and enforcement activities in areas of commercial fraud, drug trafficking, money laundering, and protecting national and international security, promoting supply chain security andw facilitation, revenue collection, and conducting relevant research in these fields.[60]

WCO organizational components focus on areas such as tariff and trade affairs, capacity building, and enforcement and compliance with this latter area emphasizing commercial fraud, counterfeiting and piracy, electronic crime, and global information and intelligence strategy.[61] Their 2011-2012 *Annual Report* stressed the increasing importance of supply chain security since 9/11 in member responsibilities, the need to identify high-risk transactions and access to early warning systems to protect against the import and export of hazardous cargoes such as WMD through member countries, and the presence of Regional Intelligence Liaison Offices (RILO) globally to provide data and trends on fraudulent trend. These RILOs are located in Cameroon, Chile, Germany, Kenya, Morocco, Poland, Russia, St. Lucia, Saudi Arabia, South Korea, and Senegal.[62]

WCO conducts conferences for member states on export control related topics. Examples of such conferences during 2011-2012 include the EastWest Institute Worldwide Security Conference in Brussels, Security of the Supply Chain and Commerce Facilitation in Sao Paulo, and Global Forum on Combating Illicit Drug Trafficking and Related Threats in Brussels.[63]

During 2010, WCO member states and personnel conducted numerous enforcement activities. They conducted 1,518 seizures of illicit tobacco products consisting of 3,180,422,391 pieces and 25,484 counterfeit product seizures consisting of 123,702,061 pieces. Transportation modal breakdowns for these product seizures were:

Airports	38%
Mail Centers	27%
Seaports	24%
Inland	7% with only 2% of seizures made at land borders.

Major transit countries where these products were seized include China, France, Germany, Hong Kong, Hungary, Italy, Mexico, the Netherlands, Poland, Russia, and the United States. These seizures were carried out by WCO nation personnel staffing of 611,318 during 2010.[64]

Zangger Committee

The Zangger Committee (ZC) is named for Swiss Professor Claude Zangger (1926-2009) and was formed between 1971-1974 to establish guidelines for implementing NPT Article 3 Section 2 covering export control provisions. Initially consisting of 15 states whose membership included both the United States and Soviet Union, ZC members who were suppliers or potential suppliers of nuclear equipment sought to reach mutual understanding instead of legally binding decisions on:

A. Defining what constituted equipment or material designed or prepared for processing, producing, special fissionable material which was not specified in NPT.

B. Determining conditions and procedures governing exports of such equipment or material to meet Article 3 Section 2 provisions on the basis of fair commercial competition.[65]

Responding to India's May 18, 1974 nuclear explosion, ZC adopted a list of controlled items or a Trigger List which attempted to govern the export of nuclear items such as highly enriched uranium, plutonium, reactors, reprocessing and enrichment plants, and components and equipment for these facilities. Trigger List stipulations are:

A. They not be used for nuclear explosives.
B. Be subject to IAEA safeguards in recipient non-nuclear states.
C. Not be re-exported unless subject to safeguards in the recipient state unless that state accepts IAEA safeguards.[66]

ZC is headquartered in Vienna and has 38 members as of late 2012. Member states include representation from all continents except Antarctica with examples including Argentina, Australia, China, France, Germany, Kazakhstan, Russia, South Africa, Turkey, and Ukraine.[67] It holds meetings each spring and fall seeking to address nuclear proliferation matters and engages in ongoing consultation with IAEA. The Trigger List was amended in 1984 to clarify entries covering isotope separation by the gas centrifuge process, 1985 amendments sought to clarify coverage of fuel reprocessing plants, and a 1992 amendment was introduced on further clarifying plants for producing heavy water, deuterium and deuterium compounds, and associated equipment.[68]

ZC works with IAEA and nuclear exporters to establish security requirements for nuclear recipient countries. It acknowledges that this is an ongoing process and a 2005 analysis acknowledged the presence of major gaps in international export controls including:

1. Some NPT states claiming they do not need to conclude an Additional Protocol giving IAEA complimentary inspection authority to that provided in NPT Safeguards Agreement.
2. Verifying physical protection of nuclear material is an ongoing challenge since only a few supplier states have appropriate inspection teams to investigate physical protection systems in recipient states.
3. States may need assistance in establishing appropriate national nuclear export controls rules and regulations and the ZC and NSG are available to help these states.[69]

ZC members have been involved in the quinquennial NPT conferences held by the United Nations on the status of this agreement. The most recent NPT was held in New York between May 3-28, 2010 and another NPT conference is scheduled for 2015. 2010 conference participants discussed recurring nonproliferation matters including nuclear disarmament, nuclear nonproliferation, accessing peaceful uses of nuclear energy, and creating a WMD free zone in the Middle East. The 2010 NPT conference succeeded in drafting a final document which reaffirmed participants commitment to these ideals. However, ongoing problems of Iranian and North Korean nuclear programs were not resolved and remain dangerous as the growth of these rogue regimes nuclear programs continues unabated.[70]

Conclusion

Ongoining problems with determining enforcement against NPT violators, which only stress diplomatic and economic sanctions, continue to be key impediments to NPT's effectiveness and to the work of organizations such as NPT. The effectiveness and relevance of the NPT given the presence of nuclear smuggling, the widespread international proliferation of nuclear knowledge, and international inability to peacefully end Iranian and North Korean nuclear aspirations leave serious questions about the effectiveness of ZC and other international export control regimes.[71] These international export control regimes mean well, have achieved some success, and provide reasonably transparent coverage of their activities. However, their absence of effective enforcement mechanisms, particularly getting international agreement on taking covert or overt military operations against conventional and WMD proliferators, the ability and willingness of individuals, nations, and transnational groups to violate international export control standards with little fear of impunity, and the understandable reluctance of most countries to surrender national sovereignty and freedom of action on critical economic and national security issues, makes these international export control mechanisms instruments of limited utility.

Notes

1. See Michael Mastanduno, *Economic Containment: CoCom and the Politics of East-West Trade*, (Ithaca: Cornell University Press, 1992); and Tor Egil Førland, *Cocom and the Forging of Strategic Export Controls*, (Dordrecht: Republic of Letters, 2009).

2. Partial examples of this field's burgeoning literature include Peter D. Zimmerman, "Proliferation: Bronze Medal Technology is Enough," *Orbis*, 38 (1)(Winter 1994): 67-82; Stephen Blank, "Russia as Rogue Proliferator," *Orbis*, 44 (1)(Winter 2000): 91-107; Seema Gahlaut and Gary K. Bertsch, "The War on Terror and the Nonproliferation Regime," *Orbis*, 48 (3)(Summer 2004): 489-504; Alexander H. Montgomery, "Ringing in Proliferation: How to Dismantle an Atomic Bomb Network," *International Security*, 30 (2)(Fall 2005): 153-187; Robert S. Ross, "The Rise of Chinese Power and the Implications for the Regional Security Order," *Orbis*, 54 (4)(Fall 2010): 525-545; and U.S. Congress, House Committee on Foreign Affairs, Subcommittee on Terrorism, Nonproliferation, and Trade, *Transshipment and Diversion: Are U.S. Trading Partners Doing Enough to Prevent the Spread of Dangerous Technologies?*, (Washington, DC: GPO, 2010); http://purl.fdlp.gov/GPO/gpo2627; Accessed December 5, 2012.

3. See United Nations Security Council (UNSC), *1540 Committee*, (New York: United Nations Security Council, 2012): 1-2; http://www.un.org/en/sc/1540/; Accessed December 14, 2012; and UNSC, *Resolution 1540 (2004)*, (New York: UNSC, 28 April 2004): 1-4; http://daccess-ods.un.org/TMP/5405232.90634155.html; Accessed December 14, 2012.

4. See The Australia Group, *Homepage,* (2012): 1; http://www.australiagroup.net/en/index.html; Accessed December 5, 2012; Ibid., *The Australia Group, Homepage, (2012): 1;* Ibid., *The Origins of the Australia Group* (2012): 1; http://www.australiagroup.net/en/origins.html; Accessed December 5, 2012; and Amy E. Smithson, *Separating Fact From Fiction: The Australia Group and the Chemical Weapons Convention*, (Washington, DC: Henry L. Stimson Center, 1997).

5. Ibid., *The Australia Group: Activities*, (2012): 1; http://www.australiagroup.net/en/activities.html; Accessed December 5, 2012. AG's Common Control Lists can be found at http://www.australiagroup.net/en/controllists.html; and include chemical weapons precursors such as thiodyglycol, pumps featuring nickels or alloys with more than 40% nickel weight; fermenters capable of cultivating pathogenic micro-organisms, biological agents such as the ebola virus; plant pathogens such as potato spindle tuber viroid; and animal pathogens such as foot and mouth disease virus.

6. Ibid., *Media Release 2012 Australia Group Plenary*, (June 15, 2012); http://www.australiagroup.net/en/media_june2012.html; Accessed December 5, 2012.

7. See Biological and Toxins Convention Website, *About the Biological and Toxin Weapons Convention*, (2012): 1; http://www.opbw.org/; Accessed December 5, 2012; and Nicholas A. Sims, *The Future of Biological Disarmament: Strengthening the Treaty Ban on Weapons*, (London: Routledge, 2009).

8. Biological Weapons Convention, *Confidence Building Measures Submitted by Norway, Switzerland, and New Zealand*, (Geneva: 1 November 2011):

1-5; http://www.opbw.org/rev_cons/7rc/BWC_CONF.VII_WP21_E.pdf; Accessed December 5, 2012.

9. See Organization for the Prohibition of Chemical Weapons (OPCW), *Genesis and Historical Development*, (The Hague: Organization for the Prohibition of Chemical Weapons, 2012): 1-6; http://www.opcw.org/chemical-weapons-convention/about-the-convention/genesis-and-historical-development/; Accessed December 5, 2012; and Jonathan Tucker, *U.S. Ratification of the Chemical Weapons Convention*, (Washington, DC: National Defense University Press, 2011): . http://purl.fdlp.gov/GPO/gpo23673; Accessed December 5, 2012.

10. Tucker, 5-22.

11. See OPCW, *Articles of the Chemical Weapons Convention*, (2012): 1; http://www.opcw.org/chemical-weapons-convention/articles/; Accessed December 5, 2012; Edward A. Tanzman, *Overview of the Chemical Weapons Convention*, (Argonne, IL: Argonne National Laboratory, 1993); . http://www.osti.gov/bridge/servlets/purl/10116174-8ufidk/native/10116174.pdf; Accessed December 5, 2012; and Michael P. Scharf, "Enforcement Through Sanctions, Force, and Criminalization," in *The New Terror: Facing the Threat of Chemical and Biological Weapons*, Sidney D. Drell, Abraham D. Sofaer, and George D. Wilson, eds., (Stanford: Hoover Institution Press, 1999): 439-479.

12. See U.S. Customs and Border Protection, *CSI In Brief*, (Washington, DC: CBP, October 7, 2011): 1; http://www.cbp.gov/xp/cgov/trade/cargo_security/csi/csi_in_brief.xml; Accessed December 6, 2012; and Public Law 109-347, "Security and Accountability for Every Port Act of 2006," 120 *U.S. Statutes at Large* 1884-1962.

13. See Ibid., *Fact Sheet: Container Security Initiative*, (Washington, DC: CBP, 2011): 1; http://www.cbp.gov/linkhandler/cgov/trade/cargo_security/csi/csi_factsheet_2011.ctt/csi_factsheet_2011.pdf; Accessed December 6, 2012; and Ibid., *How Cargo Flows Securely to the U.S.*, (Washington, DC: CBP, n.d.): 1; http://www.cbp.gov/linkhandler/cgov/trade/cargo_security/csi/csi_flows.ctt/csi_flows.pdf; Accessed December 6, 2012.

14. Ibid., "CBP Seizes Shipment of Lead-Contaminated Toys," (Washington, DC: CBP, November 26, 2012): 1-2; http://www.cbp.gov/xp/cgov/newsroom/news_releases/national/11212012.xml; Accessed December 6, 2012.

15. U.S. Department of Homeland Security, Office of Inspector General, *CBP's Container Security Initiative Has Proactive Management and Oversight But Future Direction is Uncertain*, (Washington, DC: DHS OIG, 2010): 3-5; http://purl.fdlp.gov/GPO/gpo12206; Accessed December 6, 2012.

16. U.S. Government Accountability Office, *Combating Nuclear Smuggling: Megaports Initiative Faces Funding and Sustainability Challenges*, (Washington, DC: GAO, 2012): 5-23; http://www.gao.gov/assets/650/649759.pdf; Accessed December 6, 2012.

17. See Ibid., *Supply Chain Security: CBP Needs to Conduct Regular Assessments of Its Cargo Targeting System*, (Washington, DC: GAO, 2012); http://www.gao.gov/assets/650/649695.pdf; Accessed December 6, 2012; and Ibid., *Cooperation With Many Major Drug Transit Countries Has Improved, but Better Performance Reporting and Sustainability Plans are Needed*, (Washington, DC: GAO, 2008); http://www.gao.gov/assets/280/278210.pdf; Accessed December 6, 2012.

18. See "Setting Up a Community Regime for the Control of Exports, Transfer, Brokering, and Transit of Dual-Use Items," *Official Journal of the European Union*, L 134, (29.5.2009): 1; http://trade.ec.europa.eu/doclib/docs/2009/june/tradoc_143390.pdf; Accessed December 6, 2012; Anna Wetter, *Enforcing European Union Law on Exports of Dual-Use Goods*, (Oxford: Oxford University Press, 2009); and *Sensitive Trade: The Perspective of European Union States*, Quentin Michel, ed., (New York: Peter Lang, 2011).

19. Ibid., 3, 5, 8-9.

20. Ibid., 12.

21. European Commission Trade, "Dual Use: Export Controls on Dual Use Goods," (Brussels: European Commission, 2012): 1-2; http://trade.ec.europa.eu/doclib/docs/2009/december/tradoc_145611.pdf; Accessed December 7, 2012.

22. Council of the European Union, *Council Conclusions and New Lines of Action by the European Union in Combating Proliferation of Weapons of Mass Destruction and Their Delivery Systems*, (Brussels: Council of the European Union, 2008): 7-8; http://trade.ec.europa.eu/doclib/docs/2008/december/tradoc_141740.pdf; Accessed December 7, 2012

23. See "Council Decision of 26 July 2010 Concerning Restrictive Measures Against Iran and Repealing Common Position 2007/140/CFSP," *Official Journal of the European Union*, L 195 (27.7.2010): 1-35; http://trade.ec.europa.eu/doclib/docs/2010/august/tradoc_146398.pdf; Accessed December 7, 2012; and European External Action Service, Common Foreign and Security Policy, *Sanctions or Restrictive Measures*, (Brussels: European External Action Service, 2012): 1-2; http://eeas.europa.eu/cfsp/sanctions/index_en.htm; Accessed December 13, 2012.

24. European Commission, *Green Paper: The Dual-Use Export Control System of the European Union: Ensuring Security and Competitiveness in a Changing World*, (Brussels: European Commission, 2011): 4-7, 11, 14, 19; http://trade.ec.europa.eu/doclib/docs/2011/june/tradoc_148020.pdf; Accessed December 7, 2012.

25. See European Parliament, *Dual-Use Control Items: Community Regime for the Control of Exports, Transfer, Brokering, and Transit, Update of the EU Control List*, (Strasbourg: European Parliament, 2012); http://www.europarl.europa.eu/oeil/popups/ficheprocedure.do?lang=en& reference=2010/0262(COD)#keyEvents; Accessed December 7, 2012 and "Regu-

lation EU (No. 388/2012) of the European Parliament and of the Council of 19 April 2012 Amending Council Regulation (EC) No. 428/2009 Setting Up a Community Regime for the Control of Exports , Transfer, Brokering, and Transit of Dual-Use Items," *Official Journal of the European Union*, L 129 (16.05.12): 12-280;http://eur-lex.europa.eu/LexUriServ/LexUriServ.do?uri = OJ:L: 2012:129:0012:0280:EN:PDF; Accessed December 7, 2012.

26. See International Atomic Energy Agency, "Our Work," (Vienna: IAEA, 2012): 1; http://www.iaea.org/OurWork/; Accessed December 7, 2012; *Getting Ready for a Nuclear-Ready Iran*, Henry Sokolski and Patrick Lawson, eds., (Carlisle, PA: U.S. Army War College: Strategic Studies Institute, 2005); http://www.strategicstudiesinstitute.army.mil/pubs/display.cfm?pubID = 629; Accessed December 7, 2012; *Weapons of Terror: Freeing the World From Nuclear, Biological, and Chemical* Arms, (Stockholm: The Weapons of Mass Destruction Commission, 2006); http://www.blixassociates.com/wp-content/uploads/2011/02/Weapons_of_Terror.pdf; Accessed December 7, 2012; U.S. Government Accountability Office, *Nuclear Nonproliferation: Strengthened Oversight Needed to Address Proliferation and Management Challenges in IAEA's Technical Cooperation Program*, (Washington, DC: GAO, 2009); http:// purl.access.gpo.gov/GPO/LPS113361; Accessed December 7, 2012; Gregory L. Schulte, *Strengthening the IAEA: How the Nuclear Watchdog Can Regain Its Bark*, (Washington, DC: National Defense University, 2010); http:// purl.access.gpo.gov/GPO/LPS121023; Accessed December 7, 2012; and U.S. Congress, House Committee on Foreign Affairs, *The Global Nuclear Revival and U.S. Nonproliferation Policy*, (Washington, DC: GPO, 2011); http:// purl.fdlp.gov/GPO/gpo8663; Accessed December 7, 2012.

27. See Missile Technology Control Regime, *The Missile Technology Control Regime*, (2012): 1; http://www.mtcr.info/english/index.html; Accessed December 10, 2012; Dinshaw Mistry, "Beyond the MTCR: Building a Comprehensive Regime to Contain Ballistic Missile Proliferation," *International Security*, 27 (4)(Spring 2003): 119-149; and Dinshaw Mistry, *Containing Missile Proliferation: Strategic Technology, Security Regimes, and International Cooperation in Arms Control*, (Seattle: University of Washington Press, 2003).

28. Missile Technology Control Regime, *Guidelines for Sensitive Missile-Relevant Transfers*, (2012): 1-2; http://www.mtcr.info/english/guidetext.htm; Accessed December 10, 2012.

29. Ibid., *Missile Technology Control Regime (M.T.C.R.) Equipment, Software, and Technology Annex*, (November 18, 2011); http://www.mtcr.info/english/MTCR-TEM-Technical_Annex_2011-11-18.pdf; Accessed December 10, 2012. Detailed descriptive and illustrative material on missile technology and its component parts can be found in MTCR, *Missile Technology Control Regime (MTCR) Annex Handbook 2010*, http://www.mtcr.info/english/MTCR_Annex_Handbook_ENG.pdf; Accessed December 10, 2012.

30. Minshaw, *International Security*, 120-121, 149.

31. Missile Technology Control Regime, *Plenary Meeting of the Missile Technology Control Regime Buenos Aires, Argentina 13-15 April 2011*, (2011): 1-2; http://www.mtcr.info/english/Press%20Release%20April%202011.html; Accessed December 10, 2012.

32. See Nuclear Suppliers Group, "History of the NSG," (2012); 1; http://www.nuclearsuppliersgroup.org/Leng/01-history.htm; Accessed December 10, 2012; Matthew Fuhrmann, "Spreading Temptation Proliferation and Peaceful Nuclear Cooperation Agreements," *International Security*, 34 (1)(Summer 2009): 7-41.

33. International Atomic Information Agency, *Information Circular (INFCIRC) 254/REV. 11/Part 1A, Communication Received From the Permanent Mission of the United States of America to the International Atomic Energy Agency Regarding Certain Member States' Guidelines for the Export of Nuclear Material, Equipment, and Technology*, (Vienna: International Atomic Energy Agency, November 12, 2012): 1-8; http://www.nuclearsuppliersgroup.org/Leng/PDF/infcirc254r11p1.pdf; Accessed December 10, 2012.

34. Nuclear Suppliers Group, *What Are the Activities of the NSG?*, (2012): 1; http://www.nuclearsuppliersgroup.org/Leng/04-activities.htm; Accessed December 10, 2012.

35. Ibid., *NSG Public Statement Nuclear Suppliers Group Plenary*, (Seattle: Nuclear Suppliers Group, 2012): 1-2; http://www.nuclearsuppliersgroup.org/Leng/PRESS/2012-06-Seattle_NSG_Public_Statement__FINAL_.pdf; Accessed December 10, 2012.

36. See Richard T. Cupitt and Igor Khripunov, "New Strategies for the Nuclear Suppliers Group," *Comparative Strategy*, 16 (3)(1997): 305-315; Andrew O'Neil, "Nuclear Proliferation and Global Security: Laying the Groundwork for a New Policy Agenda," *Comparative Strategy*, 24 (4)(2005): 343-359; Ian Anthony, Christer Ahlström, and Vitaly Fedchenko, *Reforming Nuclear Export Controls: The Future of the Nuclear Suppliers Group*, (Oxford: Oxford University Press, 2007); and Sharon Squassoni, "Mapping Nuclear Power's Future Spread," in Henry Sokolski, ed., *Nuclear Power's Global Expansion: Weighing Its Costs and Risks*, (Carlisle, PA: U.S. Army War College Strategic Studies Institute, 2010): 72, 75.

37. President of the United States, *National Strategy to Combat Weapons of Mass Destruction*, (Washington, DC: The White House, 2002): 3-5; http://purl.access.gpo.gov/GPO/LPS24899; Accessed December 10, 2012.

38. See U.S. Department of State, *Proliferation Security Initiative*, (Washington, DC: Department of State, (2012): 1; http://www.state.gov/t/isn/c10390.htm; Accessed December 10, 2012; and Charles Wolf, Brian G. Chow, and Gregory S. Jones, *Enhancement by Enlargement: The Proliferation Security Initiative*, (Santa Monica: The Rand Corporation, 2008).

39. Ibid., Bureau of International Security and Nonproliferation, *Proliferation Security Initiative Participants*, (Washington, DC: Department of States, 2012): 1-2; http://www.state.gov/t/isn/c27732.htm; Accessed December 10, 2012.

40. Ibid., *Proliferation Security Initiative: Statement of Interdiction Principles*, (Washington, DC: The White House, September 4, 2003): 1-3; http://www.state.gov/t/isn/c27726.htm; Accessed December 10, 2012.

41. Wolf et. al., 29-33.

42. See Mark Esper and Susan Koch, *The Proliferation Security Initiative: A Model for Future International Collaboration*, (Fairfax, VA: National Institute Press, 2009): 67-70; Rens Lee, "Why Nuclear Smuggling Matters," *Orbis*, 52 (3)(Summer 2008): 434-444.

43. Jacek Durkalek, *The Proliferation Security Initiative: Evolution and Future Prospects*, (Brussels: European Union Non-Proliferation Consortium, 2012): 1, 19-21); http://www.nonproliferation.eu/documents/nonproliferationpapers/jacekdurkalec4fcc7fd95cfff.pdf; Accessed December 11, 2012.

44. See South Eastern and European Clearinghouse for Control of Small Arms and Light Weapons (SEESAC), "About SEESAC," (Belgrade: SEESAC, 2012): 1-2; http://www.seesac.org/new-about-seesac/1/; Accessed December 11, 2012; Leonid Ryabikhin and Jevgenia Viktorova, "Weapons Transfers as a Soft Security Issue in Eastern Europe: Legal and Illicit Aspects," *European Security*, 13 (1-2)(April 2004): 73-93; and *The Politics of Security Sector Reform: Challenges and Opportunities for the European Union's Global Rule*, Magnus Ekengreen and Greg Simons, eds., (Burlington, VT: Ashgate, 2010).

45. SEESAC, "Key Activities," (Belgrade: SEESAC, 2012): 1-2; http://www.seesac.org/new-activities/1/; Accessed December 11, 2012; and Ibid. *Marking of Imported Firearms Under the UN's Firearms Protocol*, (Belgrade: Ibid.Marking of Imported Firearms Under the UN's Firearms Protocol, (Belgrade: SEESAC, 2012?); www.seesac.org/uploads/studyrep/Marking_of_Imported_Firearms.pdf; Accessed December 11, 2012. .

46. Ibid., "Key Activities," 2.

47. Ibid., *Regional Report on Arms Exports in 2010*, (Belgrade: SEESAC, 2011): 9, 48; http://www.seesac.org/uploads/armsexport/Regional_Report_on_Arms_Exports_2010.pdf; Accessed December 11, 2012.

48. United Nations Office for Disarmament Affairs, *Arms Trade Treaty*, (New York: United Nations Office for Disarmament Affairs, 2012): 1-2; https://www.un.org/disarmament/convarms/ArmsTradeTreaty/; Accessed December 12, 2012.

49. United Nations General Assembly, *Official Records*, A/64/P.55, (December 2, 2009): 15.

50. U.S. Department of State, Bureau of International Security and Nonproliferation, *U.S. Support for the Arms Trade Treaty: Fact Sheet*, (Washing-

ton, DC: U.S. Department of State, 2010): 1-2; http://www.state.gov/t/isn/rls/fs/148311.htm; Accessed December 12, 2012.

51. See *Arms Trade Treaty*, 1; and United Nations Conference on the Arms Trade Treaty, *Draft of the Arms Trade Treaty*, (New York: United Nations, August 1, 2012): 2-12; http://www.un.org/ga/search/view_doc.asp?symbol=A/CONF.217/CRP.1&Lang=E; Accessed December 12, 2012.

52. S. 2205, "Second Amendment Sovereignty Act of 2012," (Washington, DC: GPO, 2012).

53. See *Congressional Record*, 158 (108)(July 18, 2012): S5128. The text and signatories of the Senators signing this letter to Obama and Clinton can be found at United States Senate, Senator Jerry Moran, (July 26, 2012); 1-6; http://moran.senate.gov/public/index.cfm/files/serve?File_id=9cd86202-9498-47ca-8b8d-534bf60b52f7; Accessed December 12, 2012.

54. Representative Mike Kelly (R-PA), *Letter to President Obama and Secretary of State Clinton*, (June 29, 2012): 1-11; http://kelly.house.gov/sites/kelly.house.gov/files/ATT%20Letter.pdf; Accessed December, 12, 2012.

55. See Wassenaar Arrangement, *Genesis of the Wassenaar Arrangement*, (Vienna: Wassenaar Arrangement, 2012): 1-2; http://www.wassenaar.org/introduction/origins.html; Accessed December 12, 2012; U.S. Congress, Senate Committee on Governmental Affairs, *The Wassenaar Arrangement and the Future of Multilateral Export Controls*, (Washington, DC: GPO, 2000); and *Wassenaar Arrangement: Export Control and Its Role Strengthening International Security*, Dorothea Auer, ed., (Vienna: Federal Ministry for Foreign Affairs and Diplomatische AkademieWien, Vienna School of International Studies, 2005); http://www.wassenaar.org/links/Favorita_Paper.pdf; Accessed December 12, 2012.

56. Auer, 11.

57. Wassenaar Arrangement, *Participating States*, (Vienna: Wassenaar Arrangement, 2012): 1; http://www.wassenaar.org/participants/index.html; Accessed December 15, 2012.

58. See Ibid., *Guidelines and Procedures, Including the Initial Elements as As Amended and Updated in 2001, 2003, 2004, 2007, and 2011*, (Vienna: Wassenaar Arrangement, 2012); 1; http://www.wassenaar.org/guidelines/; Accessed December 12, 2012; and Auer, 23.

59. See Ibid., *Public Statement 2011 Plenary Meeting of the Wassenaar Arrangement on Export Controls for Conventional Arms and Dual-Use Goods and Technologies*, (Vienna: Wassenaar Arrangement, 2011): 1-2; http://www.wassenaar.org/publicdocuments/2011/WA%20Plenary%20 Public%20Statement%202011.pdf; Accessed December 12, 2012; and Heinz Gartner, "The Wassenaar Arrangement: How it is Broken and Needs to Be Fixed," *Defense & Security Analysis*, 24 (1)(March 2008): 53-60.

60. See World Customs Organization (WCO), *History*, (Brussels: WCO, 2012): 1-3; http://www.wcoomd.org/en/about-us/what-is-the-wco/

au_history.aspx; Accessed December 13, 2012; Ibid., *WCO Goals,* (Brussels: WCO, 2012): 1; http://www.wcoomd.org/en/about-us/what-is-the-wco/goals.aspx; Accessed December 13, 2012; and Brenda Chalfin, "Customs Regimes and the Materiality of Global Mobility: Governing the Port of Rotterdam," *American Behavioral Scientist*, 50 (12)(August 2007): 1610-1630.

61. WCO, *WCO Working Bodies,* (Brussels: WCO, 2012): 1-2; http://www.wcoomd.org/en/about-us/wco-working-bodies.aspx; Accessed December 13, 2012.

62. Ibid., *Annual Report 2011-2012*, (Brussels: WCO, 2012): 9, 15, 19, 21; http://www.wcoomd.org/en/topics/ ~ /media/WCO/Public/Global/PDF/Media/WCO%20Annual%20Report/Annual_Report_2011-12_en.ashx; Accessed December 13, 2012.

63. Ibid., 31-32.

64. Ibid., 46, 48, 52-60.

65. See Zangger Committee (ZC), *History*, (Vienna: ZC, 2010); 1; http://www.zanggercommittee.org/History/Seiten/default.aspx; Accessed December 13, 2012; and Fritz W. Schmidt, "The Zangger Committee: Its History and Future Role, *The Nonproliferation Review*, 2 (1)(Fall 1994): 38-44.

66. International Atomic Energy Agency, *Information Circular 209*, (Vienna: IAEA, September 3, 1974); http://www.iaea.org/Publications/Documents/Infcircs/Others/inf209.shtml; Accessed December 13, 2012.

67. Zanger Committee, *Members*, (Vienna: ZC, 2012): 1; http://www.zanggercommittee.org/Members/Seiten/default.aspx; Accessed December 13, 2012.

68. Schmidt, 40-42.

69. Schmidt, "Nuclear Export Controls: Closing the Gaps," *IAEA Bulletin*, 46 (2)(March 2005): 31-33; http://www.zanggercommittee.org/Documents/IAEABulletinclosingthegapsFWSchmidt.pdf; Accessed December 13, 2012.

70. See United Nations, *2010 Review Conference of the Parties to the Treaty on Nuclear Non-Proliferation of Nuclear Weapons (NPT) 3-28 May 2010*, (New York: NPT Conference, 2010); http://www.un.org/en/conf/npt/2010/; Accessed December 13, 2010 for exhaustive documentation of conference proceedings. See also Jayantha Danapala, *Evaluating the 2010 NPT Review Conference*, (Washington, DC: U.S. Institute of Peace, 2010); http://purl.fdlp.gov/GPO/gpo19409; Accessed December 13, 2012.

71. See O'Neil, 2005; Emily Cura Saunders, *Case Study: Iran, Islam, the Bomb, and NPT*, (Berkeley: Lawrence Livermore National Laboratory, 2010); Jacques E.C. Hymans, *Achieving Nuclear Ambitions: Scientists, Politicians, and Proliferation*, (Cambridge: Cambridge University Press, 2012): 11-16; and *Reviewing the Nuclear Nonproliferation Treaty*, Henry Sokolski, ed., (Carlisle: U.S. Army War College Strategic Studies Institute, 2010); http://permanent.access.gpo.gov/gpo2502/PUB987.pdf; Accessed December 13, 2012.

Conclusion

Preceding chapters have seen how the U.S. export control system has become a stovepiped and often dysfunctional bureaucracy during the six and half decades since World War II. Although U.S. export control efforts have achieved some successes, they are too disjointed to meet the realities of 21st century international economics, the diffusion of science and technology, and international security trends and developments.

American political science often uses the term iron triangle to describe the policymaking relationship between government agencies, congressional committees, and interest groups.[1] The U.S. Government's export control policymaking system and areas of collaboration and competition has expanded drastically beyond a polygonal triangle to encompass the Commerce Department, Congress, the Department of Defense, the Department of Energy and Nuclear Regulatory Commission, Department of Homeland Security, international government organizations, Justice Department, nongovernmental organizations including export oriented businesses, academic institutions, and assorted interest groups; the State Department, and the Treasury Department creating a ten sided policymaking polygon or iron decagon.[2]

Although this work has documented some successful historical and contemporary U.S. export control violation enforcement actions, making these enduring and successful is an ongoing challenge due to interagency rivalry, inconsistencies in how U.S. agencies interpret statutory law and enact administrative law, varying degrees of attention from Congress, and disagreement between non-government organizations on whether export control statutes should apply to them. Attempting to balance the desire of U.S. companies to promote exports and create jobs during protracted economic recession competes with national desires to limit the spread of conventional weapons and WMD technologies to hostile countries and transnational groups while also economically punishing regimes hostile to U.S. This problem is further exacerbated when U.S. export control policymaking interacts with comparable policymaking from other countries and multilateral international governmental organizations while simultaneously attempting to achieve some degree of cooperation with these entities.[3]

Effectively enforcing export control violations and punishing perpetrators of these violations is a major challenge once other countries become involved. An example of how difficult and complicated enforcement can be was reflected in a 2008 *Naval War College Review* article describing problems with enforcing a blockade of Mideast oil shipments to China if Beijing decided to conduct military aggression in the Western Pacific. This analysis mentioned that cargoes can be sold and resold between ports of embarkation and destination and that cargoes listed on the bill of lading as headed for South Korea could be sold to China after being inspected by the blockade and being allowed to pass. It went on to contend:

> Shipping documents can also be forged. Forgery can be quite sophisticated, especially if, (as it no doubt would be in this case) abetted by the PRC government. The blockading force would probably find no tankers will bills of lading that declared China as their destination. The Chinese government and state-owned energy companies could almost certainly offer private shippers and oil producers sufficient compensation to ensure their complicity in such a scheme.[4]

Additional enforcement problems occur with WMD smuggling due to local and regional economic, political, and security imperatives. A 2011 Senate Foreign Relations Committee report demonstrated this when it reported that Moldavia arrested 6 individuals in Chisinau on June 27, 2011 for possessing 9 kilograms of highly-enriched uranium-235 for a nuclear weapon or dirty bomb and attempting to sell these for $30 million. Selling plutonium was also an objective of these individuals and the sellers sought non-Western buyers including one believed to be from North Africa. This commodity was believed to have been enriched at various sites in Russia, transited through the Russian supported Moldovan separatist enclave of Transnistria which has weak law enforcement and border security controls, and Transnistrian residents were involved in this attempted sale. This was the second Moldovan interdiction of uranium in 2011 and the 19th unclassified international seizure of uranium and weapons grade plutonium since 1993. Porous borders between Moldova, Russia, and the Ukraine further heighten WMD proliferation possibilities and Ukranian border security officials reported a 10% increase in illicit drug, radioactive materials, and weapons interdictions over 2009.[5]

China is also a major export control challenge due to its efforts to steal advanced U.S. military technologies such as aviation, cyber technology, and space launch technology through traditional espionage and cyberespionage including an onslaught of Chinese originated computer network intrusions against U.S. private sector firms whose perpetrators are difficult to track. These efforts are also influenced by Beijing's Project 863 which seeks to develop key technologies to construct China's information infrastructure as a key national priority. This problem is further exacerbated by growing interrelationships between Chinese and U.S. companies involving employing Chinese national technical experts at U.S. facilities and off-shoring U.S. production and R&D facilities in China.[6]

North Korea is another export control challenge as its criminal regime exports drugs such as opium to finance its nuclear weapons program and cooperates with other rogue international regimes such as Iran to enhance its military capabilities through Pyongyang's Office #39 which coordinates these illegal activities through bribing customs officials, counterfeiting, licensing fraud, money laundering, creating shell companies, and using underground or illegal remittance systems involving citizens and officials from countries as diverse as Australia, China, Egypt, Malaysia, Russia, Singapore, Taiwan, South Korea, and the United States. The North Koreans have also used international criminal groups such as Chinese Triads, the Irish Republican Army, Japanese Yakuza, and the Russian Mafia to carry out their activities.[7]

Enforcing financing of terrorist organizations is an ongoing problem due to the ability of terrorist states and organizations to elude such sanctions through underground financial networks such as the Hawala system used in many Islamic countries. This makes it particularly difficult to absolutely cut off foreign financial support to Islamist terrorist groups such as Al Qaeda and its regional affiliates, the Haqqani network, the Taliban, and others because there will always be individuals and organizations willing to work around U.S. and international restrictions on terrorist financing for economic and ideological reasons.[8]

Iran has sought to evade international economic sanctions against it by using Armenian financial facilities, possibly setting up joint ventures with foreign partners in Armenia and Georgia to acquire technology for military parts and nuclear centrifuges, and participating in the regional drug trade to distribute methamphetamine and laundering money in casinos in Azerbaijan and other adjacent countries.[9]

Russia is also a major player in illegally acquiring sensitive western technology. Its skilled intelligence services make active use of cyber intelligence, human intelligence, and other operations to collect economic information and technology supporting Moscow's efforts to enhance its economic development and security. Its intelligence agencies will target Russian immigrants with advanced technical skills working for leading U.S. companies and Russia's increasing economic integration with the west will probably see a greater number of Russian companies affiliated with Russian intelligence services doing business in the U.S. with a workforce consisting of "retired" intelligence officers.[10]

Difficult international economic conditions have caused some U.S. allied countries to engage in dubious international economic and military transfers to countries of concern out of the desire to boost their own domestic industries. On January 25, 2011, France and Russia signed an agreement in which Paris agreed to sell Moscow four Mistral-class amphibious assault vehicles with the first two of these vessels priced at $1.47 billion with scheduled 2014-2015 delivery dates. Mistral-class ships are multi-mission allowing seaborne force projection, are 199 meters long, displace 22 tons and can reportedly transport up to 16 helicopters, four landing craft, 13 main battle tanks or 60-70 vehicles, and between 450-900 combat troops depending on the nature of the deployment. France claims the craft they are selling contain no military communications, command and control technology, and no NATO communications capabilities.[11]

On November 24, 2011, German defense industry company Rheinmetall announced it had signed a contract with the Russian Ministry of Defense to build an army training center in Mulino in Russia's Volga region. This simulation-supported center is to be capable of training 30,000 troops per year by 2014 and will be modeled on a high-tech army training center used by the German Bundeswehr. Its size is over 500 square kilometers and will be designed to train a reinforced mechanized infantry or armored brigade. Facility training stations will include live combat and combat training simulation along with marksmanship at modern firing ranges. This deal is worth nearly $131 million and Rheinmetall views it as potentially opening the way to additional contracts for modernizing Russian military equipment.[12]

Problems balancing export controls unique economic, political, and security quandaries has also affected the United Kingdom. During the 1980s and early 1990s, the British firm Matrix Churchill was charged with violating British export control guidelines by selling dual-use machine tool equipment to Iran and Iraq. This was against British Government policy of remaining neutral during the Iran-Iraq War and exacerbated by Matrix Churchill Managing Director Paul Henderson being an unpaid British intelligence agent. The British Foreign Office strongly opposed these sales while they were enthusiastically supported by the Department of Trade and Industry. Four company directors were put on trial for supplying Iraq equipment and knowledge, but the trial collapsed after revelations that Matrix Churchill had been advised on how to sell arms to Iraq due to the government's desire to support Britain's machine tools industry.

A British Government inquiry concluded Britain supplied no lethal weapons to Baghdad or Tehran and that the government took additional measures to prevent exporting non-lethal goods which could have exacerbated the conflict. This turned out to be a major scandal for John Major's Conservative Government, demonstrated significant weaknesses in the British parliamentary ministerial accountability system, and may have contributed to the government's 1997 election defeat against Labour lead by Tony Blair.[13]

Economic recession in western countries has produced over $100 billion defense spending declines in the U.S. and Western Europe through 2015 while defense spending and purchases are rising in east and southeast Asia, the Middle East, and South America. China and Russia have sought to fill gaps in this market by increasing their arms sales there in response to declining U.S. and European sales to these areas. The desire of European countries to retain their defense industry viability has, consequently, resulted them in seeking to enhance their arms sales to Russia and consider such sales to China despite the 1989 international arms embargo against Beijing.[14]

The Obama Administration quietly expressed objection to these arms sales, but its desire to maintain its "reset" policy on relations with Russia prevented more vocal expressions of displeasure. Factors complicating U.S. export control policy coordination with its allies toward future arms sales to Russia and elsewhere include ongoing pressure on European defense industries and governments to promote arms sales to non-NATO and EU countries; calls for increased NATO transparency on arms sales to Russia and their security implications; the role of ITAR and other conventional arms export control arrangements; and the need for rigorous enforcement and congressional oversight of U.S. arms export control laws and regulations.[15]

Multilateral export control regimes have achieved some successes but have often proved unsuccessful in preventing militarily sensitive equipment from being sold or diverted to hostile countries. In September 2012, media reports revealed that the United Nation's World Intellectual Property Organization (WIPO) had shipped U.S. made computer equipment to Iran and North Korea in violation of U.S. export control laws covering anti-terrorism, encryption, and national security. This equipment included laptop computers and a highly capable hardware firewall and network security system subject to extremely high-level U.S. licensing requirements for its dual-use capabilities. This situation is complicated by WIPO considering itself to be above national export control laws and believing that it doesn't have to adhere to UN Security Council sanctions.[16]

While we live in an interconnected global economy and security environment, these and other cases demonstrate that many international countries, individuals, and organizations do not adhere to the high ideals of open trade and knowledge exchange and will do whatever it takes to enhance their domestic political power base or augment their military capacity as the December 12, 2012 North Korean satellite launch demonstrates. These countries, individuals, and organizations will also exploit the mirror imaging idealism of western intellectuals and governments and the imprudent eagerness of businesses to sell military and dual-use weapons to any prospective buyer regardless of the consequences to their countries national interests and their own commercial interests, to acquire weapons of mass destruction, and the knowledge used to further their development of such weapons. These factors and the failure to have effective enforcement of export controls violations make this a key problem of early 21st century international security and mark as naïve those critics saying export controls have no value.[17]

Export controls involves the intersection of the debate between Die Primat der Aussenpolitik (the supremacy of foreign policy) introduced by German historian Leopold von Ranke (1795-1886) and Die Primat der Innenpolitik (the supremacy of domestic politics) adhered to by numerous scholars of international relations. Both international and domestic political factors shape national and international export control policymaking. Examining the historical record, contemporary policymaking, and speculating on the possible future evolution of export controls involves close examination of all aspects and documentation of governmental and non-governmental literature in this field including diplomatic correspondence, intelligence analysis, international agreements, congressional and parliamentary debates and hearings, trade literature, international security developments, and submissions in political, legal, and regulatory debates by interested parties.[18]

Investigating this topic leaves one hesitant to recommend a one size fits all solution to this continually evolving policymaking environment. However, the U.S. needs to improve its export control policymaking to promote more expedited licensing and processing of civilian only exports to enhance its international economic competitiveness while also promoting more rigid and more effective controls on the exports of dual-use and military items. U.S. academic institutions need to place primary emphasis on adhering to U.S. national security standards instead of idealistically promoting unrestricted access to sensitive national security information by foreign nationals from proscribed countries.

The Commerce Department should be removed from export control policymaking since its institutional mission is promoting international trade instead of protecting national security. A new U.S. Government export control policymaking entity should be established as a council consisting of DOD, DOE and the Nuclear Regulatory Commission, CBP, intelligence community representation, State, and Treasury Department making export control and economic sanctions decisions on behalf of the President with the National Security Council resolving disputes. The Justice Department would continue investigating and prosecuting those violating export control laws. Export oriented companies and non-government organizations can advocate their viewpoints on export control licensing issues through the regulations.gov portal of announcements published in the *Federal Register*.

More efficient and cost-effective congressional oversight of export controls needs to occur. This can be done by consolidating these responsibilities into a congressional select committee featuring members from appropriations committees, armed services subcommittees, armed service committees, financial services committees, foreign relations committees, homeland security committees, and intelligence committees as selected by each legislative chamber's leadership.

Export controls should be the strongest on WMD component parts and items of acute national security importance based on current and emerging threats from international terrorist organizations and countries such as China, Iran, North Korea, areas in and near Pakistan and the Gulf of Yemen, other regions of the Middle East including Syria, and the Russian Federation. Examples of critical national security controls involve advanced materials and manufacturing, aerospace and aeronautics, ballistic missile defense, capital transfers to hostile individuals, groups, and organizations, cybersecurity, electronic infrastructure security for civilian and military materials, marine systems, precision guided munitions, and space launch and space surveillance assets.[19]

Export controls are most effective when there is national and international will to enforce them and when the sanctioning country or countries have near autarkic or monopolistic control over the targeted country, individual, or transnational organization. Tough penalties must be applied against U.S. and foreign entities violating export control laws even if these penalties are unpopular domestically or internationally. Although export controls have limits to their effectiveness due to the multiplicity of diplomatic, economic, political, and security interests involved they still play an important role in contemporary and future international affairs. They will continue to be used as instruments of international coercion, diplomacy, and economics as long as individual countries or groups of countries are unable or unwilling to take covert action or overt military action to forcibly eliminate the threats or behaviors of offending nation states and groups they see as threatening national interests and international stability.

Notes

1. See Thomas L. Gais, Mark A. Peterson, and Jack L. Walker, "Interest Groups, Iron Triangles, and Representative Institutions in American National Government, *British Journal of Political Science*, 14 (2)(April 1984): 161-185; Hedrick Smith, *The Power Game: How Washington Works*, (New York: Random House, 1988); and James W. Endersby and David J. Webber, "Iron Triangle Simulation: A Role-Playing Game for Undergraduates in Congress, In-

terest Groups, and Public Policy Classes," *PS: Political Science and Politics*, 28 (3)(September 1995): 520-523.

2. Ian F. Fergusson and Paul K. Kerr, *The U.S. Export Control System and the President's Reform Initiative*, (Washington, DC: Library of Congress, Congressional Research Service, 2012).

3. See Paul Holtom and Mark Bromley, "The International Arms Trade: Difficult to Define, Measure, and Control," *Arms Control Today*, 40 (6)(July/ August 2010): 8-14; U.S. Congress, House Committee on Energy and Commerce, Subcommittee on Oversight and Investigations, *Commercial Sales of Military Technologies*, (Washington, DC: GPO, 2012); U.S. Government Accountability Office, *Export Controls: U.S. Agencies Need to Assess Control List Reform's Impact on Compliance Activities*, (Washington, DC: GAO, 2012); http://purl.fdlp.gov/GPO/gpo24893; Accessed December 21, 2012.

4. Gabriel S. Collins and William S. Murray. "No Oil for the Lamps of China," *Naval War College Review*, 62 (2)(Spring 2008): 85.

5. U.S. Congress. Senate Committee on Foreign Relations. *Enhancing Non-Proliferation Partnerships in the Black Sea Region: Minority Staff Report.* (Washington, DC: GPO, 2011): 1-3; http://purl.fdlp.gov/GPO/gpo16232; Accessed December 21, 2012.

6. See U.S. Congress, House Committee on Foreign Affairs, Subcommittee on Oversight and Investigations, *Communist Chinese Cyber-Attacks, Cyber-Espionage, and Theft of American Technology*, (Washington, DC: GPO, 2011); http://purl.fdlp.gov/GPO/gpo9687; Accessed December 21, 2012; Philip C. Saunders and Joshua K. Wiseman, *Buy, Build, or Steal: China's Quest for Advanced Military Aviation Technologies*, (Washington, DC: National Defense University Press, 2011); and U.S. Office of the National Counterintelligence Executive, *Foreign Spies Stealing U.S. Economic Secrets in Cyberspace: Annual Report to Congress on Foreign Economic Collection and Industrial Espionage, 2009-2011,* (Washington, DC: NCIX, 2011): 1, 8; www.ncix.gov/publications/reports/fecie_all/Foreign_Economic_Collection_2011.pdf; Accessed January 3, 2013.

7. Paul Rexton Kan, Bruce E. Bechtol Jr., and Robert M. Collins, *Criminal Sovereignty: Understanding North Korea's Illicit International Activities,* (Carlisle, PA: U.S. Army War College Strategic Studies Institute, 2010)

8. See Wesley J.L. Anderson, *Disrupting Threat Finances: Using Financial Information to Disrupt Terrorist Organizations,* (Hurlburt Field, FL: Joint Special Operations University Press, 2008); Matteo Vaccani, *Alternative Remittance Systems and Terrorism Financing: Issues in Risk Mitigation*, (Washington, DC: World Bank, 2010); Gretchen Peters, *Haqqani Network Financing: The Evolution of an Industry*, (West Point: U.S. Military Academy Combating Terrorism Center, 2012)

9. Ariel Cohen, "Iran Threatens U.S. Interests in the South Caucasus," in U.S. Congress, House Committee on Foreign Relations, Subcommittee on

Europe and Eurasia, *Iranian Influence in the South Caucasus and the Surrounding Region*, (Washington, DC: House Committee on Foreign Affairs, December 5, 2012): 5-6; http://foreignaffairs.house.gov/112/HHRG-112-FA14-WState-CohenA-20121205.pdf; Accessed December 21, 2012.

10. U.S. Office of the National Counterintelligence Executive, 5, 8.

11. Paul Belkin, Derek Mix, and Jim Nichol, *Recent Sales of Military Equipment and Technology by European NATO Allies to Russia*, (Washington, DC: Library of Congress, Congressional Research Service, 2012): 4-6.

12. Ibid., 7.

13. See "Arms for Iraq: Scandal Hits Fan," *The Economist*, 325 (November 14, 1992): 764; Mark Pythian and Walter Little, "Parliament and Arms Sales: Lessons of the Matrix Churchill Affair," *Parliamentary Affairs*, 46 (3)(July 1993): 293-308; Davinia Miller, *Export or Die Britain's Defence Trade With Iran and Iraq*, (London: Continuum, 1996); and Sir Richard Scott, *Inquiry into the Export of Defence Equipment and Dual-Use Goods to Iraq and Related Prosecutions*, 5 vols., (London: HMSO, 1996).

14. See Ibid., 8-9; and U.S. Congress, Senate Committee on Foreign Relations, *The Lifting of the EU Arms Embargo on China*, (Washington, DC: GPO, 2005); http://purl.access.gpo.gov/GPO/LPS63682; Accessed January 2, 2013.

15. Belkin, Mix, and Nichol, 19, 22-24.

16. See George Russell, "U.N. Shipment of High-Tech Equipment to North Korea, Iran Unjustified and Unfathomable, Say Investigators," *Fox News,* (September 13, 2012); http://www.foxnews.com/world/2012/09/13/un-shipment-high-tech-to-north-korea-iran-unjustified-and-unfathomable-say/; Accessed December 21, 2012; and World Intellectual Property Organization, *Independent External Review Report: Technical Assistance Provided to Countries Subject to United Nations Sanctions*, (Geneva: WIPO, 2012); . http://www.wipo.int/about-wipo/en/oversight/pdf/wipo_external_review_2012.pdf; Accessed December 21, 2012.

17. Examples of the phenomenon of mirror imaging in international relations and the policy failures which can occur due to this include Patrick J. Cummings, *Context, Culture, and Connection: Avoiding the Counter-Productive Effects of Mirror Imaging in Theater Security Cooperation*, M.A. Thesis, (Newport, RI: U.S. Naval War College, 2008); Jay B. Reeves, *Misunderstood Dragon or Underestimated Panda: How China Reacts to External National Security Crises*, M.A. Thesis, (Maxwell Air Force Base, AL: School of Advanced Air and Space Studies, Air University, 2009); Bo Peterrson, "Mirror, Mirror. . . : Mythmaking, Self-Images and Views of the U.S. 'Other' in Contemporary Russia," (Malmo University: Malmo University Electronic Publishing, 2012); http://muep.mah.se/bitstream/handle/2043/14000/Petersson.final.pdf?sequence=2; Accessed January 2, 2013.

18. See Theodore H. Von Laue, *Leopold Ranke: The Formative* Years, (Princeton: Princeton University Press, 1950); Jack S. Levy, "Domestic Poli-

tics and War," *The Journal of Interdisciplinary History*, 18 (4)(Spring 1988): 653-673; Gordon A. Craig, "On the Pleasure of Reading Diplomatic Correspondence," *The Journal of Contemporary History*, 26 (3/4)(September 1991): 369-384; Fareed Zakaria, "Realism and Domestic Politics: A Review Essay," *International Security*, 17 (1)(Summer 1992): 177-198; Brendan Simms, "The Return of the Primacy of Foreign Policy," *German History*, 21 (3)((July 2003): 275-291.

19. U.S. Office of the National Counterintelligence Executive, 8.

Bibliography

Joel D. Aberbach. *Keeping a Watchful Eye: The Politics of Congressional Oversight*. Washington, DC: Brookings Institution, 1990.

Kenneth W. Abbott. "Defining the Extraterritorial Reach of American Export Controls: Congress as Catalyst." *Cornell International Law Journal*, 17 (Winter 1984): 79-158.

Sherman R. Abrahamson. "Intelligence for Economic Defense." *Studies in Intelligence*, 8 (2)(Spring 1964): 33-43.

"Administrative Remedies and Procedures." 42 *Federal Register* 165 (August 25, 1977): 42851-42856.

"Amendment of the International Traffic in Arms Regulations (ITAR)-U.S. Munitions List." 48 *Federal Register* 10 (January 14, 1983): 1758.

"Amendment of the International Traffic in Arms Regulations (ITAR)-U.S. Munitions List." 48 *Federal Register* 122 (June 23, 1983): 28633.

"Amendment to the International Traffic in Arms Regulations (ITAR)." *57 Federal Register* 175 (September 9, 1992): 41077.

"Amendment to the International Traffic in Arms Regulations (ITAR)." 58 *Federal Register*, 174 (September 10, 1993): 47636.

"Amendment to the International Traffic in Arms Regulations." 59 *Federal Register* 158 (August 17, 1994): 42158.

"Amendment to the International Traffic in Arms Regulations." 59 *Federal Register* 170 (September 2, 1994): 45631-45622.

"Amendment to the International Traffic in Arms Regulations." 61 *Federal Register* 135 (July 12, 1996): 36625.

"Amendment to the International Traffic in Arms Regulations; United States Munitions List." 67 *Federal Register* 182 (September 19, 2002): 58984-58985.

"Amendment to the International Traffic in Arms Regulations: United States Munitions List." 72 *Federal Register* 136 (July 17, 2007): 39010.

"Amendment to the International Traffic in Arms Regulations: Temporary Export Exemption for Body Armor." 74 *Federal Register* 150 (August 6, 2009): 39312-39213.

"Amendment to the International Traffic in Arms Regulations: Libya." 76 *Federal Register*, 100 (May 24, 2011): 30001.

"Amendment to the List of Proscribed Items." 61 *Federal Register* 87 (May 3, 1996): 19841.

"Amendments to the International Traffic in Arms Regulations Part II." 58 *Federal Register 139* (July 22, 1993): 39280-39281.

"Amendments to the International Traffic in Arms Regulations." 63 *Federal Register* 68 (April 9, 1998): 17329-17330.

"Amendments to the International Traffic in Arms Regulations (ITAR): Control of Commercial Communications Satellites on the United States Munitions List" 64 *Federal Register* 54 (March 22, 1999): 13679.

"Amendments to the International Traffic in Arms Regulation: NATO Countries, Australia and Japan." 65 *Federal Register* 141 (July 21, 2000): 45282-45286.

American Bankers Association. "Attention: CISADA Reporting Requirements under Section 104(e), RIN 1506-AB12." June 1, 2011; http://www.regulations.gov/#!documentDetail;D=FINCEN-2011-0002-0007; Accessed November 21, 2012.

Wesley J.L. Anderson. *Disrupting Threat Finances: Using Financial Information to Disrupt Terrorist Organizations*. Hurlburt Field, FL: Joint Special Operations University Press, 2008.

American Association of Exporters and Importers. "Comments on Proposed Regulations to the Ear: Control of Aircraft and Related Items the President Determines No Longer Warrant Control Under the USML." (December 22, 2011): 2-3; http://www.regulations.gov/#!documentDetail;D=BIS-2011-0033-0016; Accessed November 20, 2012.

Gerry Argyris Andrianopolous . *Kissinger and Brzezinski: The NSC and the Struggle for U.S. National Security Policy*. New York: St. Martin's Press, 1991.

Ian Anthony, Christer Ahlström, and Vitaly Fedchenko. *Reforming Nuclear Export Controls: The Future of the Nuclear Suppliers Group*. Oxford: Oxford University Press, 2007.

Kristin Archick, Richard F. Grimmett, and Shirley A. Kan. *European Union's Arms Embargo on China: Implications and Options for U.S. Policy.* Washington, DC: Library of Congress, Congressional Research Service, 2006.

"Arms for Iraq: Scandal Hits Fan" *The Economist*, 325 (November 14, 1992): 764.

Association Connecting Electronic Industries. "Re: Proposed Revisions to the Export Administration Regulations (EAR): Control of Items the Present Determines No Longer Warrant Control Under the United States Munitions List (USML) . . . ," (September 13, 2011): http://www.regulations.gov/#!documentDetail;D=BIS-2011-0015-0031; Accessed November 20, 2012.

The Australia Group. *The Australia Group: Activities*, (2012): 1; http://www.australiagroup.net/en/activities.html; Accessed December 5, 2012.

Ibid. *Homepage*, (2012): 1; http://www.australiagroup.net/en/index. html; Accessed December 5, 2012.

Ibid. *Media Release 2012 Australia Group Plenary*, (June 15, 2012); http://www.australiagroup.net/en/media_june2012.html; Accessed December 5, 2012.

Ibid. *The Origins of the Australia Group* (2012): 1; http://www. australiagroup.net/en/origins.html; Accesssed December 5, 2012.

Norman A. Bailey. *The Strategic Plan That Won the Cold War: National Security Decision Directive 75*, (Maclean, VA: The Potomac Foundation, 1999).

James A. Baker III with Thomas M. DeFrank. *The Politics of Diplomacy: Revolution, War & Peace, 1989-1992*. New York: G.P. Putnam's Sons, 1995.

Ray Banoun, Derrick Cephas, and Larry Fruchtman. "USA Patriot Act and Other Recent Money Laundering Developments Have Broad Impact on Financial Institutions." *Journal of Taxation and Regulation of Financial Institutions*, 15 (March/April 2002): 17.

Ann Calvaresi Barr. *Export Controls: State and Commerce Have Not Taken Basic Steps to Better Insure U.S. Interests are Protected.* Washington, DC: GAO, 2008; http://www.gao.gov/assets/120/119838.pdf; Accessed August 8, 2012.

Mark Basile. "Going to the Source: Why Al Qaeda's Financial Network is Likely to Withstand the Current War on Terrorist Financing." *Studies in Conflict & Terrorism*, 27 (3)(2004): 169-185.

Esfandyar Batmanghelidj. "Sanctions, Smuggling, and the Cigarette: The Granting of Iran OFAC Licenses to Big Tobacco." *Iranian Studies*, 45 (3)(May 2012): 395-415.

Doug Beason. *The E-Bomb: How America's New Directed Energy Weapons Will Change the Way Future Wars Will Be Fought.* Cambridge, MA: Da Capo Press, 2005.

Paul Belkin, Derek Mix, and Jim Nichol. *Recent Sales of Military Equipment and Technology by European NATO Allies to Russia.* Washington, DC: Library of Congress, Congressional Research Service, 2012.

William J. Bernstein. *A Splendid Exchange: How Trade Shaped the World.* New York: Atlantic Monthly Press, 2008.

Dirk De Bièvre and Andreas Dür. "Constitutency Interests and Delegation in European and American Trade Policy." *Comparative Political Studies*, 38 (10)(December 2005): 1271-1296.

Bill Summary & Status 97th Congress (1981-1982) H.R. 7015 CRS Summary. Washington, DC: Library of Congress, Congressional Research Service, 1982; http://thomas.loc.gov/cgi-bin/bdquery/D?d097: 183:./temp/~bdlm1A:@@@D&summ2=m&|/home/Legislative Data.php?n=BSS;c=97|; Accessed November 7, 2012.

Jonathan B. Bingham and Victor C. Johnson. "A Rational Approach to Export Controls." *Foreign Affairs*, 57 (4)(Spring 1979): 894-920.

Biological Weapons Convention. *Confidence Building Measures Submitted by Norway, Switzerland, and New Zealand.* Geneva: 1 November 2011: 1-5; http://www.opbw.org/rev_cons/7rc/BWC_CONF. VII_WP21_E.pdf; Accessed December 5, 2012.

Biological and Toxins Convention Website. *About the Biological and Toxin Weapons Convention.* (2012): 1; http://www.opbw.org/; Accessed December 5, 2012.

Richard A. Bitzinger. "The Globalization of the Arms Industry: The Next Proliferation Challenge." *International Security*, 19 (2)(Autumn 1994): 170-198.

Stephen Blank. "Russia as Rogue Proliferator." *Orbis*, 44 (1)(Winter 2000): 91-107.

Morris Bornstein. *East-West Technology Transfer: The Transfer of Western Technology to the USSR.* Paris: OECD, 1985.

Nigel Bowles. *Nixon's Business: Authority and Power in Presidential Politics.* College Station: Texas A&M University Press, 2005.

Joseph C. Brada and Larry J. Wipf. "The Impact of U.S. Trade Controls on Exports to the Soviet Bloc." *Southern Economic Journal*, 41 (1)(July 1974): 47-56.

Michael J. Brenner. *Nuclear Power and Non-Proliferation: The Remaking of U.S. Policy*. Cambridge: Cambridge University Press, 1981.

Mark Bromley and Paul Holton. "The International Arms Trade: Difficult to Define, Measure, and Control." *Arms Control Today*, 40 (6)(July-August 2010): 8-14.

"Bureau of Politico-Military Affairs Amendments to the International Traffic in Arms Regulations." *56 Federal Register* 179, (September 16, 1991): 46753.

"Bureau of Political-Military Affairs; Amendment to the International Traffic in Arms Regulations." 68 *Federal Register* 31 (February 14, 2003): 7417-7418.

"Bureau of Political-Military Affairs: Revocation of Defense Export Licenses to Venezuela." 71 *Federal Register* 159 (August 17, 2006): 47554.

Matthew D. Burris. "Tilting at Windmills?: The Counterposing Policy Interest Driving The U.S. Commercial Satellite Export Control Reform Debate." *Air Force Law Review*, 66 (2010): 255-329.

Frank M. Cain. "Exporting the Cold War: British Responses to the U.S.A's Establishment of COCOM: 1947-1951." *Journal of Contemporary History*, 29 (3)(July 1994): 501-522.

Ibid. "The US-Led Trade Embargo on China: The Origins of CHIMCOM, 1947-1952." *Journal of Strategic Studies*, 18 (4)(1995): 33-54.

David Eduardo Cavazos. "Citizens and Bureaucracy: Electronic Participation in Regulatory Processes." *Electronic Government*, 8 (1)(2010): 59-72.

Center for Strategic and International Studies. *Briefing of the Working Group on the Health of the U.S. Space Industrial Base and the Impact of Export Controls*. Washington, DC: CSIS, February 2008; http://csis.org/files/media/csis/pubs/021908_csis_spaceindustry itar_final.pdf; Accessed November 19, 2012

Brenda Chalfin. "Customs Regimes and the Materiality of Global Mobility: Governing the Port of Rotterdam." *American Behavioral Scientist*, 50 (12)(August 2007): 1610-1630.

Wan-Ying Chang and Lynn M. Milan. *International Mobility and Employment Characteristics Among Recent Recipients of U.S. Doctorates*. Washington, DC: National Science Foundation, 2012; http://

www.nsf.gov/statistics/infbrief/nsf13300/nsf13300.pdf; Accessed November 19, 2012.

Emma Chanlett-Avery. *North Korea: U.S. Relations, Nuclear Diplomacy, and Internal Situation*. Washington, DC: Library of Congress, Congressional Research Service, 2012.

Dean Cheng, "Export Controls and the Hard Case of China." Washington, DC: Heritage Foundation, 2010: http://www.heritage.org/Research/Reports/2010/12/Export-Controls-and-the-Hard-Case-of-China; Accessed August 10, 2011.

Diane E. Chido. *Civilian Skills for African Military Officers to Resolve the Infrastructure, Economic Development, and Stability Crisis in Sub-Saharan Africa*. Carlisle, PA: U.S. Army War College, Strategic Studies Institute, 2011.

Duncan L. Clark and Robert J. Johnston. "U.S. Dual-Use Exports to China, Chinese Behavior, and the Israel Factor: Effective Controls?" *Asian Survey*, 39 (2)(March/April 1999): 199-213.

The Clearing House. "CISADA Reporting Requirements Under Section 104(e)." May 26, 2011; http://www.regulations.gov/#!documentDetail;D=FINCEN-2011-0002-0003; Accessed November 21, 2012.

Code of Federal Regulations: Title 15 Commerce and Foreign Trade: Parts 300 to 799. Washington, DC: GPO, 2012.

Ariel Cohen. "Iran Threatens U.S. Interests in the South Caucasus." in U.S. Congress, House Committee on Foreign Relations, Subcommittee on Europe and Eurasia. *Iranian Influence in the South Caucasus and the Surrounding Region*. (Washington, DC: House Committee on Foreign Affairs, December 5, 2012): 5-6; http://foreignaffairs.house.gov/112/HHRG-112-FA14-WState-CohenA-20121205.pdf; Accessed December 21, 2012.

Gabriel S. Collins and William S. Murray. "No Oil for the Lamps of China." *Naval War College Review*, 62 (2)(Spring 2008): 79-95.

Stephen D. Collins. "Dissuading State Support of Terrorism: Strikes or Sanctions? (An Analysis of Dissuasion Measures Employed Against Libya)." *Studies in Conflict and Terrorism*, 27 (1)(2004): 1-18.

Committee on Science, Security, and Prosperity. *Beyond "Fortress America": National Security Controls on Science and Technology in a Globalized World*. Washington, DC: National Academy Press, 2009; http://books.nap.edu/catalog.php?record_id=12567; Accessed August 9, 2012.

Doris M. Condit. *History of the Office of the Secretary of Defense Volume II: The Test of War, 1950-1953*. Washington, DC: Historical Office, Office of the Secretary of Defense, 1988.

"Congress Approves Separate Arms Sales Measure." *Congressional Quarterly Almanac 90th Congress 2nd Session*, 52 (1968): 523-525.

"Congress Declines to Block Arms Sales." *CQ Almanac*, 32 (1976): 253-256

Congressional Record, 97 (9)(August 28, 1951): 10719-10720, 10738, 10740, 10746.

Congressional Record, 100 (12)(August 20, 1954): 15666-15667.

Congressional Record, 114 (4)(February 29, 1968): 4759.

Congressional Record, 114 (20)(September 10, 1968): 26227.

Congressional Record, 114 (20)(October 10, 1968): 30403-30405.

Congressional Record, 147 (144)(October 25, 2001): S11018, 11027-11028, 11044, 11046.

Congressional Record, 152 (124)(September 28, 2006): H7697, H7704.

Congressional Record, 157 (74)(May 26, 2011): H3753.

Congressional Record, 157 (79)(June 3, 2011): H4034.

Congressional Record, 157 (183) (December 1, 2011): S8105-S8138.

Congressional Record, 158 (99)(June 28, 2012): H4420-4421.

Congressional Record, 158 (108)(July 18, 2012): S5128.

"Continuation of Export Control Regulations Executive Order 12730 of September 30, 1990." 55 *Federal Register* 192 (October 2, 1990): 40373.

Gordon Corera. *Shopping for Bombs: Nuclear Proliferation, Global Insecurity, and the Rise and Fall of the A.Q. Khan Network*. Oxford: Oxford University Press, 2006.

"Council Decision of 26 July 2010 Concerning Restrictive Measures Against Iran and Repealing Common Position 2007/140/CFSP." *Official Journal of the European Union*, L 195 (27.7.2010): 1-35; http://trade.ec.europa.eu/doclib/docs/2010/august/tradoc_146398.pdf; Accessed December 7, 2012.

Council of the European Union. *Council Conclusions and New Lines of Action by the European Union in Combating Proliferation of Weapons of Mass Destruction and Their Delivery Systems*. Brussels: Council of the European Union, 2008; http://trade.ec.europa.eu/doclib/docs/2008/december/tradoc_141740.pdf; Accessed December 7, 2012.

Gordon A. Craig. "On the Pleasure of Reading Diplomatic Correspondence." *The Journal of Contemporary History*, 26 (3/4)(September 1991): 369-384.

John R. Cranford. "Administration Eases Stand on High-Tech Exports." *CQ Weekly*, (February 24, 1990): 575.

Crockett v. Reagan, 558 F. Supp. 893 (1982).

Patrick J. Cummings. *Context, Culture, and Connection: Avoiding the Counter-Productive Effects of Mirror Imaging in Theater Security Cooperation*. M.A. Thesis. Newport, RI: U.S. Naval War College, 2008.

Richard T. Cupitt, *Reluctant Champions: U.S. Presidential Policy and Strategic Export Controls, Truman, Eisenhower, and Clinton*. London: Routledge, 2000.

Richard T. Cupitt and Igor Khripunov. "New Strategies for the Nuclear Suppliers Group." *Comparative Strategy*, 16 (3)(1997): 305-315.

Arthur I. Cyr. *After the Cold War: American Foreign Policy, Europe, and Asia*. New York: New York University Press, 1997.

Jayantha Danapala. *Evaluating the 2010 NPT Review Conference*. Washington, DC: U.S. Institute of Peace, 2010; http://purl.fdlp.gov/GPO/gpo19409; Accessed December 13, 2012.

Howard Daniel, "Economic Warfare," *The Australian Quarterly*, 15 (3)(September 1943): 62-67.

Jeffrey N. Davenport. "Freezing Terrorist Finance in its Tracks: The Fourth Amendment, Due Process, and the Office of Foreign Assets Control After Kindhearts V. Geithner." *Syracuse Law Review*, 61 (2)(2010): 173-201.

Lance Davis and Stanley Engerman." History Lessons Sanctions: Neither War nor Peace." *Journal of Economic Perspectives*, 17 (2)(Spring 2003); 187-197.

"Defense Security Cooperation Agency Strategic Plan." *DISAM Journal*, 21 (2)(Winter 1998-1999): 8-37.

David Dent and Carol O' Brien. "The Politics of the U.S. Trade Embargo of Cuba, 1959-1977. *Towson State Journal of International Affairs*, 12 (1)(1977): 43-60.

Department of Commerce. "Ferrochemie S.A Order Denying Export Privileges." 26 *Federal Register* (September 27, 1961): 9092-9094.

Ibid. "Italian Nova Works Et. Al.: Order Revoking Licenses and Denying Export Privileges." *Federal Register*, 20 (February 4, 1955): 775-777.

Ibid. "Pacific States Laboratories, Inc., Et. Al.: Ordering Revoking Export Licenses and Denying Export Privileges." *Federal Register*, 19 (August 6, 1954): 4972-4974.

"Determination and Certification Under Section 40A of the Arms Export Control Act." 67 *Federal Register* 99 (May 22, 2002): 36062.

Alan P. Dobson. "From Instrumental to Expressive: The Changing Goals of the U.S. Cold War Strategic Embargo." *Journal of Cold War Studies*, 12 (1)(Winter 2010): 98-119.

Alan P. Dobson. "The Reagan Administration, Economic Warfare, and Starting to Close Down the Cold War." *Diplomatic History*, 29 (3)(June 2005): 531-556.

Warren H. Donnelly and Barbara Rather. *Nuclear Weapons Proliferation and the International Atomic Energy Agency: An Analytical Report*. Washington, DC: Library of Congress, Congressional Research Service, 1976; http://catalog.hathitrust.org/Record/003222211; Accessed May 18, 2012.

Charles Doyle. *USA Patriot Act: A Legal Analysis*. Washington, DC: Library of Congress, Congressional Research Service, 2002.

Edward J. Drea. *History of the Office of the Secretary of Defense Volume VI: McNamara, Clifford, and the Burdens of Vietnam 1965-1969*. Washington, DC: Historical Office, Office of the Secretary of Defense, 2011.

Jacek Durkalek. The Proliferation Security Initiative: Evolution and Future Prospects. (Brussels: European Union Non-Proliferation Consortium, 2012): 1, 19-21; http://www.nonproliferation.eu/documents/nonproliferationpapers/jacekdurkalec4fcc7fd95cfff.pdf; Accessed December 11, 2012.

Dwight D. Eisenhower Presidential Library. *U.S. President's Committee to Study the United States Military Assistance Program (Draper Committee); Records, 1958-1959*. Abilene, KS: Dwight D. Eisenhower Presidential Library, 1977; http://eisenhower. archives. gov/research/finding_aids/pdf/US_Presidents_Committee_to_ Study_US_Military_Assistance_Program.pdf; Accessed August 15, 2012.

Economic Sanctions Against a Nuclear North Korea: An Analysis of United States and United Nations Actions Since 1950. Suk Hi Kim and Semoon Chang, eds. Jefferson, NC: McFarland, 2007.

James W. Endersby and David J. Webber. "Iron Triangle Simulation: A Role-Playing Game for Undergraduates in Congress, Interest Groups, and Public Policy Classes." *PS: Political Science and Politics*, 28 (3)(September 1995): 520-523.

Shawn Engbrecht. *America's Covert Warriors: Inside the World of Private Military Contractors*. Washington, DC: Potomac Books, Inc., 2010.

Stanley A. Erickson. "Economic and Technological Trends Affecting Nuclear Nonproliferation." *Nonproliferation Review*, 8 (2)(Summer 2001): 40-54

European Commission. *Green Paper: The Dual-Use Export Control System of the European Union: Ensuring Security and Competitiveness in a Changing World*. Brussels: European Commission, 2011; http://trade.ec.europa.eu/doclib/docs/2011/june/tradoc_148020.pdf; Accessed December 7, 2012.

European Commission Trade. "Dual Use: Export Controls on Dual Use Goods." (Brussels: European Commission, 2012): 1-2; http://trade.ec.europa.eu/doclib/docs/2009/december/tradoc_145611.pdf; Accessed December 7, 2012.

European External Action Service .Common Foreign and Security Policy. *Sanctions or Restrictive Measures*. Brussels: European External Action Service, 2012; http://eeas.europa.eu/cfsp/sanctions/index_en.htm; Accessed December 13, 2012.

European Parliament. *Dual-Use Control Items: Community Regime for the Control of Exports, Transfer, Brokering, and Transit, Update of the EU Control List*. Strasbourg: European Parliament, 2012) http://www.europarl.europa.eu/oeil/popups/ficheprocedure.do?lang=en&reference=2010/0262(COD)#keyEvents; Accessed December 7, 2012.

Mark Esper and Susan Koch. *The Proliferation Security Initiative: A Model for Future International Collaboration*. Fairfax, VA: National Institute Press, 2009.

European Banking Federation. "EBF Comments on the FinCEN Notice of Proposed Rulemaking (NPR) Implementing the Reporting Requirements under Section 104(c) of the Comprehensive Iran Sanctions, Accountability and Divestment Act (CISADA)." May 31, 2011; http://www.regulations.gov/#!documentDetail;D=FINCEN-2011-0002-0005; Accessed November 21, 2012.

"Executive Order." 5 *Federal Register* (April 12, 1940): 1400-1401.

"Executive Order 11432 Control of Arms Imports." 33 *Federal Register* 208, (October 24, 1968): 15701.

"Executive Order 13026 of November 15, 1996: Administration of Export Controls on Encryption Products." 61 *Federal Register* 224 (November 19, 1996): 58767-58768.

"Executive Order 13129 of July 4, 1999: Blocking Property and Prohibiting Transactions With the Taliban." 64 *Federal Register* 129 (July 7, 1999): 36759-36761.

"Executive Order 13224 of September 23, 2001." Blocking Property and Prohibiting Transactions With Persons Who Commit, Threaten to Commit, or Support Terrorism." 66 *Federal Register* 186, (September 25, 2001): 49079-49083.

"Executive Order 13288 of March 6, 2003: Blocking Property of Persons Undermining Democratic Processes or Institutions in Zimbabwe." 68 *Federal Register* 46 (March 10, 2003): 11457-11461.

"Executive Order 13558 of November 9, 2010: Export Enforcement Coordination Center." 75 *Federal Register* 219, (November 15, 2010): 69573-69574.

"Fact Sheet: Defense Technology Security Administration" *The DISAM Journal*, 19 (3)(Spring 1997): 110.

Sasan Fayazmanesh. *United States and Iran: Sanctions, Wars, and the Policy of Dual Containment*. (New York: Routledge, 2008.

Federation of American Scientists. "National Security Presidential Directives: George W. Bush Administration." Washington, DC: FAS, 2012; http://www.fas.org/irp/offdocs/nspd/index.html; Accessed August 31, 2012

Robert Feldman. "Fund Transfers-African Terrorists Blend Old and New: Hawala and Satellite Telecommunications." *Small Wars and Insurgencies*, 17 (3)(September 2006): 356-366.

Ian F. Fergusson. *The Export Administration Act: Evolution, Provisions, and Debate*. Washington, DC: Library of Congress, Congressional Research Service, 2009.

Ian F. Fergusson and Paul K. Kerr. *The U.S. Export Control System and the President's Reform Initiative*. Washington, DC: Library of Congress, Congressional Research Service, 2012.

Finding Common Ground: U.S. Export Controls in a Changed Global Environment. Washington, DC: National Academy Press, 1991.

Ronald Findlay and Kevin H. O'Rourke. *Power and Plenty: Trade, War, and the World Economy in the Second Millenium*. Princeton: Princeton University Press, 2007.

First Annual Report of the National Munitions Control Board For the Year Ending November 30, 1936. House Document 75-10. Serial 10126. Washington, DC: GPO, 1937.

Charles Fornara. "Plutarch and the Megarian Decree," in Donald Kagan, *Studies in the Greek Historians*, New York: Cambridge University Press, 2009: 213-228.

"Foreign Assistance Act of 1962: Provisions Regarding Certain Restrictions on U.S. Aid." *International Legal Materials*, 1 (1)(August 1962): 118-120.

Tor Egil Førland. Cold Economic Warfare: *CoCom and the Forging of Strategic Export Controls, 1948-1954.* Dordrecht: Republic of Letters Publishing, 2009.

Foreign Military Sales Act. House Report 90-1641. Serial 12795-4. Washington, DC: GPO, 1968.

Foreign Military Sales Act. Senate Report 90-1632. Serial 12792-5. Washington, DC: GPO, 1968

Lawrence Friedman and Efraim Karsh. *The Gulf Conflict, 1990-1991: Diplomacy and War in the New World Order.* Princeton: Princeton University Press, 1993.

From Solidarity to Martial Law The Polish Crisis of 1980-1981: A Documentary History. Andrzej Paczkowski and Malcolm Byrne, eds. Budapest: Central European University Press, 2007.

Matthew Fuhrmann. "Spreading Temptation: Proliferation and Peaceful Nuclear Cooperation Agreements." *International Security*, 34 (1)(Summer 2009): 7-41.

Seema Gahlaut and Gary K. Bertsch. "The War on Terror and the Non-proliferation Regime." *Orbis,* 48 (3)(Summer 2004): 489-504.

Seema Gahlaut and Victor Zaborsky. "Do Export Control Regimes Have Members They Really Need?" *Comparative Strategy*, 23 (1)(January-March 2004): 73-91.

Thomas L. Gais, Mark A. Peterson, and Jack L. Walker. "Interest Groups, Iron Triangles, and Representative Institutions in American National Government. *British Journal of Political Science*, 14 (2)(April 1984): 161-185.

Michael John Garcia and Charles Doyle. *Extradition To and From the United States: Overview of the Law and Recent Treaties.* Washington, DC: Library of Congress, Congressional Research Service, 2010.

Heinz Gartner. "The Wassenaar Arrangement: How it is Broken and Needs to Be Fixed." *Defense & Security Analysis,* 24 (1)(March 2008): 53-60.

Getting Ready for a Nuclear-Ready Iran. Henry Sokolski and Patrick Lawson, eds. (Carlisle, PA: U.S. Army War College: Strategic Studies Institute, 2005); http://www.strategicstudiesinstitute.army.mil/pubs/display.cfm?pubID=629; Accessed December 7, 2012.

Jonathan A. Grant. *Rulers, Guns, and Money: The Global Arms Trade in the Age of Imperialism.* Cambridge: Harvard University Press, 2007.

Great Britain. Parliament. House of Commons. *Hansard Parliamentary Debates*, Series 5, Volume 524, (February 25, 1954): column 587; http://hansard.millbanksystems.com/commons/1954/feb/25/foreign-ministers-conference-berlin; Accessed July 16, 2012.

Richard F. Grimmett. *Arms Sales: Congressional Review Process.* Washington, DC: Library of Congress, Congressional Research Service, 2007.

Ibid. *Military Technology and Conventional Export Controls: The Wassenaar Arrangement.* Washington, DC: Library of Congress, Congressional Research Service, 2006.

Peter L. Hahn. *The United States, Great Britain, and Egypt: Strategy and Diplomacy in the Early Cold War, 1945-1956.* Chapel Hill: University of North Carolina Press, 1991.

Joseph Hajda. "The Soviet Grain Embargo." *Survival*, 22 (6)(December 1980): 53-58.

C.H. Hand, Jr. "The Trading With the Enemy Act." *Columbia Law Review*, 19 (2)(April 1919): 112-139.

Joel B. Harris and Jeffrey P. Bialos. "The Strange New World of United States Export Controls under the International Emergency Economic Powers Act." *Vanderbilt Journal of Transnational Law*, 18 (Winter 1985): 71-108.

Karen M. Hayworth. "The Arms Export Control Act: Proposals to Improve Observance of American Arms Law." *New York University Journal of Law and International Politics*, 12 (1)(Spring 1979): 135-158.

John H. Henshaw. *The Origins of COCOM: Lessons for Contemporary Proliferation Control Regimes.* Washington, DC: Henry C. Stimson Center, 1993.

Stephen A. Higginson. "A Short History of the Right to Petition Government for the Redress of Grievances." *Yale Law Journal*, 96 (1)(November 1986): 142-166;

Historical Statistics of the United States Millenial Edition. Susan B. Carter et. al. eds. New York: Cambridge University Press, 2006.

Paul Holtom and Mark Bromley. "The International Arms Trade: Difficult to Define, Measure, and Control." *Arms Control Today,* 40 (6)(July/August 2010): 8-14.

Irving Louis Horowitz. *The Long Night of Dark Intent: A Half Century of Cuban Communism*. New Brunswick, NJ: Transaction Publishers, 2008.

Roy E. Horton III. *Out of (South) Africa: Pretoria's Nuclear Weapons Experience*. Colorado Springs: USAF Institute for National Security Studies, 1999.

How Sanctions Work: Lessons from South Africa. Neda C. Crawford, and Audie Klotz, eds. London: Macmillan Press Ltd., 1999.

H.R. 2004. 112th Congress, 1st Session. *"Technology Security and Anti-Boycott Act,"* Washington, DC: GPO, 2011.

H.R. 2122. 112th Congress, 1st Session. *"Export Administration Renewal Act of 2011."* Washington, DC: GPO, 2011.

H.R. 7015. 97th Congress. 2nd Session. *Office of Strategic Trade Act of 1982*. Washington, DC: GPO, 1982.

Kailai Huang. "American Business and the China Trade Embargo in the 1950s." *Essays in Economic and Business History*, 19 (2001): 33-48.

Gary Clyde Hufbauer, et. al. eds. *Economic Sanctions Reconsidered*. 3rd ed. Washington, DC: Peterson Institute for International Economics, 2007.

Robert L. Hutchings. *American Diplomacy and the End of the Cold War: An Insider's Account of U.S. Policy in Europe, 1989-1992*. Washington, DC: Woodrow Wilson Center Press, 1997.

Jacques E.C. Hymans. *Achieving Nuclear Ambitions: Scientists, Politicians, and Proliferation*. Cambridge: Cambridge University Press, 2012.

"Imposition of Foreign Policy Controls on Equipment and Technical Data Related to the Production of Chemical and Biological Weapons." *56 Federal Register* 49 (March 13, 1991): 10760-10761.

International Atomic Energy Agency. *Information Circular 209*. (Vienna: IAEA, September 3, 1974); http://www.iaea.org/Publications/Documents/Infcircs/Others/inf209.shtml; Accessed December 13, 2012.

Ibid. *Information Circular (INFCIRC) 254/REV. 11/Part 1A, Communication Received From the Permanent Mission of the United States of America to the International Atomic Energy Agency Regarding Certain Member States' Guidelines for the Export of Nuclear Material, Equipment, and Technology.* Vienna: International Atomic Energy Agency, November 12, 2012; http://www.nuclearsuppliersgroup.org/Leng/PDF/infcirc254r11p1.pdf; Accessed December 10, 2012.

Ibid. "Our Work." Vienna: IAEA, 2012: 1; http://www.iaea.org/Our Work/; Accessed December 7, 2012.

"International Traffic in Arms Regulations; Amendments." 56 *Federal Register* 208 (October 29, 1991): 55630.

"International Traffic in Arms Regulations; Exemptions for U.S. Institutions of Higher Learning." 67 *Federal Register* 61 (March 29, 2002): 15099.

Interview with Michael Reckowsky. Research Security Administrator. Purdue University. November 28, 2012.

Bruce W. Jentleson. *Pipeline Politics: The Complex Political Economy of East-West Energy Trade.* Ithaca: Cornell University Press, 1986.

Joan Johnson-Freese. "Alice in Licenseland: US Satellite Export Controls Since 1990." *Space Policy*, 16 (3)(July 2000): 195-204.

Paul Rexton Kan, Bruce E. Bechtol Jr., and Robert M. Collins. *Criminal Sovereignty: Understanding North Korea's Illicit International Activities.* Carlisle, PA: U.S. Army War College Strategic Studies Institute, 2010.

Shirley A. Kan. *China and Proliferation of Weapons of Mass Destruction and Missiles: Policy Issues.* Washington, DC: Library of Congress, Congressional Research Service, 2002.

Ibid. *China: Suspected Acquisition of U.S. Nuclear Weapons Secrets.* Washington, DC: Library of Congress, Congressional Research Service, 2000.

Lawrence S. Kaplan. *A Community of Interests: NATO and the Military Assistance Program, 1948-1951.* Washington, DC: Historical Office, Office of the Secretary of Defense, 1980.

Lawrence S. Kaplan, Ronald D. Landa, and Edward J. Drea. *History of the Office of the Secretary of Defense Volume V: The McNamara Ascendancy, 1961-1965.* (Washington, DC: Historical Office, Office of the Secretary of Defense, 2006.

Robert G. Kaufman. *In Defense of the Bush Doctrine.* Lexington: University Press of Kentucky, 2005.

Bryan Kekel, Patton Adams, and George Bakos. *Occupying the Information High Ground: Chinese Capabilities for Computer Network Operations and Cyber Espionage*. Washington, DC: Prepared by Northrup Grumman Corporation for the U.S.-China Economic and Security Review Commission, 2012; http://www.uscc.gov/RFP/2012/USCC%20Report_Chinese_CapabilitiesforComputer_Network OperationsandCyber Espionage.pdf; Accessed September 7, 2012.

Elise Keppler. "Preventing Human Rights Abuses by Regulating Arms Brokering: The U.S. Brokering Amendment to the Arms Export Control Act." *Berkeley Journal of International Law*, 19(2)(2001): 381-411.

Paul Kerr. "U.S. Stops, Then Releases Shipment of North Korean Missiles." *Arms Control Today* 33 (January/February 2003): 25.

Paul K. Kerr and Mary Beth Nikitin. *Pakistan's Nuclear Weapons: Proliferation and Security Issues*. Washington, DC: Library of Congress, Congressional Research Service, 2009.

Deborah C. Kidwell. *Public War, Private Fight?: The United States and Private Military Companies*. Fort Leavenworth, KS: Combat Studies Institute Press, 2005.

David Klein. "Memorandum for Mr. Bundy: Berlin Discussions at Geneva," Washington, DC: National Security Council, 1962: 2-3; http://www.jfklibrary.org/Asset-Viewer/Archives/JFKPOF-117-008.aspx; Accessed May 14, 2012.

Genevieve Johanna Knezo. *Counter Terrorism: Impacts on Research, Development, and Higher Education*. Hauppauge, NY: Novinka Books, 2002.

Susan J. Koch. *Proliferation Security Initiative: Origins and Evolution*. Washington, DC: National Defense University Press, 2012.

Mike Koehler. "The Façade of FCPA Enforcement." *Georgetown Journal of International Law*, 41 (4)(2010): 907-1009.

Diane B. Kunz. *Butter and Guns: America's Cold War Economic Diplomacy*. New York: Free Press, 1997.

Ibid. *The Economic Diplomacy of the Suez Crisis*. Chapel Hill: University of North Carolina Press, 1991.

Theodore H. Von Laue. *Leopold Ranke: The Formative Years*. Princeton: Princeton University Press, 1950.

Rens Lee. "Why Nuclear Smuggling Matters." *Orbis*, 52 (3)(Summer 2008): 434-444.

Richard M. Leighton. *History of the Office of the Secretary of Defense Volume III: Strategy, Money, and the New Look, 1953-1956*. Washington, DC: Historical Office, Office of the Secretary of Defense, 2001.

Peter M. Leitner. *Decontrolling Strategic Technology, 1990-1992: Creating the Military Threats of the 21st Century*. Lanham, MD: University Press of America, 1995.

Jack S. Levy. "Domestic Politics and War." *The Journal of Interdisciplinary History*, 18 (4)(Spring 1988): 653-673.

Philip I. Levy. "Sanctions on South Africa: What Did They Do?" *American Economic Review*, 89 (2)(May 1999): 415-420.

James K. Libbey. "CoCom, Comecon, and the Economic Cold War." *Russian History*, 37 (2)(2010): 133-152.

"Licenses for Export of Firearms." 42 *Federal Register* 124 (June 28, 1977): 32770.

Robert S. Litwak. *Détente and the Nixon Doctrine: American Foreign Policy and the Pursuit of Stability, 1969-1976*. Cambridge: Cambridge University Press, 1984.

William J. Long. *U.S. Export Control Policy: Executive Autonomy vs. Congressional Reform*. New York: Columbia University Press, 1989.

Robert Looney. "Hawala: The Terrorists Informal Financial Mechanism." *Middle East Policy*, 10 (1)(Spring 2003): 164-167.

Jason Luong. "Forcing Constraint: The Case for Amending the International Emergency Economic Powers Act." *Texas Law Review*, 78 (5)(April 2000): 1181-1213

Charles S. Mack. *Business, Politics, and the Practice of Government Regulations*. Westport, CT: Quorum Books, 1997.

Michael P. Malloy, Eric M. Lieberman, Dennis M. O'Connell, and Steven M. Schneebaum. "Are the U.S. Treasury's Assets Control Regulations a Fair and Effective Tool of U.S. Foreign Policy?: The Case of Cuba."*Proceedings of the Annual Meeting (American Society of International Law)*, 79 April 25-27, 1985): 169-189.

Michael Mastanduno. *Economic Containment: COCOM and the Politics of East-West Trade*. Ithaca: Cornell University Press, 1992.

Ibid. "Trade as a Strategic Weapon: American and Alliance Export Control Policy in the Early Postwar Period." *International Organization*, 42 (1)(Winter 1988): 121-150.

Allen J. Matusow. *Nixon's Economy: Booms, Busts, Dollars, and Votes*. Lawrence: University Press of Kansas, 1998.

Christopher Maynard. *Out of the Shadow: George H.W. Bush and the End of the Cold War*. College Station: Texas A&M University Press, 2008.

Jonathan Medalia. *North Korea's 2009 Nuclear Test: Containment, Monitoring, Implications*. Washington, DC: Library of Congress, Congressional Research Service, 2010.

Evan S. Medeiros. *Chasing the Dragon: Assessing China's System of Export Controls for WMD-Related Goods and Technologies*. (Santa Monica: Rand Corporation, 2005.

"Memorandum Directing the Termination of Restrictions on United States Agricultural Sales to the Soviet Union: April 24, 1981. *"Public Papers of the President Ronald Reagan 1981*. Washington, DC: National Archives and Records Service, 1982.

James A.R. Miles. *The Legacy of Tiananmen: China in Disarray*. Ann Arbor: University of Michigan Press, 1996.

Miles & Stockbridge, P.C. "Re: Continental Tire and Continental Automotive Comments on Proposed Revisions to the EAR Parts and Components of Military Vehicles Docket No: 110310188-1335-01; BIS-2011-0015." (September 12, 2011); http://www.regulations.gov/#!documentDetail;D=BIS-2011-0015-0004; Accessed November 20, 2012.

Davinia Miller. *Export or Die Britain's Defence Trade With Iran and Iraq*. London: Continuum, 1996.

Richard L. Millett. *Searching for Sustainability: The U.S. Development of Constabulary Forces in Latin America and the Philippines*. Fort Leavenworth, KS: Combat Studies Institute Press, 2010.

Missile Technology Control Regime. *Guidelines for Sensitive Missile-Relevant Transfers*. (2012); http://www.mtcr.info/english/guidetext.htm; Accessed December 10, 2012.

Ibid. *The Missile Technology Control Regime*, (2012); http://www.mtcr.info/english/index.html; Accessed December 10, 2012.

Ibid. *Missile Technology Control Regime (MTCR) Annex Handbook 2010*. http://www.mtcr.info/english/MTCR_Annex_Handbook_ENG.pdf; Accessed December 10, 2012.

Ibid. *(M.T.C.R.) Equipment, Software, and Technology Annex*. (November 18, 2011); http://www.mtcr.info/english/MTCR-TEM-Technical_Annex_2011-11-18.pdf; Accessed December 10, 2012.

Ibid. *Plenary Meeting of the Missile Technology Control Regime Buenos Aires, Argentina 13-15 April 2011*. (2011); http://www.mtcr.info/

english/Press%20Release%20April%202011.html; Accessed December 10, 2012.

Dinshaw Mistry. "Beyond the MTCR: Building a Comprehensive Regime to Contain Ballistic Missile Proliferation." *International Security*, 27 (4)(Spring 2003): 119-149.

Ibid. *Containing Missile Proliferation: Strategic Technology, Security Regimes, and International Cooperation in Arms Control*. Seattle: University of Washington Press, 2003.

The Modern Defense Industry: Political, Economic, and Technological Issues. Richard Bitzinger, ed. Santa Barbara: Praeger Security International, 2009.

Alexander H. Montgomery. "Ringing in Proliferation: How to Dismantle an Atomic Bomb Network." *International Security*, 30 (2)(Fall 2005): 153-187.

Imad Moosa. *The U.S.-China Trade Dispute: Facts, Figures, and Myths*. (Cheltenham: Edward Elgar Pub., 2012).

Lee Mordecai. *Congress vs the Bureaucracy: Muzzling Agency Public Relations*. Norman: University of Oklahoma Press, 2011.

Jere W. Morehead and David A. Dismuke. "Export Control Policies and National Security: Protecting U.S. Interests in the New Millenium." *Texas International Law Journal*, 34 (2)(Spring 1999): 173-186.

David Murphy, Sergei A. Kondrashev, and George Bailey. *Battleground Berlin: CIA vs KGB in the Cold War*. New Haven: Yale University Press, 1997.

John T. Murphy and Arthur T. Downey, "National Security, Foreign Policy and Individual Rights: The Quandry of United States Export Controls," The International and Comparative Law Quarterly, 30 (4)(October 1981): 791-834.

Mutual Security Act of 1956. House Report 84-2643. Serial 11900. Washington, DC: GPO, 1956.

Mary Beth Naitkin, Paul K. Kerr, and Steven A. Hildreth. *Proliferation Control Regimes: Background and Status*. Washington, DC: Library of Congress, Congressional Research Service, 2006.

Neutrality Act of 1937. House Report 75-363. Serial 10083. Washington, DC: GPO, 1937.

Larry A. Niksch. *North Korea's Nuclear Weapons Program*. Washington, DC: Library of Congress, Congressional Research Service, 2006.

Michael J. Noble. "Export Controls and United States Space Power." *Astropolitics*, 6 (3)(2008): 251-312.

Non-Proliferation Export Controls: Origins, Challenges, and Proposals for Stengthening. Daniel Joyner, ed. Burlington, VT: Ashgate, 2006.

Nuclear Suppliers Group. "History of the NSG." (2012); http://www.nuclearsuppliersgroup.org/Leng/01-history.htm; Accessed December 10, 2012.

Ibid. *NSG Public Statement Nuclear Suppliers Group Plenary*. Seattle: Nuclear Suppliers Group, 2012; http://www.nuclearsuppliers group.org/Leng/PRESS/2012-06-Seattle_NSG_Public_Statement _FINAL_.pdf; Accessed December 10, 2012.

Ibid. *What Are the Activities of the NSG?* (2012); http://www.nuclear suppliersgroup.org/Leng/04-activities.htm; Accessed December 10, 2012.

Office of International Affairs. National Research Council. *Dual-Use Technologies and Export Administration in the Post-Cold War Era: Documents from a Joint Program of the National Academy of Sciences and the Russian Academy of Sciences*. Washington, DC: National Academy Press, 1994.

Office of International Trade. "Revision of Export Regulations." 15 *Federal Register* (May 9, 1950): 2703-2750.

Andrew O'Neil. "Nuclear Proliferation and Global Security: Laying the Groundwork for a New Policy Agenda." Comparative Strategy, 24 (4)(2005): 343-359.

Organization for the Prohibition of Chemical Weapons (OPCW). *Articles of the Chemical Weapons Convention*. (2012): 1; http://www.opcw.org/chemical-weapons-convention/articles/; Accessed December 5, 2012.

Ibid. *Genesis and Historical Development*. The Hague: Organization for the Prohibition of Chemical Weapons, 2012: 1-6; http://www.opcw.org/chemical-weapons-convention/about-the-convention/genesis-and-historical-development/; Accessed December 5, 2012.

Vanessa Ortblad. "Criminal Prosecution in Sheep's Clothing: The Punitive Effects of OFAC Freezing Sanctions." *The Journal of Criminal Law and Criminology*, 98 (4)(Summer 2008): 1439-1466.

Robert L. Paarlberg. "Lessons of the Grain Embargo." *Foreign Affairs*, 59 (1)(Fall 1980): 144-162.

Chester J. Pach, Jr. *Arming the Free World: The Origins of the United States Military Assistance Program, 1945-1950*. Chapel Hill: University of North Carolina Press, 1991.

Panel on the Impact of National Security Controls on International Technology Transfer. *Balancing the National Interest: U.S. National Security Export Controls and Global Economic Competition.* Washington, DC: National Academy Press, 1987.

Roman Papadiuk. *The Leadership of George Bush: An Insider's View of the Forty-First President.* College Station: Texas A&M University Press, 2009.

Robert A. Pape. "Why Economic Sanctions Do Not Work." *International Security*, 22 (2)(Autumn 1997): 102, 111-112.

Katie Pavlich. *Fast and Furious: Barack Obama's Bloodiest Scandal and Its Shameless Coverup.* Washington, DC: Regnery Pub., 2012.

Graham S. Pearson, *The Search for Iraq's Weapons of Mass Destruction: Inspection, Verification, and Non-Proliferation.* Houndsmill, UK: Palgrave Macmillan, 2005.

Gregory W. Pedlow. "NATO and the Berlin Crisis of 1961: Facing the Soviets While Maintaining Unity." (Washington, DC: Central Intelligence Agency, 2011): 7-13; www.foia.cia.gov/BerlinWall/Essays/NATOandBerlinCrisis.pdf; Accessed May 15, 2012.

George Perkovich. *India's Nuclear Bomb: The Impact on Global Proliferation.* Berkeley: University of California Press, 2000.

Bo Peterrson. "Mirror, Mirror . . . : Mythmaking, Self-Images and Views of the US 'Other' in Contemporary Russia." (Malmo University: Malmo University Electronic Publishing, 2012); http://muep.mah.se/bitstream/handle/2043/14000/Petersson.final.pdf? sequence=2; Accessed January 2, 2013.

Gretchen Peters. *Haqqani Network Financing: The Evolution of an Industry.* West Point: U.S. Military Academy Combating Terrorism Center, 2012.

Alexander A. Pikayev et. al. *Russia and the U.S. Missile Technology Control Regime.* Oxford: Oxford University Press for the International Institute of Strategic Studies, 1998.

The Politics of Security Sector Reform: Challenges and Opportunities for the European Union's Global Rule. Magnus Ekengreen and Greg Simons, eds. Burlington, VT: Ashgate, 2010.

Jonathan D. Pollack. "The United States, North Korea, and the End of the Agreed Framework." *Naval War College Review*, 56 (3)(Summer 2003): 1-49.

Walter S. Poole. *History of the Joint Chiefs of Staff: The Joint Chiefs of Staff and National Policy Volume VIII: 1961-1964.* Washington, DC:

Office of Joint History, Office of the Chairman of the Joint Chiefs of Staff, 2011.

Ibid. *History of the Joint Chiefs of Staff: The Joint Chiefs of Staff and National Policy Volume IX: 1965-1968.* Washington, DC: Office of Joint History, Office of the Chairman of the Joint Chiefs of Staff, 2012.

John Duncan Powell. "Military Assistance and Militarism in Latin America." *The Western Political Quarterly*, 18 (2)(June 1965): 382-392.

Jonathan G. Pray. "Congressional Reporting Requirements: Testing the Limits of Oversight Power." *University of Colorado Law Review* 76 (1) (Winter 2005): 297-325.

Preparing for Martial Law: Through the Eyes of Col. Ryszard Kuklinski, Washington, DC: Central Intelligence Agency, 2009; http://purl.fdlp.gov/GPO/gpo15351; Accessed May 21, 2012.

Presidential Documents. "Administration of Export Controls: Executive Order 12755 of March 12, 1991." 56 *Federal Register* 51 (March 15, 1991): 11057.

Ibid. "Executive Order 12851 of June 11, 1993: Administration of Proliferation Sanctions, Middle East Arms Control, and Related Congressional Reporting Responsibilities." 58 *Federal Register* 113 (June 15, 1993): 33181-3318

Ibid. "Executive Order 12918: Prohibiting Certain Transactions With Respect to Rwanda and Delegating Authority With Respect to Other United Nations Arms Embargoes." 59 *Federal Register* 103 (May 31, 1994): 28205-28206.

Ibid. "Executive Order 12919 of June 3, 1994: National Defense Industrial Resources Preparedness," *59 Federal Register* 108 (June 7, 1994): 29525, 29529.

Ibid. "Executive Order 12946 of January 20, 1995: President's Advisory Board on Arms Proliferation Policy." 60 *Federal Register* 15 (January 24, 1995): 4829.

Ibid. "Executive Order 12981 of December 5, 1995: Administration of Export Controls." 60 *Federal Register* 236 (December 8, 1995): 62981-62982.

Ibid. "Executive Order 13026 of November 15, 1996: Administration of Export Controls on Encryption Products." 61 *Federal Register* 224 (November 19, 1996): 58767-58768.

Ibid. "Executive Order 13094 of July 28, 1998: Proliferation of Weapons of Mass Destruction." 63 *Federal Register* 146 (July 30, 1998): 40803.

Ibid. "Executive Order 13159 of June 21, 2000: Blocking Property of the Russian Federation Relating to the Disposition of Highly Enriched Uranium Extracted From Nuclear Weapons." 65 *Federal Register* 123 (June 21, 2000): 39279-39280.

Ibid. "Executive Order 13177 of December 4, 2000: National Commission on the Use of Offsets in Defense Trade and President's Council on the Use of Offsets in Commercial Trade." 65 *Federal Register* 235 (December 4, 2000): 76558-76559.

Ibid. "Executive Order 13222 of August 17, 2001: Continuation of Export Control Regulations." 66 *Federal Register* 163 (August 22, 2001): 44025-44026.

Ibid. "Executive Order 13224 of September 23, 2001: Blocking Property and Prohibiting Transactions With Persons Who Commit, Threaten to Commit, or Support Terrorism." 66 *Federal Register* 186 (September 25, 2001): 49079-49083.

Ibid. "Executive Order 13292 of March 25, 2003: Further Amendment to Executive Order 12954, as Amended, Classified National Security Information." 68 *Federal Register* 60 (March 28, 2003): 13521.

Ibid. "Executive Order 13328 of February 6, 2004." 69 *Federal Register* 28 (February 11, 2004): 6901-6903.

Ibid. "Executive Order 13382 of June 28, 2005: Blocking Property of Weapons of Mass Destruction Proliferators and Their Supporters." 70 *Federal Register* 126 (July 1, 2005): 38567-38570.

Ibid. "Executive Order 13466 of June 26, 2008: Continuing Certain Restrictions with Respect to North Korea and North Korean Nationals." 73 *Federal Register* 125 (June 27, 2008): 36787-36788.

Ibid. "Executive Order 13546 of July 2, 2010: Organizing the Security of Biological Select Agents and Toxins in the United States." 75 *Federal Register* 150 (July 8, 2010): 39439-39442.

Ibid. "Executive Order 13551: Blocking Property of Certain Persons With Respect to North Korea." 75 *Federal Register* 169 (September 1, 2010): 53837-53841.

Ibid. "Executive Order 13558 of November 9, 2010: Export Enforcement Coordination Center." 75 *Federal Register* 219 (November 15, 2010): 69573-69574.

Ibid. "Executive Order 13582 of August 17, 2011: Blocking Property of the Government of Syria and Prohibiting Certain Transactions With Respect to Syria." 76 *Federal Register* 162 (August 22, 2011): 52209-52210

Ibid. "Executive Order 13590 of November 20, 2011: Authorizing the Imposition of Certain Sanctions With Respect to the Provision of Goods, Services, Technology, or Support for Iran's Energy and Petrochemical Sectors." 76 *Federal Register* 226 (November 23, 2011): 72609-72612.

Ibid. "Executive Order 13599: Blocking Property of the Government of Iran and Iranian Financial Institutions." 77 *Federal Register* 26 (February 8, 2012): 6659-6662.

Ibid. "Executive Order 13606 of April 22, 2012: Blocking the Property and Suspending Entry into the United States of Certain Persons With Respect to Grave Human Rights Abuses by the Governments of Iran and Syria via Information Technology." 77 *Federal Register* 79 (April 24, 2012): 24571-24574.

Ibid. "Executive Order 13608: Prohibiting Certain Transactions With and Suspending Entry Into the United States of Foreign Sanctions Evaders With Respect to Iran and Syria." 77 *Federal Register* 86 (May 3, 2012): 26409-26411.

Ibid. "Executive Order 13611 of May 16, 2012: Blocking Property of Persons Threatening the Peace, Security, or Stability of Yemen." 77 *Federal Register* 97 (May 18, 2012): 29533-29535.

Ibid. "Executive Order 13617 of June 25, 2012: Blocking Property of the Russian Federation Relating to the Disposition of Highly Enriched Uranium Extracted from Nuclear Weapons." 77 *Federal Register* 124 (June 27, 2012): 38459-38461.

Ibid. "Executive Order 13622: Authorizing Additional Sanctions With Respect to Iran." 77 *Federal Register* 149 (August 2, 2012): 45897-45902.

Ibid. "Proclamation 8271 of June 26, 2008: Termination of the Exercise of Authorities Under the Trading With the Enemy Act With Respect to North Korea." 73 *Federal Register* 125 (June 27, 2008): 36785.

President of the United States. "Chemical and Biological Weapons Proliferation: Executive Order 12735 of November 16, 1990." 55 *Federal Register* 224 (November 20, 1990): 48587.

Ibid. *Continuation of Export Control Regulations.* House Document 107-114. Washington, DC: GPO, 2001; http://purl.access.gpo.gov/GPO/LPS15157; Accessed August 5, 2011.

Ibid. *Emergency Regarding Proliferation of Weapons of Mass Destruction*, House Document 107-155. Washington, DC: GPO, 2001.

Ibid. "Executive Order [8389]: Establishing the Economic Defense Board. " *Federal Register*, 6 (149)(August 1, 1941): 3823-3824.

Ibid. "Executive Order 10945: Administration of the Export Control Act of 1949" 26 *Federal Register* (May 25, 1961): 4487.

Ibid. *An Executive Order Clarifying Certain Executive Orders Blocking Property and Prohibiting Certain Executive Transactions.* House Document 109-10, (Washington, DC: GPO, 2005); http://purl.access.gpo.gov/GPO/LPS59800; Accessed May 17, 2012.

Ibid. "Executive Order 10973: Administration of Foreign Assistance and Related Programs." 26 *Federal Register* 215. (November 7, 1961): 10469-10470.

Ibid. "Executive Order 12981 of December 5, 1995: Administration of Export Control," 60 *Federal Register* 236 (December 8, 1995): 62981-62985.

Ibid. *National Policy on the Transfer of Scientific, Technological, and Engineering Information (NSDD-189).* Washington, DC: The White House, 1985; http://www.fas.org/irp/offdocs/nsdd/nsdd-189.htm; Accessed November 19, 2012.

Ibid. *A National Security Strategy of Engagement and Enlargement.* Washington, DC: The White House, 1995

Ibid. *National Security Strategy of the United States.* Washington, DC: The White House, 2002.

Ibid. *National Strategy for Global Supply Chain Security.* Washington, DC: The White House, 2012; http://www.whitehouse.gov/sites/default/files/national_strategy_for_global_supply_chain_security.pdf; Accessed September 18, 2012.

Ibid. *National Strategy to Combat Weapons of Mass Destruction.* Washington, DC: The White House, 2002; http://purl.access.gpo.gov/GPO/LPS24899; Accessed December 10, 2012.

Ibid. *Periodic Report on the National Emergency Caused by the Lapse of the Export Administration Act of 1979,* House Document 107-235. Washington, DC: GPO, 2002.

Ibid. "Proclamation 3447: Embargo on All Trade With Cuba." 27 *Federal Register* (February 7, 1962): 1085.

Ibid. *Report on the Organization and Administration of the Military Assistance Program Submitted to the President on June 3, 1959.* House Document 86-186, Serial 12228, Washington, DC: GPO, 1959.

Ibid. Title 3-The President. "Blocking Iraqi Government Property and Prohibiting Transactions With Iraq: Executive Order 12474 of August 9, 1990." 55 *Federal Register* 156 (August 13, 1990): 33089.

Professor Mike Koehler, Assistant Professor, Southern Illinois University School of Law, FCPA Professor: A Forum Devoted to the Foreign Corrupt Practices Act; www.fcpaprofessor.com/; Accessed September 20, 2012.

"Prohibition of Exports." *American State Papers Foreign Relations 03 No. 259.* Washington, DC: Gales and Seaton, 1832: 620-21.

Public Law 65-91. "An Act to Define, Regulate, and Punish Trading With the Enemy, and for Other Purposes," 40 *U.S. Statutes at Large* 411-426.

Public Law 74-479. "Neutrality Act." 49 *U.S. Statutes at Large* 1081-1085.

Public Law 75-583. "To Acquire the Registration of Certain Persons Employed by Agencies to Disseminate Propaganda in the United States and for Other Purposes." 52 *U.S. Statutes at Large* 631-633.

Public Law 76-703. "National Defense Act of 1940." 54 *U.S. Statutes at Large* 712-714.

Public Law 81-11. "Export Control Act of 1949." 63 *U.S. Statutes at Large* 7-8.

Public Law 81-329. "Mutual Defense Assistance Act of 1949." 63 *U.S. Statutes at Large* 714-721.

Public Law 81-774. "Defense Production Act of 1950." 64 *U.S. Statutes at Large* 798-822.

Public Law 82-165. "Mutual Security Act of 1951." 65 *U.S. Statutes at Large* 373-387.

Public Law 82-213. "Mutual Defense Assistance Control Act of 1951." *65 U.S. Statutes at Large* 644-647.

Public Law 83-665. "Mutual Security Act of 1954," 68 *U.S. Statutes at Large* 832-833, 848-849.

Public Law 86-108. "Mutual Security Act of 1959." 73 *U.S. Statutes at Large* 246-247.

Public Law 87-195. "Act for International Development of 1961." 75 *U.S. Statutes at Large* 424, 444-445.

Public Law 87-565. "Foreign Assistance Act of 1962." 76 *U.S. Statutes at Large* 255, 260-261.

Public Law 90-137. "Foreign Assistance Act of 1967. 81 *U.S. Statutes at Large* 455-458.

Public Law 90-629. "Foreign Military Sales Act," 82 *U.S. Statutes at Large* 1320-1328.

Public Law 91-184. "Export Administration Act of 1969." 83 *U.S. Statutes at Large* 842-844.

Public Law 91-508. "Currency and Foreign Transactions Reporting Act," 84 *U.S. Statutes at Large* 1118-1124.

Public Law 93-159. "Emergency Fuels and Fuel Allocation Act." 87 *U.S. Statutes at Large* 627.

Public Law 94-329 "International Security Assistance and Arms Export Control Act of 1976." 90 *U.S Statutes at Large* 729-769.

Public Law 95-52. "Export Administration Amendments of 1977." 91 *U.S. Statutes at Large* 235, 241.

Public Law 95-92. "International Security Assistance Act of 1977." *91 U.S. Statutes at Large* 614, 620-621.

Public Law 95-213. "Foreign Corrupt Practices Act." *91 U.S. Statutes at Large* 1495-1497.

Public Law 95-223. "With Respect to the President in Time of War or National Emergency." 91 *U.S. Statutes at Large* 1625-1628.

Public Law 95-242. "Nuclear Non-Proliferation Act of 1978." 92 *U.S. Statutes at Large* 120-121.

Public Law 95-630. "Financial Institutions Regulatory and Interest Rate Control Act." 92 *U.S. Statutes at Large* 3641, 3727.

Public Law 96-72. "Export Administration Act of 1979." 93 *U.S. Statutes at Large* 503-536.

Public Law 99-64. "Export Administration Amendments Act of 1985." 99 *U.S. Statutes at Large* 120.

Public Law 99-83. "International Security and Development Cooperation Act of 1985." 99 U.S. *Statutes at Large* 190, 267-268.

Public Law 99-440. "Comprehensive Anti-Apartheid Act of 1986." 100 *U.S. Statutes at Large* 1086, 1093, 1099.

Public Law 99-472. "Export-Amendment Bank Amendments." 100 *U.S. Statutes at Large* 1200-1203, 1210.

Public Law 100-418. "Omnibus Trade and Competitiveness Act of 1988." 102 *U.S. Statutes at Large* 1107, 1364-1366.

Public Law 101-246. "Foreign Relations Authorization Act, Fiscal Years 1990 and 1991." 104 *U.S. Statutes at Large* 15, 81, and 84.

Public Law 101-513. "Foreign Operations, Exporting Financing, and Related Programs Appropriations Act. 1991," 104 *U.S. Statutes at Large* 1979, 2042.

Public Law 102-228. "Conventional Forces in Europe Treaty Implementation Act." 105 *U.S. Statutes at Large* 1693-1694.

Public Law 102-383. "United States-Hong Kong Policy Act." 106 *U.S. Statutes at Large* 1448.

Public Law 102-484. "National Defense Authorization Act for Fiscal Year 1993." 106 *U.S. Statutes at Large* 2315, 2571-2575.

Public Law 102-558. "Defense Production Act Amendments of 1992." 106 *U.S. Statutes at Large* 4219-4220.

Public Law 103-236. "Foreign Relations Authorization Act, Fiscal Years 1994 and 1995." 108 *U.S. Statutes at Large* 382, 512, 516-519.

Public Law 104-114. "Cuban Liberty and Democratic Solidarity (LIBERTAD) Act of 1996." 110 *U.S. Statutes at Large* 785, 792-794, 798-799.

Public Law 104-132. "Antiterrorism and Effective Death Penalty Act of 1996." 110 *U.S. Statutes at Large* 1214-1215, 1247-1248, 1250, 1255-1258.

Public Law 104-164. "Foreign Assistance Act of 1961 and Arms Export Control Act Amendments," 110 *U.S. Statutes at Large* 1421, 1437-1438.

Public Law 104-172. "Iran and Libya Sanctions Act of 1996." *110 U.S. Statutes at Large* 1541-1551.

Public Law 104-294. "Economic Espionage Act of 1996." 110 *U.S. Statutes at Large* 3488-3513.

Public Law 105-261. "Strom Thurmond National Defense Authorization Act for 1999." 112 *U.S. Statutes at Large* 2174.

Public Law 105-292. "International Religious Freedom Act of 1998." 112 *U.S. Statutes at Large* 2787, 2806-2808.

Public Law 105-366. "International Anti-Bribery and Fair Competition Act of 1998." 112 *U.S. Statutes at Large* 3301-3304.

Public Law 106-65. "National Defense Authorization for Fiscal Year 2000." 113 *U.S. Statutes at Large* 953-971.

Public Law 106-113. North Korea Threat Reduction Act of 1999. 113 *U.S. Statutes at Large* 1501A-472.

Public Law 106-178. "Iran-Nonproliferation Act of 2000." 114 *U.S. Statutes at Large* 38-39, 41.

Public Law 107-56. USA Patriot Act. 115 *U.S. Statutes at Large* 292, 308-309, 330-331.

Public Law 107-99. Zimbabwe Democracy and Economic Recovery Act of 2001. 115 *U.S. Statutes at Large* 962-965.

Public Law 107-296. "Homeland Security Act of 2002," 116 *U.S. Statutes at Large* 2135-2321.

Public Law 108-175. "Syria Accountability and Lebanese Sovereignty Restoration Act of 2003." 117 *U.S. Statutes at Large* 2486-2489.

Public Law 109-177. "USA PATRIOT Improvement and Reauthorization Act." 120 *U.S. Statutes at Large* 191, 247-250.

Public Law 109-293. "Iran Freedom Support Act." 120 *U.S. Statutes at Large* 1344-1350.

Public Law 109-347. "Security and Accountability for Every Port Act of 2006." 120 *U.S. Statutes at Large* 1884-1962.

Public Law 110-49. "Foreign Investment and National Security Act of 2007." 121 *U.S. Statutes at Large* 246-260.

Public Law 111-84. "National Defense Authorization Act for Fiscal Year 2010." 123 *U.S. Statutes at Large* 2546-2547.

Public Law 111-95. "Comprehensive Iran Sanctions, Accountability, and Divestment Act of 2010." 124 *U.S. Statutes at Large* 1337.

Public Law 111-266. "Security Cooperation Act of 2010." 124 *U.S. Statutes at Large* 2797-2804.

Public Law 112-81. "National Defense Authorization Act for Fiscal Year 2012." 125 *U.S. Statutes at Large* 1636, 1647-1649.

Public Papers of the President: William J. Clinton 1993. Washington, DC: National Archives, 1994: 2:1615-1616.

Mark Pythian and Walter Little. "Parliament and Arms Sales: Lessons of the Matrix Churchill Affair." *Parliamentary Affairs*, 46 (3)(July 1993): 293-308.

Stephen Rademaker. "The Role of Export Controls in Non-Proliferation Strategy." *International Affairs: A Russian Journal of World Politics*, Diplomacy, & International Relations, 50 (6)(December 2004): 29-33.

Steven L. Reardon. *History of the Office of the Secretary of Defense Volume I: The Formative Years, 1947-1950.* Washington, DC: Historical Office, Office of the Secretary of Defense, 1984.

Jay B. Reeves. *Misunderstood Dragon or Underestimated Panda: How China Reacts to External National Security Crises*. M.A. Thesis. Maxwell Air Force Base, AL: School of Advanced Air and Space Studies, Air University, 2009.

"Regulation EU (No. 388/2012) of the European Parliament and of the Council of 19 April 2012 Amending Council Regulation (EC) No. 428/2009 Setting Up a Community Regime for the Control of Exports, Transfer, Brokering, and Transit of Dual-Use Items." *Official Journal of the European Union*, L 129 (16.05.12): 12-280; http://eur-lex.europa.eu/LexUriServ/LexUriServ.do?uri=OJ:L:2012:129:0012:0280:EN:PDF; Accessed December 7, 2012.

"Removal of Commercial Communications Satellites and Hot Section Technology from State's USML for Transfer to Commerce's CCL." 61 *Federal Register* 215 (November 5, 1996): 56894-56896.

Dianne E. Rennack. *North Korea: Economic Sanctions*. Washington, DC: Library of Congress, Congressional Research Service, 2003.

Reviewing the Nuclear Nonproliferation Treaty. Henry Sokolski, ed. Carlisle: U.S. Army War College Strategic Studies Institute, 2010; http://permanent.access.gpo.gov/gpo2502/PUB987.pdf; Accessed December 13, 2012.

"Revision of Controls on Exports of Munitions List Articles to the People's Republic of China." 46 *Federal Register* 239 (December 14, 1981): 60820.

"Revision of the International Traffic in Arms Regulations." 49 *Federal Register* 236 (December 6, 1984): 47682-47712.

"Revisions to the United States Munitions List." 75 *Federal Register* 237 (December 10, 2010): 76935, 76937.

Frank Reynolds. *Managing Exports: Navigating the Complex Rules, Controls, Barriers, and Laws*. Hoboken, NJ: J. Wiley, 2003.

Condoleezza Rice. "Promoting the National Interest." *Foreign Affairs*, 79(1)(January/February 2000): 45-62.

John C. Rood. "Improvements to the Defense Export Trade Control System." *DISAM Journal*, 30 (4)(December 2008): 83-89.

Richard Rosecrance. *The Rise of the Trading State: Commerce and Conquest in the Modern World*. New York: Basic Books, Inc., 1985.

Robert S. Ross. "The Rise of Chinese Power and the Implications for the Regional Security Order." *Orbis*, 54 (4)(Fall 2010): 525-545.

John Roth, Douglas Greenburg, and Serena Wille. *Monograph on Terrorist Financing: Staff Report to the Commission*. (Washington, DC:

U.S. National Commission on Terrorist Attacks Upon the United States, 2004); http://govinfo.library.unt.edu/911/staff_statements/911_TerrFin_Monograph.pdf; Accessed October 9, 2012.

Trifin J. Roule. "Post 9-11 Financial Freeze Dries Up Hamas Funding." *Jane's Intelligence Review*, 14 (5)(May 2002): 17-19.

Jalil Roshandel and Nathan Chapman Lean. *Iran, Israel, and the United States: Regime Security vs. Political Legitimacy*. Santa Barbara: Praeger, 2011.

George Russell. "U.N. Shipment of High-Tech Equipment to North Korea, Iran Unjustified and Unfathomable, Say Investigators." Fox News, (September 13, 2012); http://www.foxnews.com/world/2012/09/13/un-shipment-high-tech-to-north-korea-iran-unjustified-and-unfathomable-say/; Accessed December 21, 2012.

Leonid Ryabikhin and Jevgenia Viktorov, "Weapons Transfers as a Soft Security Issue in Eastern Europe: Legal and Illicit Aspects." European Security, 13 (1-2)(April 2004): 73-93.

"S. 2205 Second Amendment Sovereignty Act of 2012" Washington, DC: GPO, 2012.

Eligar Sadeh, "Viewpoint: Bureaucratic Politics and the Case of Satellite Export Controls." *Astropolitics: The International Journal of Space Politics & Policy,* 5 (3)(2007): 289-302.

Rajib Sanyal. "Determinants of Bribery in International Business: The Cultural and Economic Factors." *Journal of Business Ethics,* 59 (1/2)(June 2005): 139-145.

Emily Cura Saunders. *Case Study: Iran, Islam, the Bomb, and NPT.* Berkeley: Lawrence Livermore National Laboratory, 2010.

Philip C. Saunders and Joshua K. Wiseman. *Buy, Build, or Steal: China's Quest for Advanced Military Aviation Technologies.* Washington, DC: National Defense University Press, 2011.

Michael P. Scharf. "Enforcement Through Sanctions, Force, and Criminalization." in *The New Terror: Facing the Threat of Chemical and Biological Weapons.* Sidney D. Drell, Abraham D. Sofaer, and George D. Wilson, eds. (Stanford: Hoover Institution Press, 1999): 439-479.

Wendy J. Schiller. "Trade Politics in the American Congress: A Study of the Interaction of Political Geography and Interest Group Behavior." *Political Geography*, 18 (7)(1999): 769-789.

Joseph A. Schorl, "Clicking the 'Export' Button: Cloud Data Storage and U.S. Dual-Use Export Controls," *George Washington University Law Review*, 80 (2)(February 2012): 633-667.

Fritz W. Schmidt. "Nuclear Export Controls: Closing the Gaps,. *IAEA Bulletin*, 46 (2)(March 2005): 31-33; http://www.zanggercommit tee.org/Documents/IAEABulletinclosingthegapsFWSchmidt.pdf; Accessed December 13, 2012.

Ibid. "The Zangger Committee: Its History and Future Role. *The Nonproliferation Review*, 2 (1)(Fall 1994): 38-44.

Gregory L. Schulte. *Strengthening the IAEA: How the Nuclear Watchdog Can Regain Its Bark*. Washington, DC: National Defense University, 2010; http://purl.access.gpo.gov/GPO/LPS121023; Accessed December 7, 2012.

Sir Richard Scott. *Inquiry into the Export of Defence Equipment and Dual-Use Goods to Iraq and Related Prosecutions*. 5 vols. London: HMSO, 1996.

Security Assistance: U.S. and International Historical Perspectives. Kendall G. Gott and Michael G. Brooks, eds. Fort Leavenworth, KS: Combat Studies Institute Press, 2006.

Sensitive Trade: The Perspective of European Union States. Quentin Michel, ed. New York: Peter Lang, 2011.

"Setting Up a Community Regime for the Control of Exports, Transfer, Brokering, and Transit of Dual-Use Items." *Official Journal of the European Union*, L 134, (29.5.2009): 1; http://trade.ec.europa.eu/doclib/docs/2009/june/tradoc_143390.pdf; Accessed December 6, 2012.

Dingli Shen. "Can Sanctions Stop Proliferation?" *The Washington Quarterly*, 31 (3)(Summer 2008): 89-100.

Ronald J. Sievert. "Urgent Message to Congress—Nuclear Triggers to Libya, Missile Guidance to China, Air Defense to Iraq, Arms Suppliers to the World: Has the Time Arrived to Overhaul the U.S. Export Regime?—The Case for Immediate Reform of our Outdated, Ineffective, and Self-Defeating Export Control System." *Texas International Law Journal*, 37 (1)(Winter 2002): 89-109.

Brendan Simms. "The Return of the Primacy of Foreign Policy." *German History*, 21 (3)(July 2003): 275-291.

Paul H. Silverstone. "The Export Control Act of 1949: Extraterritorial Enforcement." *University of Pennsylvania Law Review*, 107 (3)(January 1959): 331-362.

Nicholas A. Sims. *The Future of Biological Disarmament: Strengthening the Treaty Ban on Weapons*. London: Routledge, 2009.

Sixth Annual Report of the National Munitions Control Board for the Year Ended December 31, 1940. House Document 77-127. Serial 10581. Washington, DC: GPO, 1941.

Hedrick Smith. *The Power Game: How Washington Works*. New York: Random House, 1988.

Joseph P. Smaldone. "U.S. Commercial Arms Exports: Policy, Process, and Patterns." In *Marketing Security Assistance: New Perspectives on Arms Sales*. David J. Louscher and Michael D. Salamone, eds. Lexington, MA: Lexington Books, 1987.

Amy E. Smithson. *Separating Fact From Fiction: The Australia Group and the Chemical Weapons Convention*. Washington, DC: Henry L. Stimson Center, 1997.

Henry D. Sokolski. *Best of Intentions: America's Campaign Against Strategic Weapons Proliferation*. Westport, CT: Praeger, 2001.

South Eastern and European Clearinghouse for Control of Small Arms and Light Weapons (SEESAC). "About SEESAC." Belgrade: SEESAC, 2012: 1-2; http://www.seesac.org/new-about-seesac/1/; Accessed December 11, 2012.

Ibid. "Key Activities." Belgrade: SEESAC, 2012: 1-2; http://www.seesac.org/new-activities/1/; Accessed December 11, 2012.

Ibid. *Marking of Imported Firearms Under the UN's Firearms Protocol*. Belgrade: SEESAC, 2012?; www.seesac.org/uploads/studyrep/Marking_of_Imported_Firearms.pdf; Accessed December 11, 2012.

Ibid. *Regional Report on Arms Exports in 2010*. Belgrade: SEESAC, 2011; 9, 48. http://www.seesac.org/uploads/armsexport/Regional_Report_on_Arms_Exports_2010.pdf; Accessed December 11, 2012

Sharon Squassoni. "Mapping Nuclear Power's Future Spread," in Henry Sokolski, ed. *Nuclear Power's Global Expansion: Weighing Its Costs and Risks*. Carlisle, PA: U.S. Army War College Strategic Studies Institute, 2010: 53-92.

Timothy J. Stapleton. *A Military History of South Africa from the Dutch-Khoi Wars to the End of Apartheid*. (Santa Barbara: Praeger, 2010.

"Statement of Allan I. Mendolowitz. Associate Director, National Security and International Affairs Division, Before the Senate Committee on Foreign Relations on Foreign Policy Export Controls," Washington, DC: GAO, 1983; http://archive.gao.gov/d40t12/121773.pdf; Accessed August 3, 2011.

John J. Stemlau. *The International Politics of the Nigerian Civil War 1967-1970.* Princeton: Princeton University Press, 1977.

J. Terrence Stender. "Too Many Secrets: Challenges to the Control of Strong Crypto and the National Security Perspective." *Case Western Reserve Journal of International Law*, 30 (1)(Winter 1998): 287-337.

Reginald C. Stuart. "Special Interests and National Authority in Foreign Policy: American-British Provincial Links During the Embargo and the War of 1812." *Diplomatic History*, 8 (4)(October 1984): 311-328.

Jeremi Suri. *Henry Kissinger and the American Century.* Cambridge: Belknap Press of Harvard University Press, 2007.

"Survivability of West Berlin." *In On the Front Lines of the Cold War Intelligence War in Berlin 1946 to 1961.* Donald Steury, ed. (Washington, DC: Center for the Study of Intelligence, 1999): 633-634.

"Suspension of Munitions Export Licenses to Yugoslavia." 56 *Federal Register* 139 (July 19, 1991): 33322.

Peter Swan. "A Road Map to Understanding Global Export Controls: National Security in a Changing Global Environment." *American Business Law Journal*, 30 (4)(February 1993): 616.

Edward A. Tanzman. *Overview of the Chemical Weapons Convention.* Argonne, IL: Argonne National Laboratory, 1993; http://www.osti. gov/bridge/servlets/purl/10116174-8ufidk/native/10116174.pdf; Accessed December 5, 2012.

W. Andrew Terrill. *The Conflicts in Yemen and U.S. National Security.* Carlisle, PA: U.S. Army War College, Strategic Studies Institute, 2011.

"Title 31: Money and Finance: Treasury Chapter V-Foreign Assets Control, Department of the Treasury." 15 *Federal Register* 245 (December 19, 1950): 9040-9055.

Peter K. Tompa. "The Arms Export Control Act and Congressional Codetermination Over Arms Sales. *American University International Journal of International Law and Policy*, 1 (1)(Summer 1986): 291-330.

Jonathan Tucker. *U.S. Ratification of the Chemical Weapons Convention.* Washington, DC: National Defense University Press, 2011; http://purl.fdlp.gov/GPO/gpo23673; Accessed December 5, 2012.

Christopher Tuplin. "Thucydides 1.42.2 and the Megarian Decree," *The Classical Quarterly*, 29 (2)(1979): 301-307.

United Nations. *2010 Review Conference of the Parties to the Treaty on Nuclear Non-Proliferation of Nuclear Weapons (NPT) 3-28 May 2010.* (New York: NPT Conference, 2010); http://www.un.org/en/conf/npt/2010/; Accessed December 13, 2010.

United Nations Conference on the Arms Trade Treat. *Draft of the Arms Trade Treaty.* New York: United Nations, August 1, 2012: 2-12; http://www.un.org/ga/search/view_doc.asp?symbol=A/CONF.217/CRP.1&Lang=E; Accessed December 12, 2012.

United Nations. Department for Disarmament Affairs. Report of the Secretary General. *South Africa's Nuclear-Tipped Ballistic Missile Capability.* New York: United Nations, 1991.

United Nations General Assembly. *Official Records, A/64/P.55.* (December 2, 2009): 15.

United Nations Office for Disarmament Affairs. *Arms Trade Treaty.* New York: United Nations Office for Disarmament Affairs, 2012: 1-2; https://www.un.org/disarmament/convarms/ArmsTradeTreaty/; Accessed December 12, 2012.

United Nations Security Council. *Resolution 418 of 1977 of November 4, 1977.* New York: United Nations Security Council, 1977: 5-6; http://daccess-dds-ny.un.org/doc/RESOLUTION/GEN/NR0/297/01/IMG/NR029701.pdf?OpenElement; Accessed May 16, 2012.

Ibid. *Resolution 1540* (2004), New York: UNSC, 28 April 2004: 1-4; http://daccess-ods.un.org/TMP/5405232.90634155.html; Accessed December 14, 2012.

Ibid. *1540 Committee.* (New York: United Nations Security Council, 2012): 1-2; http://www.un.org/en/sc/1540/; Accessed December 14, 2012.

U.S. Air Force. "Subchapter E—Security Part 850 Safeguarding Classified Information: Miscellaneous Amendments." 30 *Federal Register* 155 (August 12, 1965): 10046-10047.

U.S. Assistant Secretary of Defense (Installations and Logistics). "Department of Defense Shipments by Foreign-Flag Vessels in the Cuban Trade." 28 *Federal Register* 40 (February 27, 1963): 1797.

U.S. Bureau of East-West Trade. *Export Administration Report: 113th Report on U.S. Export Controls to the President and the Congress Semiannual: October 1975-March 1976.* Washington, DC: U.S. Department of Commerce, 1976; http://catalog.hathitrust.org/Record/007395801; Accessed July 23, 2012.

Ibid."Organization and Functions." 41 *Federal Register* 133 (July 9, 1976): 28335.

U.S. Bureau of Export Administration. *Annual Report to Congress Fiscal Year 1996*. Washington, DC: Dept. of Commerce, 1996: I-1 to I-2; www.bis.doc/gov/news/publications/bxachap1.pdf; Accessed August 8, 2012.

Ibid. "Commercial Communications Satellites and Hot Section Technology for the Development, Production or Overhaul of Commercial Aircraft Engines." 61 *Federal Register* 204 (October 21, 1996): 54540-54541.

Ibid. "Definition of Supercomputer." 53 *Federal Register* 233 (December 5, 1988): 48932.

Ibid. "Export Administration Regulation; Simplification of Export Administration Regulations." 61 *Federal Register* 58 (March 25, 1996): 12714-13041.

Ibid. "Leif Kare Johansen, Constitutionsvel 21, 4085 Hundvaag, Norway; Respondent; Decision and Order." 61 *Federal Register* 32 (February 15, 1996): 5980-5981.

Ibid. "Removal of Commercial Communication Satellites and Related Items from the Department of Commerce's Commerce Control List for Retransfer to the Department of State's United States Munitions List." 64 *Federal Register* 52 (March 18, 1999): 13338-13340.

Ibid. "Removal of National Security Controls for Exports of Certain Prepeg Production Equipment." 56 *Federal Register* 106 (June 3, 1991): 25023-25024.

Ibid. "Revisions to the Commerce Control List: Equipment Related to the Production of Chemical and Biological Weapons; Biological Agents." 57 *Federal Register* 136 (July 15, 1992): 31309-31312.

U.S. Bureau of Foreign and Domestic Commerce, Department of Commerce. "Exportations Requiring License and Applications for Licenses." 14 *Federal Register* (October 12, 1949): 6167-6169.

Ibid. Department of Commerce. "Part 37-Scope of Export Control by Department of Commerce." 14 *Federal Register* (August 31, 1949): 5389-5390.

U.S. Bureau of International Commerce, Department of Commerce,."Subchapter B-Export Regulations." 36 *Federal Register* 95 (May 15, 1971): 8932-8933.

Ibid. 37 *Federal Register* 84 (April 29, 1972): 8659-8660/

Ibid. "Continuation of Short Supply Controls on Petroleum and Petroleum Products for the Fourth Quarter 1975." 40 *Federal Register*
191 (October 1, 1975): 45159-45162.

U.S. Census Bureau. *Statistical Abstract of the United States 1993.* Washington, DC: GPO, 1993.

Ibid. *Trade in Goods With China.* (2012); http://www.census.gov/for-
eign-trade/balance/c5700.htm; Accessed August 6, 2012.

Ibid. *Trade in Goods With Russia.* (2012); http://www.census.gov/for-
eign-trade/balance/c4621.html; Accessed August 6, 2012.

Ibid. "U.S. Trade in Goods and Services-Balance of Payments (BOP)
Basis 1960 thru 2011." Washington, DC: U.S. Census Bureau, 2012;
http://www.census.gov/foreign-trade/statistics/historical/gands.txt;
Accessed November 6, 2012

U.S. Census Bureau. Foreign Trade Division. "U.S. Trade in Goods
and Services-Balance of Payments (BOP) Basis." (2012)
www.census.gov/foreign-trade/statistics/historical/gands.pdf; Accessed April 11, 2012.

U.S. Central Intelligence Agency. *Consequences of a Relaxation of Non-
Communist Controls on Trade With the Soviet Bloc, NIE 100-3-54.*
Washington, DC: CIA, 1954; http://www.foia.cia.gov/docs/
DOC_0000269320/DOC_0000269320.pdf; Accessed August 15,
2012.

Ibid. *Dependence of Soviet Military Power on Economic Relations With
the West, Special National Intelligence Estimate 3/11-4-81.* Washington, DC: CIA, 1981; http://www.foia.cia.gov/docs/DOC_000068
1971/DOC_0000681971.pdf; Accessed August 22, 2012.

Ibid. *Notes on Soviet Vulnerabilities.*" (Washington, DC: CIA, July 7,
1961): 9-13; www.foia.cia.gov/BerlinWall/1961-Summer/1961-97-
07d.pdf; Accessed May 15, 2012.

Ibid. *Probable Effects on the Soviet Bloc of Certain Courses of Action
Directed at the Internal and External Commerce of Communist China,
Special Estimate (SE) 37.* Washington, DC: Central Intelligence
Agency, 1953; http://www.foia.cia.gov/docs/DOC_0000269301/
DOC_0000269301.pdf; Accessed August 15, 2012.

Ibid. *Soviet Acquisition of Militarily Significant Western Technology: An
Update.* Washington, DC: CIA, 1985; http://www.foia.cia.gov/docs/
DOC_0000500561/DOC_0000500561.pdf; Accessed August 22,
2012.

Ibid. *Soviet Acquisition of Western Technology*. Washington, DC: CIA, 1982.

Ibid. *Strategic Warning & the Role of Intelligence: Lessons Learned from the 1968 Soviet Invasion of Czechoslovakia*. Washington, DC: CIA, 2010(?); http://permanent.access.gpo.gov/gpo15421/Soviet%20-%20Czech%20Invasion%20Booklet.pdf; Accessed July 20, 2012.

Ibid. *Unclassified Report to Congress on the Acquisition of Technology Relating to Weapons of Mass Destruction and Advanced Conventional Munitions 1 January to 31 December 2006*. Washington, DC: CIA, 2006.

United States-China Economic and Security Review Commission. *China's Proliferation Practices and the Development of its Cyber and Space Warfare Capabilities*. Washington, DC: GPO, 2008.

U.S. Commission on the Intelligence Capabilities of the United States Regarding Weapons of Mass Destruction. *Report*. (Washington, DC: The Commission, 2005.

U.S. Commission to Assess the Organization of the Federal Government to Combat the Proliferation of Weapons of Mass Destruction. *Report*. Washington, DC: GPO, 1999.

U.S. Committee on Balancing Scientific Openness and National Security. *Balancing Scientific Openness and National Security Controls at the Nation's Nuclear Weapons Laboratories*. Washington, DC: National Academy Press, 1999.

U.S. Committee on Public Information. *Official Bulletin*, 1 (40)(June 26, 1917): 1.

U.S. Committee on Science, Engineering, and Public Policy. *Balancing the National Interest: U.S. National Security on Export Controls and Global Economic Competition*. Washington, DC: National Academy Press, 1987; http://books.nap.edu/catalog.php?record_id=987; Accessed August 2, 2012.

U.S. Congress. *Reports to Be Made to Congress: Communication From the Clerk*. U.S. House of Representatives . House Document 112-79. Washington, DC: GPO, 2012.

U.S. Congress. House Committee on Appropriations. *Financial Services and General Government Appropriations Bill, 2013*. House Report 112-550. Washington, DC: GPO, 2012.

Ibid. House Committee on Appropriations. *Semiannual Report of Committee Activities*. House Report 112-145. (Washington, DC: GPO, 2011.

U.S. Congress. House Committee on Armed Services. *Economic Impacts of Defense Sequestration*. Washington, DC: GPO, 2012.

Ibid. *First Semiannual Report of the Activities of the Committee on Armed Services*. House Report 112-123 Washington, DC: GPO, 2011.

U.S. Congress. House Committee on Banking and Currency. *Export Control Act Extension: Report Together With Supplemental Views To Accompany H.R. 4293*. House Report 91-524. Serial 12837-3. Washington, DC: GPO, 1969.

U.S. Congress. House Committee on Banking and Currency. Subcommittee on International Trade. *To Extend and Amend the Export Control Act of 1949*. Washington, DC: GPO, 1969.; http://catalog.hathitrust.org/Record/008466898; Accessed May 16, 2012.

U.S. Congress. House Committee on Commerce. Subcommittee on Finance and Hazardous Materials. *The International Anti-Bribery and Fair Competition Act of 1998*. Washington, DC: GPO, 1999.

U.S. Congress. House Committee on Energy and Commerce. Subcommittee on Oversight and Investigations. *Commercial Sales of Military Technologies*. Washington, DC: GPO, 2012.

Ibid. Subcommittee on Telecommunications, Consumer Protection, and Finance. *Foreign Corrupt Practices Act-Oversight*. Washington, DC: GPO, 1982.

U.S. Congress. House Committee on Financial Services. *First Semiannual Report on the Activities of the Committee on Financial Services*. House Report 112-121. Washington, DC: GPO, 2011.

Ibid. Subcommittee on Oversight and Investigations. *Oversight of the Department of Treasury*. Washington, DC: GPO, 2004.

Ibid. *Weapons of Mass Destruction: Stopping the Funding—The OFAC Role*. Washington, DC: GPO, 2006.

U.S. Congress. House Committee on Foreign Affairs. *Export Controls, Arms Sales, and Reform: Balancing U.S. Interests: Part I*. (Washington, DC: GPO, 2011).

Ibid. *The Foreign Military Sales Act*. Washington, DC: GPO, 1968.

Ibid. *The Global Nuclear Revival and U.S. Nonproliferation Policy*. (Washington, DC: GPO, 2011); http://purl.fdlp.gov/GPO/gpo8663; Accessed December 7, 2012.

Ibid. *Legislative Review and Oversight Activities*. House Report 112-126. Washington, DC: GPO, 2011.

Ibid. *Nuclear Cooperation and Non-Proliferation after Khan and Iran*. Washington, DC: GPO, 2010.

Ibid. *U.S. Post-Cold War Foreign Policy*. Washington, DC: GPO, 1993.

Ibid. Subcommittees on Arms Control, International Security and Science and International Economic Policy and Trade. *Missile Proliferation: The Need for Controls (MTCR)*. Washington, DC: GPO, 1990.

Ibid. House Committee on Foreign Affairs. Subcommittee on Foreign Economic Policy. *East-West Trade*. Washington, DC: GPO, 1954.

Ibid. House Committee on Foreign Affairs. Subcommittee on International Economic Policy and Trade. *The Foreign Trade Practices Act*. Washington, DC: GPO, 1985.

Ibid. *Technology Exports: Department of Defense Organization and Performance*. Washington, DC: GPO, 1980; http://babel.hathitrust.org/cgi/pt?id=mdp.39015082336663; Accessed August 14, 2012.

Ibid. Subcommittee on Oversight and Investigations. *Communist Chinese Cyber-Attacks, Cyber-Espionage, and Theft of American Technology*. Washington, DC: GPO, 2011; http://purl.fdlp.gov/GPO/gpo9687; Accessed December 21, 2012.

Ibid. Subcommittee on Terrorism, Nonproliferation, and Trade. *Exports Controls: Are We Protecting Security and Facilitating Exports?* Washington, DC: GPO, 2007.

Ibid. *Transshipment and Diversion: Are U.S. Trading Partners Doing Enough to Prevent the Spread of Dangerous Technologies?* Washington, DC: GPO, 2010; http://purl.fdlp.gov/GPO/gpo2627; Accessed December 5, 2012.

U.S. Congress. House Committee on Government Operations. *Strengthening the Export Licensing System: First Report*. House Report 102-137 Washington, DC: GAO, 1991.

U.S. Congress. House Committee on Government Operations. Subcommittee on Commerce, Consumer, and Monetary Affairs. *U.S. Government Controls on Sales to Iraq*. Washington, DC: GPO, 1991.

U.S. Congress. House Committee on Government Oversight and Reform. *IG Report: The Department of Justice's Office of the Inspector General Examines the Failures of Operation Fast and Furious*. Washington, DC: GPO. 2012. http://purl.fdlp.gov/GPO/gpo31471; Accessed January 30, 2013.

U.S. Congress. House Committee on Government Oversight and Reform. *Operation Fast and Furious: Reckless Decisions, Tragic Outcomes*. Washington, DC: GPO, 2011.

Ibid. *Operation Fast and Furious: The Other Side of the Border*. Washington, DC: GPO, 2012.

U.S. Congress. House Committee on Homeland Security. *Report on Legislative and Oversight Activities*. House Report 112-127. Washington, DC: GPO, 2011.

U.S. Congress. House Committee on International Relations. *Arms Export Control Act*. (Washington, DC: GPO, 1976; http://catalog.hathi trust.org/Record/003220393; Accessed May 17, 2012.

Ibid. *Export Licensing of Advanced Technology: A Review*. Washington, DC: GPO, 1976.

Ibid. *International Security Assistance and Arms Export Control Act of 1976*. (Washington, DC: GPO, 1976; http://catalog.hathitrust.org/Record/003220332; Accessed May 17, 2012.

Ibid. *Munitions List Export Licensing Issues*. Washington, DC: GPO, 2000, http://purl.access.gpo.gov/GPO/LPS8616; Accessed August 5, 2011.

U.S. Congress. House Committee on International Regulations and Library of Congress, Congressional Research Service. *Administration of Export Controls*. Washington, DC: GPO, 1976.

U.S. Congress. House Committee on International Relations. Subcommittee on Africa. *U.S.-South Africa Relations: Nuclear Cooperation*. (Washington, DC: GPO, 1978.

United States Congress. House Committee on International Relations. Subcommittees on Africa and International Organizations. *United States Policy Toward South Africa*. Washington, DC: GPO, 1978.

U.S. Congress. House Committee on International Relations. Subcommittee on International Economic Policy and Trade. *Department of Defense Policy Statement on Export Control of United States Technology*. Washington, DC: GPO, 1977; http://catalog.hathitrust.org/Record/002943097; Accessed August 21, 2012.

U.S. Congress. House Committee on International Relations. Subcommittee on International Economic Policy and Trade. *Emergency Controls on International Economic Transactions*. Washington, DC: GPO, 1977; http://catalog.hathitrust.org/Record/002939966; Accessed November 6, 2012.

Ibid. *Encryption: Individual Right to Privacy Vs. National Security*. Washington, DC: GPO, 1998.

Ibid. *Helms-Burton; Two Years Later*. Washington, DC: GPO, 1998.

Ibid. *Interfering With U.S. National Security Interests: The World Trade Organization and European Union Challenge to the Helms-Burton Law*. Washington, DC: GPO, 1997.

Ibid. *Issues in Export Control*. Washington, DC: GPO, 1995.

Ibid. Subcommittee on International Terrorism and Nonproliferation. *Venezuela: Terrorism Hub of South America?* (Washington, DC: GPO, 2006); http://purl.access.gpo.gov/GPO/LPS74890; Accessed August 5, 2011.

Ibid. Subcommittee on International Trade and Commerce. *Trading With the Enemy: Legislative and Executive Documents Concerning Regulation of International Transactions in Time of Declared National Emergency*. Washington, DC: GPO, 1976; http://catalog.hathitrust.org/Record/003220307; Accessed May 17, 2012.

Ibid. Subcommittee on the Middle East and Central Asia. *Syria Accountability and Lebanese Sovereignty Restoration Act Two Years Later*. Washington, DC: GPO, 2006.

U.S. Congress. Subcommittee on the Western Hemisphere. *Democracy in Venezuela*. Washington, DC: GPO, 2006; < http://purl.access.gpo.gov/GPO/LPS72914; Accessed August 5, 2011.

U.S. Congress. House Committee on Interstate and Foreign Commerce. Subcommittee on Oversight and Investigations. *Foreign Corrupt Practices Act*. Washington, DC: GPO, 1979.

U.S. Congress. House Committee on the Judiciary. *First Semiannual Report on the Activities of the Committee on the Judiciary*. House Report 112-119. Washington, DC: GPO, 2011.

U.S. Congress. House Committee on National Security and House Committee on International Relations. *United States Policy Regarding the Export of Satellites to China*. Washington, DC: GPO, 1999.

U.S. Congress. House Committee on Oversight and Government Reform. *The Department of Justice's Operation Fast and Furious: The Other Side of the Border*. Washington, DC: GPO, 2012; http://purl.fdlp.gov/GPO/gpo19478; Accessed January 29, 2013.

U.S. Congress,.House Committee on Oversight and Government Reform. *Implementation of Iran Sanctions*. Washington, DC: GPO, 2011.

U.S. Congress. House Permanent Select Committee on Intelligence, *Semiannual Report of the Activity of the House Permanent Select Committee on Intelligence*. House Report 112-134. Washington, DC: GPO, 2011.

U.S. Congress. House Committee on Science, Space, and Technology. *The Effect of Changing Export Controls on Cooperation in Science and Technology*. Washington, DC: GPO, 1991.

Ibid. *Impacts of U.S. Export Control Policies on Science and Technology Activities and Competitiveness*. (Washington, DC: GPO, 2009.

U.S. Congress. House Committee on Ways and Means. *Report on the Legislative and Oversight Activities*. House Report 112-130. Washington, DC: GPO, 2011.

Ibid. Subcommittee on Oversight. *Administration and Enforcement of U.S. Export Control Programs*. Washington, DC: GPO, 1992.

Ibid. Subcommittee on Trade. *Legislation to Prohibit the Importation of Products Made by Toshiba Corp. and Kongsberg Vaapenfabrik Co.* Washington, DC: GPO, 1987.

U.S. Congress. House Select Committee on Export Control. *Investigation and Study of the Administration, Operation and Enforcement of the Export Control Act of 1949, and Related Acts*. House Report 87-1753. Serial 12430. Washington, DC: GPO, 1962.

U.S. Congress. House Select Committee on U.S. National Security and Military Concerns with the People's Republic of China. *Report*. House Report 105-851. Washington, DC: GPO, 1998.

U.S. Congress. Joint Economic Committee. *Soviet Pipeline Sanctions: The European Perspective*. Washington, DC: GPO, 1983; http://catalog.hathitrust.org/Record/011336860.

U.S. Congress. Office of Technology Assessment. *Export Controls and Nonproliferation Policy*. Washington, DC: OTA, 1994.

U.S. Congress. Representative Mike Kelly. *Letter to President Obama and Secretary of State Clinton*, (June 29, 2012): 1-11; http://kelly.house.gov/sites/kelly.house.gov/files/ATT%20Letter.pdf ; Accessed December 12, 2012.

U.S. Congress. Senate Committee on Agriculture, Nutrition, and Forestry. *Embargo on Grain Sales to the Soviet Union*. Washington, DC: GPO, 1980.

U.S. Congress. Senate Committee on Appropriations. *Subcommittee Jurisdiction by Program, Senate Print 110-11*. Washington, DC: GPO, 2007.

U.S. Congress. Senate Committee on Armed Services. *Report of the Activities*. Senate Report 112-2. Washington, DC: GPO, 2011.

Ibid. *U.S. Export Control and Nonproliferation Policy and the Role and Responsibility of the Department of Defense.* Washington, DC: GPO, 1998.

U.S. Congress. Senate Committee on Banking and Currency. *Export Control Act of 1949: Report to Accompany S. 548.* Senate Report 81-31. Washington, DC: GPO, 1949.

Ibid. *Extension of Export Control Act of 1949.* Senate Report 87-1576. Serial 12417. Washington, DC: GPO, 1962.

U.S. Congress. Senate Committee on Banking, Housing, and Urban Affairs. *Controls on the Export of Capital From the United States.* Washington, DC: GPO, 1986

Ibid. *Establishing an Effective Modern Framework for Export Controls.* Washington, DC: GPO, 2002.

Ibid. *Export Control Issues in the Cox Report.* Washington, DC: GPO, 2000.

Ibid. *Department of Commerce's First Annual Report on Foreign Policy Export Controls.* (Washington, DC: GPO, 1986; http://catalog. hathitrust.org/Record/007604044; Accessed May 25, 2012.

Ibid. *Report on the Activities of the Committee on Banking, Housing, and Urban Affairs.* Senate Report 112-7. Washington, DC: GPO, 2011.

Ibid. *U.S. Export Control Policy and Extension of the Export Administration Act.* Washington, DC: GPO, 1979; http://catalog.hathitrust. org/Record/002947441; Accessed May 21, 2012.

U.S. Congress. Senate Committee on Banking, Housing, and Urban Affairs. Subcommittee on International Finance. *Amending the Trading With the Enemy Act.* Washington, DC: GPO, 1977; http:// catalog.hathitrust.org/Record/002941349; Accessed May 17, 2012.

Ibid. *Arab Boycott.* Washington, DC: GPO, 1977.

Ibid. *The Export Administration Act of 1996 [H.R. 361].* Washington, DC: GPO, 1997.

Ibid. Subcommittee on International Finance and Monetary Policy. *Agricultural Embargoes and the Sanctity of Contracts.* Washington, DC: GPO, 1982,

U.S. Congress. Senate Committee on Banking, Housing, and Urban Affairs. Subcommittee on International Finance and Monetary Policy. *International Affairs Functions of the Treasury and Export Administration Act.* Washington, DC: GPO, 1981.

Ibid. *Toshiba-Kongsberg Technology Diversion Case.* Washington, DC: GPO, 1987.

U.S. Congress. Senate Committee on Energy and Natural Resources. Subcommittee on Energy Research and Development. *Nuclear Non-Proliferation Policy Act of 1977*, Washington, DC: GPO, 1977.

U.S. Congress. Senate Committee on Finance. *Extending Most-Favored-Nation Status for China*. Washington, DC: GPO, 1991.

Ibid. *Report on the Activities of the Committee on Finance*. Senate Report 112-11. Washington, DC: GPO, 2011.

U.S. Congress. Senate Committee on Foreign Relations. *Arms Sales and Foreign Policy*. Washington, DC: GPO, 1967.

Ibid. *Arms Sales and Foreign Policy: Staff Study*. Washington, DC: GPO, 1967.

Ibid. *Enhancing Non-Proliferation Partnerships in the Black Sea Region: Minority Staff Report*. Washington, DC: GPO, 2011; http://purl.fdlp.gov/GPO/gpo16232; Accessed December 21, 2012.

Ibid. *Foreign Military Sales: Hearing, Ninetieth Congress, Second Session, on S. 3093 to Consolidate and Revise Foreign Assistance Legislation Relating to Reimbursable Military Exports*. Washington, DC: GPO, 1968.

Ibid. *Interpreting the Pressler Amendment: Commercial Military Sales to Pakistan*. Washington, DC: GPO, 1992.

Ibid. *Iran's Political/Nuclear Ambitions and U.S. Policy Options: A Compilation of Statements by Witnesses*. Washington, DC: GPO, 2006.

Ibid. *The Lifting of the EU Arms Embargo on China*. Washington, DC: GPO, 2005; http://purl.access.gpo.gov/GPO/LPS63682; Accessed January 2, 2013.

Ibid. *Membership and Jurisdiction of Subcommittees*. Senate Print 111-3. Washington, DC: GPO, 2009.

Ibid. *Mutual Security Act of 1959. Hearings on S. 1451 to Amend Further the Mutual Security Act of 1954, as Amended, and for Other Purposes. . .* Washington, DC: GPO, 1959. http://catalog.hathitrust.org/Record/009862897; Accessed May 10, 2012.

U.S. Congress. Senate Committee on Government Operations. Permanent Subcommittee on Investigations. *East-West Trade Pt. 1-3*. Washington, DC: GPO, 1956.

Ibid. *East-West Trade: Report Together With Minority Views*. Senate Report 84-2621. Serial 11890 Washington, DC: GPO, 1956.

U.S. Congress. Senate Committee on Governmental Affairs. The *Wassenaar Arrangement and the Future of Multilateral Export Controls*. Washington, DC: GPO, 2000.

Ibid. Subcommittee on Federal Services, Post Office, and Civil Service. *A Review of Arms Export Licensing*. (Washington, DC: GPO, 1994).

Ibid. Senate Committee on Governmental Affairs. Subcommittee on International Security, Proliferation, and Federal Services. *The Role of Bilateral and Multilateral Arms Control Agreements in Controlling Threats from the Proliferation of Weapons of Mass Destruction*. Washington, DC: GPO, 2003.

Ibid. *Russia and China: Non-Proliferation Concerns and Export Controls*. Washington, DC: GPO, 2003.

U.S. Congress. Senate Committee on Governmental Affairs. Permanent Subcommittee on Investigations. *Role of U.S. Correspondent Banking in International Money Laundering*. 5 vols. Washington, DC: GPO, 2001.

Ibid. *Transfers of Technology and the Dresser Industries Export Licensing Actions*. Washington, DC: GPO, 1976; http://catalog.hathitrust.org/Record/002948072; Accessed July 27, 2011.

U.S. Congress. Senate Committee on Homeland Security and Governmental Affairs. *Iran Sanctions: Why Does the U.S. Government Do Business With Companies Doing Business in Iran?* Washington, DC: GPO, 2011.

Ibid. *Nuclear Terrorism: Assessing the Threat to the Homeland*. Washington, DC: GPO, 2010.

Ibid. *Rules and Procedures*. Senate Print 112-11. Washington, DC: GPO, 2011.

Ibid. Permanent Subcommittee on Investigations. *U.S. Vulnerabilities to Money Laundering, Drugs, and Terrorist Financing: HSBC Case History: Majority and Minority Staff Report*. Washington, DC: GPO, 2012; http://www.hsgac.senate.gov/subcommittees/investigations/hearings/us-vulnerabilities-to-money-laundering-drugs-and-terrorist-financing-hsbc-case-history; Accessed October 9, 2012.

Ibid. Subcommittee on Oversight of Government Management, the Federal Workforce, and the District of Columbia Subcommittee. *Beyond Control: Reforming Export Licensing Agencies for National Security and Economic Interests*. Washington, DC: GPO, 2009.

U.S. Congress. Senate Committee on the Judiciary. *Report of the Activities of the Committee on the Judiciary.* Senate Print 112-5. Washington, DC: GPO, 2011.

U.S. Congress. Senate Permanent Select Committee on Intelligence and Senate Committee on the Judiciary. Subcommittee on Terrorism, Technology, and Government Information. *Economic Espionage.* Washington, DC: GPO, 1996.

U.S. Congress. Senate Committee on Intelligence. *Report of the Select Committee on Intelligence on the U.S. Intelligence Community's Prewar Intelligence Assessments on Iraq Together With Additional Views.* Washington, DC: GPO, 2004.

Ibid. *Report of the Select Committee on Intelligence.* Senate Report 112-3. Washington, DC: GPO, 2011.

U.S. Congress. Senate Special Committee Investigating the Munitions Industry, *Hearings 40 Pts.* Washington, DC: GPO, 1935-1936.

U.S. Congressional Budget Office. *Domestic Costs of Sanctions on Foreign Commerce.* Washington, DC: CBO, 1999.

U.S. Constitution. *Article 1, Sections 8-9.*

U.S. Constitution. *First Amendment, Clause Six.*

U.S. Customs and Border Protection. "CBP Officers Arrest Woman on Alien Smuggling Charges, Seize 6,486 Rounds of High Powered Ammunition." (Washington, DC: CBP, December 31, 2009); http://www.cbp.gov/xp/cgov/newsroom/news_releases/archives/2009_news_releases/dec_2009/12312009_6.xml; Accessed September 18, 2012.

Ibid. *CBP Seizes Shipment of Lead-Contaminated Toys.* (Washington, DC: CBP, November 26, 2012): 1-2; http://www.cbp.gov/xp/cgov/newsroom/news_releases/national/11212012.xml; Accessed December 6, 2012.

Ibid. *CSI In Brief.* (Washington, DC: CBP, October 7, 2011): http://www.cbp.gov/xp/cgov/trade/cargo_security/csi/csi_in_brief.xml; Accessed December 6, 2012.

Ibid. *Export Control and Related Border Security (EXBS) Program Overview.* Washington, DC: DHS, 2008); http://www.cbp.gov/xp/cgov/border_security/international_operations/international_training/exbs.xml; Accessed September 19, 2012.

Ibid. *Fact Sheet: Container Security Initiative.* (Washington, DC: CBP, 2011): http://www.cbp.gov/linkhandler/cgov/trade/cargo_security/

csi/csi_factsheet_2011.ctt/csi_factsheet_2011.pdf; Accessed December 6, 2012.

Ibid. *How Cargo Flows Securely to the U.S.* (Washington, DC: CBP, n.d.): 1; http://www.cbp.gov/linkhandler/cgov/trade/cargo_security/csi/csi_flows.ctt/csi_flows.pdf; Accessed December 6, 2012.

Ibid. "Secure Freight Initiative Begins Data Transmission for Radiation Scanning in Pakistan." (Washington, DC: CBP, May 2, 2007); http://www.cbp.gov/xp/cgov/newsroom/news_releases/archives/2007_news_releases/052007/05022007.xml; Accessed September 18, 2012.

Ibid. *Summary of Laws and Regulations Enforced by CBP.* (Washington, DC: CBP, n.d.); http://www.cbp.gov/xp/cgov/trade/legal/summary_laws_enforced/; Accessed September 18, 2012.

Ibid. *United States Border Patrol: Border Patrol Agent Staffing by Fiscal Year (Oct. 1st through Sept. 30th).* (Washington, DC: DHS, 2011); http://www.cbp.gov/linkhandler/cgov/border_security/border_patrol/usbp_statistics/staffing_92_10.ctt/staffing_92_11.pdf; Accessed September 19, 2012.

Ibid. *United States Border Patrol: Enacted Border Patrol Program Budget by Fiscal Year (Dollars in Thousands)*, Washington, DC: DHS, 2011); http://www.cbp.gov/linkhandler/cgov/border_security/border_patrol/usbp_statistics/budget_stats.ctt/budget_stats.pdf; Accessed September 19, 2012.

U.S. Customs Service. *Mission and Organization.* Washington, DC: U.S. Customs Service, Office of the Comptroller, 1988.

U.S. Deemed Export Advisory Committee. *The Deemed Export Rule in the Era of Globalization.* Washington, DC: Dept. of Commerce, 2007; http://tac.bis.doc.gov/2007/deacreport.pdf; Accessed August 8, 2012.

U.S. Defense Board. *Report to the Secretary of Defense: Task Force Group on Best Practices for Export Controls.* Washington, DC: Defense Business Board, 2008; http://dbb.defense.gov/pdf/Task_Group_on_Best_Practices_for_Export_Controls_Final_Report.pdf; Accessed

U.S. Defense Institute for Security Assistance Management."DISAM Mission." (2012);

Ibid. *The Management of Security Assistance.* Wright-Patterson Air Force Base, OH: Defense Institute of Security Assistance Management, 1990http://www.disam.dsca.mil/pages/disam/mission.aspx; Accessed September 7, 2012September 6, 2012.

U.S. Defense Science Board. *An Analysis of the Export Control of U.S. Technology*. Washington, DC: Defense Science Board, 1976.

Ibid. *Defense Science Board Task Force on Directed Energy Weapons*. Washington, DC: Office of the Undersecretary of Defense for Acquisition, Technology, and Logistics, 2007; http://purl.access.gpo. gov/GPO/LPS91811; Accessed August 5, 2011.

Ibid. U.S. Defense Science Board Task Force on the Export of U.S. Technology. *An Analysis of Export Control of U.S. Technology-A DOD Perspective*. Washington, DC: DOD, 1976i; www.dtic.mil/ dtic/tr/fulltext/u2/a022029.pdf; Accessed August 21, 2012.

U.S. Defense Technology Security Administration,. "Licensing Directorate." (2012); http://www.dtsa.mil/Directorates/Licensing; Accessed September 6, 2012.

Ibid. "Policy Directorate." (2012); http://www.dtsa.mil/Directorates/ Policy; Accessed September 6, 2012.

Ibid. "Space Directorate." (2012); http://www.dtsa.mil/Directorates/ Space; Accessed September 6, 2012.

U.S. Department of Agriculture. Departmental Management. *Militarily Critical Technologies List, (n.d.)*; http://www.dm.usda.gov/ocpm/ Security%20Guide/T1threat/Mctl.htm; Accessed August 21, 2012.

U.S. Department of Commerce. *Export Control Reform "Dashboard."* (2012); http://export.gov/ecr/; Accessed August 9, 2012.

U.S. Department of Commerce. *President's Export Control Reform Initiative*. Washington, DC: Department of Commerce, 2012; http:// export.gov/ECR/; Accessed November 7, 2012.

Ibid. "Restriction of Exports to the Republic of South Africa and Namibia." 43 *Federal Register* 36 (February 22, 1978): 7311.

U.S. Department of Commerce. Bureau of Economic Analysis. "News Release: Gross Domestic Product: Fourth Quarter and Annual 2011 (Third Estimate) Corporate Profits: Fourth Quarter and Annual 2011." (March 29, 2012); www.bea.gov/newsreleases/national/gdp/2012/ pdf/gdp4q11_3rd.pdf; Accessed April 13, 2012.

U.S. Department of Commerce. Bureau of Export Administration. "Establishment of New General License for Shipments to Country Groups QWY and the People's Republic of China." 59 *Federal Register* 64 (April 4, 1994): 15621.

U.S. Department of Commerce. Bureau of Export Administration. "Guidelines for Export Transactions Involving Equipment, Materials, and Technical Data for Producing Biological Weapons." 55 *Federal Register* 242 (December 17, 1990): 51740.

U.S. Department of Commerce. Bureau of Industry and Security. *Annual Report Fiscal Year 2002*. Washington, DC: Department of Commerce, 2002; http://www.bis.doc.gov/news/2003/annualreport/ printableversion.pdf; Accessed August 8, 2012.

Ibid. *Annual Report to the Congress for Fiscal Year 2010*. Washington, DC: Department of Commerce, 2011(?); https://www.bis.doc.gov/ news/2011/bis_annual_report_2010.pdf; Accessed August 10, 2012.

Ibid. "BIS Program Offices." (2012); https://www.bis.doc.gov/about/ programoffices.htm; Accessed August 10, 2012.

Ibid. "Computer Technology and Software Eligible for Export or Reexport Under License Exception TSR (Technology and Software Under Restriction)." 67 *Federal Register* 111 (June 10, 2002): 39675-39676.

Ibid. "Establishment of New License Exception for the Export or Reexport to U.S. Persons in Libya of Certain Items Controlled for Anti-Terrorism Reasons Only on the Commerce Control List." 70 *Federal Register* 220 (November 16, 2005): 64932-64935.

Ibid. *2011 Foreign Policy Report on Export-Based Controls* . Washington, DC: Department of Commerce, 2012 ; https://www.bis.doc.gov/ news/2011/2011_fpreport.pdf; Accessed August 10, 2012.

Ibid. "Imposition and Expansion of Controls on Designated Terrorists." 68 *Federal Register* 109 (June 6, 2003): 34192-34196.

Ibid. "In the Matter of MUTCO International Kelenbergweg 37 1101 EX Amsterdam, Netherlands; Respondent." 71 *Federal Register* 128 (July 5, 2006): 38133-38135.

Ibid. "In the Matter of: Suburban Guns (Pty) Ltd., 119 Mail Road, Plumstead 7800, Cape Town, South Africa. Respondent." 70 *Federal Register* 219 (November 15, 2005): 69314-69316.

Ibid. "Industry and Security Programs; Change of Agency Names." 67 *Federal Register* 81 (April 26, 2002): 20630-29632.

Ibid. "Proposed Revisions to the Export Administration Regulations (EAR): Control of Items the President Determines No Longer Warrant Control Under the United States Munitions List (USML). 76 *Federal Register* 136 (July 15, 2011): 41958-41985.

Ibid. "Revisions to the Export Administration Regulations (EAR): Control of Aircraft and Related Items the President Determines No Longer

Warrant Control Under the United States Munitions List (USML), 76 Federal Register 215 (November 7, 2011): 68675-68690

U.S. Department of Commerce. Industry and Trade Administration. "Restriction of Exports to the Republic of South Africa and Namibia." 43 *Federal Register* 56 (February 22, 1978): 7311-7315.

Ibid. "U.S. Trade Status with Communist Countries." (September 20, 1978): 1; http://catalog.hathitrust.org/Record/006259584; Accessed July 24, 2012.

U.S. Department of Commerce. International Trade Administration. "Amendment of Oil and Gas Controls to the U.S.S.R." 47 *Federal Register* 122 (June 24, 1982): 27250-27254.

Ibid. "Order Temporarily Denying Export Privileges." 47 *Federal Register* 113 (June 11, 1982): 25396-25398.

U.S. Department of Commerce. Office of Budget. *Bureau of Industry and Security Fiscal Year 2013 President's Submission.* (Washington, DC: U.S.

Dept. of Commerce, 2012): 4, 37; http://www.osec.doc.gov/bmi/budget/fy13cbj/BIS_FY2013_Congressional%20Justification-FINAL.pdf; Accessed August 10, 2012.

U.S. Department of Commerce. Office of the Inspector General. *Bureau of Industry and Security: Deemed Export Controls May Not Stop the Transfer of Sensitive Technology to Foreign Nationals in the U.S,* Washington, DC: U.S. Dept. of Commerce OIG, 2004; www.oig.doc.gov/OIGPublications/IPE-16176.pdf; Accessed August 8, 2012.

Ibid. *Improvements Are Needed for Effective Web Security Management.* Washington, DC: U.S. Department of Commerce OIG, 2011); http://www.oig.doc.gov/OIGPublications/OIG-12-002-A.pdf; Accessed August 10, 2012.

U.S. Defense Security Cooperation Agency (DSCA). *Foreign Military Sales, Foreign Military Construction Sales and Other Security Cooperation Historical Facts As of September 30, 2010.* Washington, DC: DSCA, 2010; www.dsca.mil/programs/biz-ops/factsbook/default; Accessed August 20, 2012.

U.S. Defense Threat Reduction Agency. *Defense's Nuclear Agency 1947-1997.* Washington, DC: DTRA, 2002.

U.S. Department of Defense. *Annual Defense Department Report FY 1978.* Washington, DC: DOD, 1977; http://catalog.hathitrust.org/Record/006748275; Accessed August 21, 2012.

Ibid. *Annual Report to Congress Secretary of Defense: Fiscal Year 1983.* Washington, DC: DOD, 1982; http://catalog.hathitrust.org/Record/000078603; Accessed August 22, 2012.

Ibid. *Annual Report to Congress: Fiscal Year 1990.* Washington, DC: DOD, 1989.

Ibid. *Directive 5132.03 DoD Policy and Responsibilities Relating to Security Cooperation.* (Washington, DC: DOD, 2008); www.dtic.mil/directives/corres/pdf/513203p.pdf; Accessed August 15, 2012; originally issued July 22, 1957.

Ibid. *DOD Directive 5105.72: Defense Technology Security Administration.*" Washington, DC: Washington Headquarters Service, July 28, 2005; http://www.dtic.mil/whs/directives/corres/pdf/510572p.pdf; Accessed September 5, 2012.

Ibid. "DOD Directive 5111.5: Assistant Secretary of Defense for Nuclear Security and Counterproliferation." 58 *Federal Register* 139 (July 22, 1993): 39365.

Ibid. *DOD Instruction 2040.02: International Transfers of Technology, Articles, and Services.* Washington, DC: Washington Headquarters Service, July 10, 2008); http://www.dtic.mil/whs/directives/corres/pdf/204002p.pdf; Accessed September 5, 2012.

Ibid. *DOD Instruction 5000.60: Defense Industrial Capabilities Assessment.* Washington, DC: Washington Headquarters Service, October 15, 2009; http://www.acq.osd.mil/mibp/docs/ida_study-export_controls_%20us_def_ib.pdf; Accessed September 7, 2012.

Ibid. "Initial Militarily Critical Technologies List." 45 *Federal Register* 192 (October 1, 1980): 65014-65019.

Ibid. Office of Manufacturing and Industrial Base Policy. "Our Mission." (2012); < www.acq.osd.mil/mibp/about.shtml; Accessed September 7, 2012.

Ibid. "Organization: Responsibilities and Relationships in International Security Affairs." 17 *Federal Register* 196 (October 7, 1952): 8961.

Ibid. *Report of the Secretary of Defense to the President and Congress.* Washington, DC: GPO, 1991.

Ibid. *Report of the Secretary of Defense to the President and the Congress.* Washington, DC: GPO, 1992.

Ibid. *Report on the Department of Defense's Plans to Reform the Export Control System.* Washington, DC: DOD, 2011.

Ibid. *Selling to Allies: A Guide for U.S. Firms.* Washington, DC: GPO, 1990.

Ibid. *The Technology Security Program: A Report to the 99th Congress.* Washington, DC: DOD, 1986; http://www.dtic.mil/dtic/tr/fulltext/u2/a194106.pdf; Accessed August 22, 2012.

Ibid. Assistance Secretary of Defense (International Security Affairs). "Delegation of Authority Regarding Strategic Security Trade Controls on Foreign Excess Personal Property." 24 *Federal Register* 81 (April 25, 1959): 3255-3256.

U.S. Department of Defense. *Export Controls: Controls Over Exports to China.* Washington, DC: DODIG, 2006; http://www.dodig.mil/audit/reports/FY06/06-067.pdf; Accessed September 5, 2012.

Ibid. *Followup Audit on Recommendations for Controls Over Exporting Sensitive Technologies to Countries of Concern* Washington, DC: DODIG, 2007; http://www.dodig.mil/audit/reports/FY07/07-131.pdf; Accessed September 5, 2012.

Ibid. *Review of the DOD Export Licensing Processes for Dual-Use Commodities and Munitions.* Washington, DC: DODIG, 1999; http://www.dodig.mil/Audit/reports/fy99/99-186.pdf; Accessed August 29, 2012.

U.S. Departments of Defense and State. *Report to Congress: Section 1248 of the National Defense Authorization Act for Fiscal Year 2010 (Public Law 111-84) Risk Assessment of United States Space Export Control Policy.* Washington, DC: Departments of Defense and State, 2011; http://www.defense.gov/home/features/2011/0111_nsss/docs/1248_Report_Space_Export_Control.pdf; Accessed January 29, 2013.

U.S. Department of Energy. "Defense Programs; List of Energy Related Militarily Critical Technologies." 45 *Federal Register* 192 (October 1, 1980): 65152-65175.

Ibid. "Unclassified Activities in Foreign Atomic Energy Programs." 47 *Federal Register* 181 (September 17, 1982): 41320-41327.

U.S. Department of Energy. Chief Financial Officer. *Department of Energy FY 2013 Congressional Budget Request: Budget Highlights.* Washington, DC: DOE, 2012; http://www.cfo.doe.gov/budget/13budget/Content/Highlights.pdf; Accessed September 28, 2012.

Ibid. *Department of Energy FY 2013 Congressional Budget Request National Nuclear Security Administration: Office of the Administrator Weapons Activities Defense Nuclear Nonproliferation Naval Reactors.* Washington, DC: DOE, 2012; http://www.cfo.doe.gov/budget/13budget/Content/Volume1.pdf; Accessed October 1, 2012.

U.S. Department of Energy. National Nuclear Security Administration. *Office of the Second Line of Defense: Megaports Initiative.* Washington, DC: NNSA, 2010; http://nnsa.energy.gov/sites/default/files/nnsa/inlinefiles/singlepages_9-15-2010.pdf; Accessed December 18, 2012.

U.S. Department of Energy. Office of Inspector General. *Contractor Compliance With Deemed Export Controls.* (Washington, DC: DOE IG, 2004): 1-2; http://energy.gov/sites/prod/files/igprod/documents/CalendarYear2004/ig-0645.pdf; Accessed September 28, 2012.

Ibid. *The Department of Energy's Export Licensing Process For Dual-Use and Munitions Commodities.* Washington, DC: DOE IG, 1999; http://energy.gov/sites/prod/files/igprod/documents/CalendarYear1999/ig-0445.pdf; Accessed September 28, 2012.

Ibid. *The Department of Energy's Review of Chemical and Biological Export License Applications.* Washington, DC: DOE IG 2005; http://energy.gov/sites/prod/files/igprod/documents/CalendarYear2005/ig-0682.pdf; Accessed September 28, 2012.

Ibid. *The Department of Energy's Review of Export License Applications for China.* Washington, DC: DOE IG, 2006; http://energy.gov/sites/prod/files/igprod/documents/CalendarYear2006/IG-0723.pdf; Accessed September 28, 2012.

Ibid. *The Department's Unclassified Foreign Visits and Assignments Program.* (Washington, DC: DOE IG, 2008; http://energy.gov/sites/prod/files/igprod/documents/IG-0791.pdf; Accessed September 28, 2012.

Ibid. *The Global Threat Reduction Initiative's Molybdenum-99 Program.* Washington, DC: DOE IG, 2012; http://energy.gov/sites/prod/files/OAS-L-12-07.pdf; Accessed January 3, 2013.

Ibid. *Inspection of the Department of Energy's Role in the Commerce Control List and the U.S. Munitions List.* Washington, DC: DOE IG, 2001; http://energy.gov/sites/prod/files/igprod/documents/CalendarYear2001/inso0103.pdf; Accessed September 28, 2012.

U.S. Department of Homeland Security. *Annual Performance Report: Fiscal Years 2011-2013 Appendix A: Measure Descriptions and Data Collection Methodologies.* Washington, DC: DHS, 2012); www.dhs.gov/xlibrary/assets/mgmt/cfo_apr_fy2011_appa.pdf; Accessed September 18, 2012.

Ibid. *Privacy Impact Assessment for the Exodus Accountability Referral System (EARS).* Washington, DC: DHS, 2010); http://www.dhs.gov/

xlibrary/assets/privacy/privacy_pia_ice_ears.pdf; Accessed September 17, 2012.

U.S. Department of Homeland Security. Office of Inspector General. *Audit of Export Controls for Activities Related to China.* Washington, DC: DHS OIG, 2006.

Ibid. *CBP's Container Security Initiative Has Proactive Management and Oversight But Future Direction is Uncertain.* Washington, DC: DHS OIG, 2010: http://purl.fdlp.gov/GPO/gpo12206; Accessed December 6, 2012.

Ibid. *Effectiveness of Customs and Border Protection's Procedures to Detect Uranium In Two Smuggling Incidents.* Washington, DC: DHS OIG, 2004; www.oig.dhs.gov/assets/Mgmt/OIG-04-40.pdf; Accessed September 18, 2012.

Ibid. *Review of Controls over the Export of Chemical and Biological Commodities (Redacted).* Washington, DC: DHS OIG, 2005.

U.S. Department of Justice. "Foreign Agents Registration Act." www.fara.gov/; Accessed September 20, 2012.

Ibid. *Summary of Major U.S. Export Enforcement and Embargo-Related Criminal Prosecutions: 2007 to the Present.* Washington, DC: Department of Justice, 2011; www.justice.gov/nsd/docs/summary-eaca.pdf; Accessed April 13, 2012.

U.S. Department of Justice. Executive Office of for United States Attorneys. "Terrorist Financing," U.S. Attorneys Bulletin, 51 (4)(July 2003);

U.S. Department of Justice. Federal Bureau of Investigation. *Higher Education and National Security: The Targeting of Sensitive, Proprietary and Classified Information on Campuses of Higher Education.* Washington, DC: FBI, 2011; http://www.fbi.gov/about-us/investigate/counterintelligence/higher-education-national-security; Accessed November 28, 2012.

Ibid. Justice Management Division. *Department of Justice FY 2013 Congressional Budget Submission: National Security Division (NSD).* Washington, DC: U.S. Department of Justice, 2012; http://www.justice.gov/jmd/2013summary/pdf/fy13-nsd-bud-summary.pdf; Accessed September 26, 2012.

U.S. Department of Justice. "National Security Division," About the Division. Washington, DC: USDOJ, n.d.: 1; http://www.justice.gov/nsd/about-nsd.html; Accessed September 20, 2012.

Ibid. "Sections and Offices," http://www.justice.gov/nsd/list-view.html; Accessed September 20, 2012.

Ibid. *Summary of Major U.S. Export Enforcement, Economic Espionage, Trade Secret and Embargo-Related Criminal Cases (January 2007 to the present: updated September 6, 2012.* Washington, DC: U.S. Department of Justice, 2012: 74; www.justice.gov/nsd/docs/export-case-fact-sheet.pdf; Accessed September 21, 2012.

Ibid. Office of the Inspector General. *A Review of ATF's Operation Fast and Furious and Related Matters*, Washington, DC: OIG, 2012; http://www.justice.gov/oig/reports/2012/s1209.pdf; Accessed September 26, 2012.

U.S. National Performance Review. *From Red Tape to Results: Creating a Government that Works Better & Costs Less: Department of Commerce*. Washington, DC: Office of the Vice President, 1993.

U.S. National Nuclear Security Administration. Office of Global Security Engagement and Cooperation. *International Nonproliferation Export Control Program*. Washington, DC: NNSA, 2008; http://nnsa.energy.gov/sites/default/files/nnsa/inlinefiles/INECP_Brochure.pdf; Accessed September 26, 2012.

U.S. Department of State. Bureau of International Security and Nonproliferation. *U.S. Support for the Arms Trade Treaty: Fact Sheet,* (Washington, DC: U.S. Department of State, 2010): 1-2; http://www.state.gov/t/isn/rls/fs/148311.htm; Accessed December 12, 2012.

U.S. Department of State. Bureau of Politico-Military Affairs. "Amendment to the International Traffic in Arms Regulations (ITAR)." 56 *Federal Register* 97 (May 20, 1991): 20320.

U.S. Department of State. "D&CP-Political-Military Affairs: Resource Summary." (n.d.); www.state.gov/documents/organization/123563.pdf; Accessed August 5, 2011.

Ibid. "Defense Trade Advisory G roup Terms of Reference." (2006) www.pmddtc.state.gov/DTAG/documents/reference_terms_06.pdf; 1-2; Accessed August 3, 2011.

U.S. Department of State. *Documents on Germany, 1944-1985*. (Washington, DC: U.S. Department of State, 1986): 773-775.

Ibid. *Fighting Global Corruption: Business Risk Management Information for Global Businesses and Organizations Navigating the International Anticorruption Environment*. Washington, DC: Department of State, 2000.

U.S. Department of State. *Foreign Relations of the United States (FRUS) 1950: Volume IV: Central and Eastern Europe; the Soviet Union.* Rogers P. Churchill, Charles S. Sampson, and William Z. Slany, eds. Washington, DC: GPO, 1980.

Ibid. *FRUS, 1952-1954, Volume I Part II General Economic and Political Matters.* William Z. Slany, Editor-in-Chief. Washington, DC: GPO, 1983

Ibid. *FRUS, 1952-1954, Volume II Part I National Security Affairs.* Lisle H. Rose and Neil H. Peterson, eds. Washington, DC: GPO, 1984.

Ibid. *FRUS, 1952-1954: Volume VI Part I, Western Europe and Canada.* William Z. Slany, ed. Washington, DC: GPO, 1986.

Ibid. *FRUS, 1955-1957: Foreign Aid and Economic Defense Policy Volume X.* Robert J. McMahon, William F. Sanford, and Sherrill B. Wells, eds. Washington, DC: GPO, 1989.

Ibid. *FRUS, 1955-1957, Volume IX: Foreign Economic Policy; Foreign Information Program.* John P. Glennon. Editor-in-Chief, (Washington, DC: GPO, 1987

Ibid. *FRUS, 1955-1957, Suez Crisis, July 26-December 31, 1956 Volume XVI.* Nina J. Noring, ed. Washington, DC: GPO, 1990.

Ibid. *FRUS, 1955-1957: Volume XX: Regulations of Armaments, Atomic Energy.* David S. Patterson, ed. Washington, DC: GPO, 1990.

Ibid. *FRUS, 1958-1960 Volume IV: Foreign Economic Policy.* Suzanne E. Koffman, Edward C. Kieffer, Harriett Dashiell Schwar, and Glenn W. LaFantasie, eds. Washington, DC: GPO, 1992.

Ibid. *FRUS, 1961-1963 Volume IX: Foreign Economic Policy.* Glenn W. LaFantasie, ed. Washington, DC: GPO, 1995.

Ibid. *FRUS, 1961-1963, Volume X, Cuba, January 1961-September 1962.* Louis J. Smith, ed. Washington, DC: GPO, 1997.

Ibid. *FRUS, 1961-1963 Volume XI: Cuban Missile Crisis and Aftermath.* David S. Patterson, ed. Washington, DC: GPO, 1996.

Ibid. *FRUS, 1961-1963: Volume XIV: Berlin, 1961-1963.* Charles S. Sampson, ed. Washington, DC: GPO, 1993.

Ibid. *FRUS, 1964-1968: Volume IX: International Development and Economic Defense Policy; Commodities.* David S. Patterson, Evan Duncan, and Carolyn B. Yee, eds. Washington, DC: GPO, 1997.

Ibid. *FRUS, 1964-1968 Volume XI: Arms Control and Disarmament.* Evans Gerkas, David B. Patterson, and Carolyn B. Yee, eds. Washington, DC: GPO, 1997.

Ibid. *FRUS, 1964-1968 Volume XV: South Asia.* Gabrielle S. Mallon and Louis J. Smith, eds. Washington, DC: GPO, 2001

Ibid. *FRUS, 1964-1968: Volume XXIV, Africa.* Nina Davis Howland, ed. (Washington, DC: GPO, 1999): 610-690.

Ibid. *FRUS, 1969-1976, Volume E-5, Part I, Documents on Sub-Saharan Africa, 1969-1972.* Joseph Hilts and David C. Humphrey, eds. Washington, DC: GPO, 2005; http://history.state.gov/historicaldocuments/frus1969-76ve05p1; Accessed May 16, 2012.

Ibid. *FRUS, 1969-1976 Volume IV: Foreign Assistance, International Development, Trade Policies, 1969-1972.* Bruce F. Duncombe, ed. Washington, DC: GPO, 2002.

Ibid. *FRUS, 1969-1976 Volume XXVIII: Southern Africa.* Myra F. Burton, ed. Washington, DC: GPO, 2011.

Ibid. *FRUS, 1973-1976, Volume XXXI, Foreign Economic Policy.* Edward C. Keefer, ed. Washington, DC: GPO, 2009.

U.S. Department of State. *Incoming Telegram To: Secretary of State.*" (Washington, DC: U.S. Department of State, February 18, 1962): 1; http://www.jfklibrary.org/Asset-Viewer/Archives/JFKPOF-117-008.aspx; Accessed May 14, 2012.

U.S. Department of State. "International Traffic in Arms Regulations." 56 *Federal Register* 203 (October 21, 1991): 53608.

U.S. Department of State. *Papers Relating to Foreign Relations of the United States: The Lansing Papers 1914-1920.* Washington, DC: GPO, 1940): 2: 10-11.

U.S. Department of State. *Patterns of Global Terrorism 1999.* Washington, DC: GPO, 2000.

Ibid. *Proliferation Security Initiative.* Washington, DC: Department of State, (2012); http://www.state.gov/t/isn/c10390.htm; Accessed December 10, 2012.

Ibid. "Proliferation Security Initiative: Statement of Interdiction Principles." Washington, DC: Department of State, September 4, 2003; http://www.state.gov/t/isn/c27726.htm; Accessed August 31, 2012.

U.S. Department of State. *The 1958 Revision of East-West Trade Controls Mutual Defense Assistance Control Act of 1951: Twelfth Report to Congress.* Washington, DC: GPO, 1959.

U.S. Department of State. *Siberian Gas Pipeline and U.S. Export Controls.* Washington, DC: Department of State, 1982.

U.S. Department of State and the Broadcasting Board of Governors Office of Inspector General. *Report of Audit: Export Licensing of Chemi-*

cal and Biological Commodities. Washington, DC: Department of State, 2005; http://oig.state.gov/documents/organization/126942.pdf; Accessed August 5, 2011.

Ibid. *Review of Export Controls*. Washington, DC: Department of State, 2006; http://oig.state.gov/documents/organization/104037.pdf; Accessed August 5, 2011.

Ibid. *Review of Export Controls for Foreign Persons Employed at Companies and Universities*. Washington, DC: Department of State, 2004; http://oig.state.gov/documents/organization/104036.pdf; Accessed August 5, 2011.

Ibid. *A Review of U.S. Policy Toward Venezuela November 2001-April 2002*. Washington, DC: Department of State, 2002); http://oig.state.gov/documents/organization/13682.pdf; Accessed August 5, 2011.

U.S. Department of State. Bureau of International Security and Nonproliferation. *Proliferation Security Initiative Participants*. Washington, DC: Department of States, 2012; http://www.state.gov/t/isn/c27732.htm; Accessed December 10, 2012.

Ibid. *Proliferation Security Initiative: Statement of Interdiction Principles*. Washington, DC: The White House, September 4, 2003; http://www.state.gov/t/isn/c27726.htm; Accessed December 10, 2012.

U.S. Department of State. Bureau of Politico-Military Affairs. "Director, Office of Munitions Control: Redelegation of Authority." 35 *Federal Register* 63 (April 1, 1970): 5423-5424.

Ibid. "Revocation of Munitions Export Licenses to Iraq; Suspension of Munitions Exports to Kuwait." 55 *Federal Register* 150 (August 3, 1990): 31808.

U.S. Department of State. Directorate of Defense Trade Controls. "Congressional Notifications." (2011): 1; www.pmddtc.state.gov/reports/intro_congnotify.html; Accessed August 9, 2011.

Ibid. "Consent Agreement 1978: Olin Corporation." http://www.pmddtc.state.gov/compliance/consent_agreements/OlinCorp.htm;Accessed July 27, 2011.

Ibid. "Consent Agreements 1992: Japan Aviation Electronics Industry Ltd." http://www.pmddtc.state.gov/compliance/consent_agreements/OlinCorp.htm; Accessed July 27, 2011.

Ibid. "Consent Agreements 2010: XE Services LLC." http://www.pmd dtc.state.gov/compliance/consent_agreements/XeServicesLLC.html; Accessed July 27, 2011.

Ibid. "End-Use Monitoring of Defense Articles and Defense Services Commercial Exports FY 2009." (2010): 4; www.pmddtc.state.gov/ reports/documents/End_Use_FY_2009.pdf; Accessed August 9, 2011.

Ibid. "License Processing Times." (2011): 1; http://www.pmddtc.state. gov/metrics/index.html; Accessed August 9, 2011.

Ibid. "Licensing Processing Times." (2013); 1; http://www.pmddtc. state.gov/metrics/; Accessed January 3, 2013.

Ibid. "Section 655 Annual Military Assistance Reports (2011): 1; http: //www.pmddtc.state.gov/reports/655_intro.html; Accessed August 9, 2011.

Ibid. *Unclassified Report by the Department of State Pursuant to Section 655 of the Foreign Assistance Act, As Amended Direct Commercial Sales Authorizations for Fiscal Year 2010*. (2010): 1; www.pmddtc. state.gov/report/documents/rpt655_FY10.pdf; Accessed August 9, 2011.

U.S. Department of State. Office of the Coordinator for Counterterrorism. "Designation of Foreign Terrorist Organizations," 62 *Federal Register* 195, (October 8, 1997): 52650-52651.

Ibid. "Designations of Terrorists and Terrorist Organizations Pursuant to Executive Order 13324 of September 23, 2001." 67 *Federal Register* 53 (March 19, 2002): 12633.

U.S. Department of State. Office of the Historian. "Assistant Secretaries of State for Politico-Military Affairs." (n.d.); http://history.state.gov/ departmenthistory/people/principalofficers/assistant-secretary-for-politico-military-affairs; Accessed July 26, 2011.

U.S. Department of the Treasury. "Blocking Extended to Vietnam." 40 *Federal Register* 86 (May 2, 1975): 9202-9203.

Ibid. "Cuban Assets Control Regulations: Control of Financial and Commercial Transactions Involving Cuba or Nationals Thereof." 28 *Federal Register* (July 9, 1963): 974.

Ibid. "Cuban Assets Control Regulations." 39 *Federal Register* 133 (July 10, 1974): 25317-25319.

Ibid. *Departmental Offices-S&E FY 2013 President's Budget Submission*. Washington, DC: Department of the Treasury, 2012: DO-3; http://www.treasury.gov/about/budget-performance/Documents/

2%20-%20FY%202013%20DO%20SE%20CJ.pdf; Accessed October 23, 2012.

Ibid. "Iranian Assets Control Regulations." 44 *Federal Register* 222 (November 15, 1979): 65956-65958.

Ibid. "List of Specially Designated Nationals." 51 *Federal Register* 237 (December 10, 1986): 44549.

U.S. Department of the Treasury. Committee on Foreign Investment in the United States. *Annual Report to Congress: CY 2010.* Washington, DC: CFIUS, 2011; http://www.treasury.gov/resource-center/international/foreign-investment/Documents/2011%20CFIUS%20Annual%20Report%20FINAL%20PUBLIC.pdf; Accessed October 10, 2012.

U.S. Department of the Treasury. Financial Crimes Enforcement Network. "Financial Crimes Enforcement Network: Comprehensive Iran Sanctions, Accountability, and Divestment Act of 2010 ("CISADA") Reporting Requirements Under Section 104 (e)." 76 *Federal Register* 84 (May 2, 2011): 24410-24421.

U.S. Department of the Treasury. "Terrorism and Financial Intelligence Office of Foreign Assets Control (OFAC): Mission." Washington, DC: OFAC, 2012; http://www.treasury.gov/about/organizational-structure/offices/Pages/Office-of-Foreign-Assets-Control.aspx; Accessed October 5, 2012.

Ibid. "Resource Center: United States Statutes." (2012); http://www.treasury.gov/resource-center/sanctions/Pages/statutes-links.aspx; Accessed October 5, 2012.

U.S. Department of the Treasury. Office of Foreign Assets Control. "About," (2012); http://www.treasury.gov/about/organizational-structure/offices/Pages/Office-of-Foreign-Assets-Control.aspx; Accessed April 13, 2012.

Ibid. *Civil Penalties and Enforcement Information: 2012 Enforcement Information.* (Washington, DC: OFAC, 2012); 1-2; http://www.treasury.gov/resource- center/sanctions/CivPen/Pages/civpen-index2.aspx; Accessed October 23, 2012.

Ibid. "Certain Transactions Incident to Travel to and Inland Mainland China." 34 *Federal Register* 156 (August 15, 1969): 13277.

Ibid. *Enforcement Information for June 12, 2012.* Washington, DC: OFAC, 2012; http://www.treasury.gov/resource-center/sanctions/CivPen/Documents/06122012_ing.pdf; Accessed October 23, 2012.

Ibid. *Enforcement Information for October 19, 2012*. Washington, DC: OFAC, 2012; http://www.treasury.gov/resource-center/sanctions/Civ Pen/Documents/20121019_brasseler.pdf; Accessed October 23, 2012.

Ibid. *Frequently Asked Questions and Answers*. Washington, DC: OFAC, 2007; http://www.treasury.gov/resource-center/faqs/Sanctions/Pages/answer.aspx; Accessed October 23, 2012.

Ibid. "Iraqi Sanctions Regulations; Census of Blocked Iraqi Government Assets and Claims Against Iraq and Iraqi Government Entities." 56 *Federal Register* 128 (February 11, 1991): 5636.

Ibid. "Regulations Prohibiting Transactions Involving the Shipment of Certain Merchandise Between Foreign Countries." 30 Federal Register 25 (February 6, 1965): 1284.

Ibid. "Specially Designated Nations and Blocked Persons List" (October 4, 2012); www.treasury.gov/ofac/downloads/t11sdn.pdf; Accessed October 8, 2012.

U.S. Department of the Treasury. Office of the Inspector General. *Combating Terrorism: Treasury Provides Terrorism Information for Consolidated Watchlist Purposes Through Its Specially Designated Nationals List*. Washington, DC: TIG, 2007; http://www.treasury.gov/about/organizational-structure/ig/Documents/oig08022.pdf; Accessed October 10, 2012.

Ibid. *Financial Assets Control: Actions Have Been Taken to Better Ensure Financial Institution Compliance With OFAC Sanction Programs, But Their Effectiveness Cannot Yet Be Determined*. Washington, DC: TIG, 2007; http://www.treasury.gov/about/organizational-structure/ig/Documents/OFAC%20Final%20Report%209-20-07.pdf; Accessed October 10, 2012.

Ibid. *Foreign Assets Control: OFAC's Ability to Monitor Financial Institution Compliance is Limited Due to Legislative Impairments*. Washington, DC: TIG, 2002); http://www.treasury.gov/about/organizational-structure/ig/Documents/oig02082.pdf; Accessed October 10, 2012.

Ibid. *Foreign Assets Control: Hundreds of OFAC Civil Penalty Cases Expired Before Enforcement Action Could be Completed*. Washington, DC: TIG, 2007; http://www.treasury.gov/about/organizational-structure/ig/Documents/oig07032.pdf; Accessed October 10, 2012

Ibid. *Foreign Assets Control: OFAC Should Have Better and More Timely Documented its Review of Potential Sanctions Violations*. Washington, DC: TIG, 2010; http://www.treasury.gov/about/organizational-

structure/ig/Documents/OIG10045%20%28Fedwire%29-Not%20
SBU%20%282%29.pdf; Accessed October 23, 2012.

Ibid. *Foreign Investments: Review of Treasury's Failure To Provide Congress Required Quadrennial Reports in 1998 and 2002 on Foreign Acquisitions and Industrial Espionage Activity Involving U.S. Critical Technology Companies.* Washington, DC: TIG, 2008; http:// www.treasury.gov/about/organizational-structure/ig/Documents/ oig08031.pdf; Accessed October 10, 2012.

Ibid. *Terrorist Financing/Money Laundering: OTS Examinations of Thrifts for Bank Secrecy Act and Patriot Act Compliance Were Often Limited.* Washington, DC: TIG, 2008; http://www.treasury.gov/about/ organizational-structure/ig/Documents/oig08034.pdf; Accessed October 10, 2012.

Ibid. *Terrorist Financing/Money Laundering: Responsibility for Bank Secrecy Act is Spread Across Many Organizations.* Washington, DC: TIG, 2008; http://www.treasury.gov/about/organizational-structure/ ig/Documents/oig0830.pdf; Accessed October 10, 2012.

U.S. Federal Interagency Working Group on Hazardous Substances Export Policy, "Draft Report," 45 Federal Register 157 (August 12, 1980): 53754-53787.

U.S. General Accounting Office. *Arms Control: U.S. and International Efforts to Ban Chemical Weapons.* Washington, DC: GAO, 1991; . http://archive.gao.gov/t2pbat7/114972.pdf; Accessed August 3, 2011.

Ibid. *Arms Control: U.S. Efforts to Control the Transfer of Nuclear-Capable Missile Technology.* Washington, DC: GAO, 1990; http:// www.gao.gov/assets/220/212558.pdf; Accessed August 6, 2012.

Ibid. *Arms Exports: Licensing Reviews for Exporting Military Items Can Be Improved.* Washington, DC: GAO, 1987; http://archive.gao.gov/ d29t5/133904.pdf; Accessed August 3, 2011.

Ibid. *Commercial Offices Abroad Need Substantial Improvements to Assist U.S. Export Objectives.* Washington, DC: GAO, 1972; www.gao. gov/assets/210/203611.pdf; Accessed July 23, 2012.

Ibid. *Controls Over Importing and Exporting Munitions Items.* Washington, DC: GAO, 1973; www.gao.gov/assets/210/200273.pdf; Accessed July 23, 2012.

Ibid. *Defense Conversion.* Washington, DC: GAO, 1996; http://www. gao.gov/assets/90/85988.pdf; Accessed August 27, 2012.

Ibid. *Economic Sanctions: Effectiveness as Tools of Foreign Policy.* Washington, DC, GAO, 1992.

Ibid. *An Evaluation of the Administration's Proposed Nuclear Non-Proliferation Strategy: Report to the Congress.* (Washington, DC: GAO, 1977); http://catalog.hathitrust.org/Record/011408757; Accessed May 18, 2012.

Ibid. "Export Control of Commercial Goods and Technology: Statement of Allan I. Mendelowitz, National Security and International Affairs Division." Washington, DC: GPO, 1987); http://www.gao.gov/assets/110/101591.pdf; Accessed August 2, 2012.

Ibid. *Export Controls: Better Interagency Coordination Needed on Satellite Exports.* Washington, DC: GAO, 1999; http://www.gao.gov/assets/230/228230.pdf; Accessed August 7, 2012.

Ibid. *Export Controls: Clarification of Jurisdiction for Missile Technology Items Needed.* Washington, DC: GAO, 2001; http://purl.access.gpo.gov/GPO/LPS46638; Accessed August 5, 2011.

Ibid. *Export Controls: Concerns Over Stealth-Related Exports.* Washington, DC: GAO, 1995; http://www.gao.gov/assets/230/221232.pdf; Accessed August 27, 2012.

Ibid. *Export Controls: Extent of DOD Influence on Licensing Decisions.* Washington, DC: GAO, 1989; http://www.gao.gov/assets/150/147857.pdf; Accessed August 24, 2012.

Ibid. *Export Controls: License Screening and Compliance Procedures Need Strengthening.* Washington, DC: GAO, 1994; www.gao.gov/assets/220/219754/pdf; Accessed August 7, 2012.

Ibid. *Export Controls: Need to Clarify Policy and Simplify Administration.* Washington, DC: GAO, 1979; http://www.gao.gov/assets/130/125687.pdf; Accessed August 22, 2012.

Ibid. *Export Controls: Reengineering Business Processes Can Improve Efficiency of State Department License Reviews.* Washington, DC: GAO, 2001; http://purl.access.gpo.gov/GPO/LPS44344; Accessed August 5, 2011.

Ibid. *Export Controls: Sensitive Machine Tool Exports to China.* Washington, DC: GAO, 1996; http://www.gao.gov/assets/230/223443.pdf; Accessed August 27, 2012.

Ibid. *Export Controls: Some Controls Over Missile-Related Technology Exports to China are Weak.* Washington, DC: GAO, 1995; www.gao.gov/archive/1995/ns95082.pdf; Accessed August 4, 2011.

Ibid. *Export-Licensing: Commerce-Defense Review of Applications to Certain Free World Nations.* Washington, DC: GAO, 1986; http://www.gao.gov/assets/150/144632.pdf; Accessed August 3, 2012.

Ibid. *Export Licensing: Number of Applications Reviewed by the Defense Department Washington*. DC: GAO, 1988; http://www.gao.gov/assets/90/88087.pdf; Accessed August 22, 2012.

Ibid. *Foreign Military Sales—A Growing Concern: Departments of State and Defense*. Washington, DC: GAO, 1976; www.gao.gov/assets/120/115630.pdf; Accessed August 21, 2012.

Ibid. *Foreign Technologies: Federal Agencies Efforts to Track Developments*. Washington, DC: GAO, 1989; http://www.gao.gov/assets/220/211477.pdf; Accessed August 6, 2012.

Ibid. *The Government's Role in East-West Trade-Problems and Issues*. Washington, DC: GAO, 1976; www.gao.gov/assets/120/116411.pdf; Accessed July 23, 2012.

Ibid. *Hong Kong's Reversion to China: Effective Monitoring Critical to Assessing U.S. Nonproliferation Risks*. Washington, DC: GAO, 1997; http://www.gao.gov/assets/230/224198.pdf; Accessed August 7, 2012.

Ibid. *Improper Blocking of U.S. Funds by Office of Foreign Assets Control*. Washington, DC: GAO, 1979; http://www.gao.gov/assets/130/127865.pdf; Accessed October 23, 2012.

Ibid. *Overview of Nuclear Export Policies of Major Foreign Supplier Nations*. Washington, DC: GAO, 1977; http://www.gao.gov/assets/130/120163.pdf; Accessed August 22, 2012.

Ibid. *Treasury Should Keep Better Track of Blocked Foreign Assets*. Washington, DC: GAO, 1980; http://www.gao.gov/assets/140/130936.pdf; Accessed October 23, 2012.

Ibid. *U.S. Should Systematically Assess Terrorists Use of Alternative Financial Systems*. Washington, DC: GAO, 2003; http://www.gao.gov/assets/250/240616.pdf; Accessed October 23, 2012.

Ibid. Weapons of Mass Destruction: Defense Threat Reduction Agency Addresses Broad Range of Threats, but Performance Reporting Can Be Improved, (Washington, DC: GAO, 2004; http://www.gao.gov/assets/250/241416.pdf; Accessed September 5, 2012.

Ibid. *Weapons of Mass Destruction: DOD's Actions to Combat Weapons Use Should Be More Integrated and Focused*. Washington, DC: GAO, 2000; http://www.gao.gov/assets/230/229156.pdf; Accessed August 29, 2012.

U.S. Government Accountability Office. *Combating Nuclear Smuggling: Megaports Initiative Faces Funding and Sustainability Challenges*.

(Washington, DC: GAO, 2012): 5-23; http://www.gao.gov/assets/ 650/649759.pdf; Accessed December 6, 2012.

Ibid. *Competing Priorities Enforcing Cuban Embargo*, Washington, DC: GAO, 2007: ; http://www.gao.gov/assets/270/269849.pdf; Accessed October 23, 2012.

Ibid. *Cooperation With Many Major Drug Transit Countries Has Improved, but Better Performance Reporting and Sustainability Plans are Needed.* Washington, DC: GAO, 2008; http://www.gao.gov/ assets/280/278210.pdf; Accessed December 6, 2012.

Ibid. *Defense Technologies: DOD's Critical Technology Lists Rarely Inform Export Control and Other Policy Decisions.* Washington, DC: GAO, 2006; http://purl.access.gpo.gov/GPO/LPS73050; Accessed August 14, 2012.

Ibid. *Defense Trade: Clarification and More Comprehensive Oversight of Export Exemptions Certified by DOD are Needed,* (Washington, DC: GAO, 2007; http://www.gao.gov/assets/270/268269.pdf; Accessed September 5, 2012.

Ibid. *Efforts to Combat Arms Trafficking to Mexico.* Washington, DC: GAO, 2009); www.gao.gov/assets/300/291223.pdf; Accessed September 21, 2012.

Ibid. *Export Controls: Agencies Should Assess Vulnerabilities and Improve Guidance for Protecting Export-Controlled Information at Universities.* Washington, DC: GAO, 2006; http://purl.access.gpo. gov/GPO/LPS77457; Accessed August 5, 2011.

Ibid. *Export Controls: Challenges Exist in Enforcement of an Inherently Complex System.* Washington, DC: GAO, 2006; http://www.gao.gov/ new.items/d07265.pdf; Accessed September 17, 2012.

Ibid. *Export Controls: Improvements Needed to Prevent Unauthorized Technology Releases to Foreign Nationals in the United States,* Washington, DC: GAO, 2011; http://www.gao.gov/assets/320/315496.pdf; Accessed August 10, 2012.

Ibid. *Export Controls: Observations on Selected Countries' Systems and Proposed Treaties.* Washington, DC: GAO, 2010; www.gao.gov/ new.items/d10557.pdf; Accessed August 8, 2011.

Ibid. *Export Controls: U.S. Agencies Need to Assess Control List Reform's Impact on Compliance Activities.* Washington, DC: GAO, 2012; http:/ /purl.fdlp.gov/GPO/gpo24893; Accessed December 21, 2012.

Ibid. U.S. Government Accountability Office, "High-Risk Series: An Update," (Washington, DC: GAO, 2013): 192; http://www.gao.gov/ assets/660/652133.pdf; Accessed March 4, 2013. From p. 232.

Ibid. *Iran Sanctions: Impact in Furthering U.S. Objectives is Unclear and Should Be Reviewed.* Washington, DC: GAO, 2007; http://www. gao.gov/new.items/d0858.pdf; Accessed June 18, 2012.

Ibid. *Nonproliferation: Agencies Could Improve Information Sharing and End-Use Monitoring on Unmanned Aerial Vehicle Exports.* Washington, DC: GAO, 2012.

Ibid. *Nuclear Nonproliferation: Comprehensive U.S. Planning and Better Foreign Cooperation Needed to Secure Vulnerable Nuclear Materials Worldwide.* Washington, DC: GAO, 2010; http://www.gao. gov/assets/320/313961.pdf; Accessed October 1, 2012.

Ibid. *Nuclear Nonproliferation: DOE's International Radiological Threat Reduction Program Needs to Focus Future Efforts on Securing the Highest Priority Radiological Sources.* Washington, DC: GAO, 2007); http://www.gao.gov/assets/260/256110.pdf; Accessed October 1, 2012.

Ibid. *Nuclear Nonproliferation: DOE Needs to Address Uncertainties with and Strengthen Independent Safety Oversight of Its Plutonium Disposition Program.* Washington, DC: GAO, 2010; http://www.gao. gov/assets/310/302279.pdf; Accessed October 1, 2012.

Ibid. *Nuclear Nonproliferation: Further Actions Needed by U.S. Agencies to Secure Vulnerable Nuclear and Radiological Materials.* Washington, DC: GAO, 2012; http://www.gao.gov/assets/590/589345.pdf; Accessed October 1, 2012.

Ibid. *Nuclear Nonproliferation: Strengthened Oversight Needed to Address Proliferation and Management Challenges in IAEA's Technical Cooperation Program.* Washington, DC: GAO, 2009; http://purl. access.gpo.gov/GPO/LPS113361; Accessed December 7, 2012.

Ibid. *Nuclear Nonproliferation: U.S. Agencies Have Limited Ability to Account for, Monitor, and Evaluate Security of U.S. Nuclear Material Overseas.* Washington, DC: GAO, 2011; http://www.gao.gov/ assets/330/323043.pdf; Accessed October 1, 2012.

Ibid. *Persian Gulf: U.S. Agencies Need to Improve Licensing Data and Document Reviews of Arms Transfers for U.S. Foreign Policy and National Security Goals.* Washington, DC: GAO, 2010; http:// www.gao.gov/assets/310/309821.pdf; Accessed September 7, 2012.

Ibid. *Supply Chain Security: CBP Needs to Conduct Regular Assessments of Its Cargo Targeting System.* Washington, DC: GAO, 2012; http://www.gao.gov/assets/650/649695.pdf; Accessed December 6, 2012.

Ibid. *Treasury's Office of Terrorism and Financial Intelligence Could More Effectively Manage Its Mission.* Washington, DC: GAO, 2009; http://www.gao.gov/assets/300/295922.pdf; Accessed October 23, 2012.

Ibid. *U.S. Embargo on Cuba: Recent Regulatory Changes and Potential Presidential or Congressional Action.* Washington, DC: GAO, 2009; http://purl.access.gpo.gov/GPO/LPS119709; Accessed May 10, 2012

Ibid. U.*S. Faces Challenges in Recovering Assets, Has Financial Mechanisms.* Washington, DC: GAO, 2004; http://www.gao.gov/assets/250/244163.pdf; Accessed October 23, 2012.

U.S. International Trade Administration. "Amendment of Oil and Gas Controls to the U.S.S.R." 47 *Federal Register* 122, (June 24, 1982): 47250-47252.

Ibid. *Electricity Imports/Exports-International Electricity Regulation.* Washington, DC: ITA, 2009); 1; http://export.gov/regulation/eg_main_018222.asp; Accessed September 26, 2012.

Ibid. *Export Licenses.* Washington, DC: ITA, 2011): 1; http://export.gov/regulation/eg_main_0 18219.asp; Accessed September 26, 2012.

Ibid. "General Orders: Suspension of Licensing for All Orders to the U.S.S.R." 47 *Federal Register* 2 (January 5, 1982): 141-146.

Ibid. "Request for Comments on Effects of Foreign Policy Controls." 45 *Federal Register* 173, (September 4, 1980): 58562.

Ibid. "Revisions to Reflect Identification and Continuation of Foreign Policy Export Controls." *45 Federal Register* 5, (January 8, 1980): 1595-1598.

U.S. International Trade Commission. *Overview and Analysis of the Economic Impact of U.S. Sanctions With Respect to India and Pakistan, Investigation 332-406.* Washington, DC: USITC, 1999.

U.S. Joint Chiefs of Staff. "Statements of Generals Watson and Clarke on Berlin Wall Situation 13-31, August 1961." (Washington, DC: Joint Chiefs of Staff, 1962): 3; http://www.jfklibrary.org/Asset-Viewer/Archives/JFKPOF-117-008.aspx; Accessed May 14, 2012.

U.S. National Archives and Records Administration. *Code of Federal Regulations Title 22: Foreign Relations: Parts 1-299.* (Washington,

DC: National Archives and Records Administration, 2011): 464-571.

Ibid. "Guide to Federal Records in the National Archives of the United States. "Records of the Bureau of Foreign and Domestic Commerce RG 151." http://www.archives.gov/research/guide-fed-records/groups/151.html; Accessed July 12, 2012.

Ibid. "Records of the International Trade Administration RG 489." http://www.archives.gov/research/guide-fed-records/groups/489.html; Accessed July 12, 2012.

Ibid. "Records of the Office of Foreign Assets Control RG 265." Washington, DC: National Archives, 1995; http://www.archives.gov/research/guide-fed-records/groups/265.html; Accessed October 5, 2012.

Ibid. "Records of the War Trade Board RG 182." (Washington, DC: National Archives and Records Administration, 1995); http://www.archives.gov/research/guide-fed-records/groups/182.html#182.1; Accessed May 3, 2012;

Ibid. *United States Government Manual*. Washington, DC: GPO, 2011; http://www.gpo.gov/fdsys/pkg/GOVMAN-2011-10-05/xml/GOVMAN-2011-10-05-113.xml; Accessed July 12, 2012.

Ibid. Office of the Federal Register. "Export Administration Bureau," (2012); https://www.federalregister.gov/agencies/export-administration-bureau; Accessed August 2, 2012.

U.S. National Archives and Records Service. *Public Papers of the Presidents of the United States Richard Nixon 1973*. Washington, DC: GPO, 1975.

Ibid. *Public Papers of the Presidents of the United States Jimmy Carter 1978: Book II June 30-December 31, 1978*. Washington, DC: GPO, 1979.

U.S. National Research Council. *Beyond "Fortress America": National Security Controls on Science and Technology in a Globalized World*. Washington, DC: National Academies Press, 2009.

Ibid. *Export Control Challenges Associated With Securing the Homeland*. Washington, DC: National Academies Press, 2012.

U.S. National Security Council. "East-West Trade Controls." (July 6, 1981); www.foia.cia.gov/Reagan/19810706.pdf; Accessed August 2, 2012.

Ibid. "East-West Trade Controls." (July 9, 1981); ; www.foia.cia.gov/Reagan/19810709.pdf; Accessed August 2, 2012.

Ibid. "NSDD-75 on U.S. Relations With the USSR," Washington, DC: The White House, 1983: 3; www.fas.org/irp/offdocs/nsdd/nsdd-75. pdf; Accessed May 24, 2012

Ibid. *National Security Decision Memorandum 15: East-West Trade.* Washington, DC: The White House, May 28, 1969); http://www. nixonlibrary.gov/virtuallibrary/documents/nsdm/nsdm_015.pdf; Accessed August 20, 2012.

Ibid. *National Security Decision Memorandum 235: NSSM 150, United States Policy on Transfer of Highly Enriched Uranium for Fueling Power* Reactors." Washington, DC: The White House, October 4, 1973; http://www.nixonlibrary.gov/virtuallibrary/documents/nsdm/ nsdm_235.pdf; Accessed August 20, 2012.

Ibid. *National Security Decision Memorandum 261: Nuclear Sales to the PRC.*" Washington, DC: The White House, July 22, 1974); http:// www.nixonlibrary.gov/virtuallibrary/documents/nsdm/nsdm_261. pdf; Accessed August 20, 2012.

Ibid. *National Security Decision Memorandum 275: COCOM Position on the Return of Depleted Uranium (Tails) from the USSR.* Washington, DC: White House, October 10, 1974; http://www.fordlibrary museum.gov/library/document/0310/nsdm275.pdf; Accessed August 21, 2012.

Ibid. *National Security Decision Memorandum 289: U.S. Military Supply Policy to Pakistan and India.*" (Washington, DC: The White House, March 24, 1975; http://www.fordlibrarymuseum.gov/library/ document/0310/nsdm289.pdf; Accessed August 21, 2012.

Ibid. *National Security Decision Memorandum 298: FRG Reactor Sale to the USSR.*" Washington, DC: The White House, June 14, 1975; http://www.fordlibrarymuseum.gov/library/document/0310/nsdm 298.pdf; Accessed August 21, 2012.

U.S. Nuclear Regulatory Commission. "Export and Import of Nuclear Equipment and Fuel." 49 *Federal Register* 142 (March 1, 1984): 7572-7583.

Ibid. "Export and Import of Nuclear Equipment and Fuel." *49 Federal Register* 233 (December 3, 1984): 41791-41796.

U.S. Office of the Director of National Intelligence. *Background Briefing with Senior U.S. Officials on Syria's Covert Nuclear Reactor and North Korea's Involvement.* Washington, DC: ODNI, 2008; http:// www.dni.gov/interviews/20080424_interview.pdf; Accessed June 19, 2012.

U.S. Office of the National Counterintelligence Executive. *Foreign Spies Stealing U.S. Economic Secrets in Cyberspace: Annual Report to Congress on Foreign Economic Collection and Industrial Espionage, 2009-2011*. Washington, DC: NCIX, 2011; www.ncix.gov/publications/reports/fecie_all/Foreign_Economic_Collection_2011.pdf; Accessed January 3, 2013.

U.S. Secretary of Defense. *Annual Report to the President and the Congress*. Washington, DC: DOD, 1997.

Ibid. *Report of the Quadrennial Defense Review*. Washington, DC: DOD, 1997.

U.S. Senate. Senator Jerry Moran. *Letter to President Barack Obama and Secretary of State Hillary Clinton*. (July 26, 2012); 1-6; http://moran.senate.gov/public/index.cfm/files/serve?File_id=9cd86202-9498-47ca-8b8d-534bf60b52f7; Accessed December 12, 2012.

U.S. War Trade Board. *Report of the War Trade Board, June 1917-June 1919*. Washington, DC: GPO, 1920; http://babel.hathitrust.org/cgi/pt?id=mdp.39015006987500; Accessed May 3, 2012

U.S. Treasury Department Foreign Funds Control. *Administration of the Wartime Financial and Property Controls of the United States Government*. Washington, DC: Treasury Department, 1942; http://catalog.hathitrust.org/Record/001122826; Accessed May 3, 2012.

"United States v. Curtiss-Wright Export Corp. 1936." in *Judging Executive Power: Sixteen Supreme Court Cases That Have Shaped the American Presidency*. Richard J. Ellis, ed. Lanham, MD: Rowman and Littlefield Publishers, 2009: 87-94.

Ibid. 299 *U.S.* 304.

U.S. v. Da Chuan Zeng et. al. 590 F. Supp. 274 (1984).

U.S. v. Reed, 790 F.2d 208 (1986).

U.S. v. Yakou, 428 F.3d 241 (2005).

U.S. v. Zhen Zou Wu, Chitron Corporation, 668 F. Supp. 2d 298 (2011).

Matteo Vaccani. *Alternative Remittance Systems and Terrorism Financing: Issues in Risk Mitigation*. Washington, DC: World Bank, 2010.

Jiri Valenti. Soviet Intervention in Czechoslovakia: Anatomy of a Decision. Baltimore: Johns Hopkins University Press, 1991.

Richard Van Atta. *Export Controls and the U.S. Industrial Base*. Alexandria, VA: Institute for Defense Analyses, 2007; http://www.acq.osd.mil/mibp/docs/ida_study-export_controls_%20us_def_ib.pdf; Accessed September 7, 2012.

Mitchell B. Wallerstein. "Losing Controls." *Foreign Affairs*, 88 (6)(November/December 2009): 11-18.

Teng Kun Wang. "Lobbying Paradox of Strategic Export Policy in a Differentiated Duopoly." *International Economics and Economic Policy*, 8 (3)(September 2011): *323-336*.

Wassenaar Arrangement: Export Control and Its Role Strengthening International Security. Dorothea Auer, ed. (Vienna: Federal Ministry for Foreign Affairs and Diplomatische AkademieWien, Vienna School of International Studies, 2005); http://www.wassenaar.org/links/Favorita_Paper.pdf; Accessed December 12, 2012.

Wassenaar Arrangement. *Genesis of the Wassenaar Arrangement*. Vienna: Wassenaar Arrangement, 2012: 1-2; http://www.wassenaar.org/introduction/origins.html; Accessed December 12, 2012.

Ibid. *Guidelines and Procedures, Including the Initial Elements as Amended and Updated in 2001, 2003, 2004, 2007, and 2011*. Vienna: Wassenaar Arrangement, 2012; 1; http://www.wassenaar.org/guidelines/; Accessed December 12, 2012.

Ibid. *Participating States*. Vienna: Wassenaar Arrangement, 2012: 1; http://www.wassenaar.org/participants/index.html; Accessed December 15, 2012.

Ibid. *Public Statement 2011 Plenary Meeting of the Wassenaar Arrangement on Export Controls for Conventional Arms and Dual-Use Goods and Technologies*. Vienna: Wassenaar Arrangement, 2011): 1-2; http://www.wassenaar.org/publicdocuments/2011/WA%20Plenary%20Public%20Statement%202011.pdf; Accessed December 12, 2012.

Robert J. Watson. *History of the Office of the Secretary of Defense Volume IV: Into the Missile Age, 1956-1960*. Washington, DC: Historical Office, Office of the Secretary of Defense, 1997.

Weapons of Terror: Freeing the World From Nuclear, Biological, and Chemical Arms. Stockholm: The Weapons of Mass Destruction Commission, 2006; http://www.blixassociates.com/wp-content/uploads/2011/02/Weapons_of_Terror.pdf; Accessed December 7, 2012.

David L. Weimer. "The Puzzle of Private Rulemaking: Expertise, Flexibility, and Blame Avoidance in U.S. Regulation." *Public Administration Review*, 66 (4)(July/August 2006): 569-582.

Kenneth G. Weiss. "Space Dragon: Long March, Missile Proliferation, and Sanctions." *Comparative Strategy*, 18 (4)(October-December 1999): 335-359.

Stuart L. Weiss. "American Foreign Policy and Presidential Power: The Neutrality Act of 1935." *The Journal of Politics,* 30 (3)(August 1968): 672-695.

Anna Wetter. *Enforcing European Union Law on Exports of Dual-Use Goods.* Oxford: Oxford University Press, 2009.

White House. *Counterproliferation: Presidential Decision Directive PDD/ NSC 18.* Washington, DC: The White House, December 7, 1993; http://www.fas.org/irp/offdocs/pdd18.htm; Accessed August 27, 2012.

Ibid. *National Security Action Memorandum No. 220: U.S. Government Shipments by Foreign-Flagged Vessels in the Cuban Trade.* Washington, DC: The White House, February 5, 1963; http://www.jfk library.org/Asset-Viewer/AD4Yc0VgwEexd3-punOIoA.aspx; Accessed August 16, 2012.

Ibid. *National Security Action Memorandum 294: U.S. Nuclear and Strategic Delivery System to France."* (Washington, DC: The White House, April 20, 1964); http://www.lbjlib.utexas.edu/johnson/archives.hom/nsams/nsam294.asp; Accessed August 17, 2012.

Ibid. *National Security Action Memorandum 312: National Policy on Release of Inertial Guidance Technology to Germany.* Washington, DC: The White House, July 10, 1964; http://www.lbjlib.utexas.edu/johnson/archives.hom/nsams/nsam312.asp; Accessed August 17, 2012.

Ibid. *National Security Decision Memorandum 247: U.S. Policy on the Export of Computers to Communist Countries.* Washington, DC: National Security Council, 1974; http://nixon.archives.gov/virtual library/documents/nsdm/nsdm_247.pdf; Accessed July 23, 2012.

Ibid. *National Security Directive 24: Chemical Weapons Control Initiatives.* Washington, DC: National Security Council,, September 26, 1989; http://bushlibrary.tamu.edu/research/pdfs/nsd/nsd24.pdf; Accessed August 23, 2012.

Ibid. *National Security Directive 53: Interagency Review and Disposition of Export Control Licenses Issued by the Department of Commerce.* Washington, DC: National Security Council, December 10, 1990); http://bushlibrary.tamu.edu/research/pdfs/nsd/nsd53.pdf; Accessed August 23, 2012.

Ibid. *National Security Directive 70: United States Nonproliferation Policy.* Washington, DC: National Security Council, July 10, 1992; http://

bushlibrary.tamu.edu/research/pdfs/nsd/nsd70.pdf; Accessed August 23, 2012.

Ibid. *Nonproliferation Science and Technology Strategy: Presidential Decision Directive PDD/NSC 27.* Washington, DC: The White House, August 1994; http://www.fas.org/irp/offdocs/pdd27.htm; Accessed August 27, 2012.

Ibid. *NSPD-19: Review of Defense Trade Export Policy and National Security: Fact Sheet.* Washington, DC: The White House, November 21, 2002; http://www.fas.org/irp/offdocs/nspd/deftrade.html; Accessed August 31, 2012.

Ibid. *NSPD-20: Counterproliferation Interdiction.* (Washington, DC: The White House, 2002?; http://www.fas.org/irp/offdocs/nspd/index.html; Accessed August 31, 2012.

Ibid. *National Security Presidential Directive NSPD-41: Maritime Security Policy.* Washington, DC: The White House, December 21, 2004; http://www.fas.org/irp/offdocs/nspd/nspd41.pdf; Accessed August 31, 2012.

Ibid. *National Strategy for Countering Biological Threats.* Washington, DC: NSC, 2009; http://www.whitehouse.gov/sites/default/files/National_Strategy_for_Countering_BioThreats.pdf; Accessed September 6, 2012.

Ibid. *PDD 34: Criteria for Decisionmaking on U.S. Arms Exports."* Washington, DC: The White House, February 17, 1995; http://www.fas.org/irp/offdocs/pdd34.htm; Accessed August 27, 2012.

Ibid. *PDD 47: Nuclear Scientific and Technical Cooperation With Russia Related to Stockpile Safety and Security and Compehensive Test Ban Treaty (CTBT) Monitoring and Verification.* Washington, DC: The White House, March 21, 1996; http://www.fas.org/irp/offdocs/pdd-pdd47.pdf; Accessed August 27, 2012.

Ibid. "President Obama Lays the Foundation for a New Export Control System to Strengthen National Security and the Competitiveness of Key U.S. Manufacturing and Technology Sectors." Washington, DC: The White House, 2010; http://www.whitehouse.gov/the-press-office/2010/08/30/president-obama-lays-foundation-a-new-export-control-system-strengthen-n; Accessed August 9, 2012.

Ibid. *Presidential Policy Directive 2: Implementation of the National Security Strategy for Countering Biological Threats.* Washington, DC: The White House, 2009; www.fas.org/irp/offdocs/ppd/ppd-2.pdf; Accessed September 6, 2012.

Charles Wolf, Brian G. Chow, and Gregory S. Jones. *Enhancement by Enlargement: The Proliferation Security Initiative*. Santa Monica: The Rand Corporation, 2008.

Amy F. Woolf. *Nonproliferation and Threat Reduction Assistance: U.S. Programs in the Former Soviet Union*. Washington, DC: Library of Congress, Congressional Research Service, 2008.

World Customs Organization. *Annual Report 2011-2012*. (Brussels: WCO, 2012): http://www.wcoomd.org/en/topics/ ~ /media/WCO/ Public/Global/PDF/Media/WCO%20Annual%20Report/Annual_ Report_2011-12_en.ashx; Accessed December 13, 2012.

Ibid. *WCO Goals*. Brussels: WCO, 2012; 1; http://www.wcoomd.org/ en/about-us/what-is-the-wco/goals.aspx; Accessed December 13, 2012.

Ibid. *History*. Brussels: WCO, 2012; 1-3; http://www.wcoomd.org/en/ about-us/what-is-the-wco/au_history.aspx; Accessed December 13, 2012.

Ibid. *WCO Working Bodies*. Brussels: WCO, 2012; 1-2; http://www.wco omd.org/en/about-us/wco-working-bodies.aspx; Accessed December 13, 2012.

World Intellectual Property Organization. *Independent External Review Report: Technical Assistance Provided to Countries Subject to United Nations Sanctions*. Geneva: WIPO, 2012; http://www.wipo.int/about-wipo/en/oversight/pdf/wipo_external_review_2012.pdf; Accessed December 21, 2012.

Fareed Zakaria. "Realism and Domestic Politics: A Review Essay." *International Security*, 17 (1)(Summer 1992): 177-198.

Zangger Committee (ZC). *History*. Vienna: ZC, 2010; 1; http://www. zanggercommittee.org/History/Seiten/default.aspx; Accessed December 13, 2012.

Ibid. *Members*. Vienna: ZC, 2012: 1; http://www.zanggercommittee.org/ Members/Seiten/default.aspx; Accessed December 13, 2012.

Philip Zelikow and Condoleezza Rice. *Germany Unified and Europe Transformed: A Study in Statecraft*. Cambridge: Harvard University Press, 1995.

Peter D. Zimmerman. "Proliferation: Bronze Medal Technology is Enough." *Orbis*, 38 (1)(Winter 1994): 67-82.

Index

About the Author

B ert Chapman is Government Information, Political Science, and Economics Librarian and Professor of Library Science at Purdue University in West Lafayette, IN. He is the author of four previous books including *Geopolitics: A Guide to the Issues*.

His research interests include government and scholarly literature on national and international security, foreign policy, and various aspects of diplomatic, economic, military, and political history.